Tamaki Nozomu Presents Dance In The Vampire Bund 2

DANCE IN THE VAMPIRE BUND

2

NOZOMU TAMAKI

Homme, si, le cœur plein de joie ou d'amertume,

Tu passais vers midi dans les champs radieux,

Fuis! la Nature est vide et le Soleil consume:

Rien n'est vivant ici, rien n'est triste ou joyeux.

Viens! Le Soleil te parle en paroles sublimes;

Dans sa flamme implacable absorbe-toi sans fin;

Et retourne à pas lents vers les cités infimes,

Le cœur trempé sept fois dans le Néant divin.

Humans, if you choose to allow your hearts to
shake with joy and sink with sadness,
And go down the bright mid-day trail, then flee, for
nature is inane, and the sun will burn your flesh.
For all living things, there is neither joy nor sadness.

Cometh! The sun shall beckon you with noble words.
Sink into those fires of hell for eternity, and then with
d back to your humble town.
times in the nihilism that is God.

Lisle, Poèmes antiques

Dance In The Vampire Bund 2

Contents

Chapter 7: To a New Battlefield

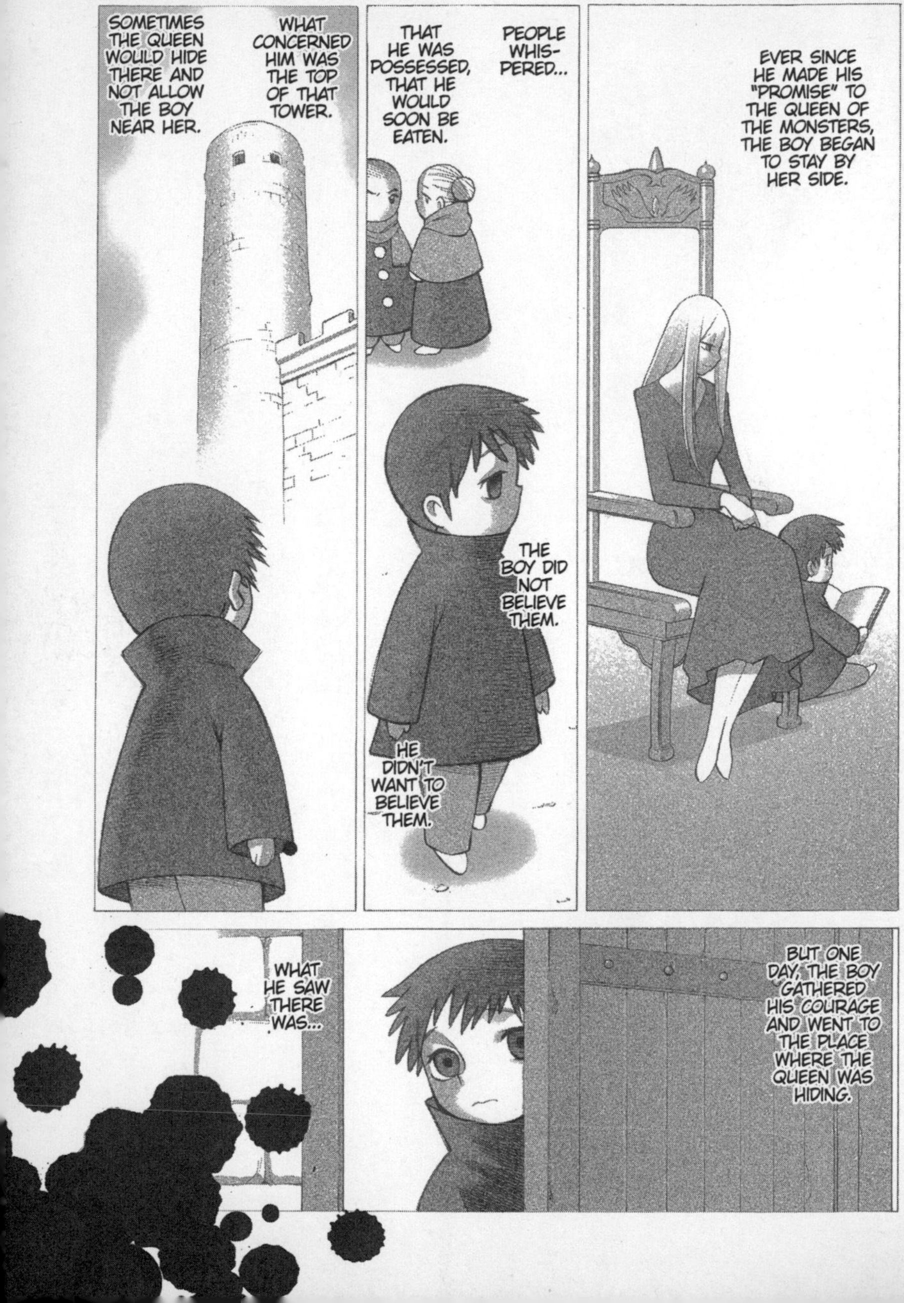
EVER SINCE HE MADE HIS "PROMISE" TO THE QUEEN OF THE MONSTERS, THE BOY BEGAN TO STAY BY HER SIDE.
PEOPLE WHISPERED...
THAT HE WAS POSSESSED, THAT HE WOULD SOON BE EATEN.
THE BOY DID NOT BELIEVE THEM.
HE DIDN'T WANT TO BELIEVE THEM.
WHAT CONCERNED HIM WAS THE TOP OF THAT TOWER.
SOMETIMES THE QUEEN WOULD HIDE THERE AND NOT ALLOW THE BOY NEAR HER.
BUT ONE DAY, THE BOY GATHERED HIS COURAGE AND WENT TO THE PLACE WHERE THE QUEEN WAS HIDING.
WHAT HE SAW THERE WAS...

Chapter 7: To a New Battlefield

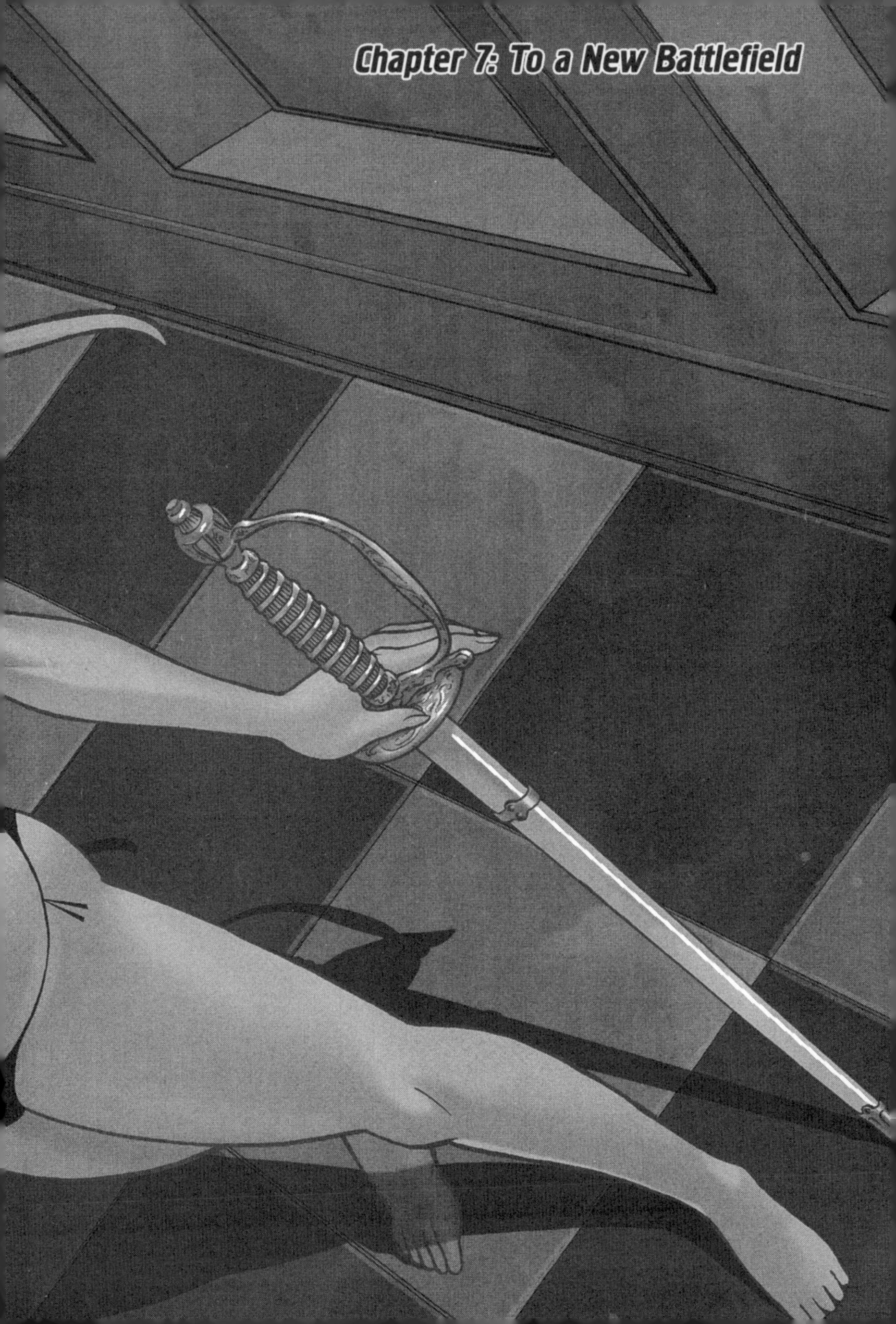

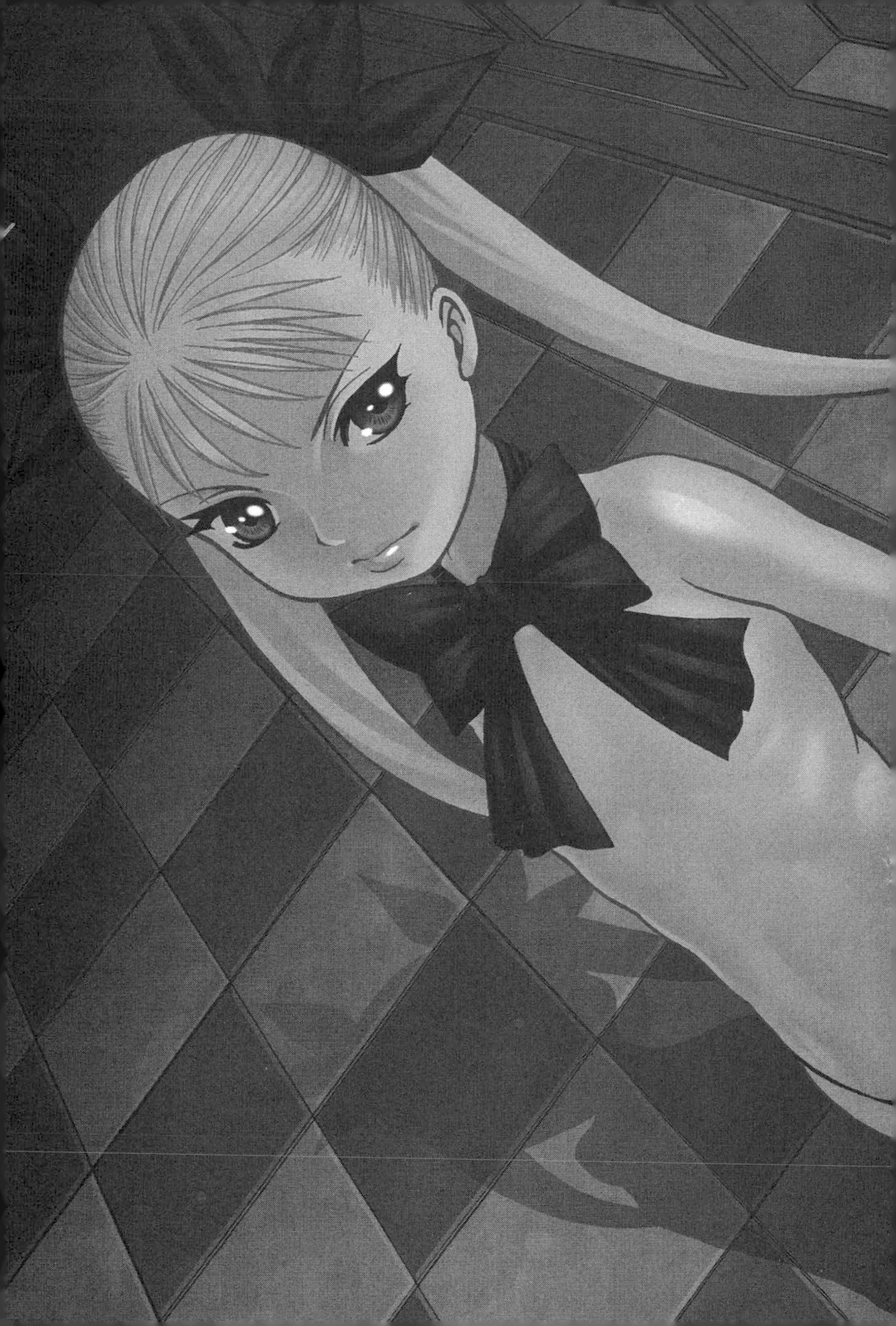

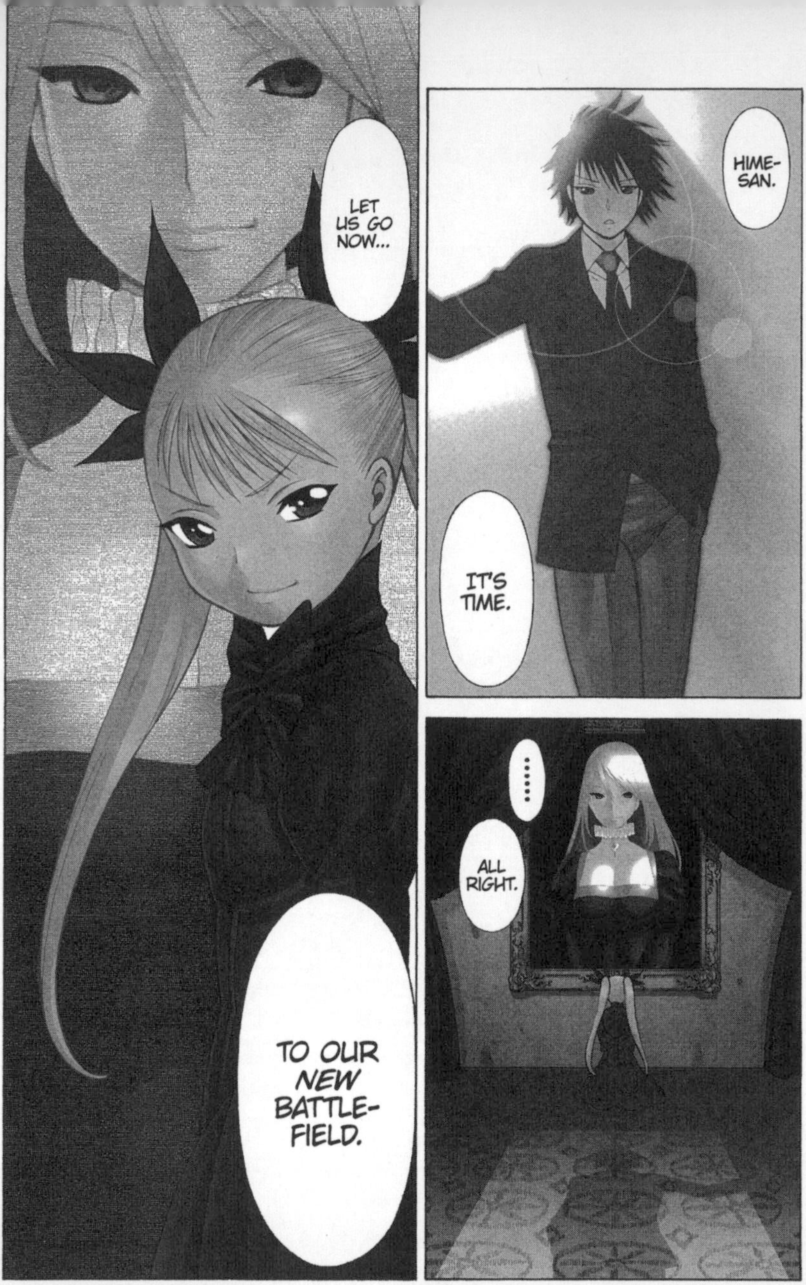
HIME-SAN.
IT'S TIME.
......
ALL RIGHT.
LET US GO NOW...
TO OUR NEW BATTLE-FIELD.

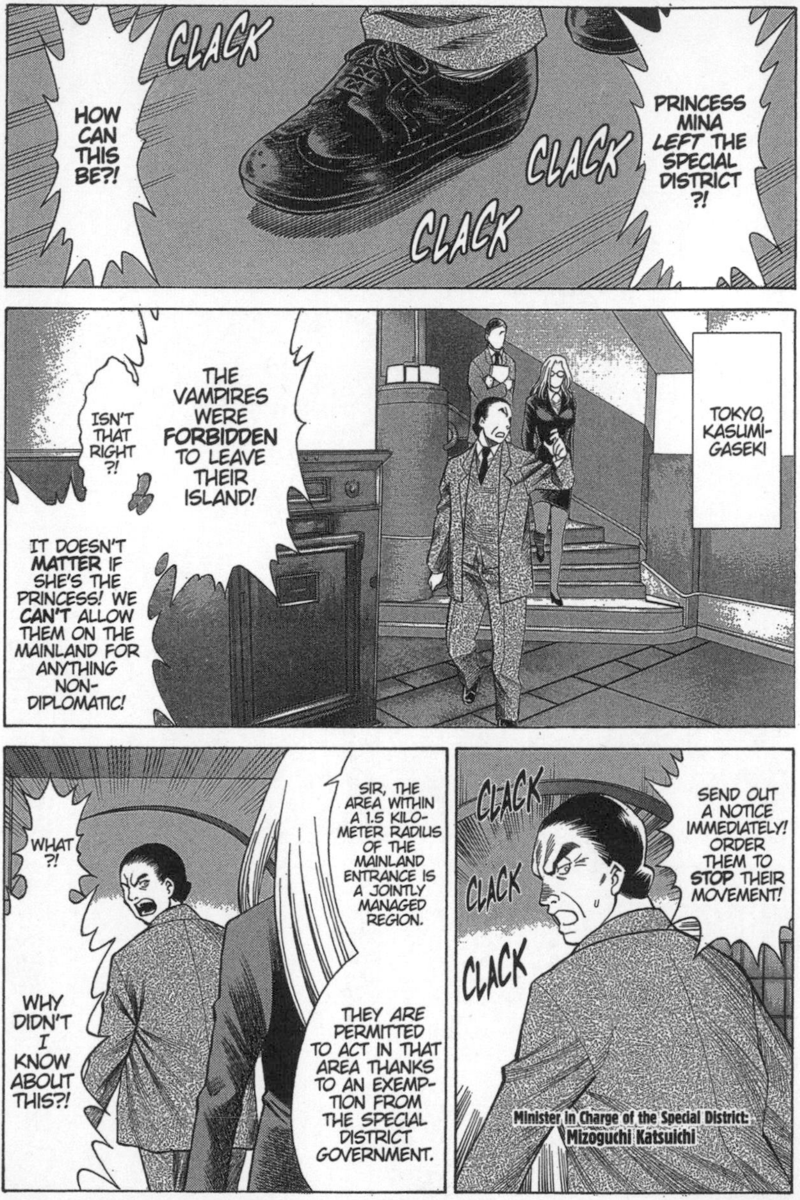
PRINCESS MINA LEFT THE SPECIAL DISTRICT ?!
CLACK
CLACK
CLACK
HOW CAN THIS BE?!
TOKYO, KASUMI-GASEKI
THE VAMPIRES WERE FORBIDDEN TO LEAVE THEIR ISLAND!
ISN'T THAT RIGHT ?!
IT DOESN'T MATTER IF SHE'S THE PRINCESS! WE CAN'T ALLOW THEM ON THE MAINLAND FOR ANYTHING NON-DIPLOMATIC!
SEND OUT A NOTICE IMMEDIATELY! ORDER THEM TO STOP THEIR MOVEMENT!
CLACK
CLACK
CLACK
Minister in Charge of the Special District: Mizoguchi Katsuichi
SIR, THE AREA WITHIN A 1.5 KILO-METER RADIUS OF THE MAINLAND ENTRANCE IS A JOINTLY MANAGED REGION.
WHAT ?!
THEY ARE PERMITTED TO ACT IN THAT AREA THANKS TO AN EXEMP-TION FROM THE SPECIAL DISTRICT GOVERNMENT.
WHY DIDN'T I KNOW ABOUT THIS?!

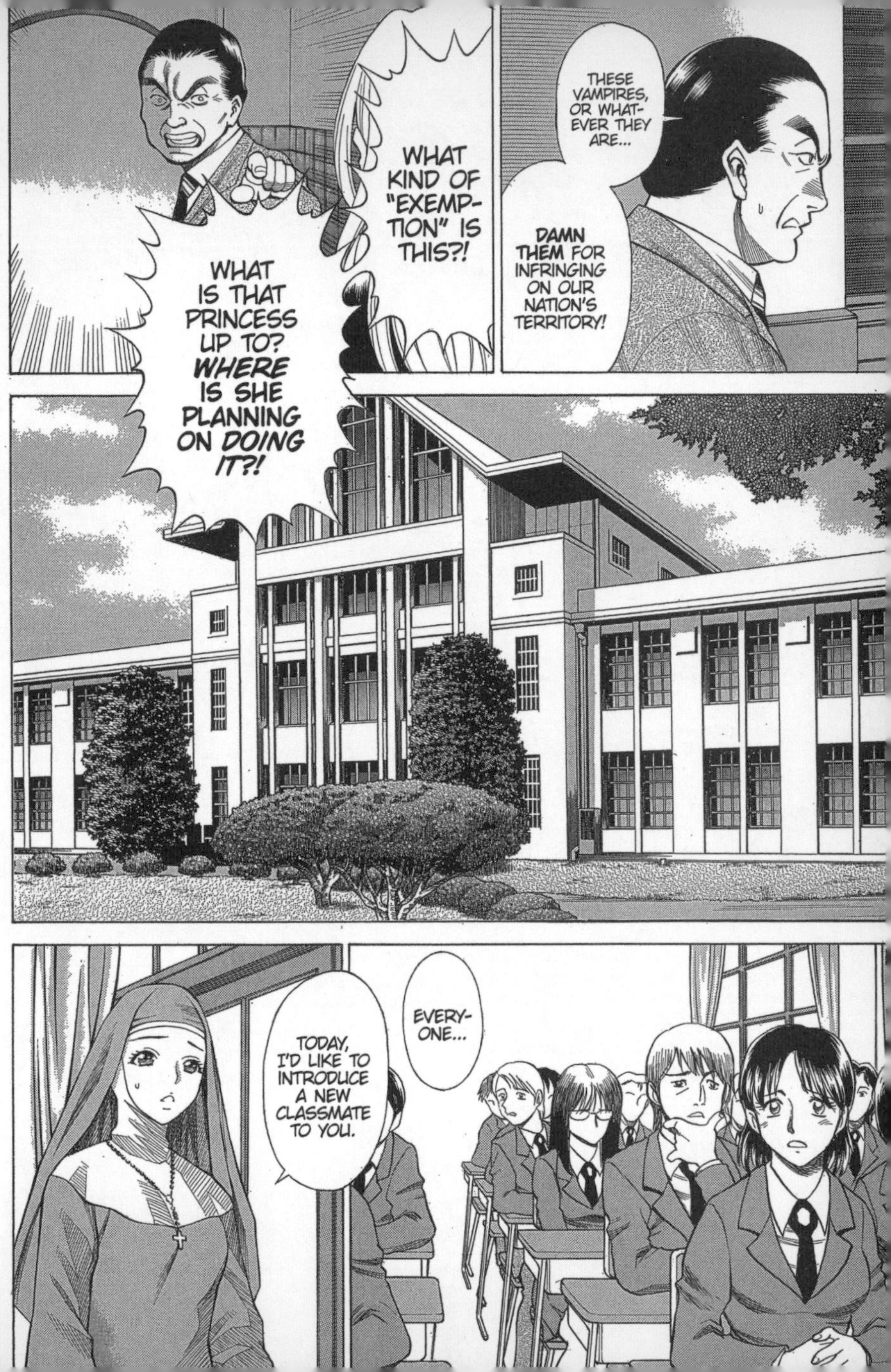
THESE VAMPIRES, OR WHATEVER THEY ARE...
DAMN THEM FOR INFRINGING ON OUR NATION'S TERRITORY!
WHAT KIND OF "EXEMPTION" IS THIS?!
WHAT IS THAT PRINCESS UP TO? *WHERE* IS SHE PLANNING ON *DOING IT*?!
EVERYONE...
TODAY, I'D LIKE TO INTRODUCE A NEW CLASSMATE TO YOU.

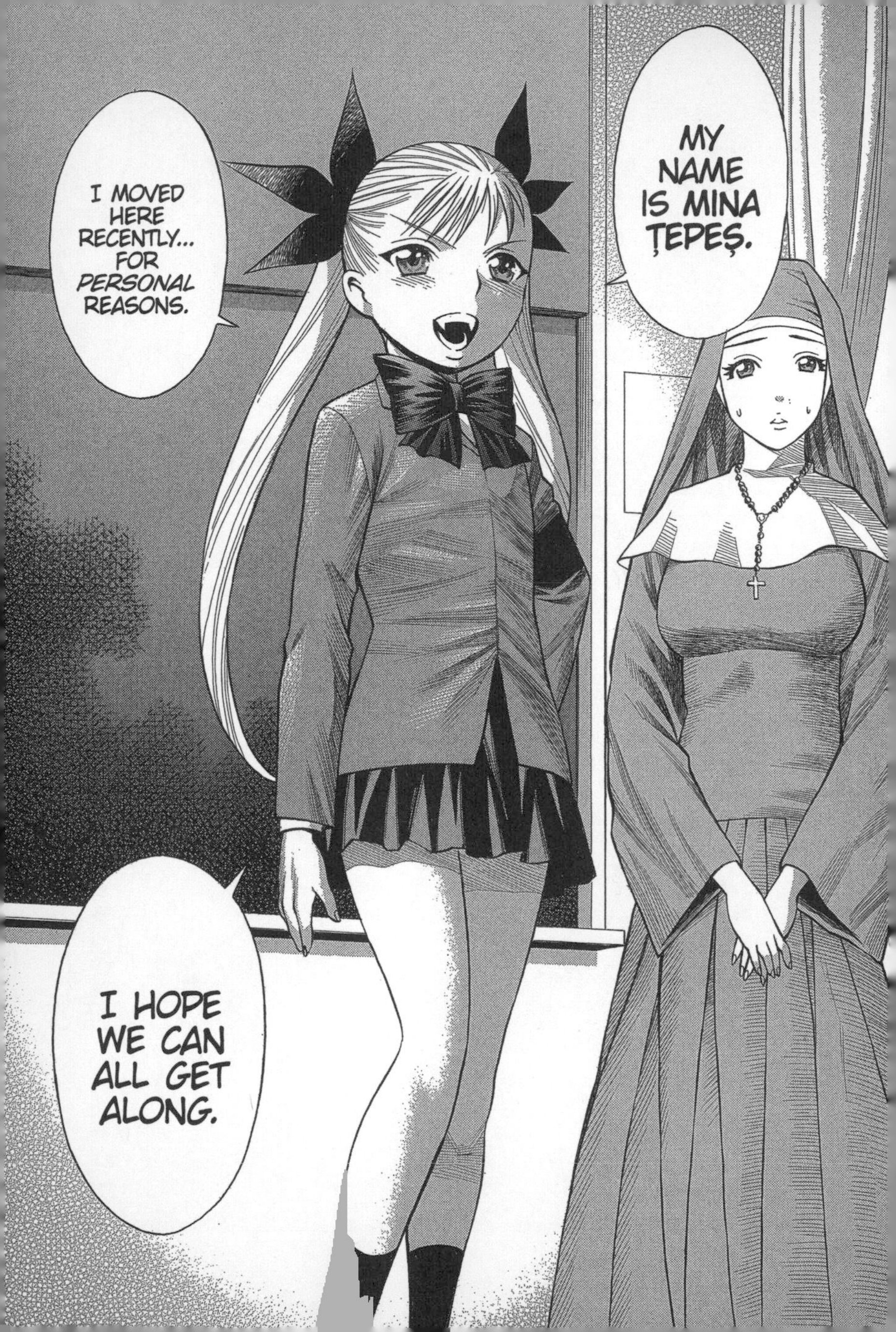
MY NAME IS MINA ȚEPEȘ.
I MOVED HERE RECENTLY... FOR PERSONAL REASONS.
I HOPE WE CAN ALL GET ALONG.

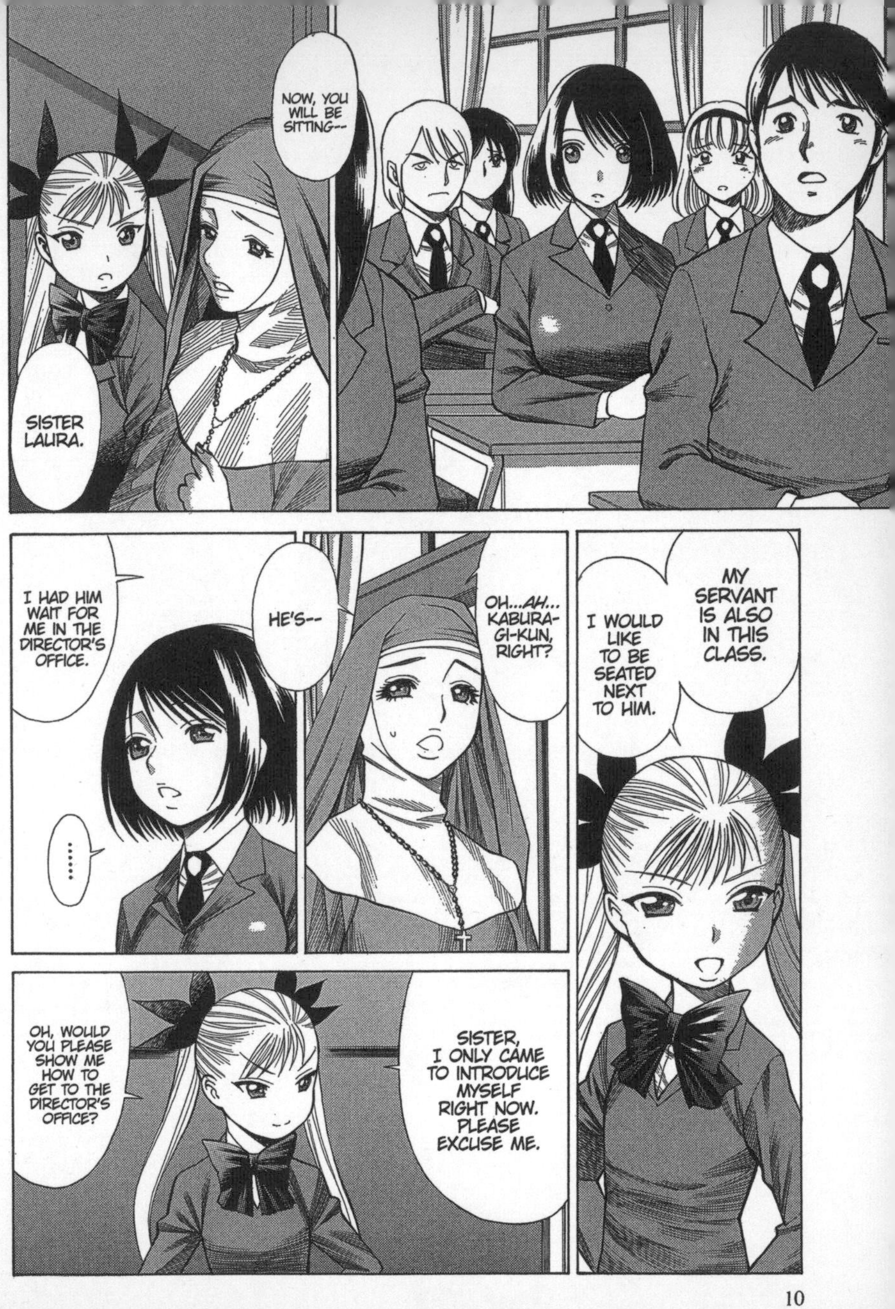
NOW, YOU WILL BE SITTING--
SISTER LAURA.
MY SERVANT IS ALSO IN THIS CLASS.
I WOULD LIKE TO BE SEATED NEXT TO HIM.
OH...AH... KABURAGI-KUN, RIGHT?
HE'S--
I HAD HIM WAIT FOR ME IN THE DIRECTOR'S OFFICE.
......
SISTER, I ONLY CAME TO INTRODUCE MYSELF RIGHT NOW. PLEASE EXCUSE ME.
OH, WOULD YOU PLEASE SHOW ME HOW TO GET TO THE DIRECTOR'S OFFICE?

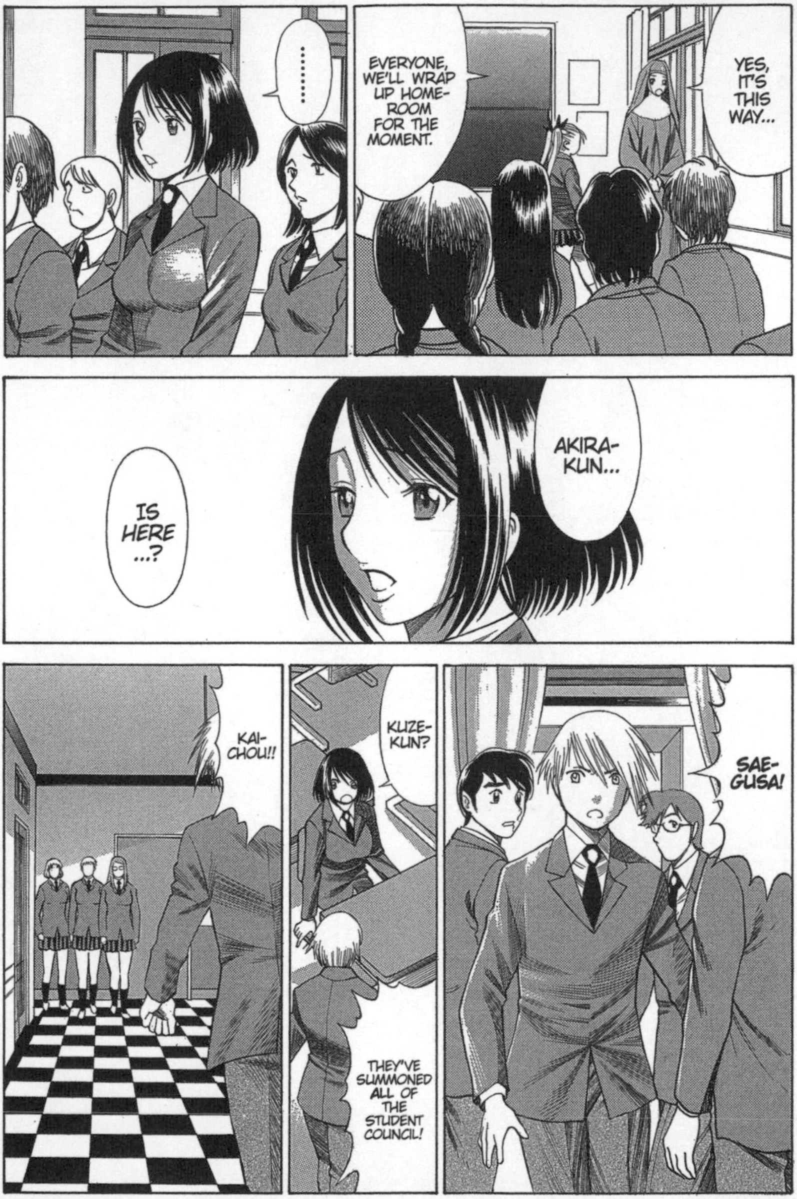
YES, IT'S THIS WAY...
EVERYONE, WE'LL WRAP UP HOME-ROOM FOR THE MOMENT.
......
AKIRA-KUN...
IS HERE ...?
SAE-GUSA!
KUZE-KUN?
THEY'VE SUMMONED ALL OF THE STUDENT COUNCIL!
KAI-CHOU!!

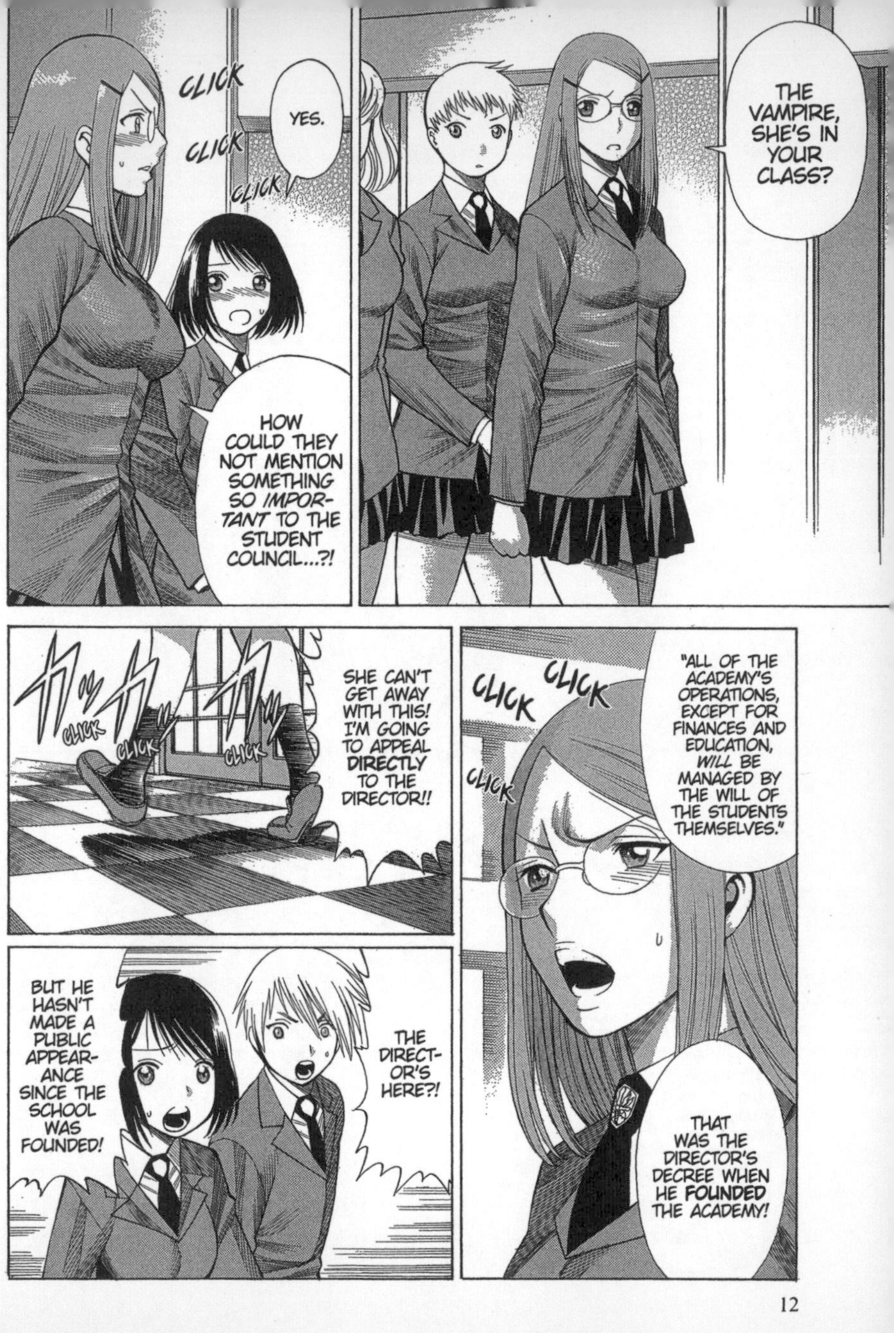
THE VAMPIRE, SHE'S IN YOUR CLASS?
YES.
CLICK
CLICK
CLICK
HOW COULD THEY NOT MENTION SOMETHING SO *IMPORTANT* TO THE STUDENT COUNCIL...?!
CLICK
CLICK
"ALL OF THE ACADEMY'S OPERATIONS, EXCEPT FOR FINANCES AND EDUCATION, *WILL* BE MANAGED BY THE WILL OF THE STUDENTS THEMSELVES."
CLICK
THAT WAS THE DIRECTOR'S DECREE WHEN HE **FOUNDED** THE ACADEMY!
SHE CAN'T GET AWAY WITH THIS! I'M GOING TO APPEAL **DIRECTLY** TO THE DIRECTOR!!
カッ カッ カッ
CLICK
CLICK
CLICK
THE DIRECTOR'S HERE?!
BUT HE HASN'T MADE A PUBLIC APPEARANCE SINCE THE SCHOOL WAS FOUNDED!

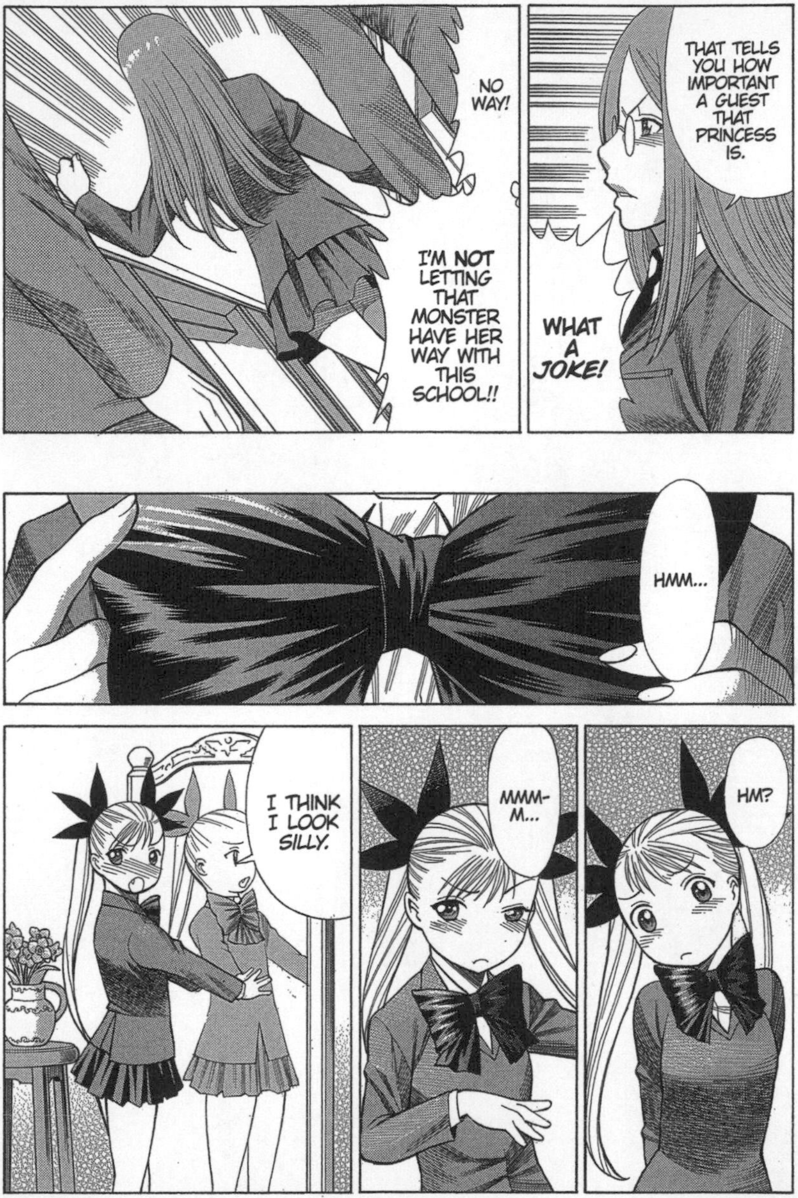
THAT TELLS YOU HOW IMPORTANT A GUEST THAT PRINCESS IS.
WHAT A JOKE!
NO WAY!
I'M NOT LETTING THAT MONSTER HAVE HER WAY WITH THIS SCHOOL!!
HMM...
HM?
MMMM-M...
I THINK I LOOK SILLY.

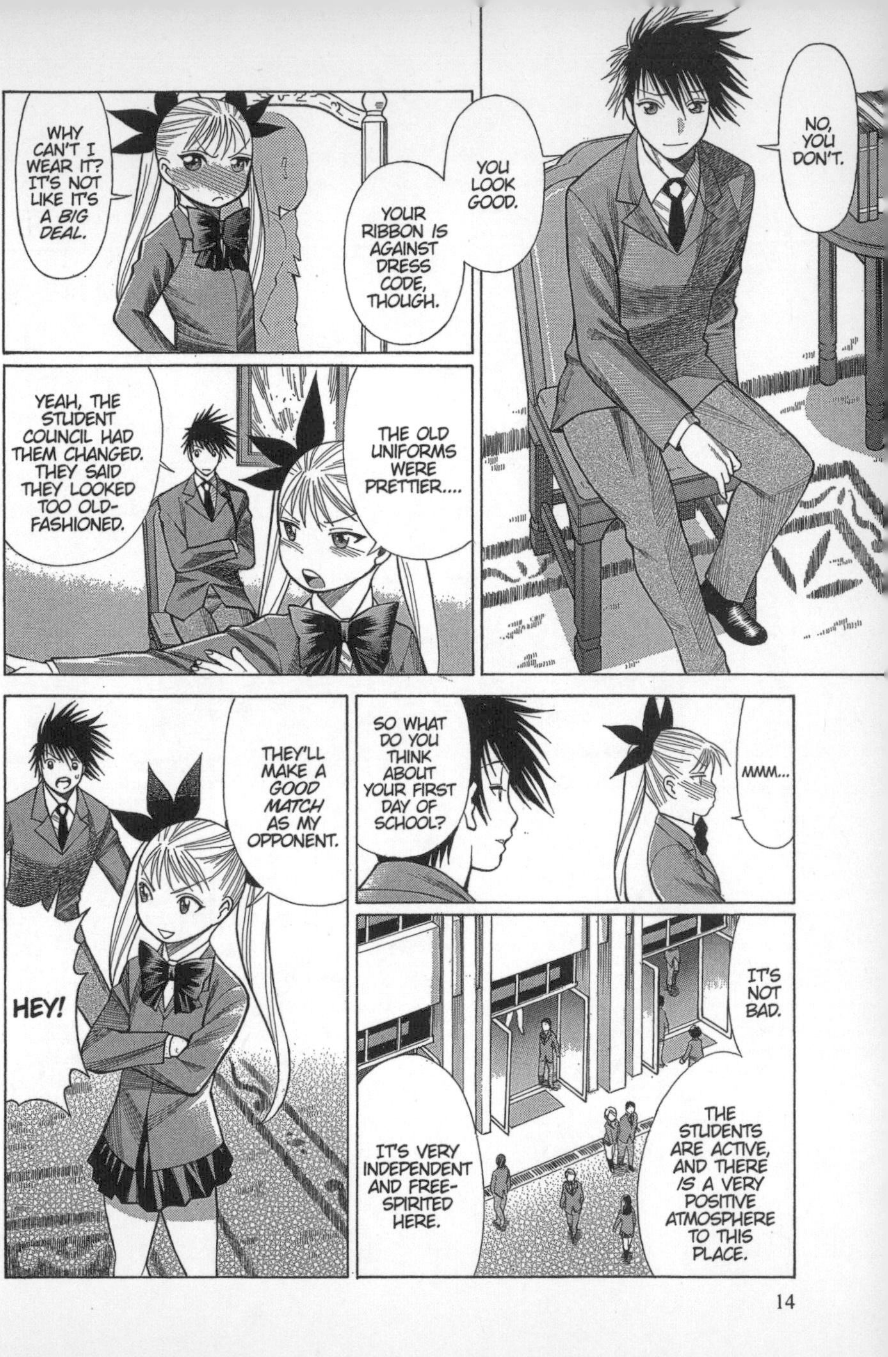
NO, YOU DON'T.
YOU LOOK GOOD.
YOUR RIBBON IS AGAINST DRESS CODE, THOUGH.
WHY CAN'T I WEAR IT? IT'S NOT LIKE IT'S A *BIG DEAL*.
THE OLD UNIFORMS WERE PRETTIER....
YEAH, THE STUDENT COUNCIL HAD THEM CHANGED. THEY SAID THEY LOOKED TOO OLD-FASHIONED.
MMM...
SO WHAT DO YOU THINK ABOUT YOUR FIRST DAY OF SCHOOL?
IT'S NOT BAD.
THE STUDENTS ARE ACTIVE, AND THERE *IS* A VERY POSITIVE ATMOSPHERE TO THIS PLACE.
IT'S VERY INDEPENDENT AND FREE-SPIRITED HERE.
THEY'LL MAKE A *GOOD MATCH* AS MY OPPONENT.
HEY!

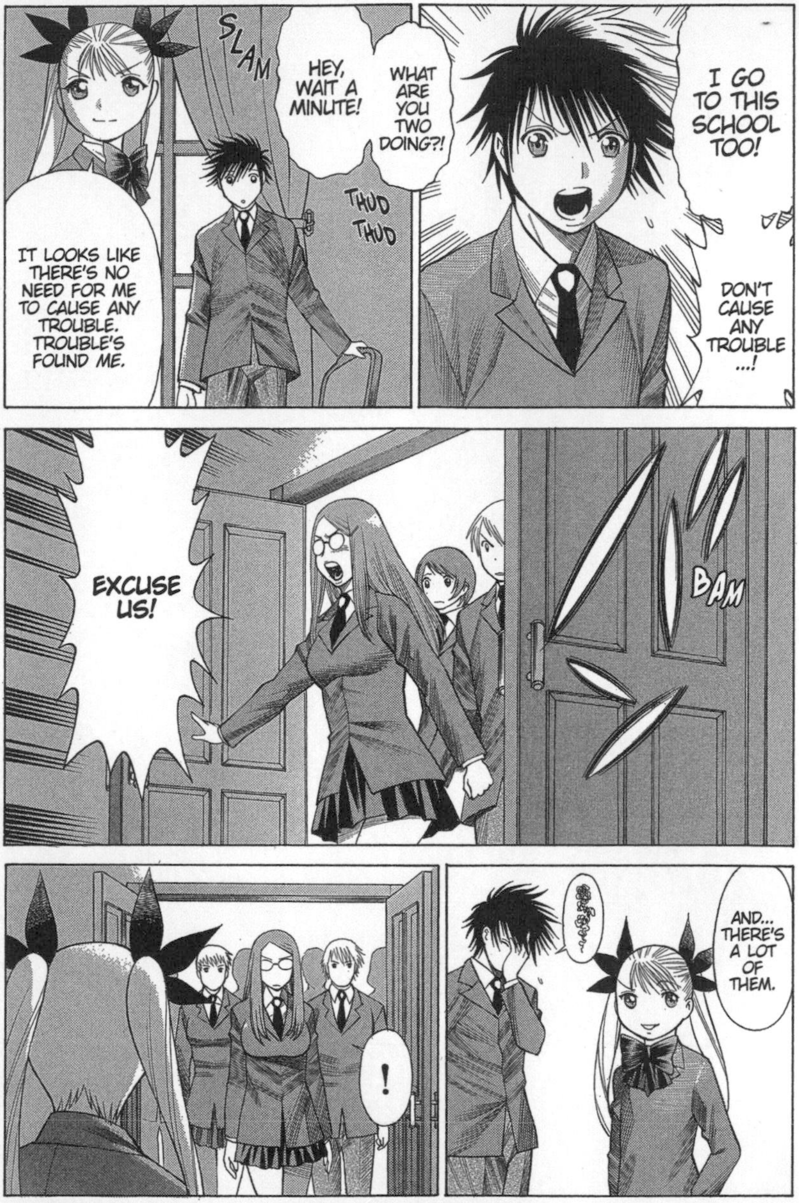
I GO TO THIS SCHOOL TOO!
DON'T CAUSE ANY TROUBLE ...!
WHAT ARE YOU TWO DOING?!
HEY, WAIT A MINUTE!
SLAM
THUD THUD
IT LOOKS LIKE THERE'S NO NEED FOR ME TO CAUSE ANY TROUBLE. TROUBLE'S FOUND ME.
BAM
EXCUSE US!
AND... THERE'S A LOT OF THEM.
!

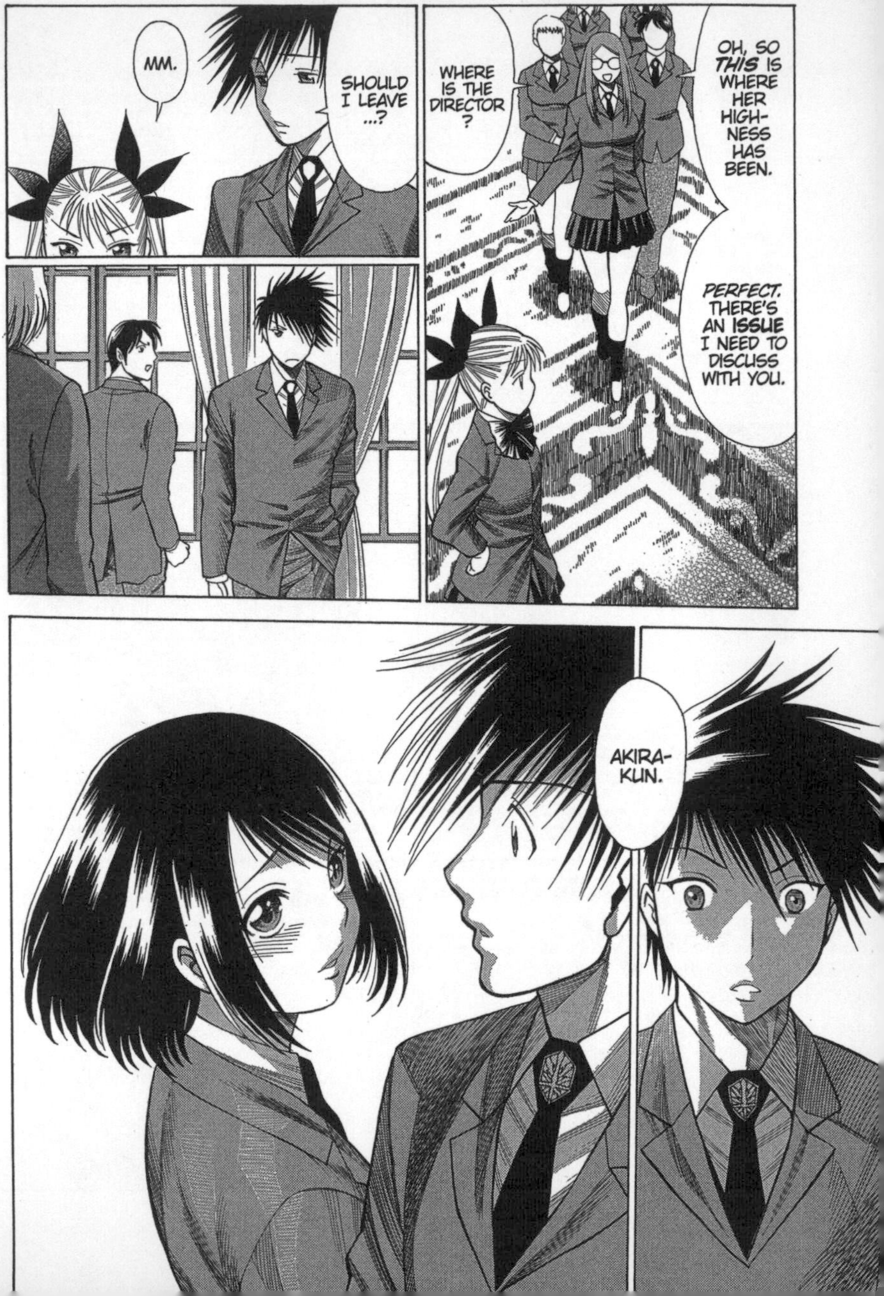
OH, SO THIS IS WHERE HER HIGHNESS HAS BEEN.
WHERE IS THE DIRECTOR?
PERFECT. THERE'S AN ISSUE I NEED TO DISCUSS WITH YOU.
SHOULD I LEAVE ...?
MM.
AKIRA-KUN.

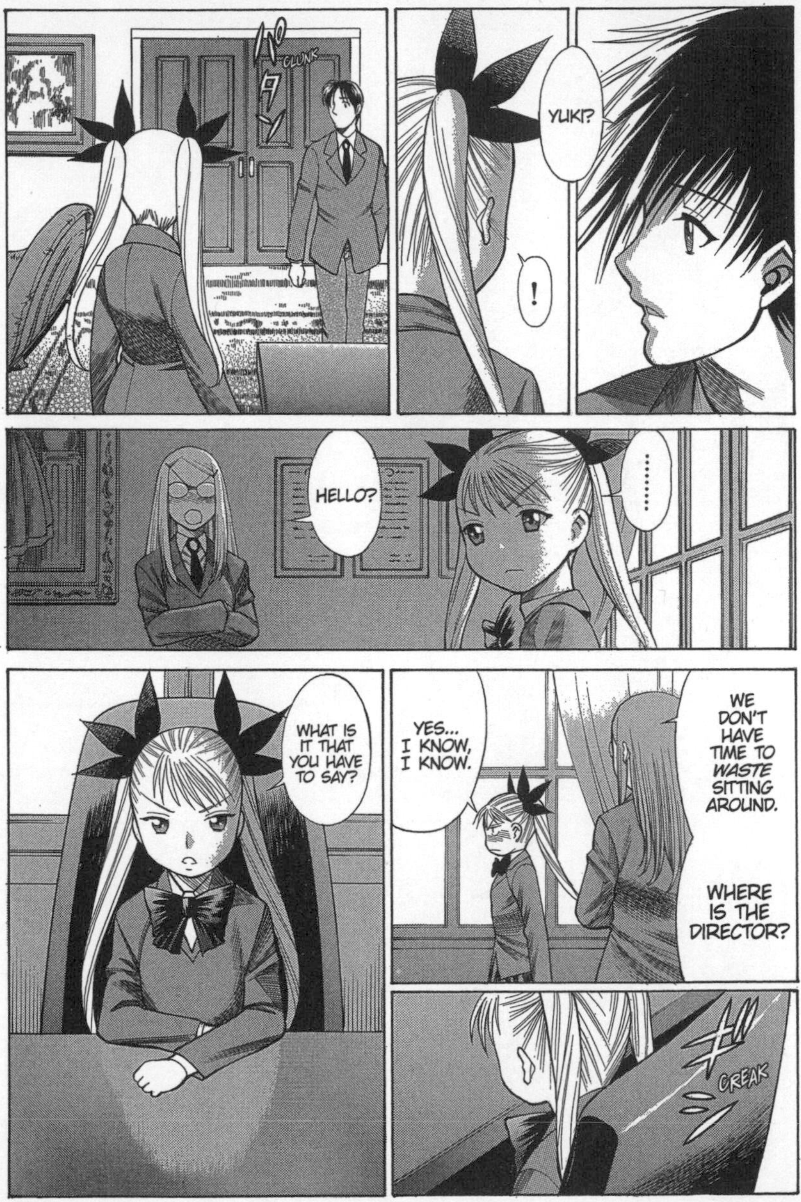
YUKI?
!
CLUNK
……
HELLO?
WE DON'T HAVE TIME TO *WASTE* SITTING AROUND.
WHERE IS THE DIRECTOR?
YES... I KNOW, I KNOW.
CREAK
WHAT IS IT THAT YOU HAVE TO SAY?

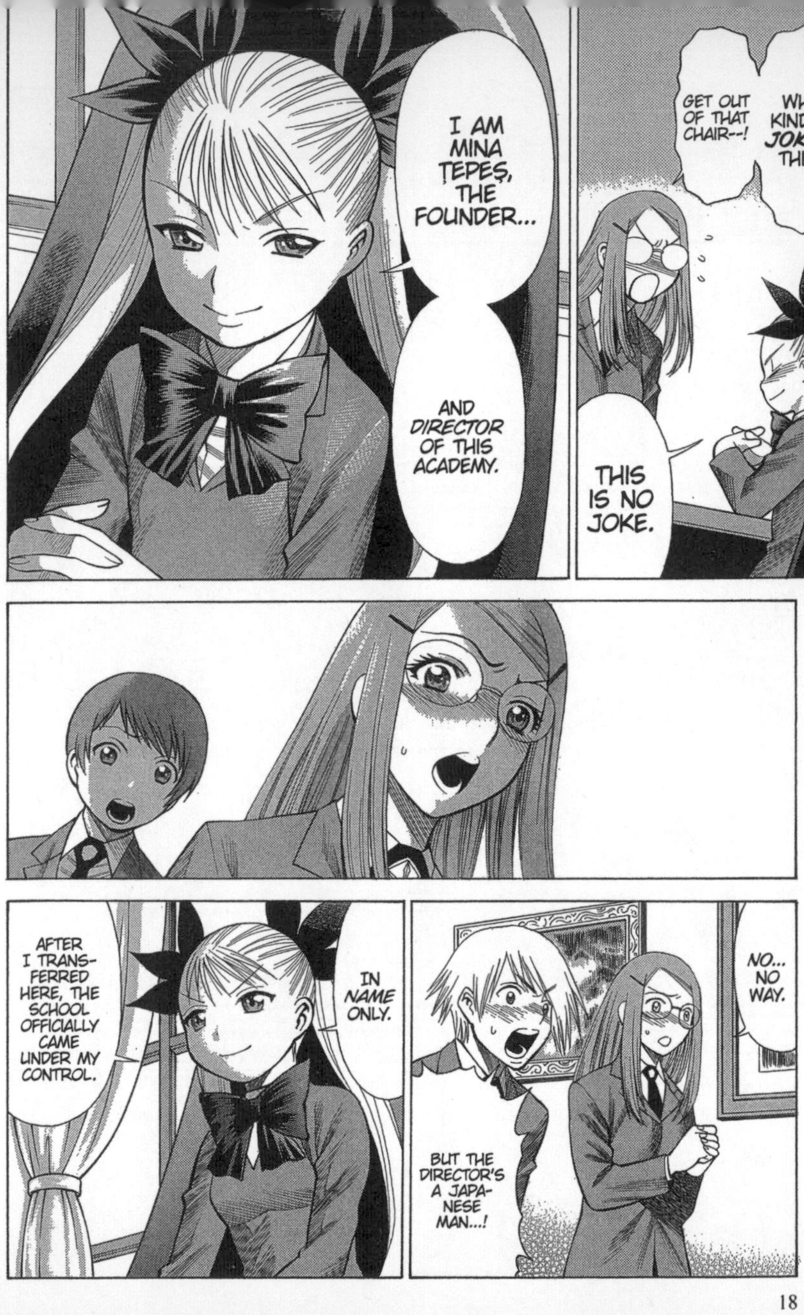
WHAT KIND OF JOKE IS THIS?!
GET OUT OF THAT CHAIR--!
THIS IS NO JOKE.
I AM MINA ŢEPEŞ, THE FOUNDER...
AND DIRECTOR OF THIS ACADEMY.
NO... NO WAY.
BUT THE DIRECTOR'S A JAPANESE MAN...!
IN NAME ONLY.
AFTER I TRANSFERRED HERE, THE SCHOOL OFFICIALLY CAME UNDER MY CONTROL.

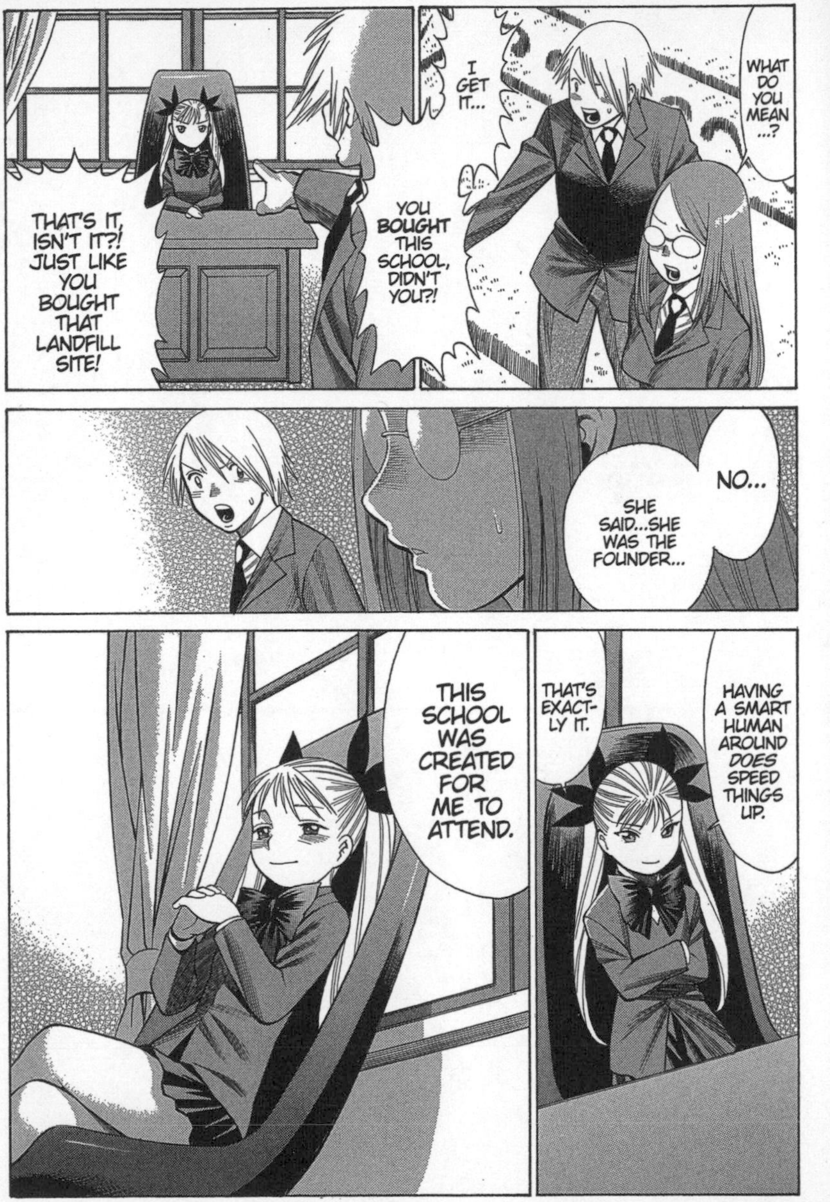
WHAT DO YOU MEAN...?
I GET IT...
YOU BOUGHT THIS SCHOOL, DIDN'T YOU?!
THAT'S IT, ISN'T IT?! JUST LIKE YOU BOUGHT THAT LANDFILL SITE!
NO...
SHE SAID...SHE WAS THE FOUNDER...
HAVING A SMART HUMAN AROUND *DOES* SPEED THINGS UP.
THAT'S EXACT-LY IT.
THIS SCHOOL WAS CREATED FOR ME TO ATTEND.

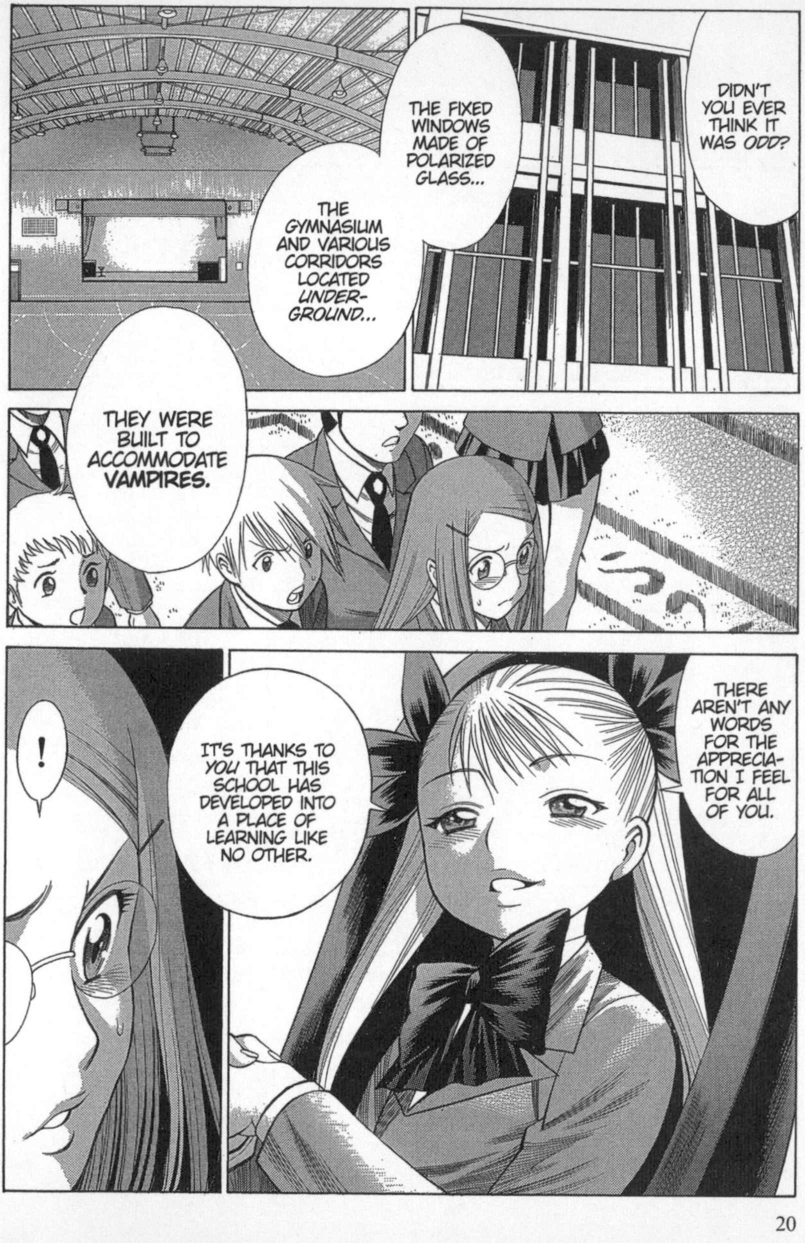
DIDN'T YOU EVER THINK IT WAS *ODD?*
THE FIXED WINDOWS MADE OF POLARIZED GLASS...
THE GYMNASIUM AND VARIOUS CORRIDORS LOCATED UNDER-GROUND...
THEY WERE BUILT TO ACCOMMODATE **VAMPIRES.**
THERE AREN'T ANY WORDS FOR THE APPRECIA-TION I FEEL FOR ALL OF YOU.
IT'S THANKS TO *YOU* THAT THIS SCHOOL HAS DEVELOPED INTO A PLACE OF LEARNING LIKE NO OTHER.
!

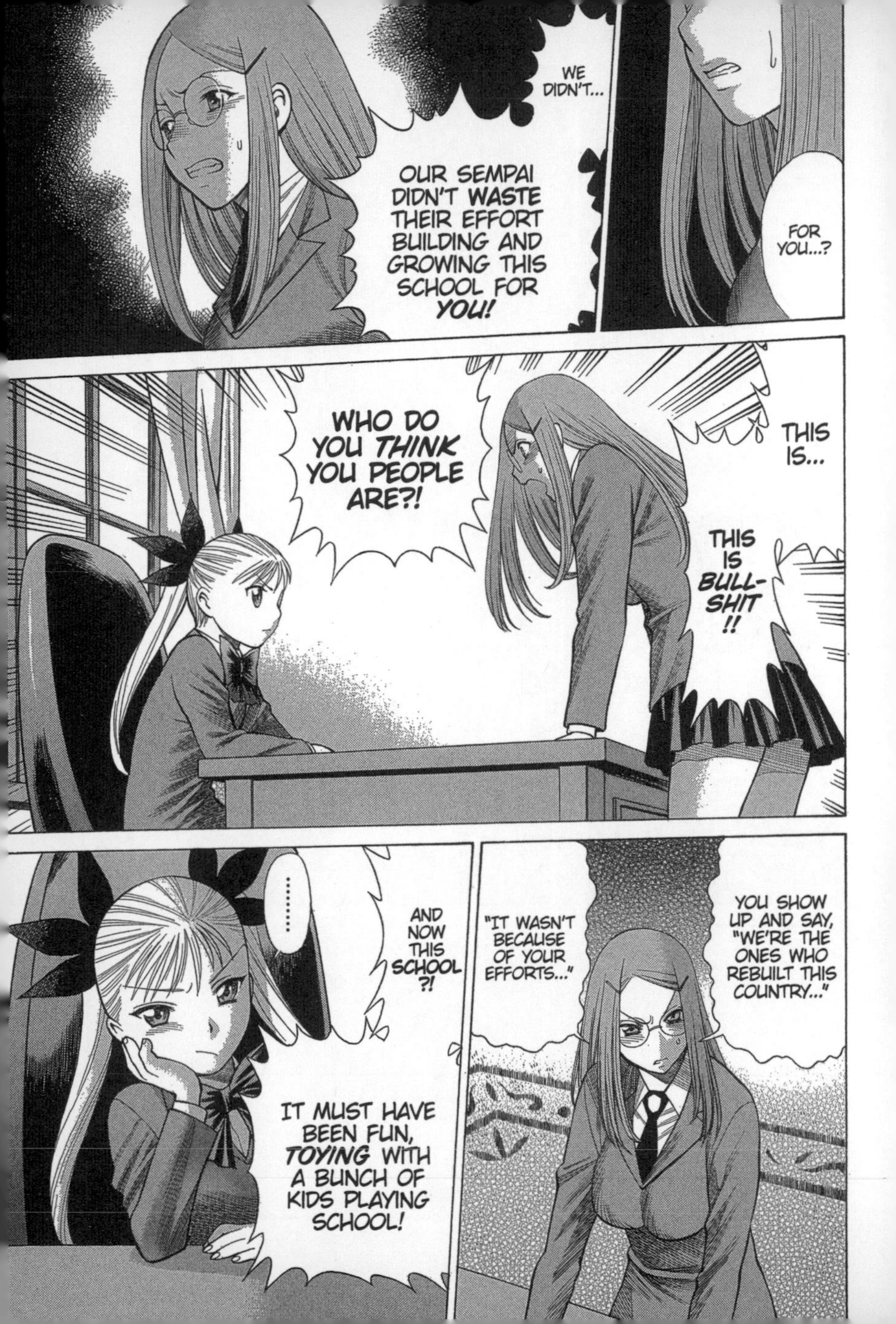
FOR YOU...?
WE DIDN'T...
OUR SEMPAI DIDN'T WASTE THEIR EFFORT BUILDING AND GROWING THIS SCHOOL FOR YOU!
THIS IS...
THIS IS BULLSHIT!!
WHO DO YOU THINK YOU PEOPLE ARE?!
YOU SHOW UP AND SAY, "WE'RE THE ONES WHO REBUILT THIS COUNTRY..."
"IT WASN'T BECAUSE OF YOUR EFFORTS..."
AND NOW THIS SCHOOL?!
IT MUST HAVE BEEN FUN, TOYING WITH A BUNCH OF KIDS PLAYING SCHOOL!
....

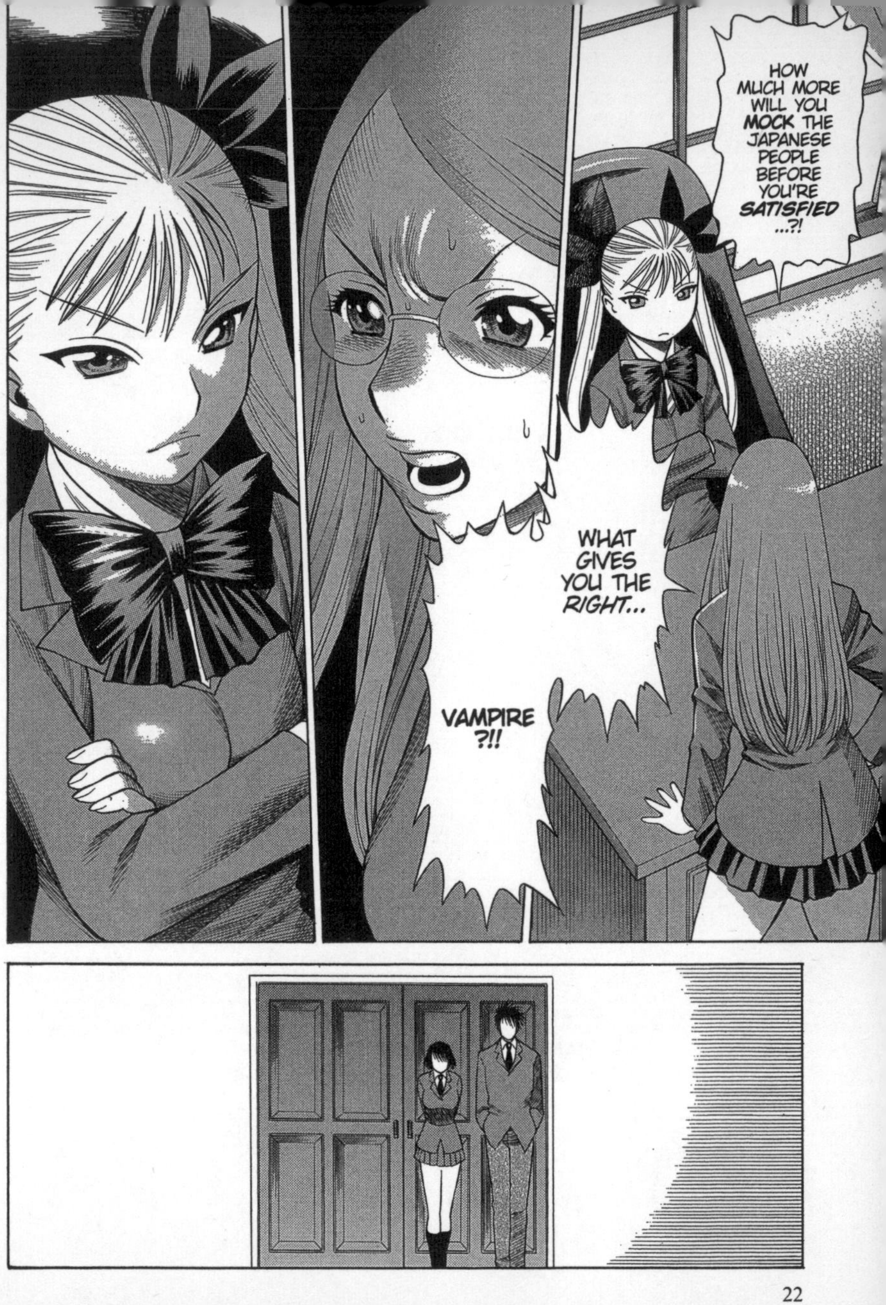

HOW MUCH MORE WILL YOU MOCK THE JAPANESE PEOPLE BEFORE YOU'RE SATISFIED ...?!
WHAT GIVES YOU THE RIGHT...
VAMPIRE ?!!

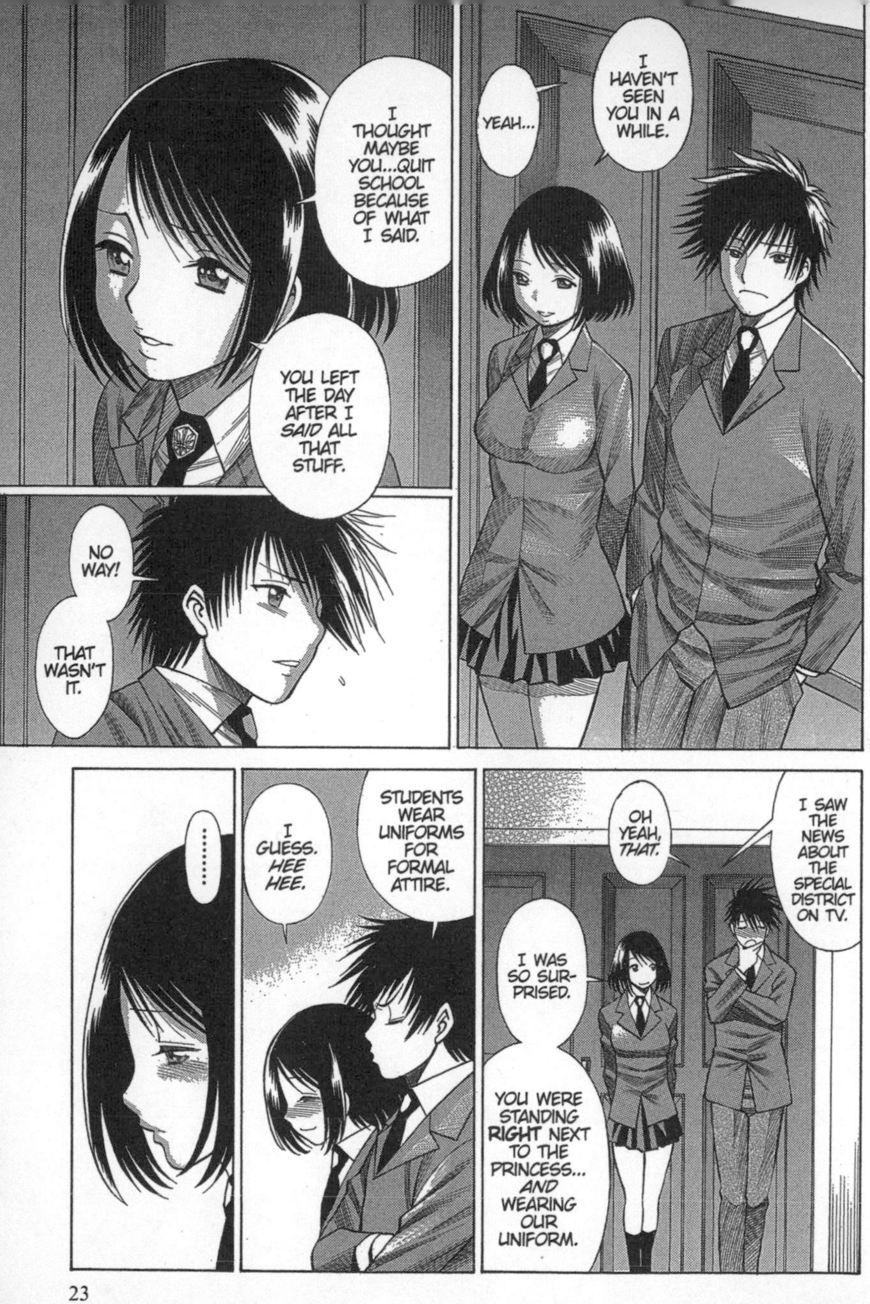
I HAVEN'T SEEN YOU IN A WHILE.
YEAH...
I THOUGHT MAYBE YOU...QUIT SCHOOL BECAUSE OF WHAT I SAID.
YOU LEFT THE DAY AFTER I *SAID* ALL THAT STUFF.
NO WAY!
THAT WASN'T IT.
I SAW THE NEWS ABOUT THE SPECIAL DISTRICT ON TV.
OH YEAH, *THAT.*
I WAS SO SUR-PRISED.
YOU WERE STANDING **RIGHT** NEXT TO THE PRINCESS... *AND* WEARING OUR UNIFORM.
STUDENTS WEAR UNIFORMS FOR FORMAL ATTIRE.
I GUESS. *HEE HEE.*
....

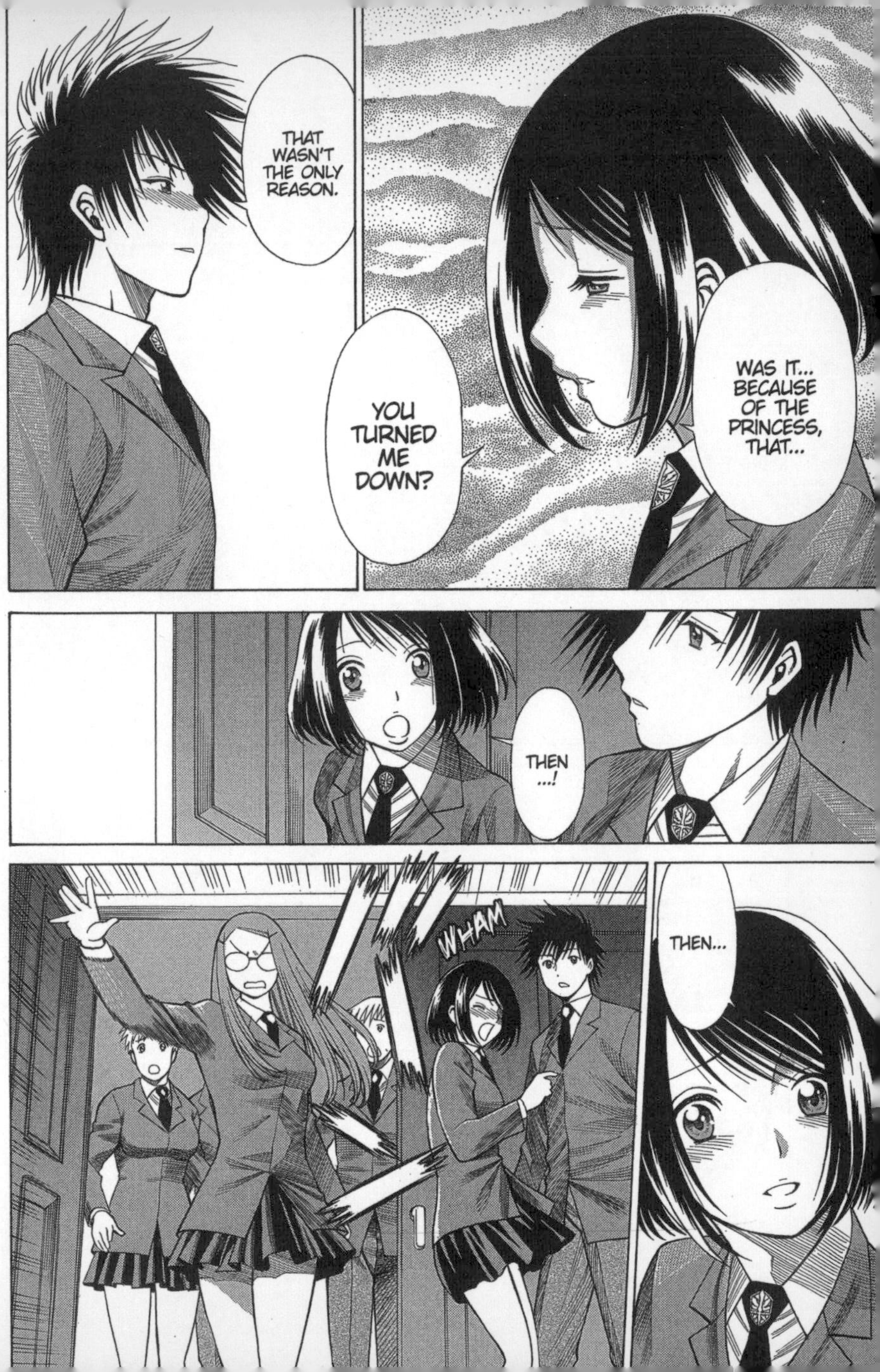
WAS IT... BECAUSE OF THE PRINCESS, THAT...
YOU TURNED ME DOWN?
THAT WASN'T THE ONLY REASON.
THEN ...!
THEN...
WHAM

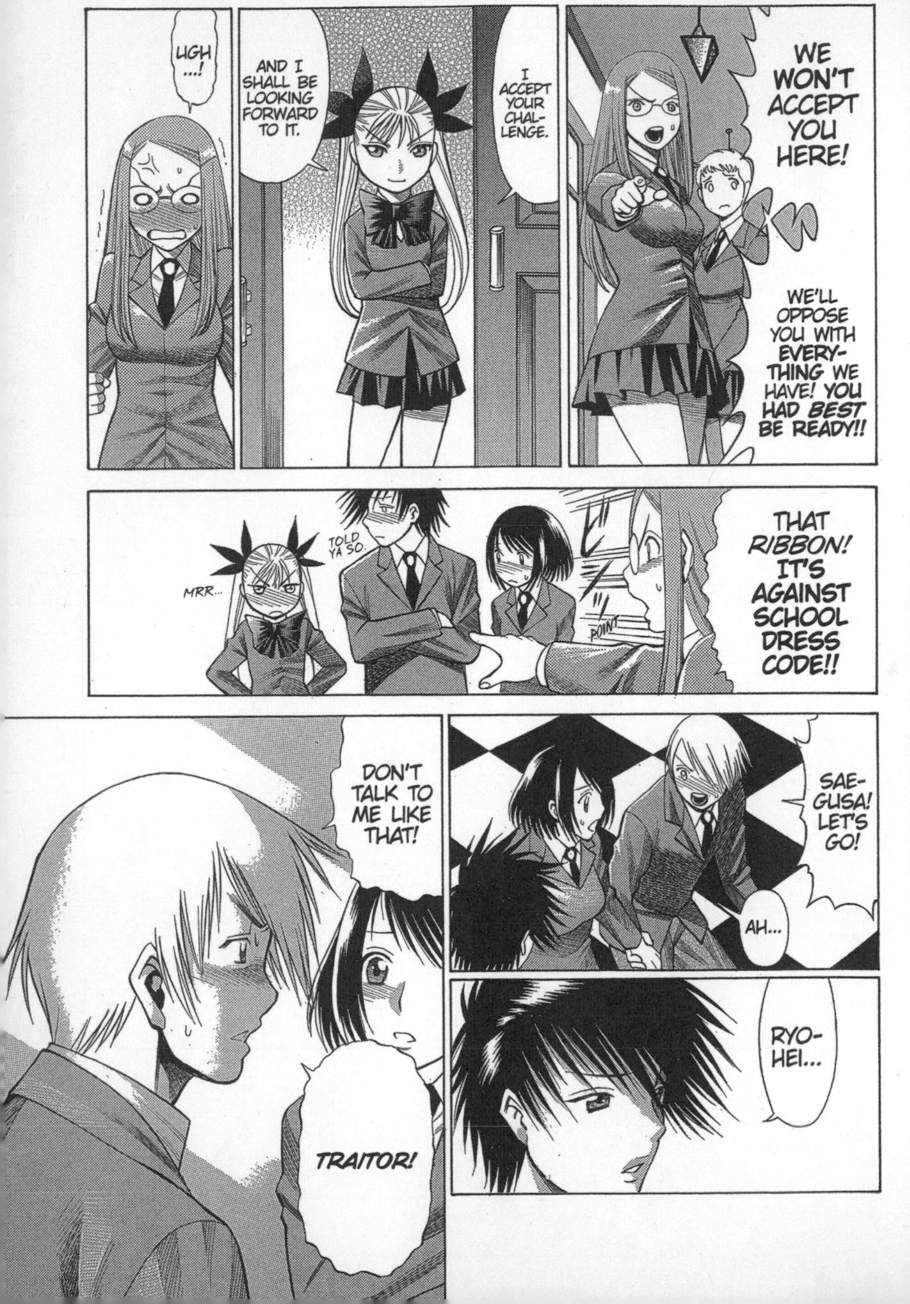
WE WON'T ACCEPT YOU HERE!
WE'LL OPPOSE YOU WITH EVERY-THING WE HAVE! YOU HAD *BEST* BE READY!!
I ACCEPT YOUR CHAL-LENGE.
AND I SHALL BE LOOKING FORWARD TO IT.
UGH ...!
THAT *RIBBON!* IT'S AGAINST SCHOOL DRESS CODE!!
POINT
TOLD YA SO.
MRR...
SAE-GUSA! LET'S GO!
AH...
RYO-HEI...
DON'T TALK TO ME LIKE THAT!
TRAITOR!

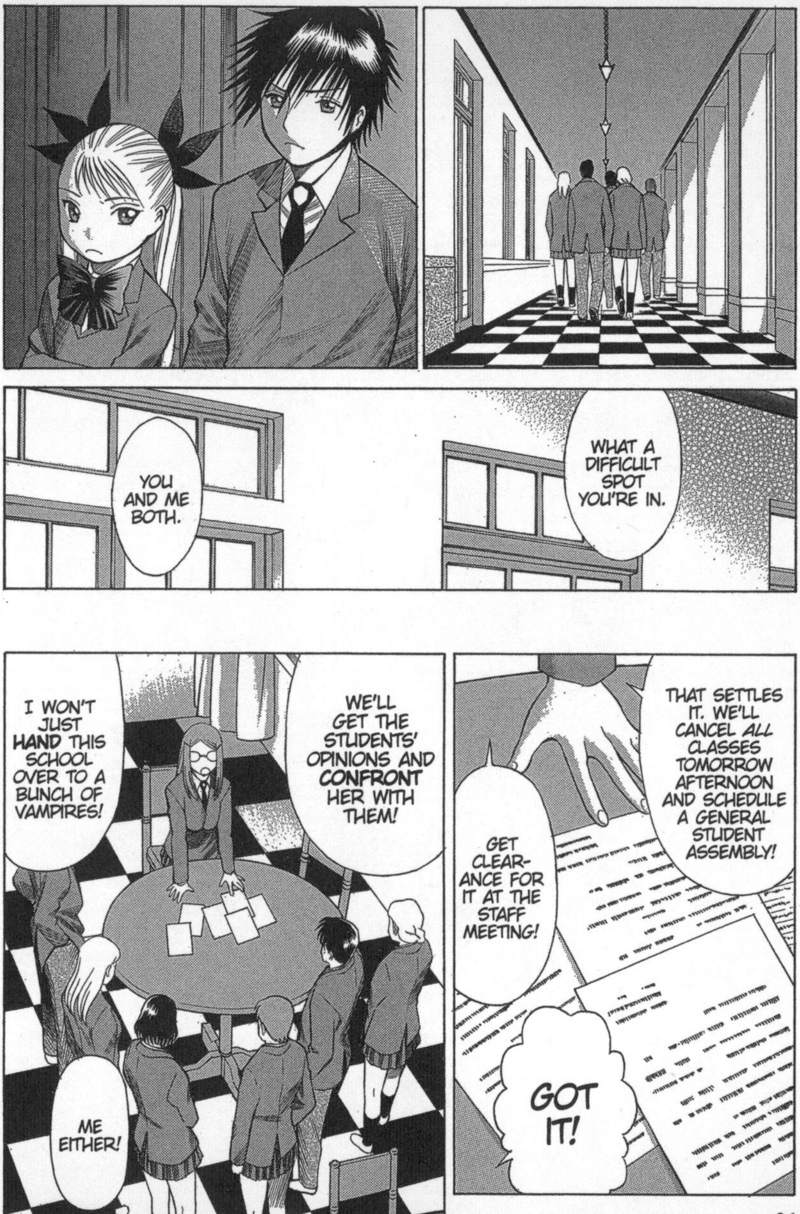
WHAT A DIFFICULT SPOT YOU'RE IN.
YOU AND ME BOTH.
THAT SETTLES IT. WE'LL CANCEL ALL CLASSES TOMORROW AFTERNOON AND SCHEDULE A GENERAL STUDENT ASSEMBLY!
GET CLEARANCE FOR IT AT THE STAFF MEETING!
GOT IT!
WE'LL GET THE STUDENTS' OPINIONS AND CONFRONT HER WITH THEM!
I WON'T JUST HAND THIS SCHOOL OVER TO A BUNCH OF VAMPIRES!
ME EITHER!

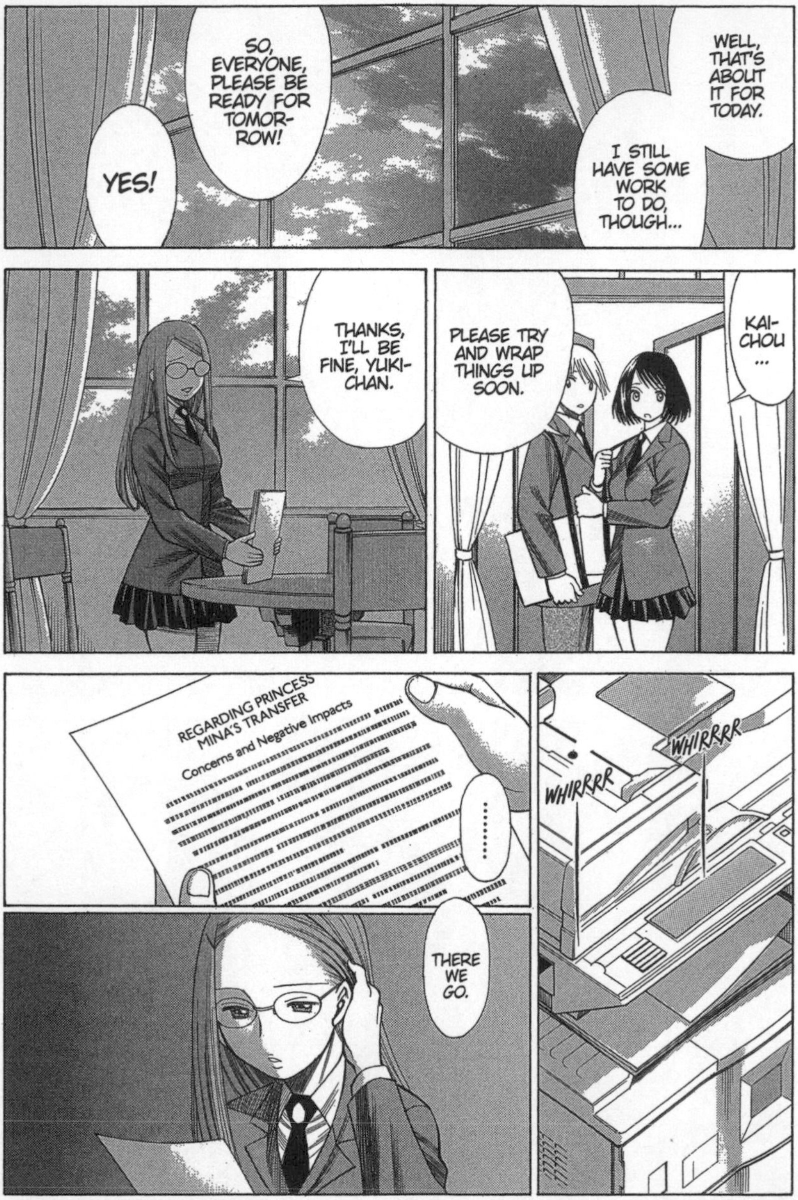
WELL, THAT'S ABOUT IT FOR TODAY.
I STILL HAVE SOME WORK TO DO, THOUGH...
SO, EVERYONE, PLEASE BE READY FOR TOMORROW!
YES!
KAI-CHOU ...
PLEASE TRY AND WRAP THINGS UP SOON.
THANKS, I'LL BE FINE, YUKI-CHAN.
WHIRRRR
WHIRRRR
REGARDING PRINCESS MINA'S TRANSFER
Concerns and Negative Impacts
....
THERE WE GO.

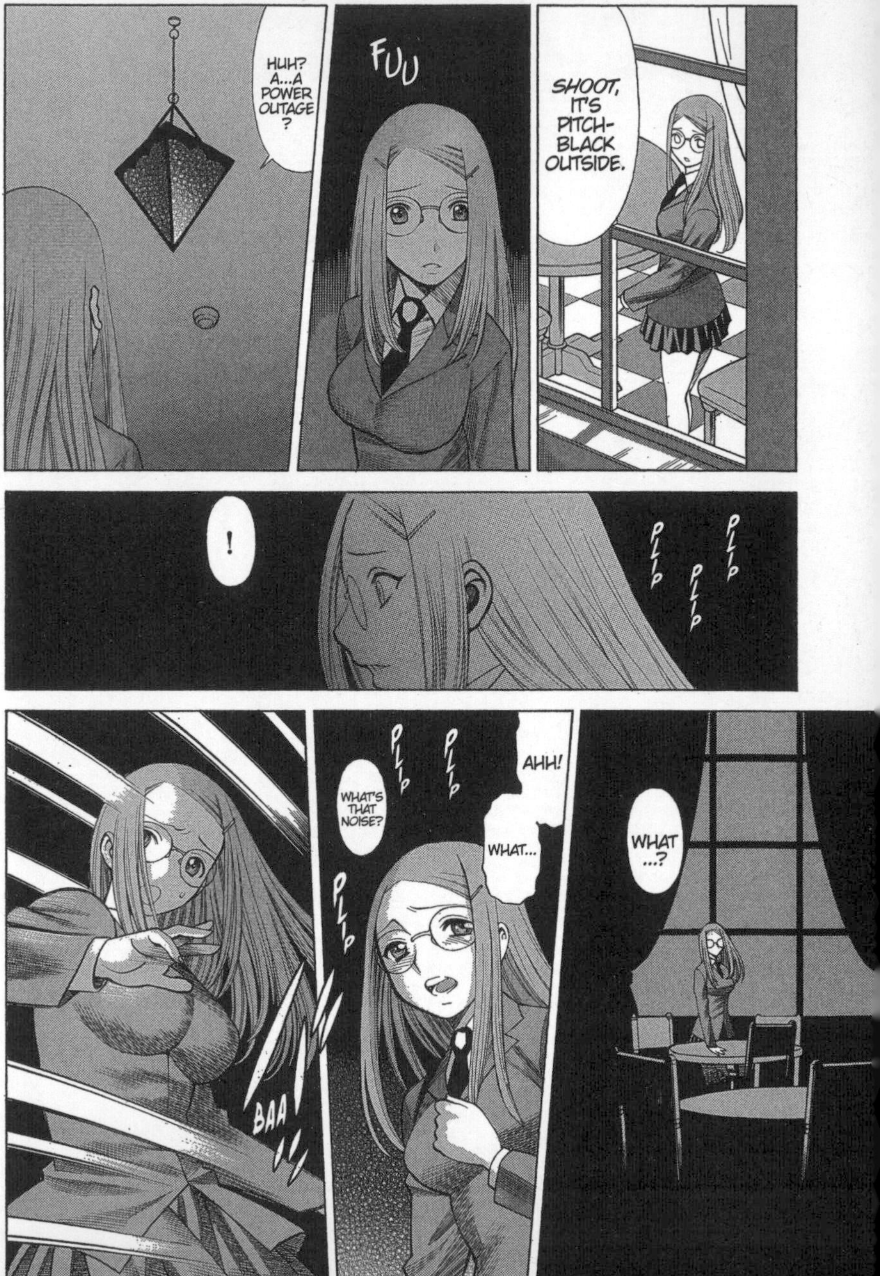
SHOOT, IT'S PITCH-BLACK OUTSIDE.
FUU
HUH? A...A POWER OUTAGE?
PLIP
PLIP
PLIP
!
WHAT ...?
AHH!
WHAT...
PLIP
PLIP
WHAT'S THAT NOISE?
PLIP
BAA

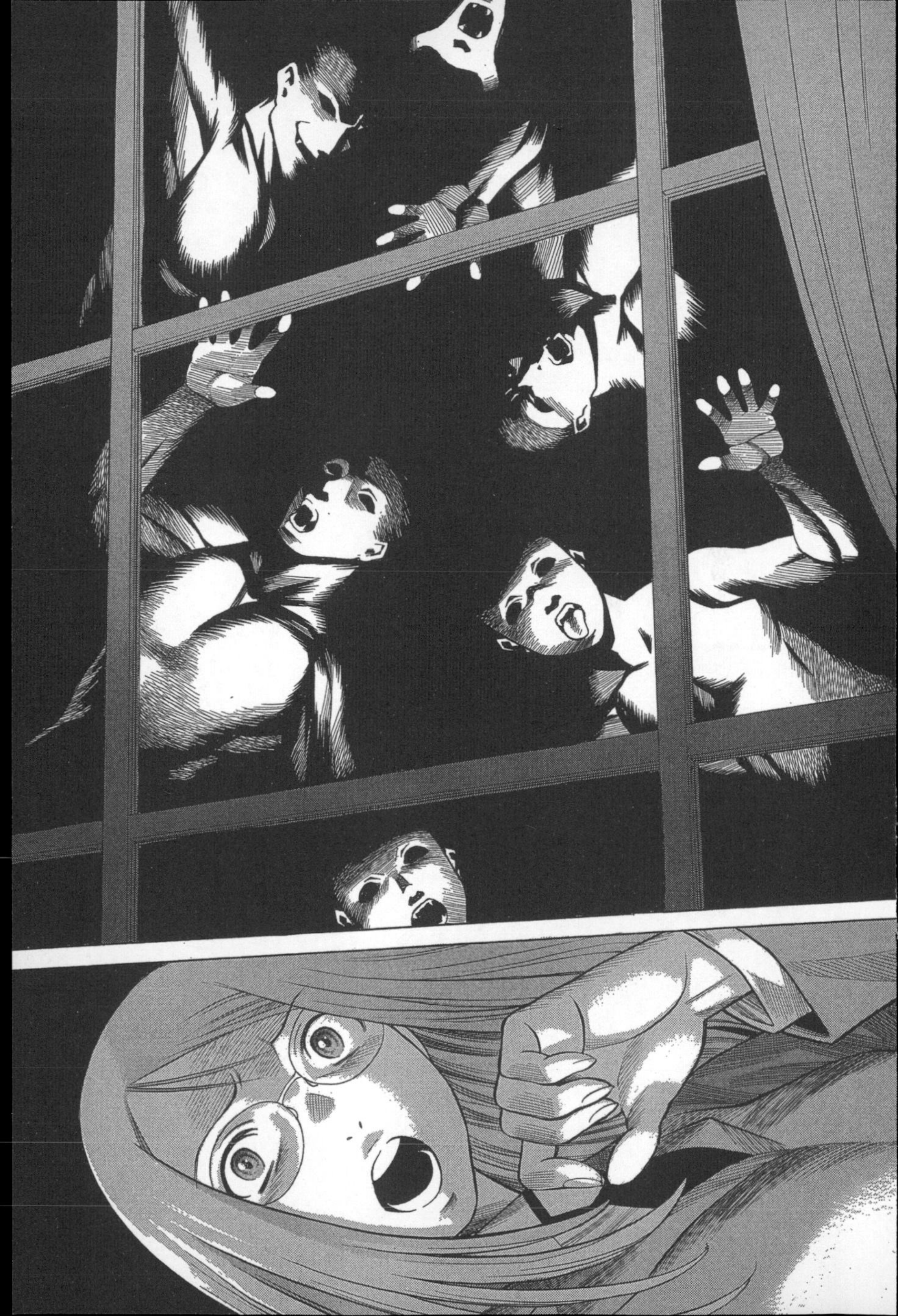

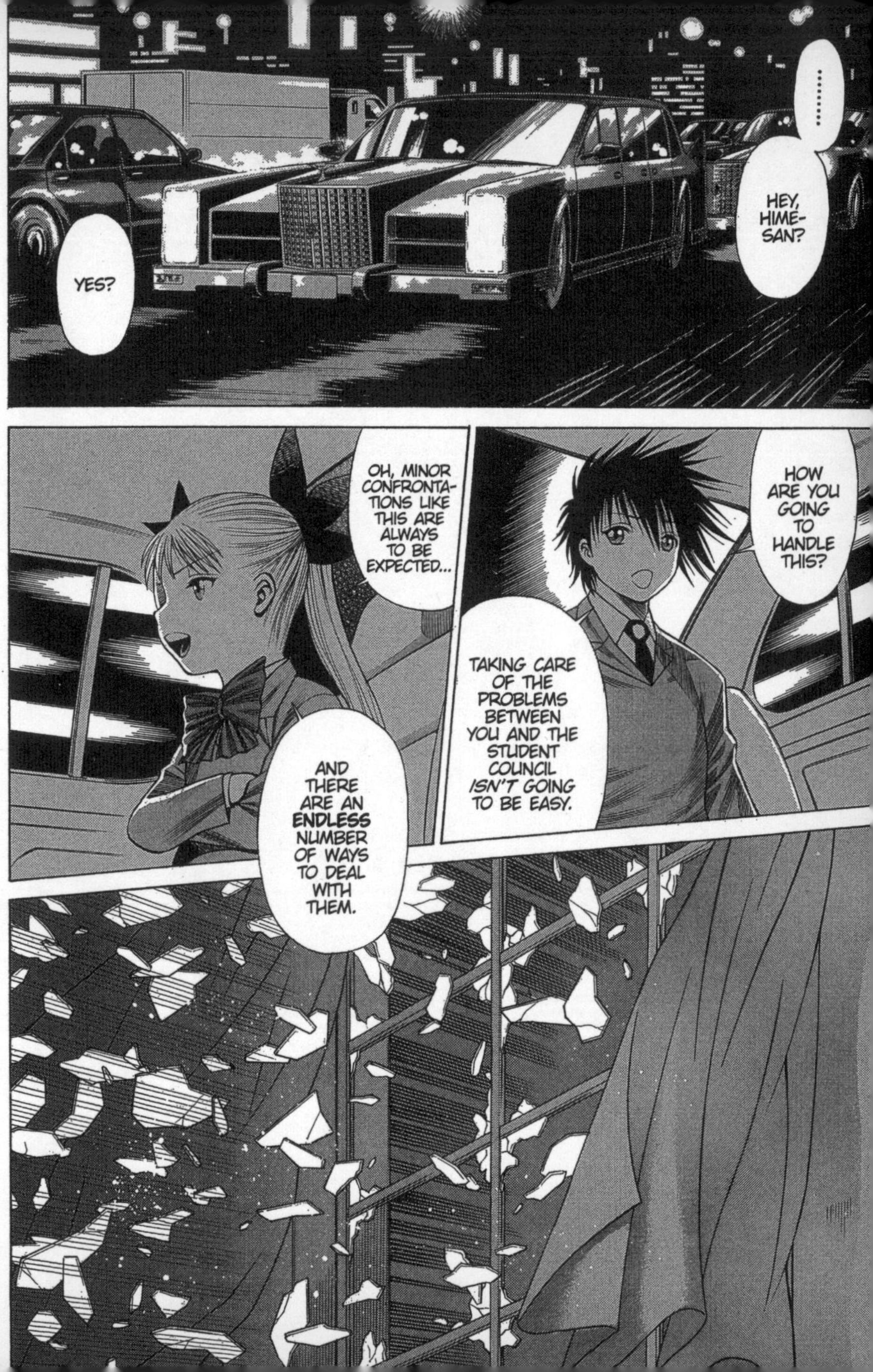
......
HEY, HIME-SAN?
YES?
HOW ARE YOU GOING TO HANDLE THIS?
TAKING CARE OF THE PROBLEMS BETWEEN YOU AND THE STUDENT COUNCIL *ISN'T* GOING TO BE EASY.
OH, MINOR CONFRONTATIONS LIKE THIS ARE ALWAYS TO BE EXPECTED...
AND THERE ARE AN **ENDLESS** NUMBER OF WAYS TO DEAL WITH THEM.

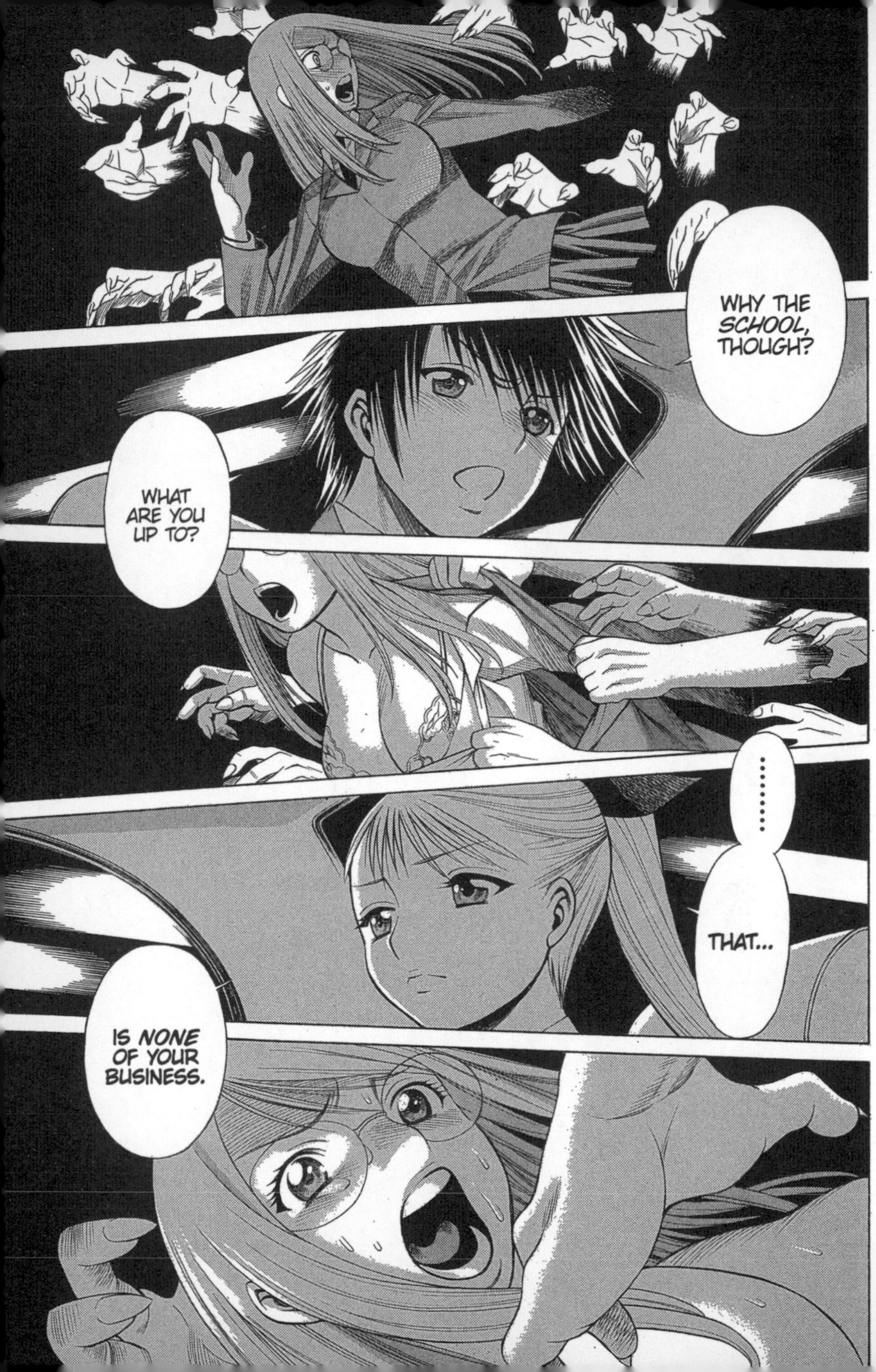
WHY THE SCHOOL, THOUGH?
WHAT ARE YOU UP TO?
......
THAT...
IS NONE OF YOUR BUSINESS.

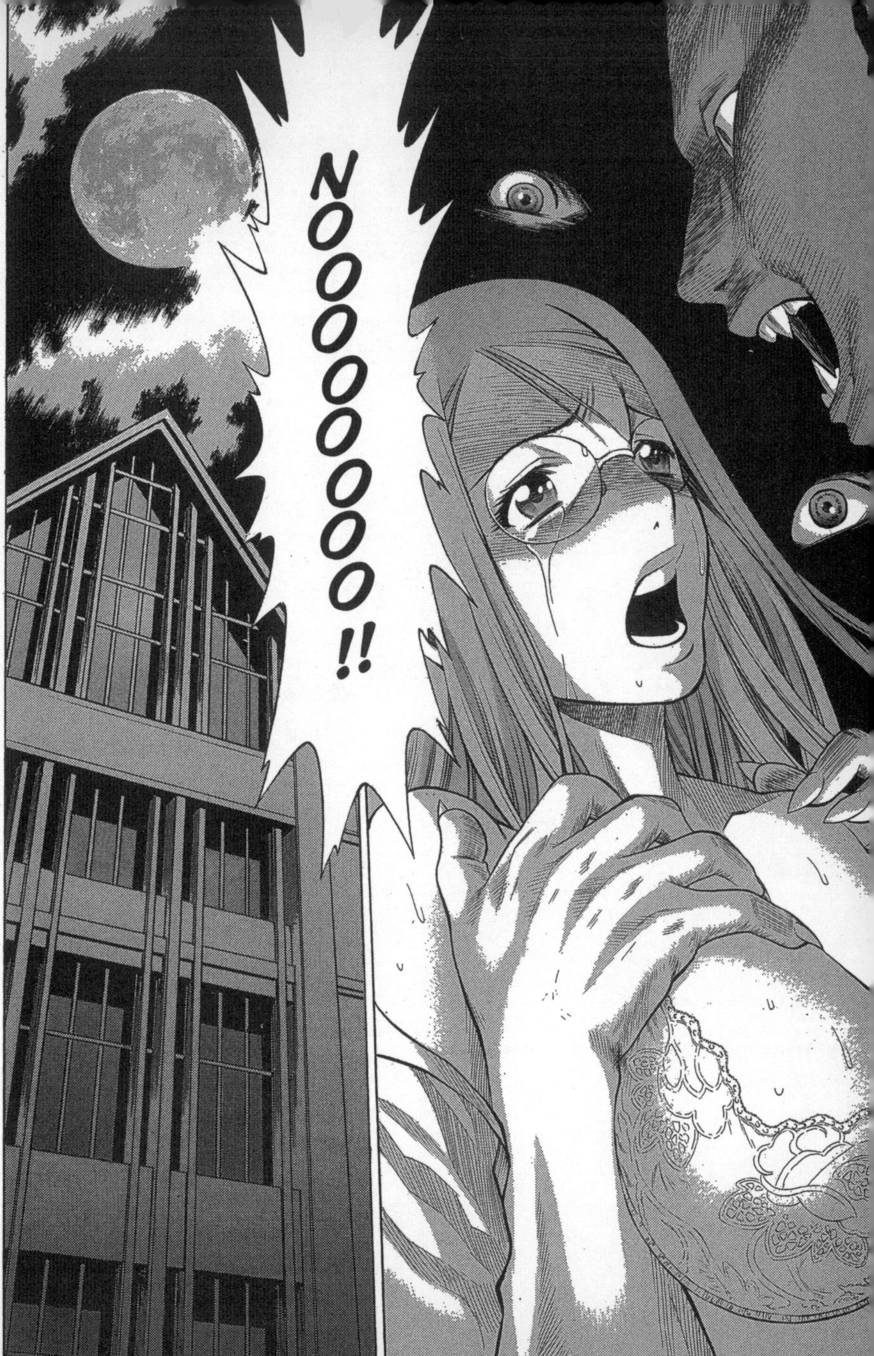
NOOOOOOOOO!!

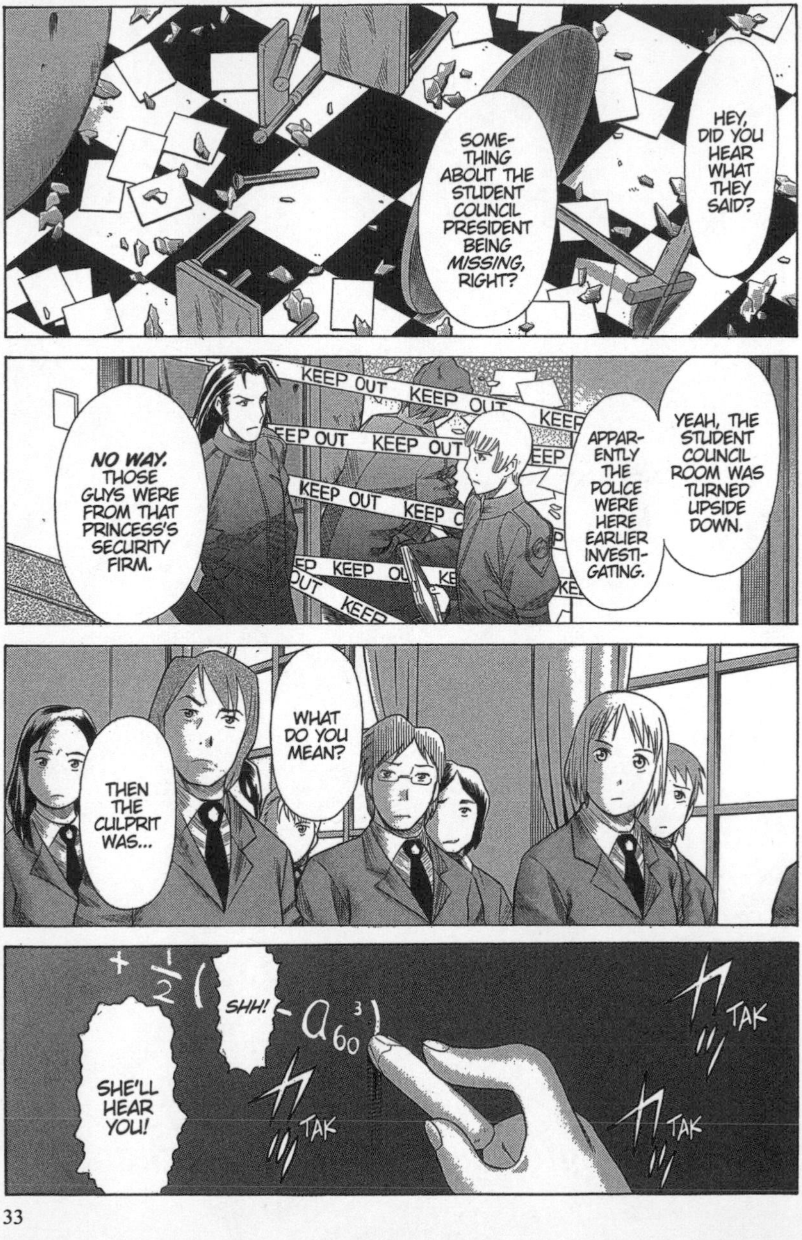
HEY, DID YOU HEAR WHAT THEY SAID?
SOME-THING ABOUT THE STUDENT COUNCIL PRESIDENT BEING *MISSING*, RIGHT?
KEEP OUT
YEAH, THE STUDENT COUNCIL ROOM WAS TURNED UPSIDE DOWN.
APPAR-ENTLY THE POLICE WERE HERE EARLIER INVESTI-GATING.
NO WAY. THOSE GUYS WERE FROM THAT PRINCESS'S SECURITY FIRM.
WHAT DO YOU MEAN?
THEN THE CULPRIT WAS...
TAK
TAK
TAK
SHH!
SHE'LL HEAR YOU!

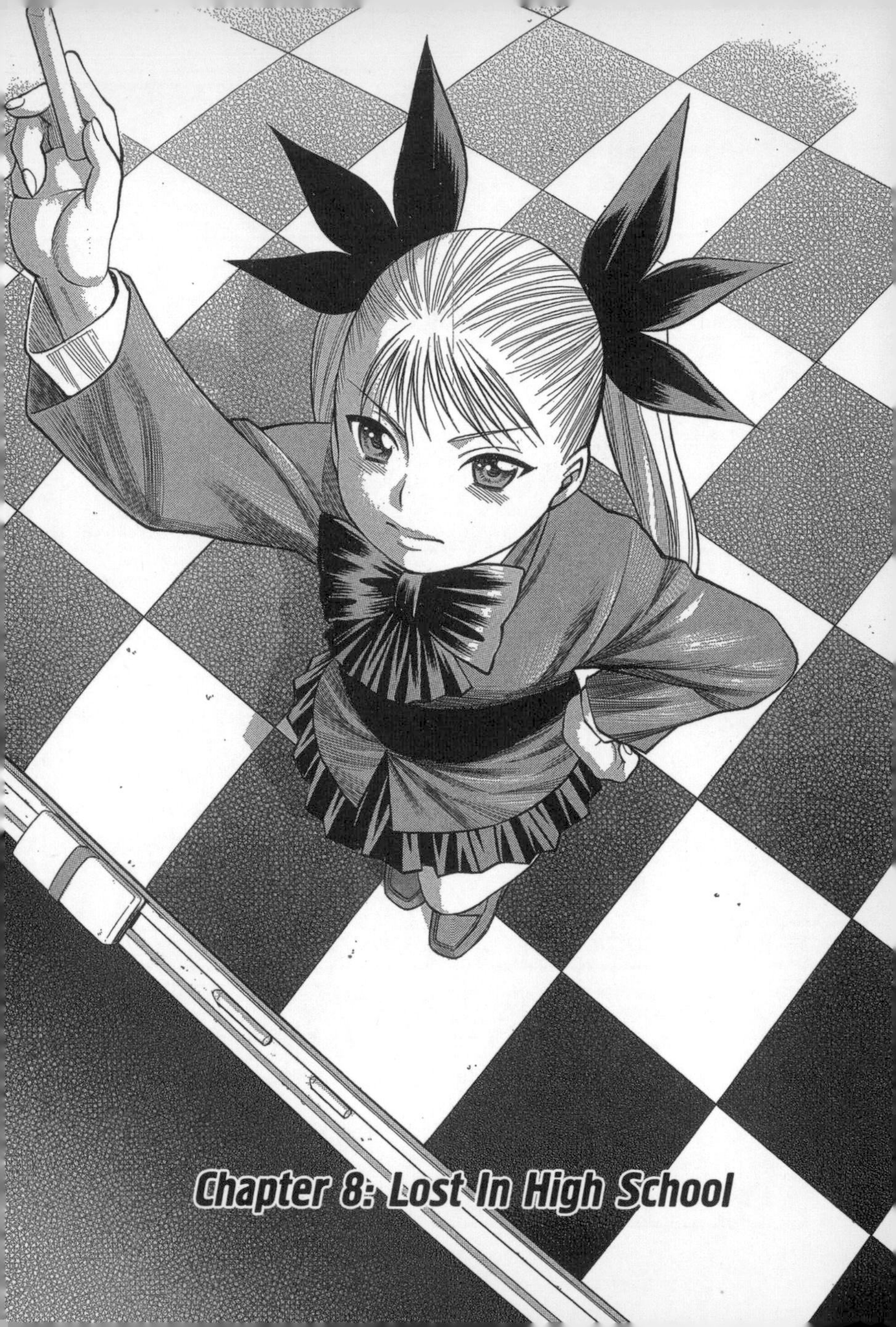

Chapter 8: Lost In High School

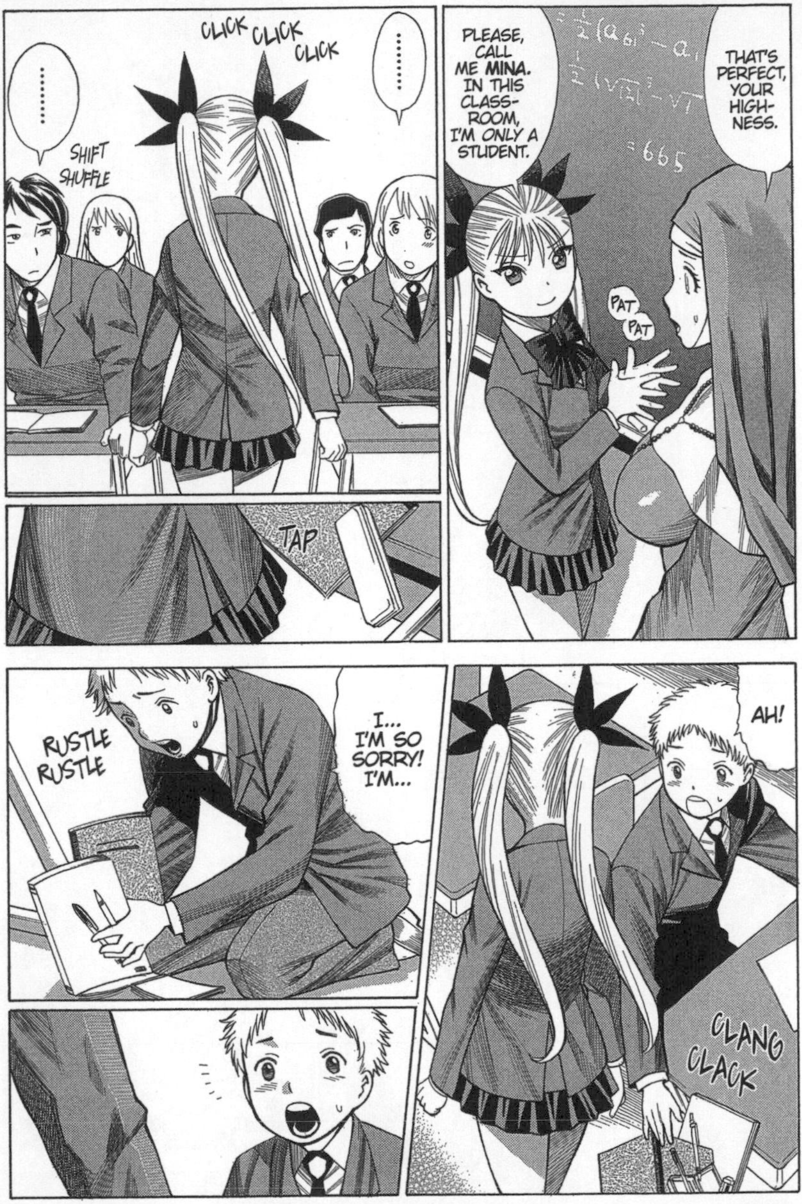
THAT'S PERFECT, YOUR HIGHNESS.
PLEASE, CALL ME **MINA**. IN THIS CLASSROOM, I'M ONLY A STUDENT.
PAT PAT
......
CLICK CLICK CLICK
......
SHIFT SHUFFLE
TAP
AH!
CLANG CLACK
I... I'M SO SORRY! I'M...
RUSTLE RUSTLE

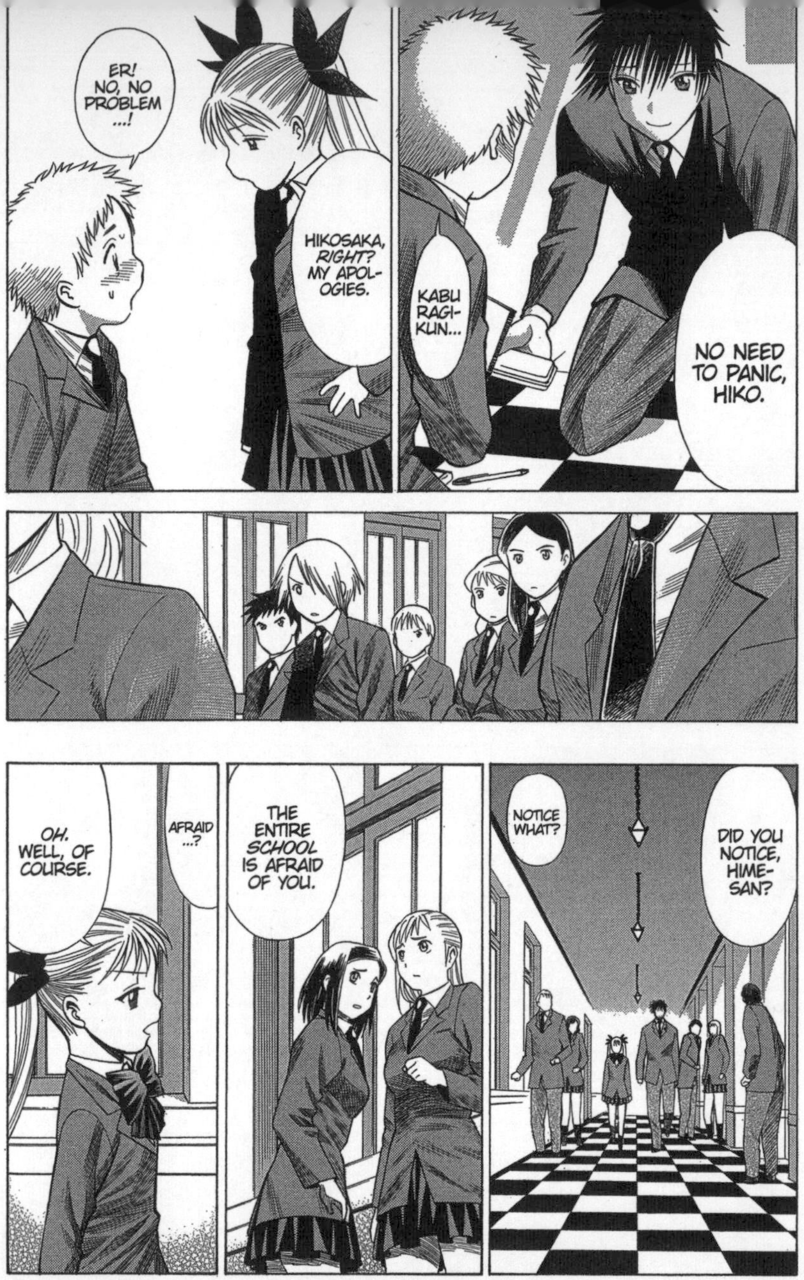
NO NEED TO PANIC, HIKO.
KABURAGI-KUN...
HIKOSAKA, *RIGHT?* MY APOLOGIES.
ER! NO, NO PROBLEM ...!
DID YOU NOTICE, HIME-SAN?
NOTICE WHAT?
THE ENTIRE *SCHOOL* IS AFRAID OF YOU.
AFRAID ...?
OH. WELL, OF COURSE.

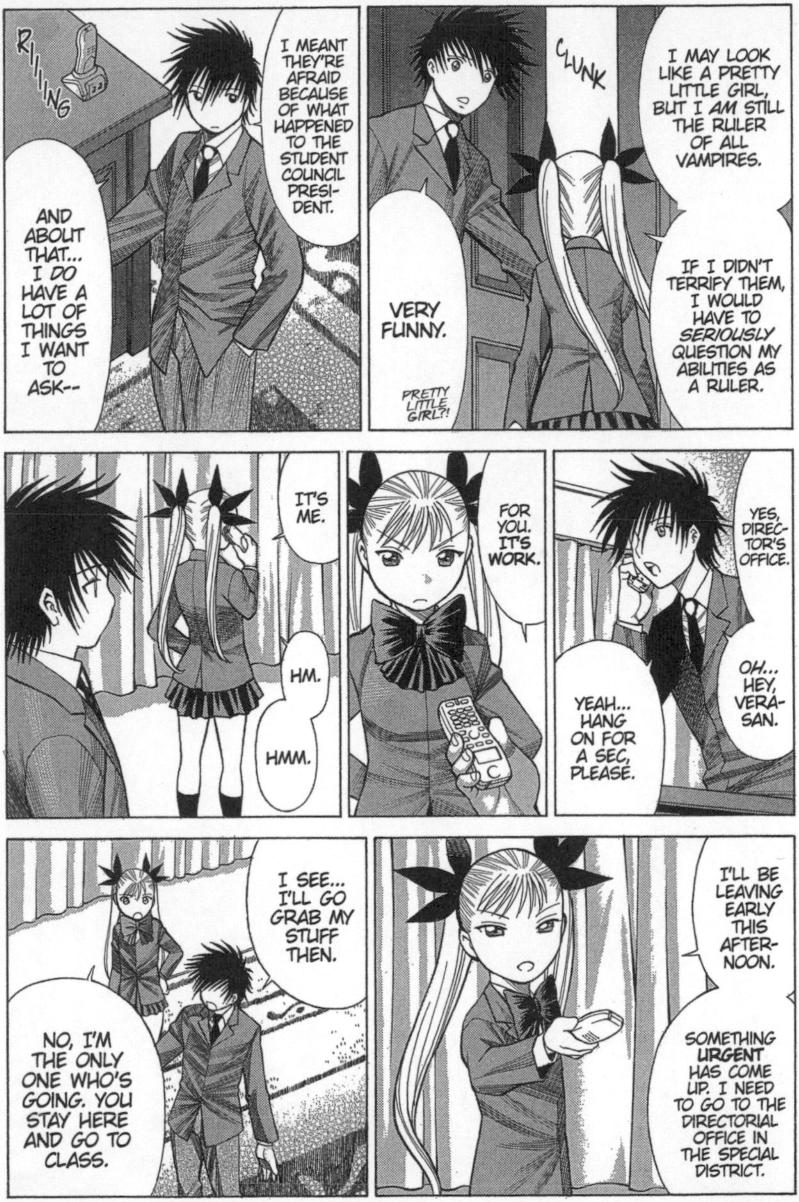
CLUNK
I MAY LOOK LIKE A PRETTY LITTLE GIRL, BUT I AM STILL THE RULER OF ALL VAMPIRES.
IF I DIDN'T TERRIFY THEM, I WOULD HAVE TO SERIOUSLY QUESTION MY ABILITIES AS A RULER.
VERY FUNNY.
PRETTY LITTLE GIRL?!
RIIIING
I MEANT THEY'RE AFRAID BECAUSE OF WHAT HAPPENED TO THE STUDENT COUNCIL PRESIDENT.
AND ABOUT THAT... I DO HAVE A LOT OF THINGS I WANT TO ASK--
YES, DIRECTOR'S OFFICE.
OH... HEY, VERA-SAN.
YEAH... HANG ON FOR A SEC, PLEASE.
FOR YOU. IT'S WORK.
IT'S ME.
HM.
HMM.
I'LL BE LEAVING EARLY THIS AFTERNOON.
SOMETHING URGENT HAS COME UP. I NEED TO GO TO THE DIRECTORIAL OFFICE IN THE SPECIAL DISTRICT.
I SEE... I'LL GO GRAB MY STUFF THEN.
NO, I'M THE ONLY ONE WHO'S GOING. YOU STAY HERE AND GO TO CLASS.

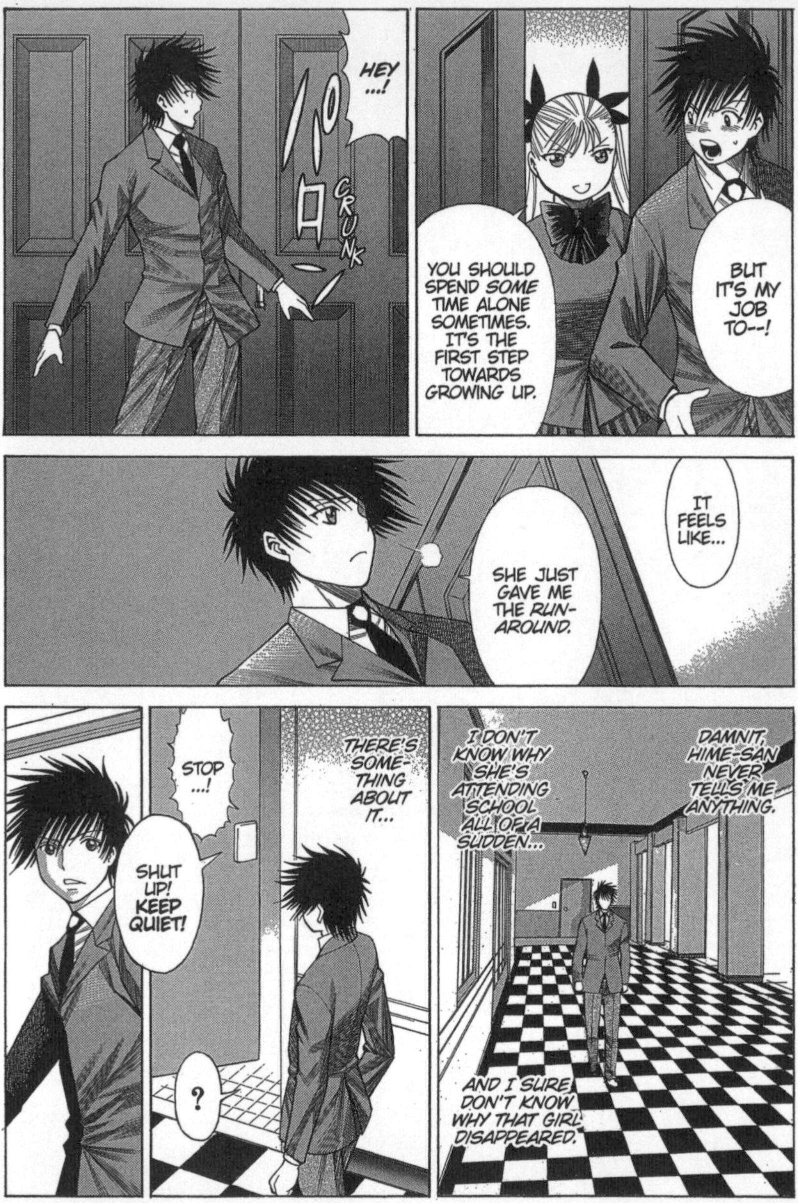
BUT IT'S MY JOB TO--!
YOU SHOULD SPEND SOME TIME ALONE SOMETIMES. IT'S THE FIRST STEP TOWARDS GROWING UP.
HEY ...!
CRUNK
IT FEELS LIKE...
SHE JUST GAVE ME THE RUN-AROUND.
DAMNIT, HIME-SAN NEVER TELLS ME ANYTHING.
I DON'T KNOW WHY SHE'S ATTENDING SCHOOL ALL OF A SUDDEN...
AND I SURE DON'T KNOW WHY THAT GIRL DISAPPEARED.
THERE'S SOMETHING ABOUT IT...
STOP ...!
?
SHUT UP! KEEP QUIET!

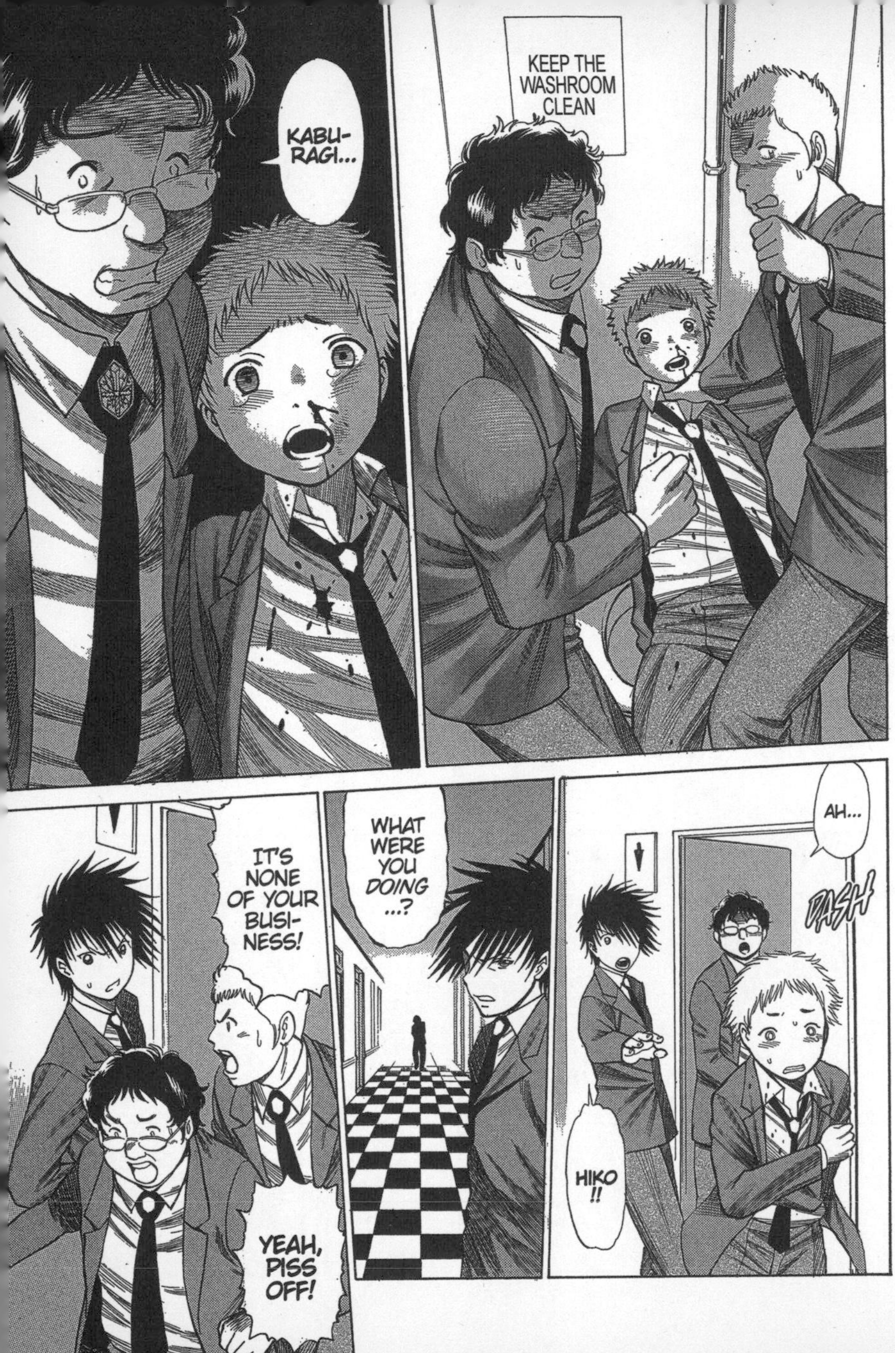
KEEP THE WASHROOM CLEAN
KABU-RAGI...
AH...
DASH
HIKO!!
WHAT WERE YOU DOING ...?
IT'S NONE OF YOUR BUSI-NESS!
YEAH, PISS OFF!

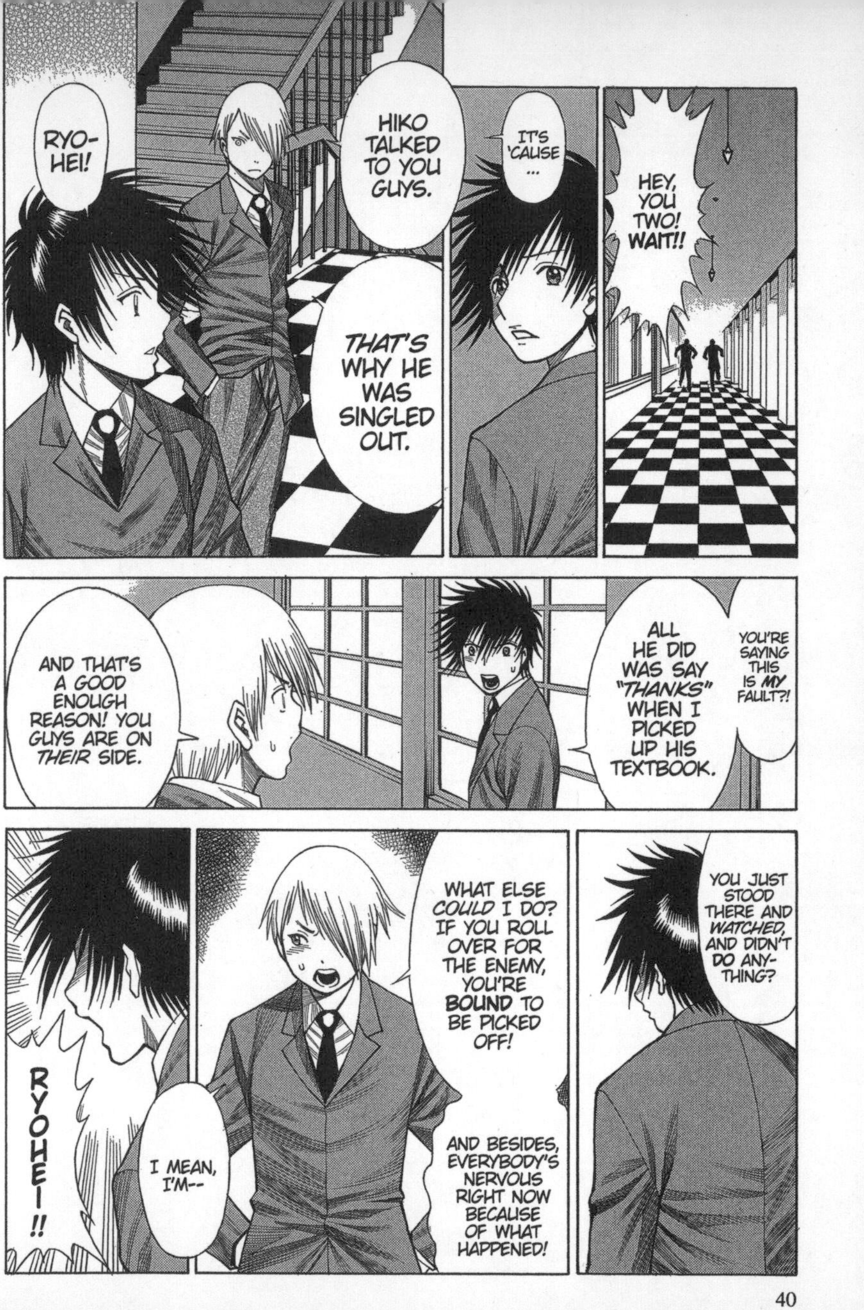
HEY, YOU TWO! WAIT!!
IT'S 'CAUSE ...
HIKO TALKED TO YOU GUYS.
THAT'S WHY HE WAS SINGLED OUT.
RYO-HEI!
YOU'RE SAYING THIS IS MY FAULT?!
ALL HE DID WAS SAY "THANKS" WHEN I PICKED UP HIS TEXTBOOK.
AND THAT'S A GOOD ENOUGH REASON! YOU GUYS ARE ON THEIR SIDE.
YOU JUST STOOD THERE AND WATCHED, AND DIDN'T DO ANYTHING?
WHAT ELSE COULD I DO? IF YOU ROLL OVER FOR THE ENEMY, YOU'RE BOUND TO BE PICKED OFF!
AND BESIDES, EVERYBODY'S NERVOUS RIGHT NOW BECAUSE OF WHAT HAPPENED!
I MEAN, I'M--
RYOHEI!!

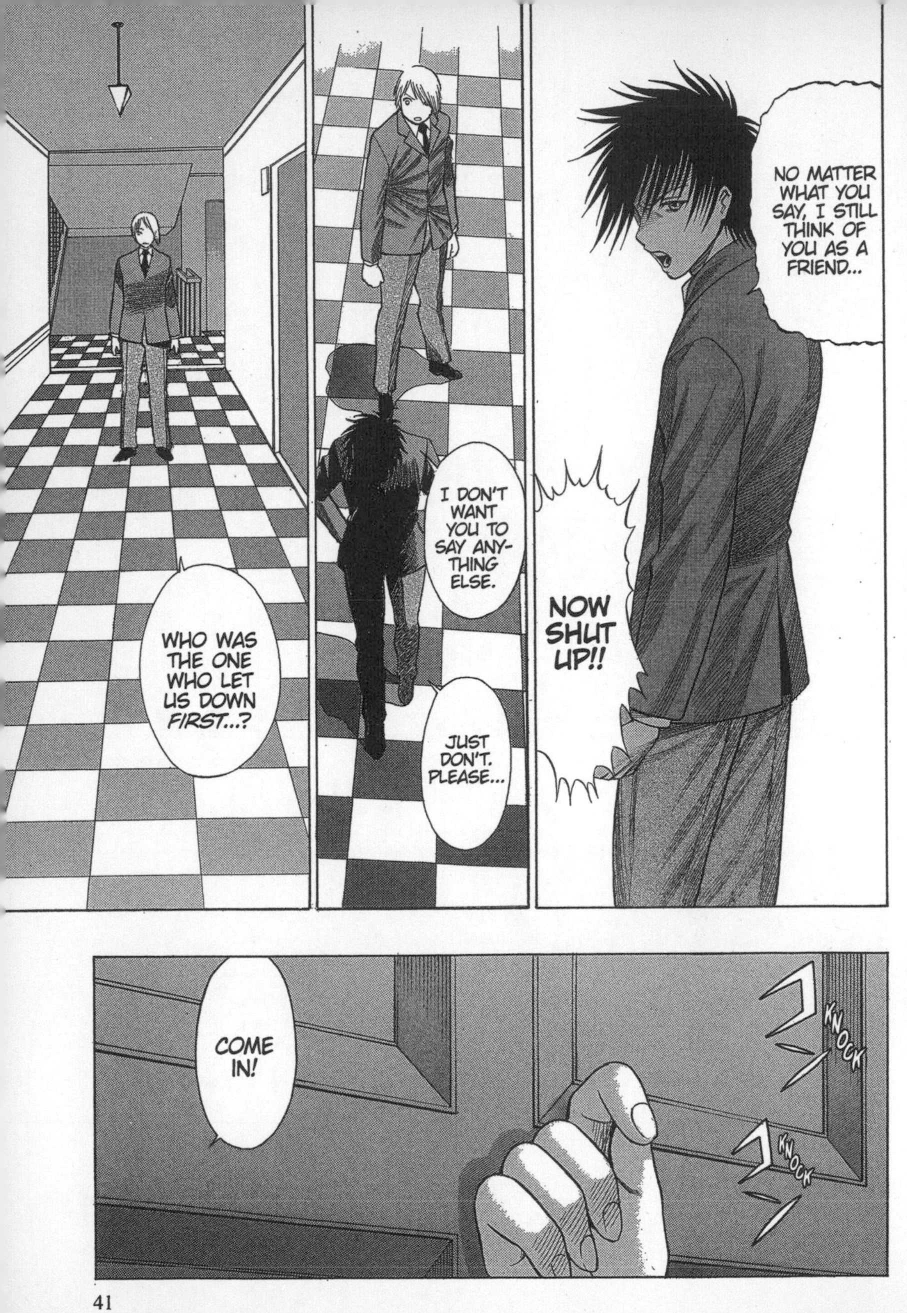

NO MATTER WHAT YOU SAY, I STILL THINK OF YOU AS A FRIEND...
NOW SHUT UP!!
I DON'T WANT YOU TO SAY ANY-THING ELSE.
JUST DON'T. PLEASE...
WHO WAS THE ONE WHO LET US DOWN *FIRST*...?
KNOCK
KNOCK
COME IN!

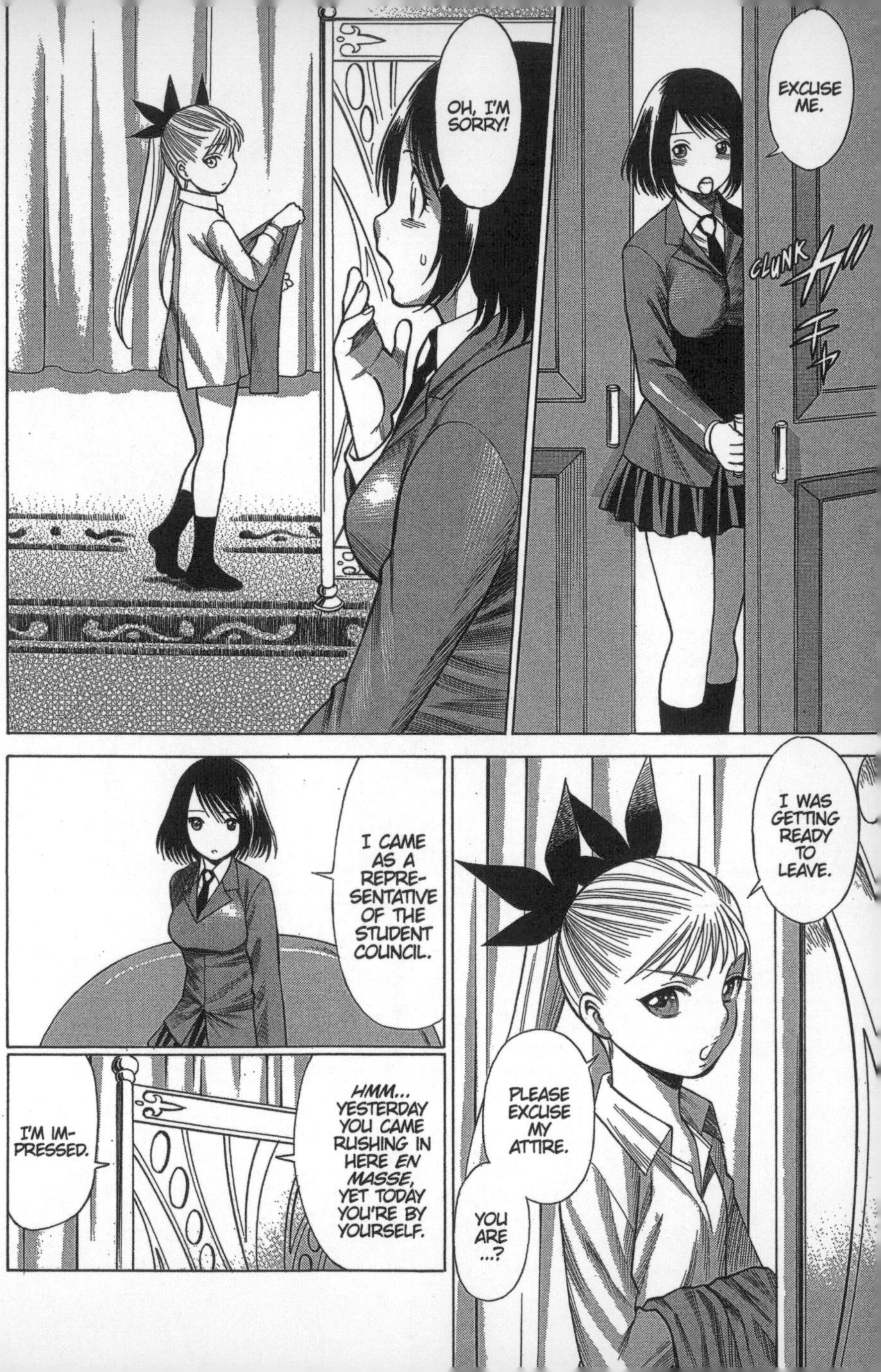
EXCUSE ME.
CLUNK
OH, I'M SORRY!
I WAS GETTING READY TO LEAVE.
PLEASE EXCUSE MY ATTIRE.
YOU ARE ...?
I CAME AS A REPRESENTATIVE OF THE STUDENT COUNCIL.
HMM... YESTERDAY YOU CAME RUSHING IN HERE *EN MASSE*, YET TODAY YOU'RE BY YOURSELF.
I'M IMPRESSED.

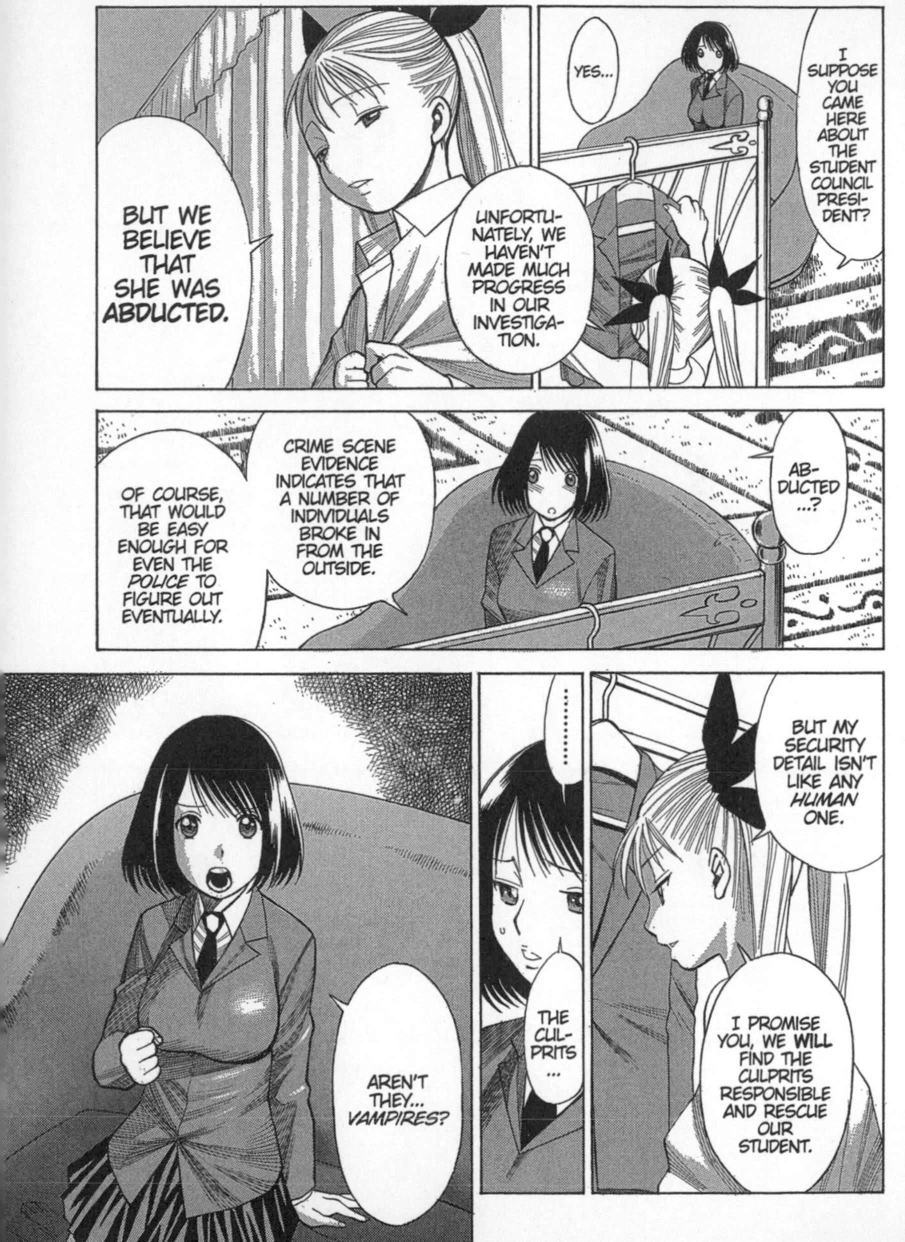
I SUPPOSE YOU CAME HERE ABOUT THE STUDENT COUNCIL PRESIDENT?
YES...
UNFORTUNATELY, WE HAVEN'T MADE MUCH PROGRESS IN OUR INVESTIGATION.
BUT WE BELIEVE THAT SHE WAS ABDUCTED.
ABDUCTED...?
CRIME SCENE EVIDENCE INDICATES THAT A NUMBER OF INDIVIDUALS BROKE IN FROM THE OUTSIDE.
OF COURSE, THAT WOULD BE EASY ENOUGH FOR EVEN THE *POLICE* TO FIGURE OUT EVENTUALLY.
BUT MY SECURITY DETAIL ISN'T LIKE ANY *HUMAN* ONE.
....
I PROMISE YOU, WE **WILL** FIND THE CULPRITS RESPONSIBLE AND RESCUE OUR STUDENT.
THE CULPRITS...
AREN'T THEY... *VAMPIRES?*

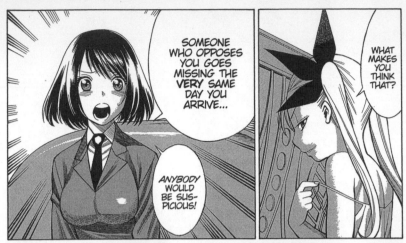

WHAT MAKES YOU THINK THAT?
SOMEONE WHO OPPOSES YOU GOES MISSING THE VERY SAME DAY YOU ARRIVE...
ANYBODY WOULD BE SUSPICIOUS!
SUSPICIOUS?
OF WHAT?
THAT I ORDERED THE KIDNAPPING...?
YES.
AH HA HA HA!
YOU'RE BRAVER THAN YOU LOOK!

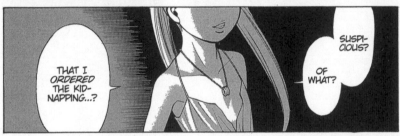

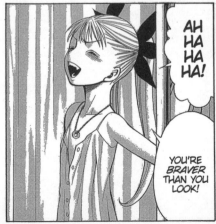

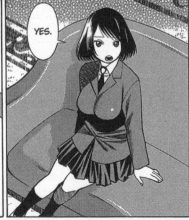

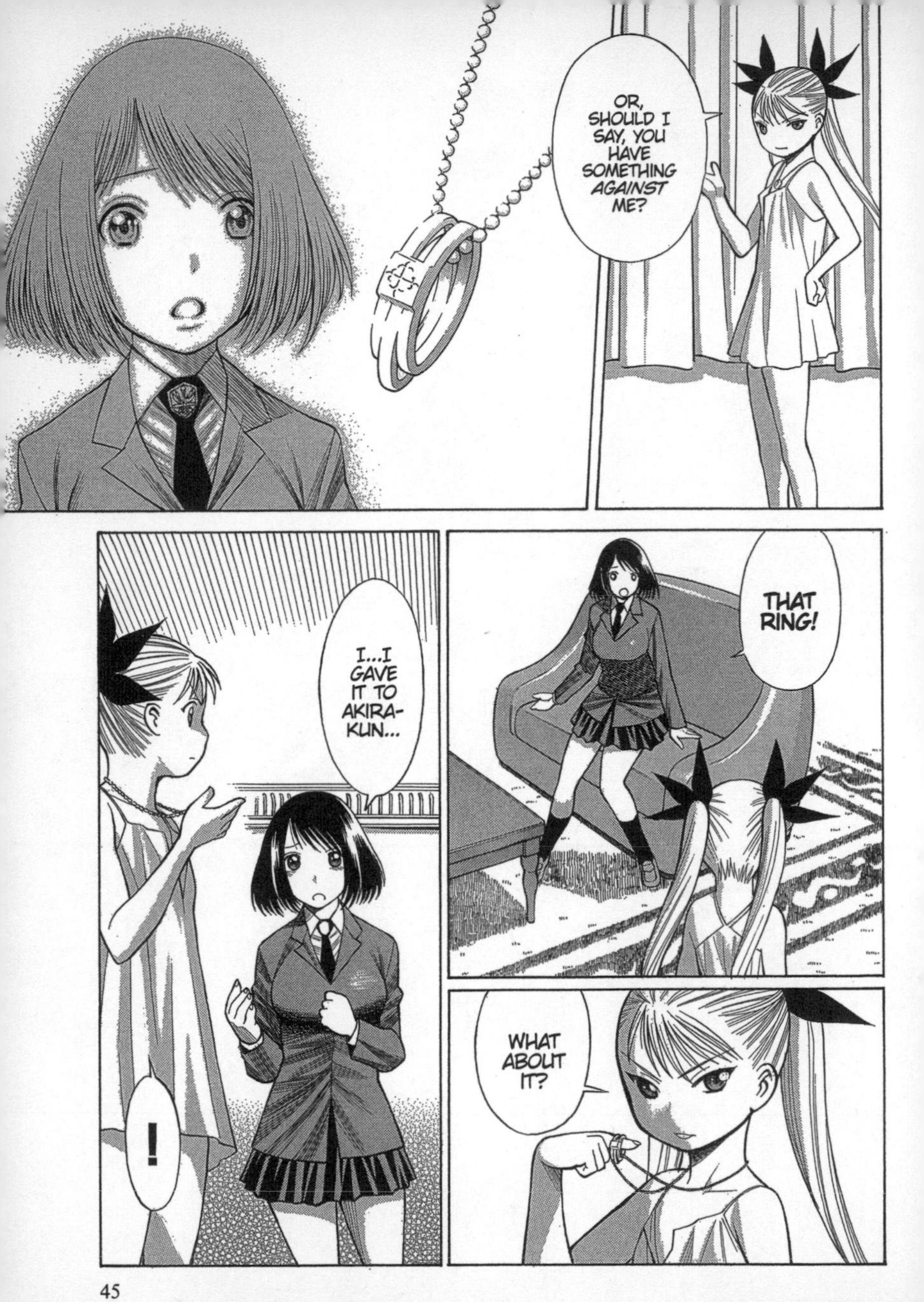
OR, SHOULD I SAY, YOU HAVE SOMETHING *AGAINST* ME?
THAT RING!
WHAT ABOUT IT?
I...I GAVE IT TO AKIRA-KUN...
!

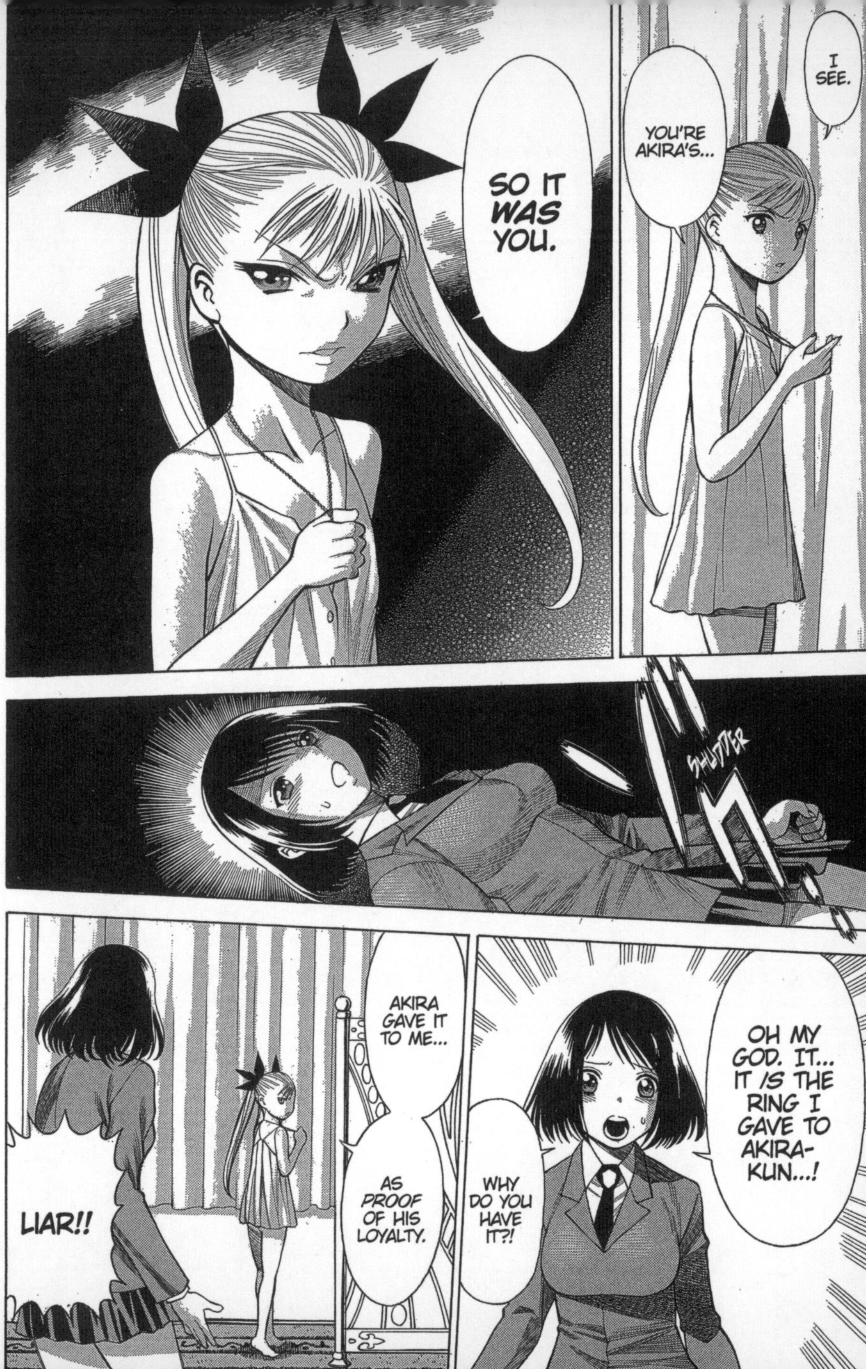
I SEE.
YOU'RE AKIRA'S...
SO IT WAS YOU.
SHUDDER
OH MY GOD. IT... IT IS THE RING I GAVE TO AKIRA-KUN...!
WHY DO YOU HAVE IT?!
AKIRA GAVE IT TO ME...
AS PROOF OF HIS LOYALTY.
LIAR!!

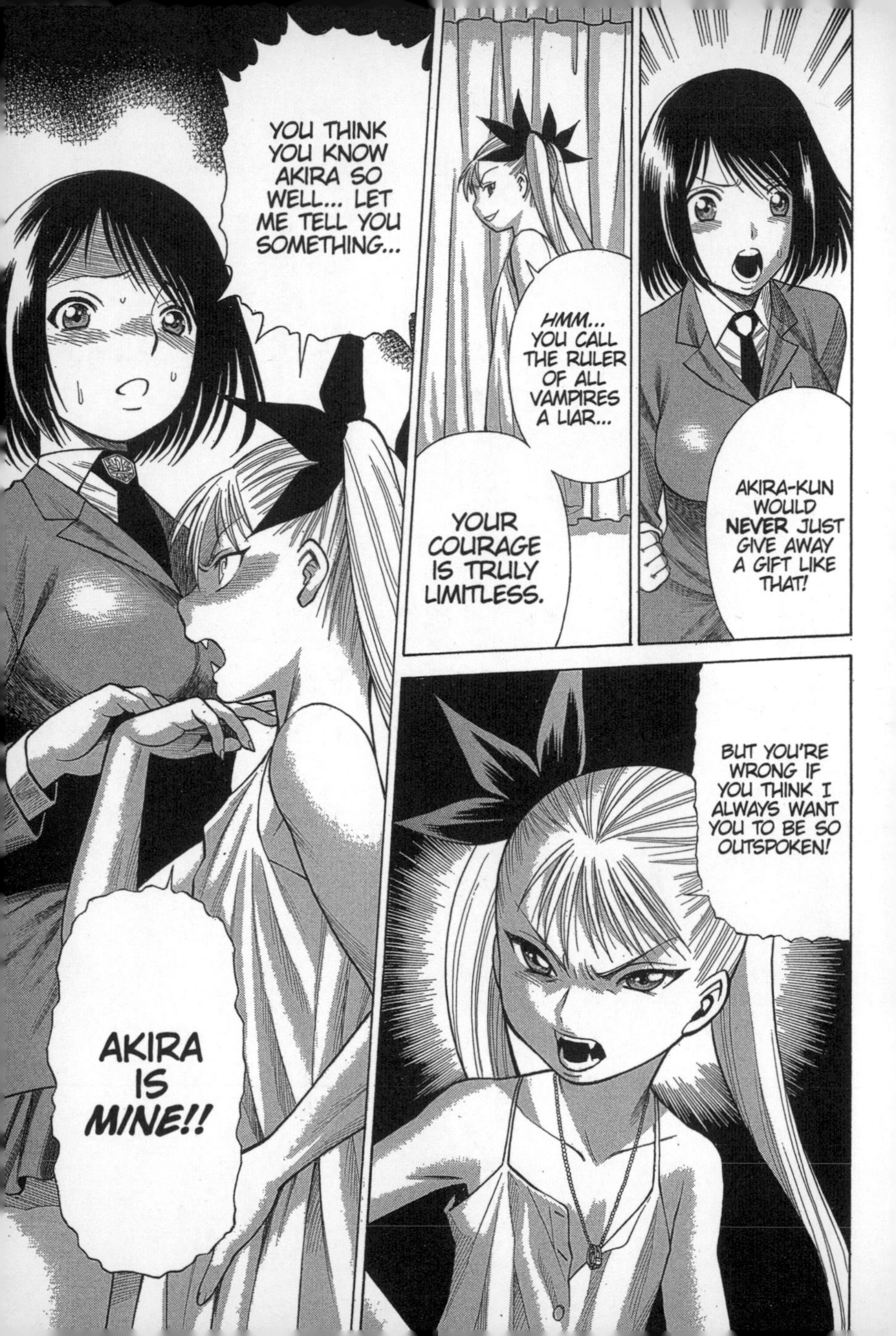
AKIRA-KUN WOULD NEVER JUST GIVE AWAY A GIFT LIKE THAT!
HMM... YOU CALL THE RULER OF ALL VAMPIRES A LIAR...
YOUR COURAGE IS TRULY LIMITLESS.
BUT YOU'RE WRONG IF YOU THINK I ALWAYS WANT YOU TO BE SO OUTSPOKEN!
YOU THINK YOU KNOW AKIRA SO WELL... LET ME TELL YOU SOMETHING...
AKIRA IS MINE!!

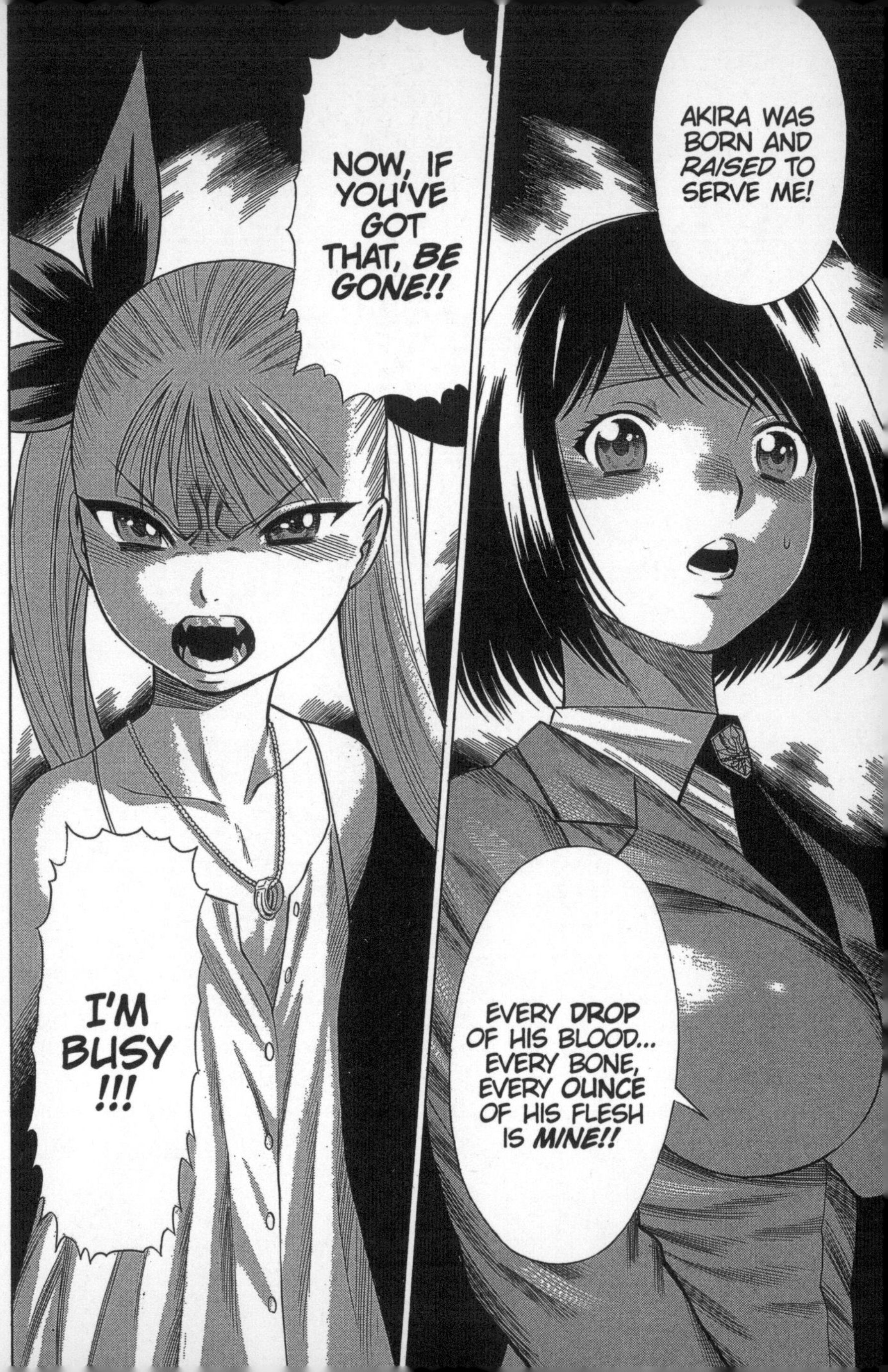
AKIRA WAS BORN AND RAISED TO SERVE ME!
EVERY DROP OF HIS BLOOD... EVERY BONE, EVERY OUNCE OF HIS FLESH IS MINE!!
NOW, IF YOU'VE GOT THAT, BE GONE!!
I'M BUSY !!!

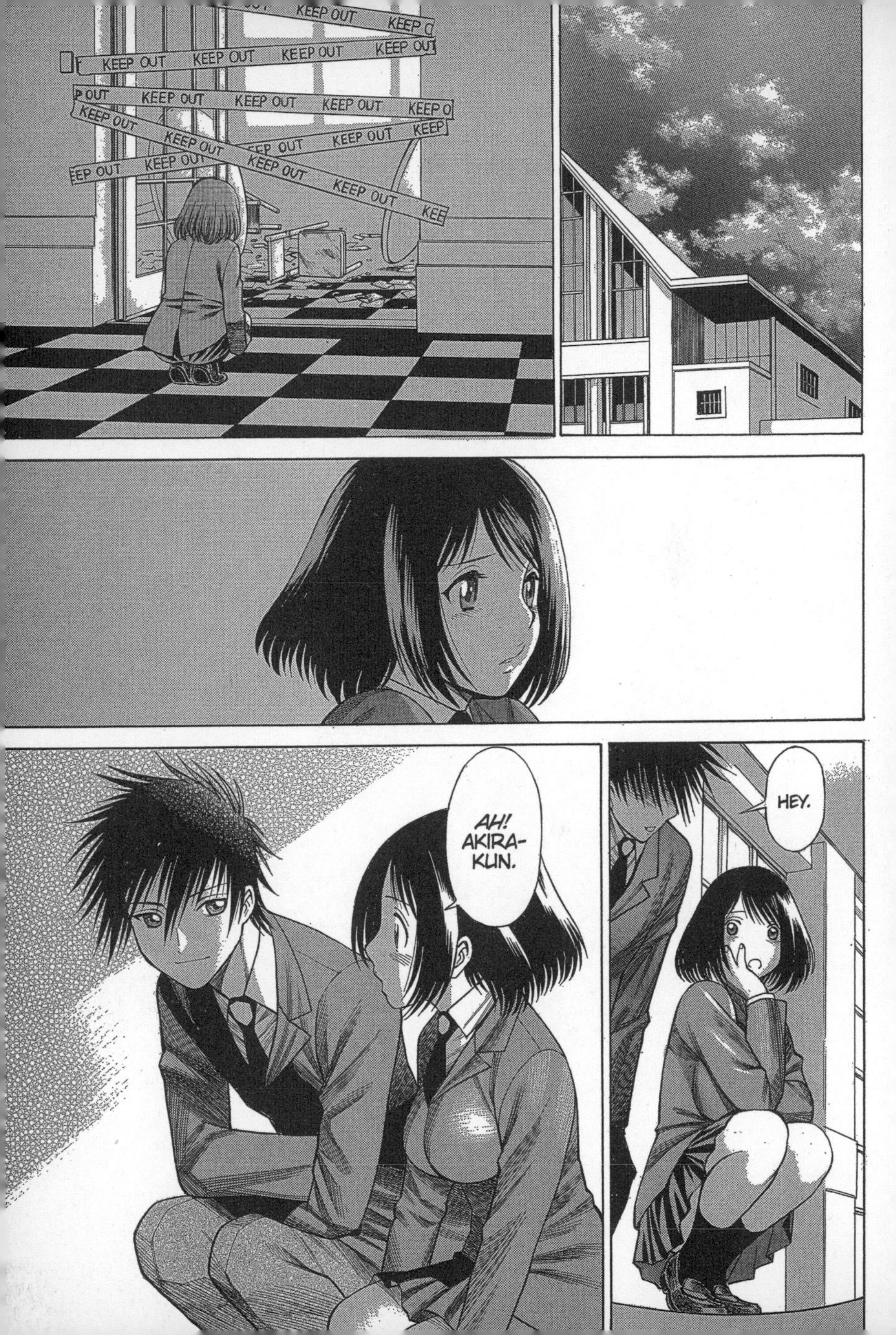
KEEP OUT
KEEP OUT
KEEP OUT
KEEP OUT
KEEP OUT
KEEP OUT
KEEP OUT
KEEP OUT
KEEP OUT
KEEP OUT
KEEP OUT
HEY.
AH! AKIRA-KUN.

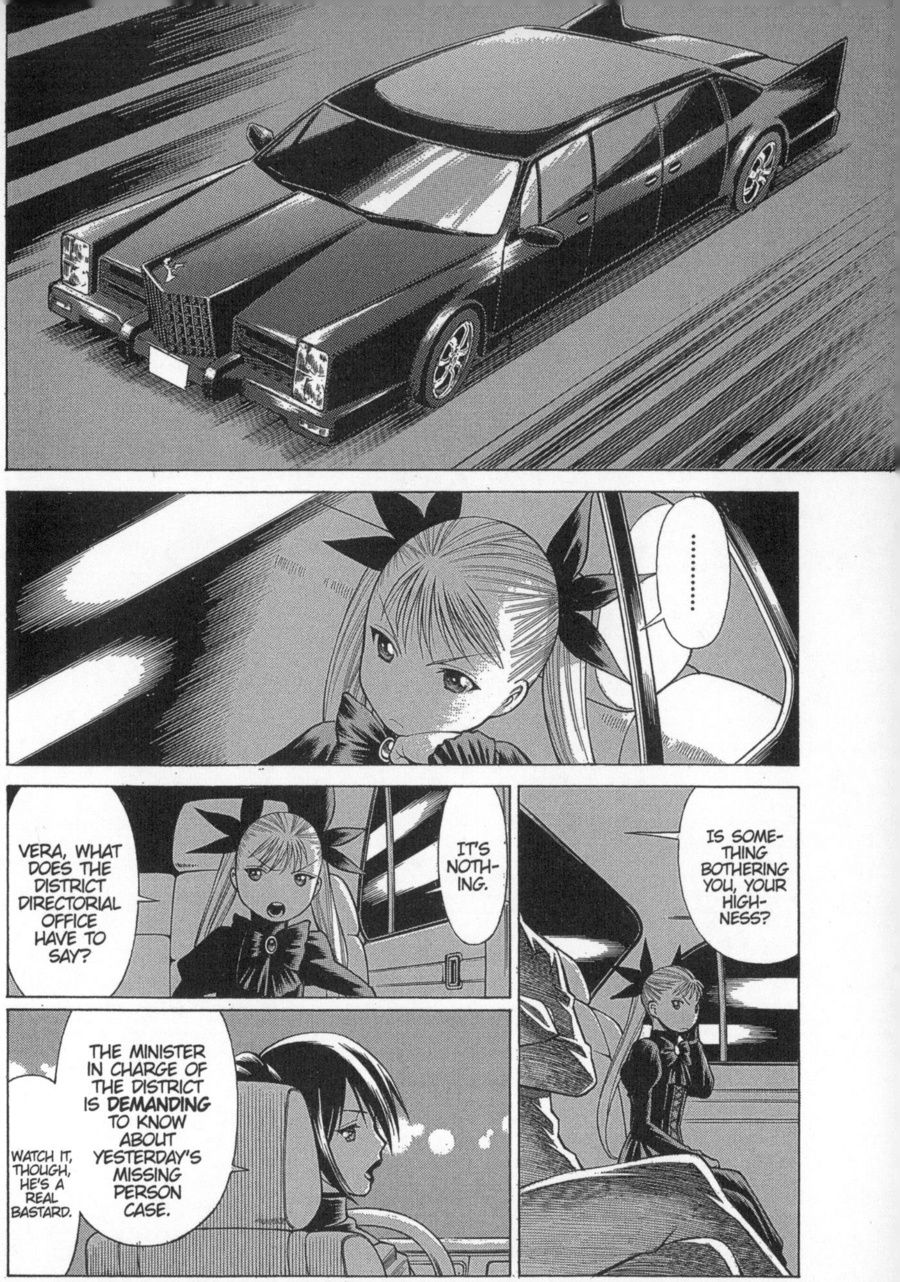
......
IS SOME-THING BOTHERING YOU, YOUR HIGH-NESS?
IT'S NOTH-ING.
VERA, WHAT DOES THE DISTRICT DIRECTORIAL OFFICE HAVE TO SAY?
THE MINISTER IN CHARGE OF THE DISTRICT IS **DEMANDING** TO KNOW ABOUT YESTERDAY'S MISSING PERSON CASE.
WATCH IT, THOUGH, HE'S A REAL BASTARD.

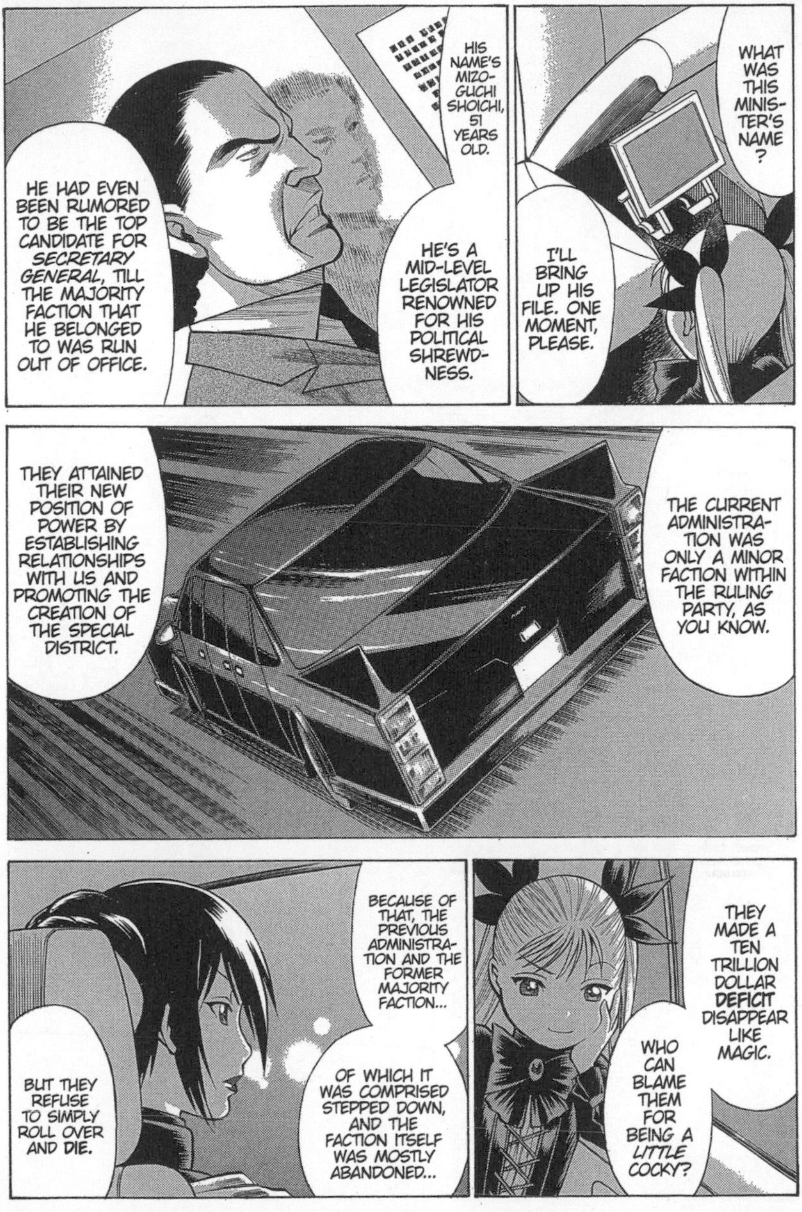
WHAT WAS THIS MINISTER'S NAME?
I'LL BRING UP HIS FILE. ONE MOMENT, PLEASE.
HIS NAME'S MIZOGUCHI SHOICHI, 51 YEARS OLD.
HE'S A MID-LEVEL LEGISLATOR RENOWNED FOR HIS POLITICAL SHREWDNESS.
HE HAD EVEN BEEN RUMORED TO BE THE TOP CANDIDATE FOR *SECRETARY GENERAL*, TILL THE MAJORITY FACTION THAT HE BELONGED TO WAS RUN OUT OF OFFICE.
THE CURRENT ADMINISTRATION WAS ONLY A MINOR FACTION WITHIN THE RULING PARTY, AS YOU KNOW.
THEY ATTAINED THEIR NEW POSITION OF POWER BY ESTABLISHING RELATIONSHIPS WITH US AND PROMOTING THE CREATION OF THE SPECIAL DISTRICT.
THEY MADE A TEN TRILLION DOLLAR **DEFICIT** DISAPPEAR LIKE MAGIC.
WHO CAN BLAME THEM FOR BEING A *LITTLE* COCKY?
BECAUSE OF THAT, THE PREVIOUS ADMINISTRATION AND THE FORMER MAJORITY FACTION...
OF WHICH IT WAS COMPRISED STEPPED DOWN, AND THE FACTION ITSELF WAS MOSTLY ABANDONED...
BUT THEY REFUSE TO SIMPLY ROLL OVER AND **DIE**.

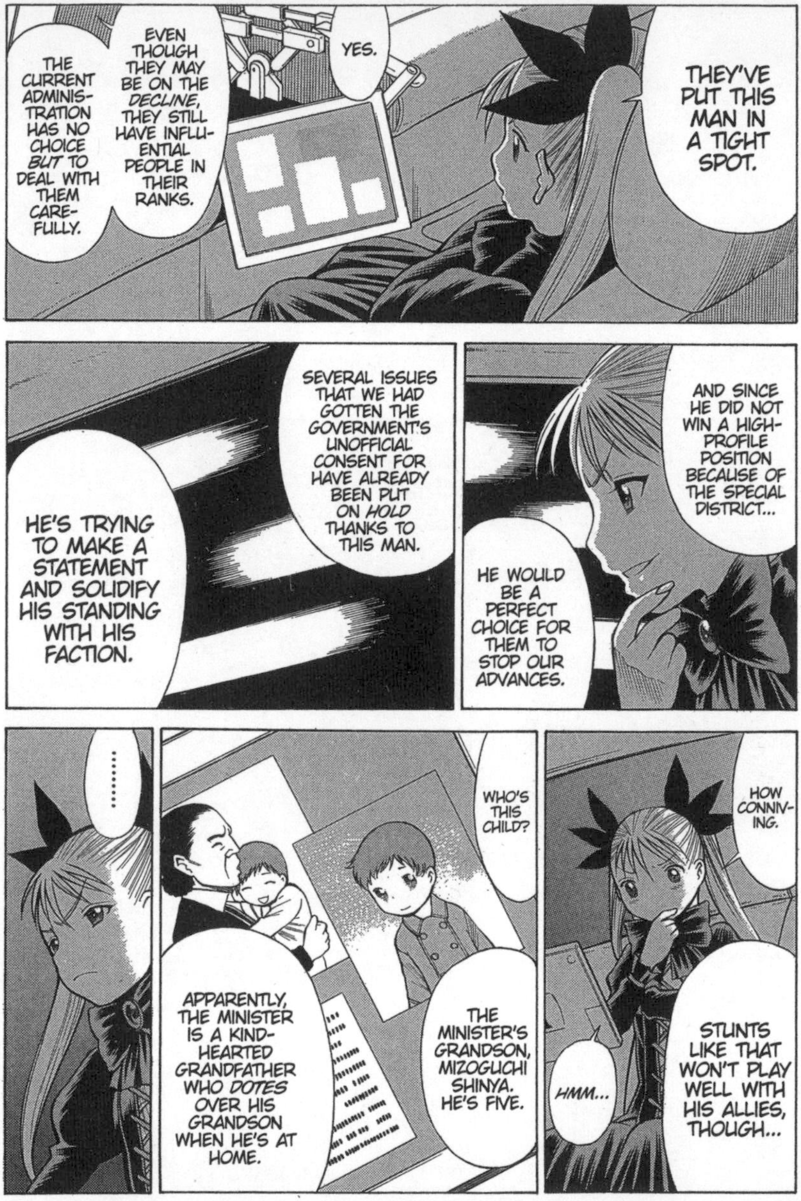
THEY'VE PUT THIS MAN IN A TIGHT SPOT.
YES.
EVEN THOUGH THEY MAY BE ON THE *DECLINE*, THEY STILL HAVE INFLUENTIAL PEOPLE IN THEIR RANKS.
THE CURRENT ADMINISTRATION HAS NO CHOICE *BUT* TO DEAL WITH THEM CAREFULLY.
AND SINCE HE DID NOT WIN A HIGH-PROFILE POSITION BECAUSE OF THE SPECIAL DISTRICT...
HE WOULD BE A PERFECT CHOICE FOR THEM TO STOP OUR ADVANCES.
SEVERAL ISSUES THAT WE HAD GOTTEN THE GOVERNMENT'S UNOFFICIAL CONSENT FOR HAVE ALREADY BEEN PUT ON *HOLD* THANKS TO THIS MAN.
HE'S TRYING TO MAKE A STATEMENT AND SOLIDIFY HIS STANDING WITH HIS FACTION.
HOW CONNIVING.
STUNTS LIKE THAT WON'T PLAY WELL WITH HIS ALLIES, THOUGH...
WHO'S THIS CHILD?
HMM...
THE MINISTER'S GRANDSON, MIZOGUCHI SHINYA. HE'S FIVE.
APPARENTLY, THE MINISTER IS A KIND-HEARTED GRANDFATHER WHO *DOTES* OVER HIS GRANDSON WHEN HE'S AT HOME.
......

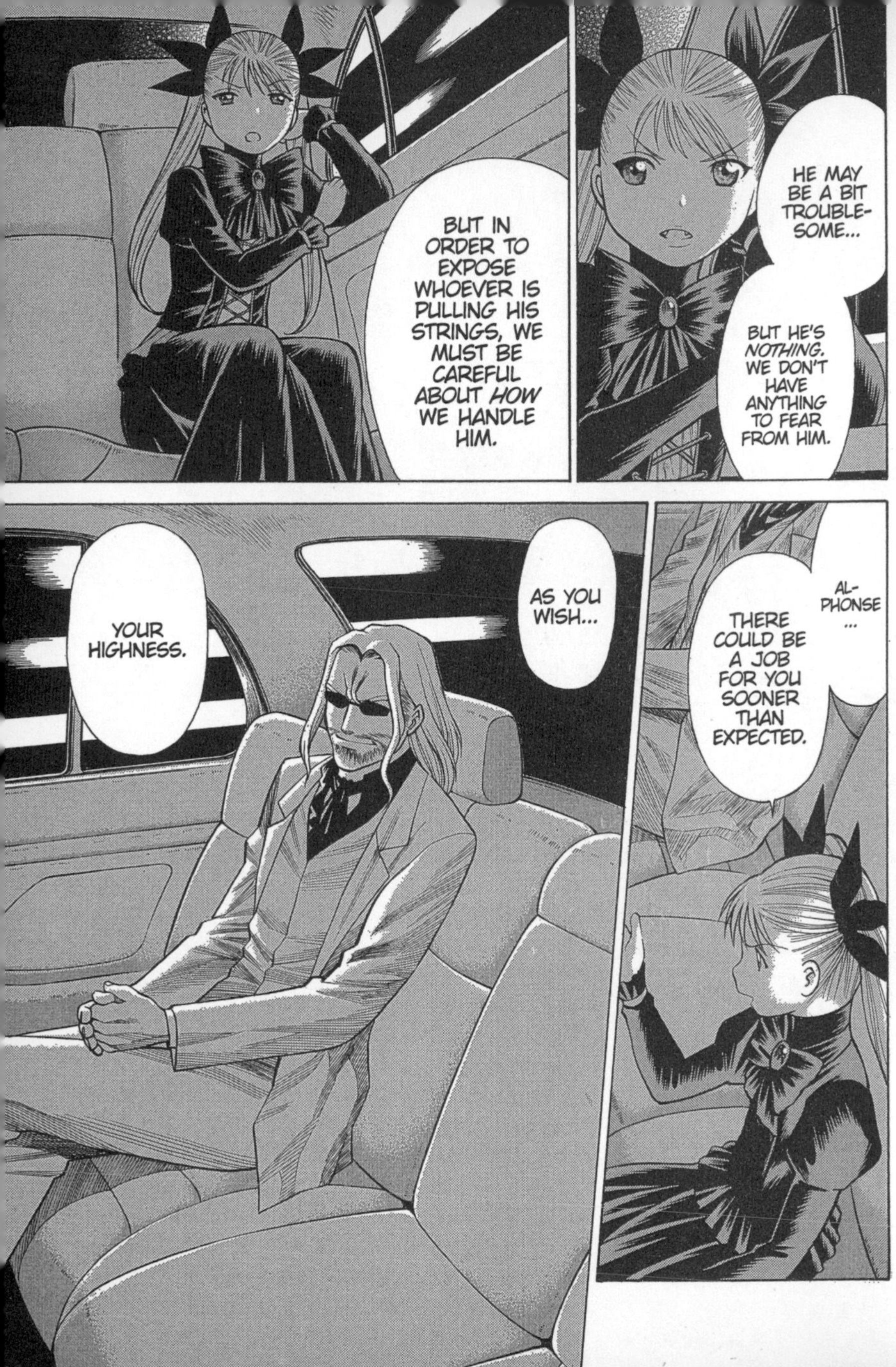
HE MAY BE A BIT TROUBLE-SOME...
BUT HE'S *NOTHING*. WE DON'T HAVE ANYTHING TO FEAR FROM HIM.
BUT IN ORDER TO EXPOSE WHOEVER IS PULLING HIS STRINGS, WE MUST BE CAREFUL ABOUT *HOW* WE HANDLE HIM.
AL-PHONSE ...
THERE COULD BE A JOB FOR YOU SOONER THAN EXPECTED.
AS YOU WISH...
YOUR HIGHNESS.

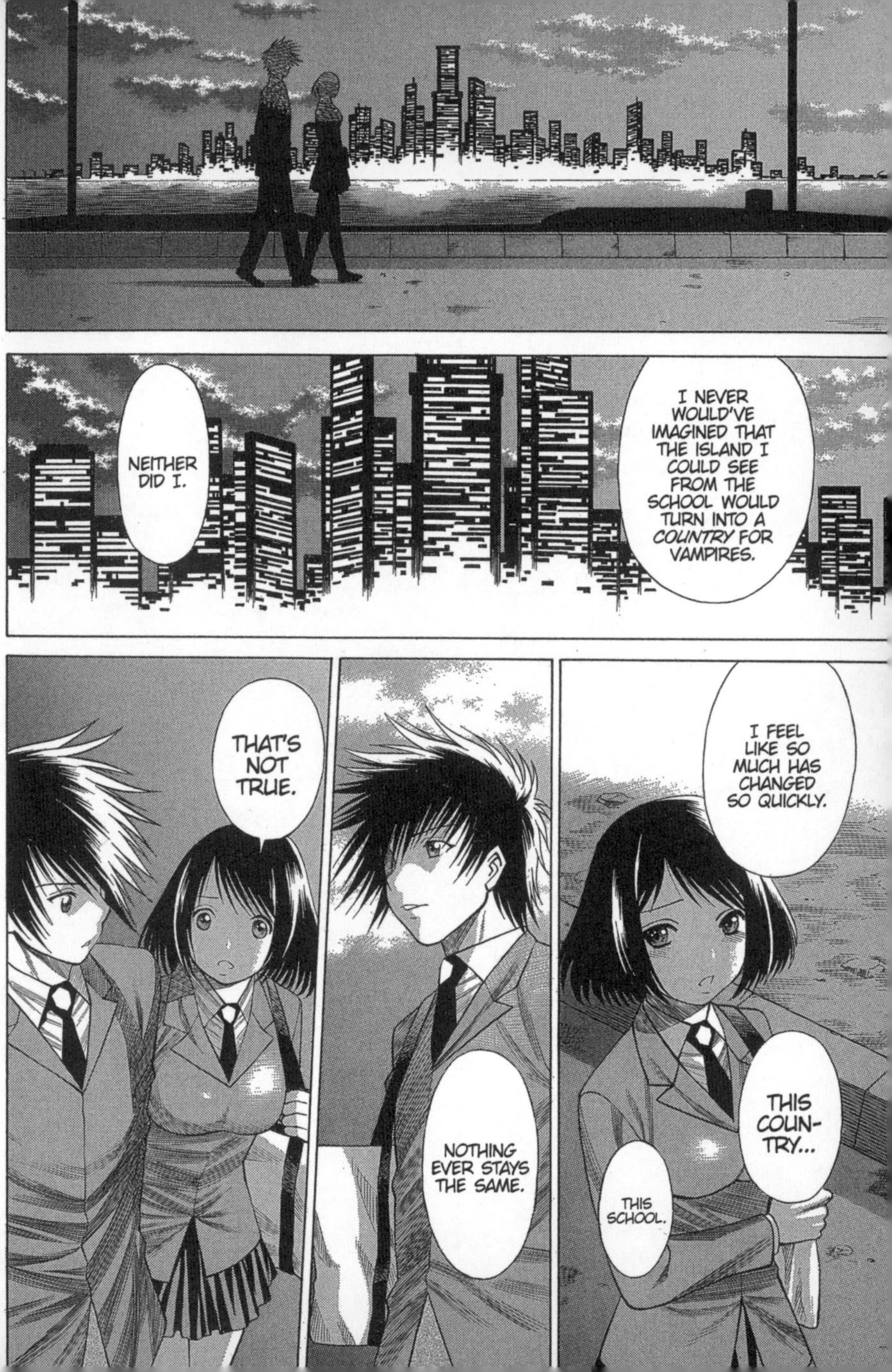
I NEVER WOULD'VE IMAGINED THAT THE ISLAND I COULD SEE FROM THE SCHOOL WOULD TURN INTO A *COUNTRY* FOR VAMPIRES.
NEITHER DID I.
I FEEL LIKE SO MUCH HAS CHANGED SO QUICKLY.
THIS COUN-TRY...
THIS SCHOOL.
NOTHING EVER STAYS THE SAME.
THAT'S NOT TRUE.

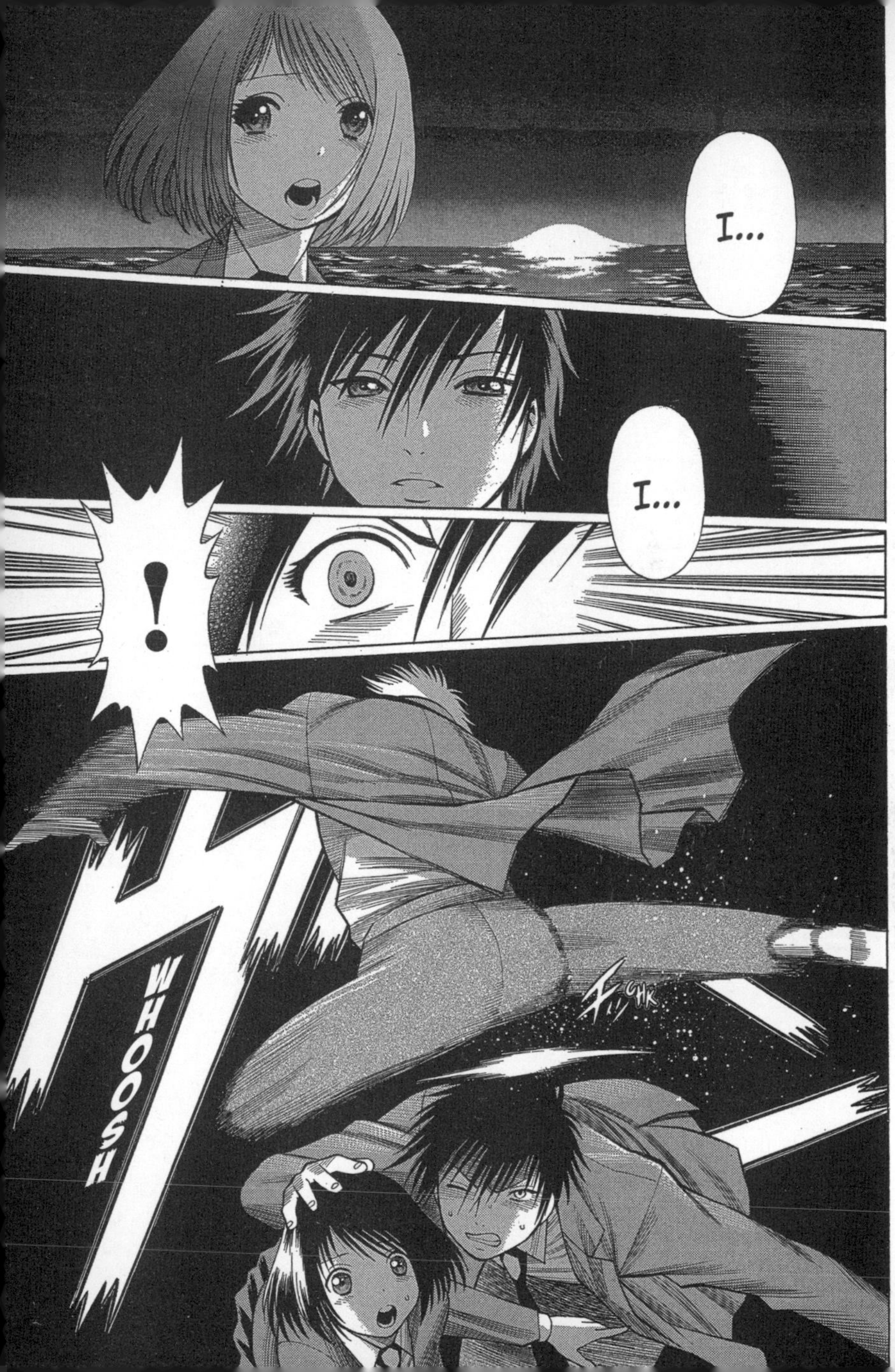
I...
I...
!
WHOOSH
CHK

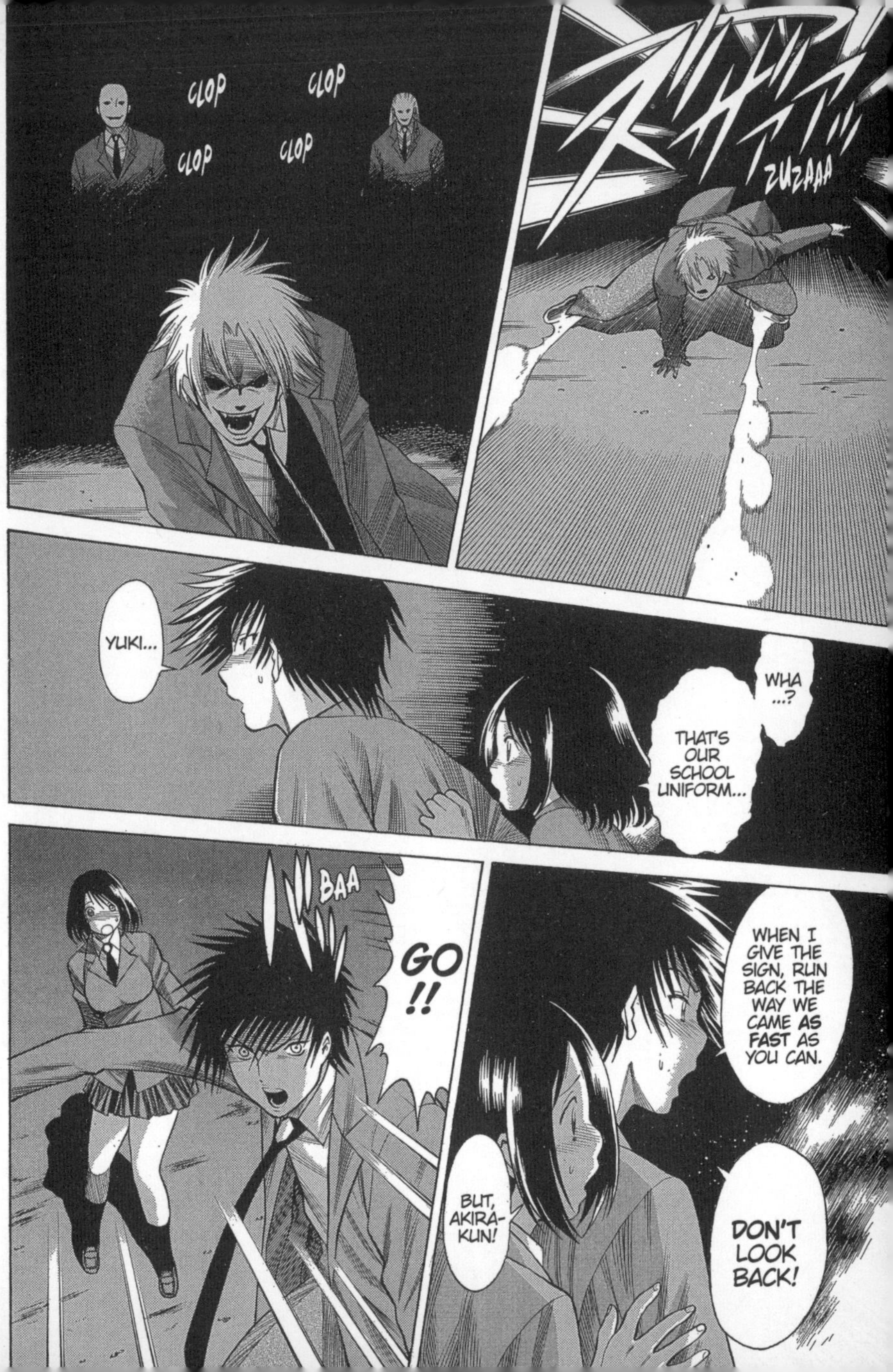
ZUZAAA
CLOP
CLOP
CLOP
CLOP
YUKI...
WHA ...?
THAT'S OUR SCHOOL UNIFORM...
WHEN I GIVE THE SIGN, RUN BACK THE WAY WE CAME AS FAST AS YOU CAN.
DON'T LOOK BACK!
BUT, AKIRA-KUN!
BAA
GO !!

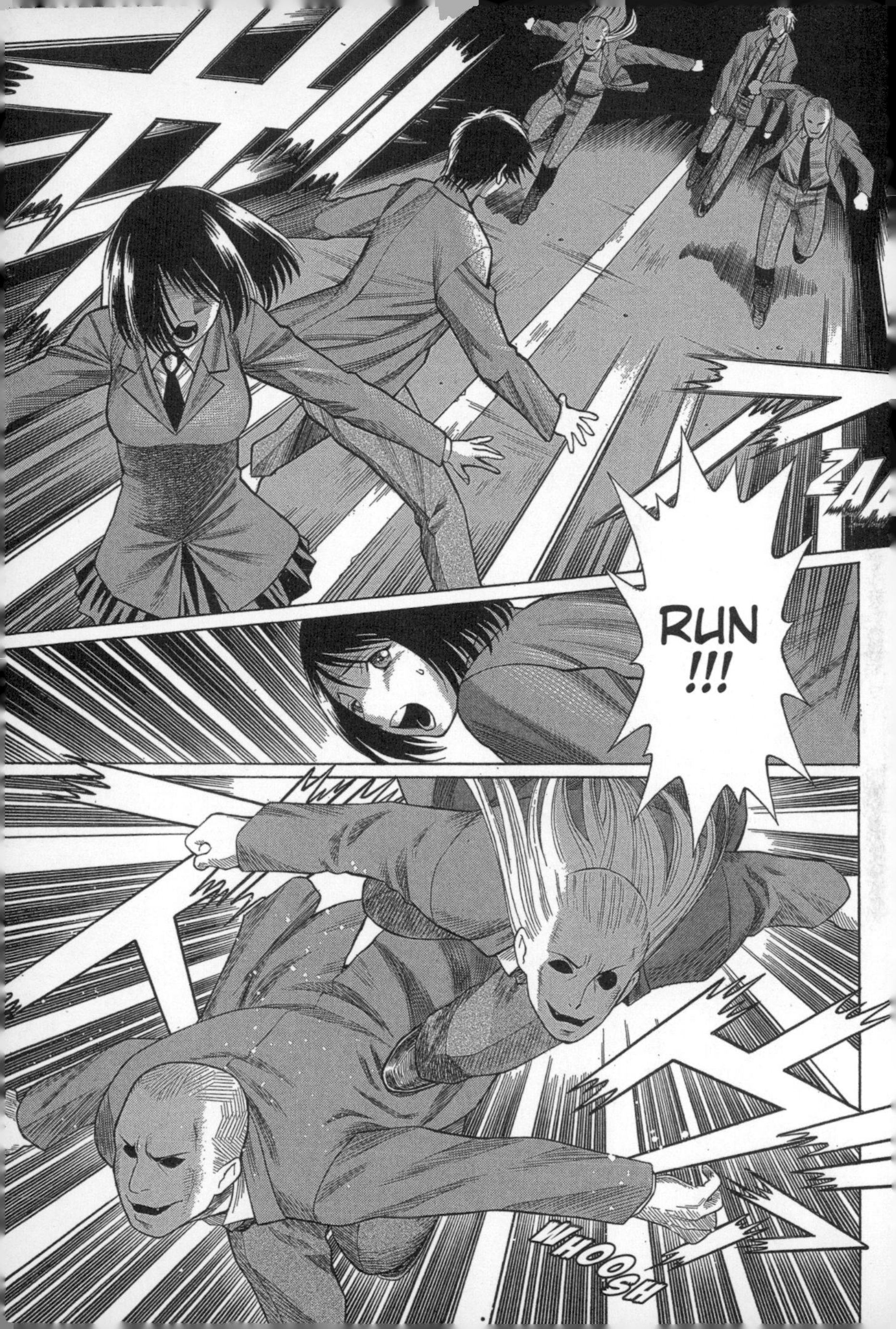
ZAA
RUN !!!
WHOOSH

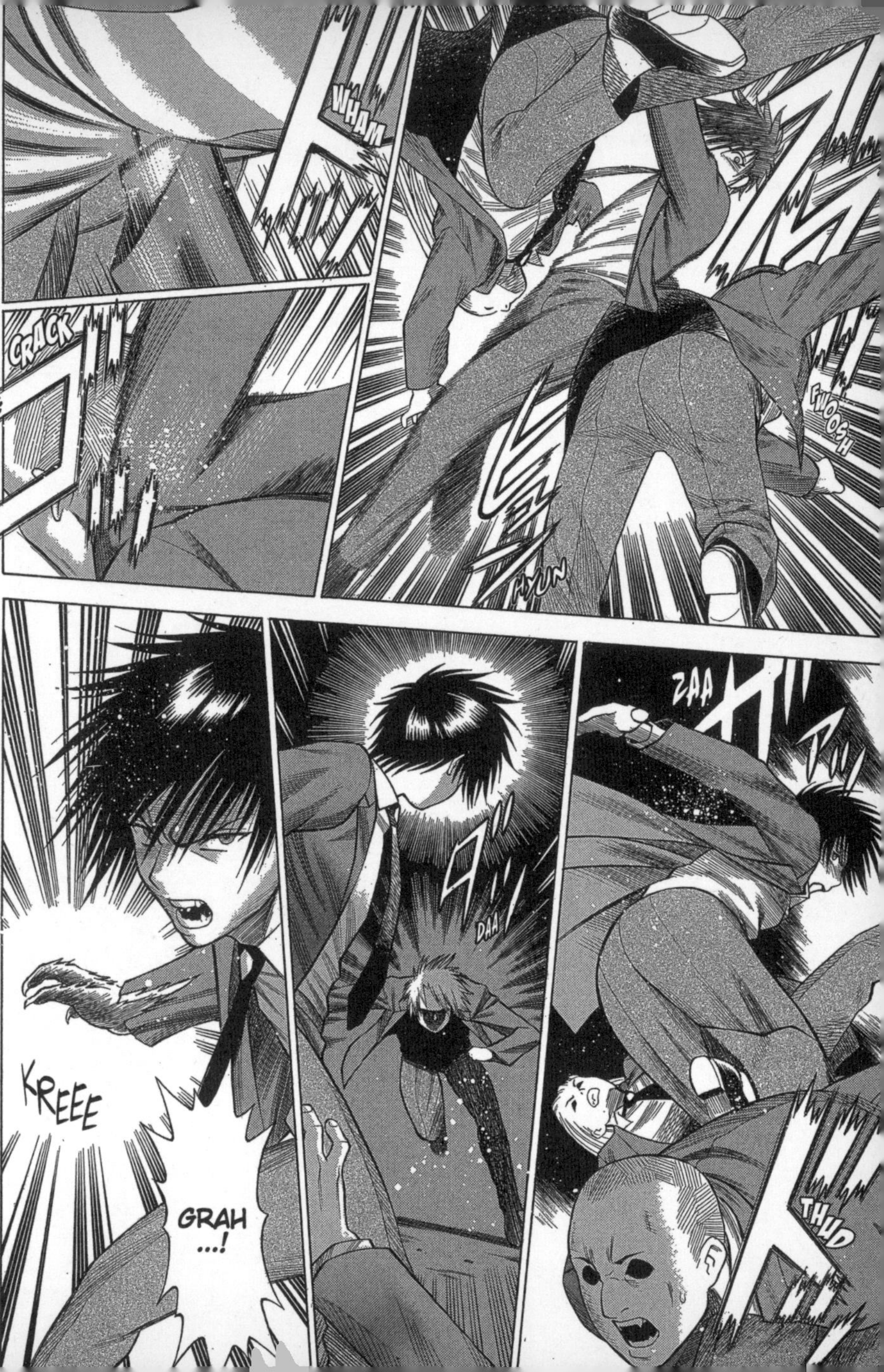
FWOOSH
HYUN
WHAM
CRACK
ZAA
THUD
DAA
KREEE
GRAH
...!

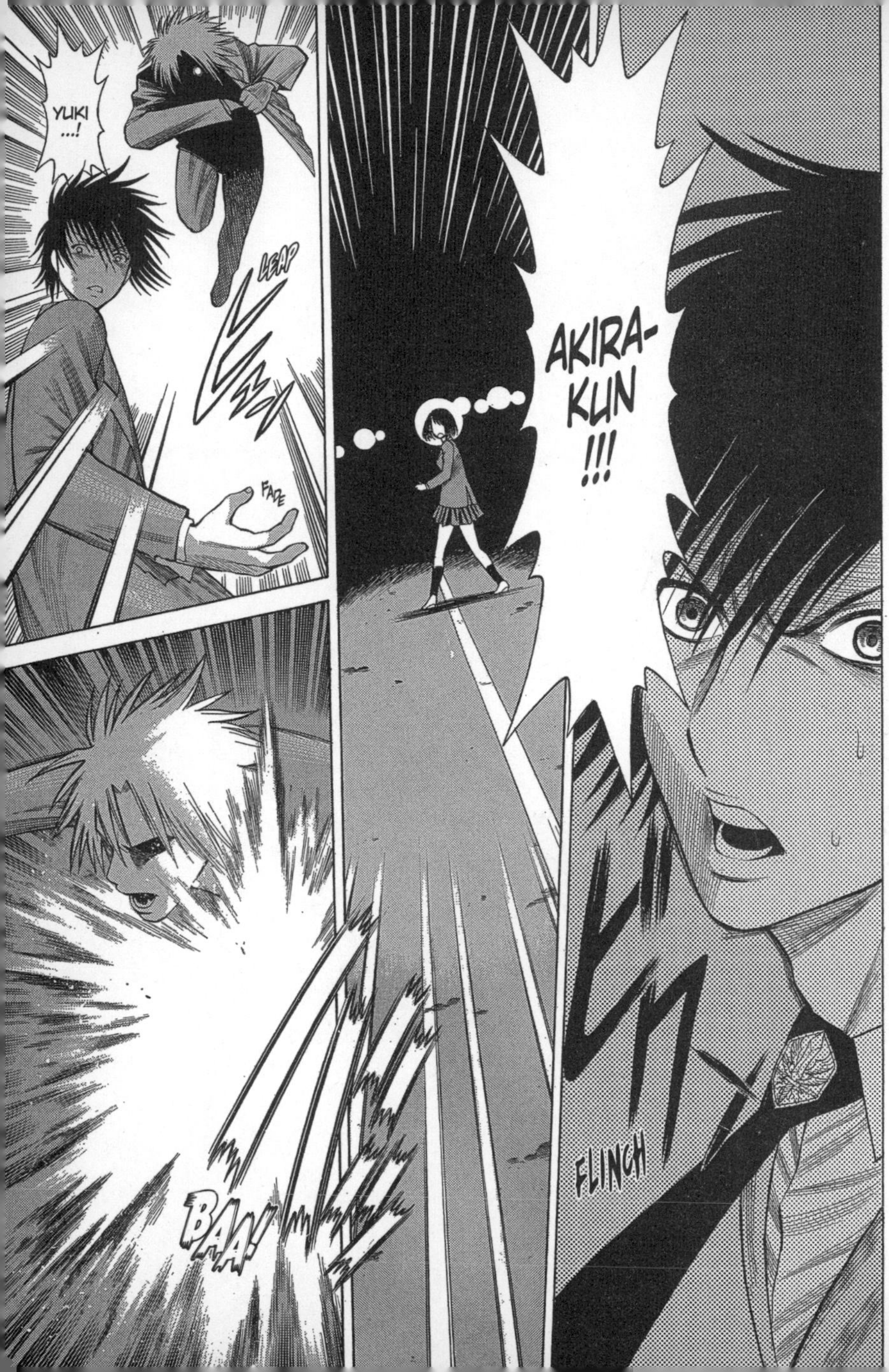
AKIRA-KUN!!!
FLINCH
YUKI...!
LEAP
FADE
BAA!

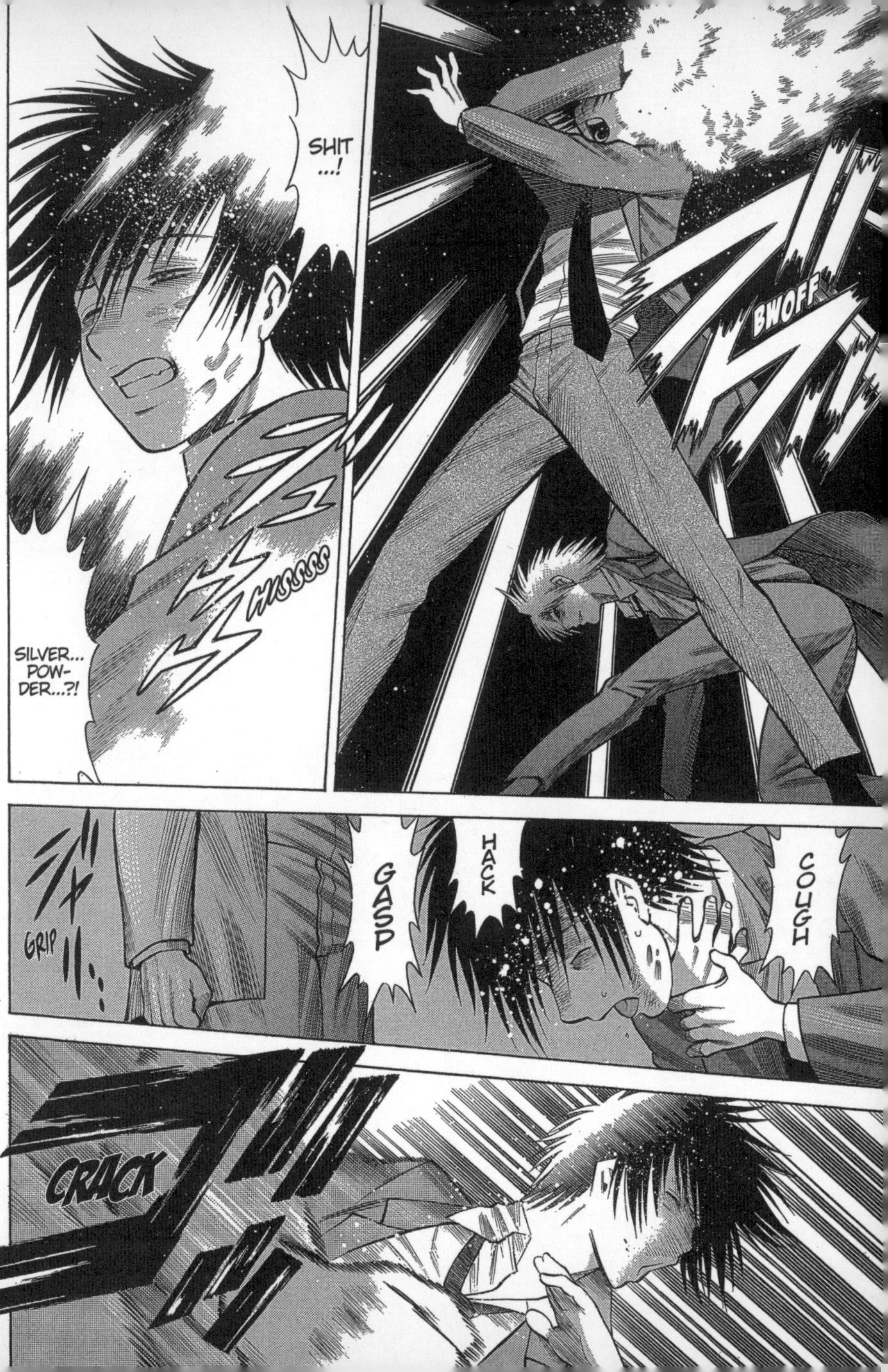
BWOFF
SHIT ...!
HISSSS
SILVER... POW-DER...?!
COUGH
HACK
GASP
GRIP
CRACK

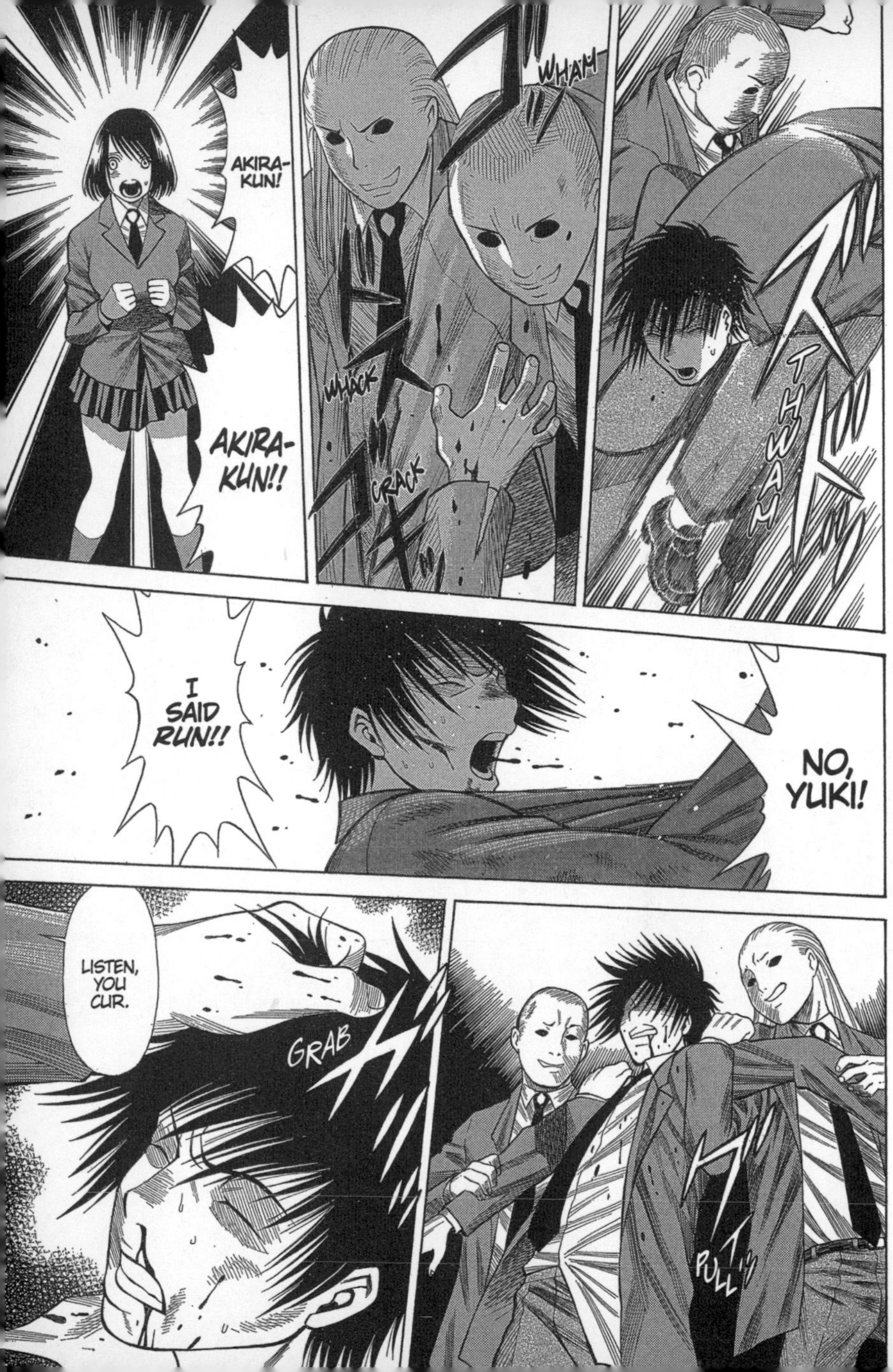
THWAM
WHAM
WHACK
CRACK
AKIRA-KUN!
AKIRA-KUN!!
NO, YUKI!
I SAID RUN!!
PULL
LISTEN, YOU CUR.
GRAB

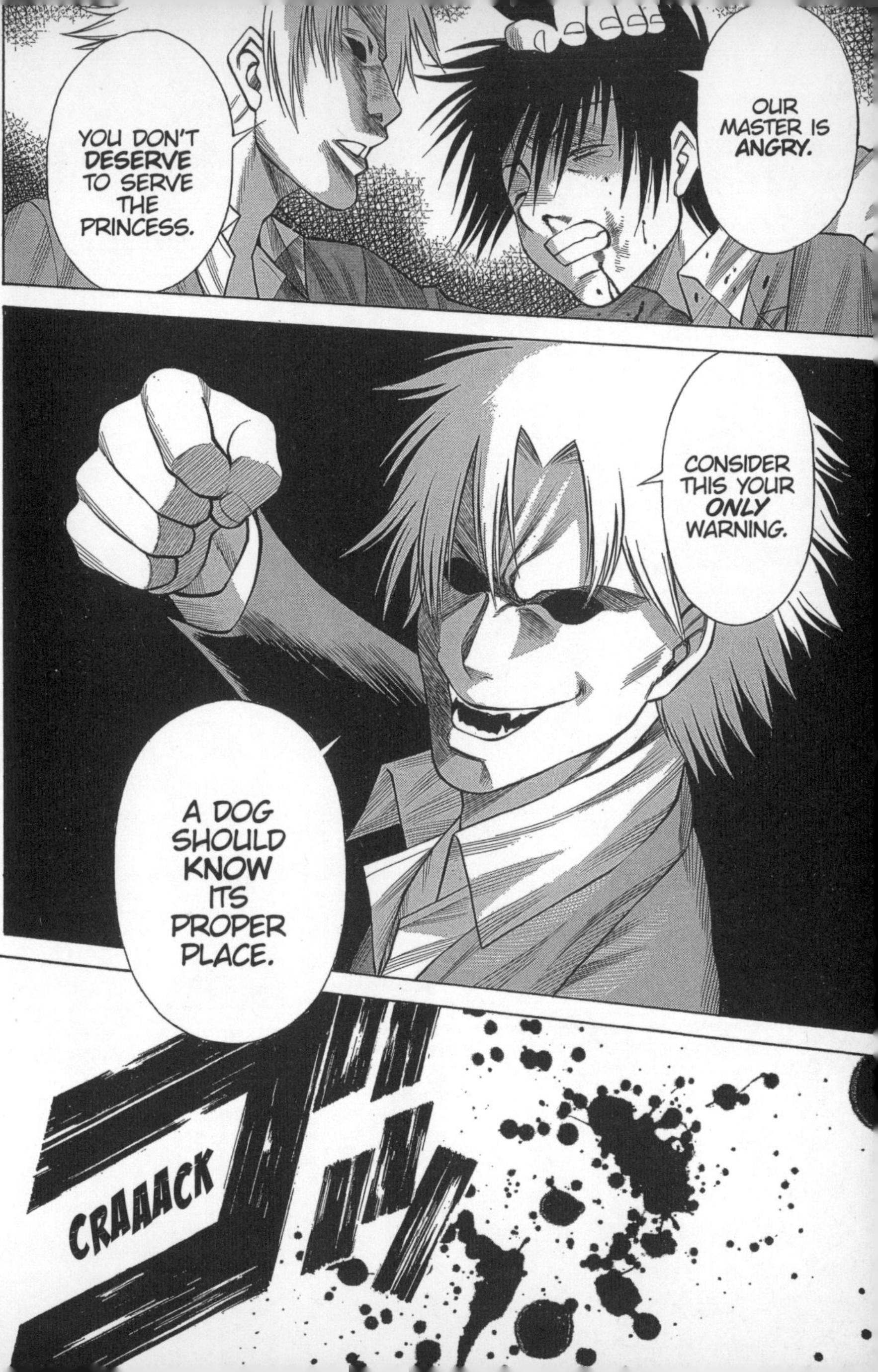
OUR MASTER IS ANGRY.
YOU DON'T DESERVE TO SERVE THE PRINCESS.
CONSIDER THIS YOUR ONLY WARNING.
A DOG SHOULD KNOW ITS PROPER PLACE.
CRAAACK

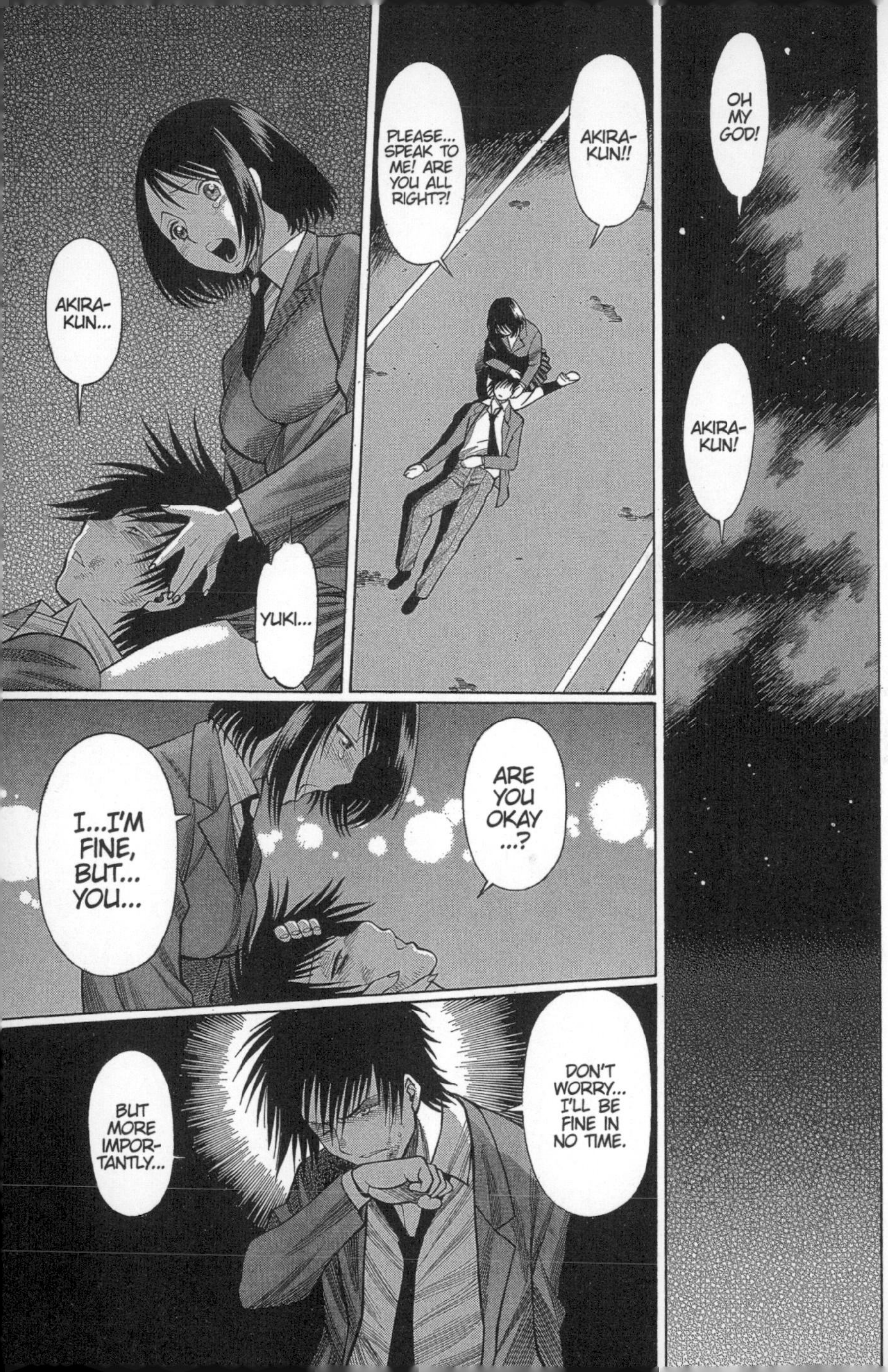
OH MY GOD!
AKIRA-KUN!
AKIRA-KUN!!
PLEASE... SPEAK TO ME! ARE YOU ALL RIGHT?!
YUKI...
AKIRA-KUN...
ARE YOU OKAY ...?
I...I'M FINE, BUT... YOU...
DON'T WORRY... I'LL BE FINE IN NO TIME.
BUT MORE IMPOR-TANTLY...

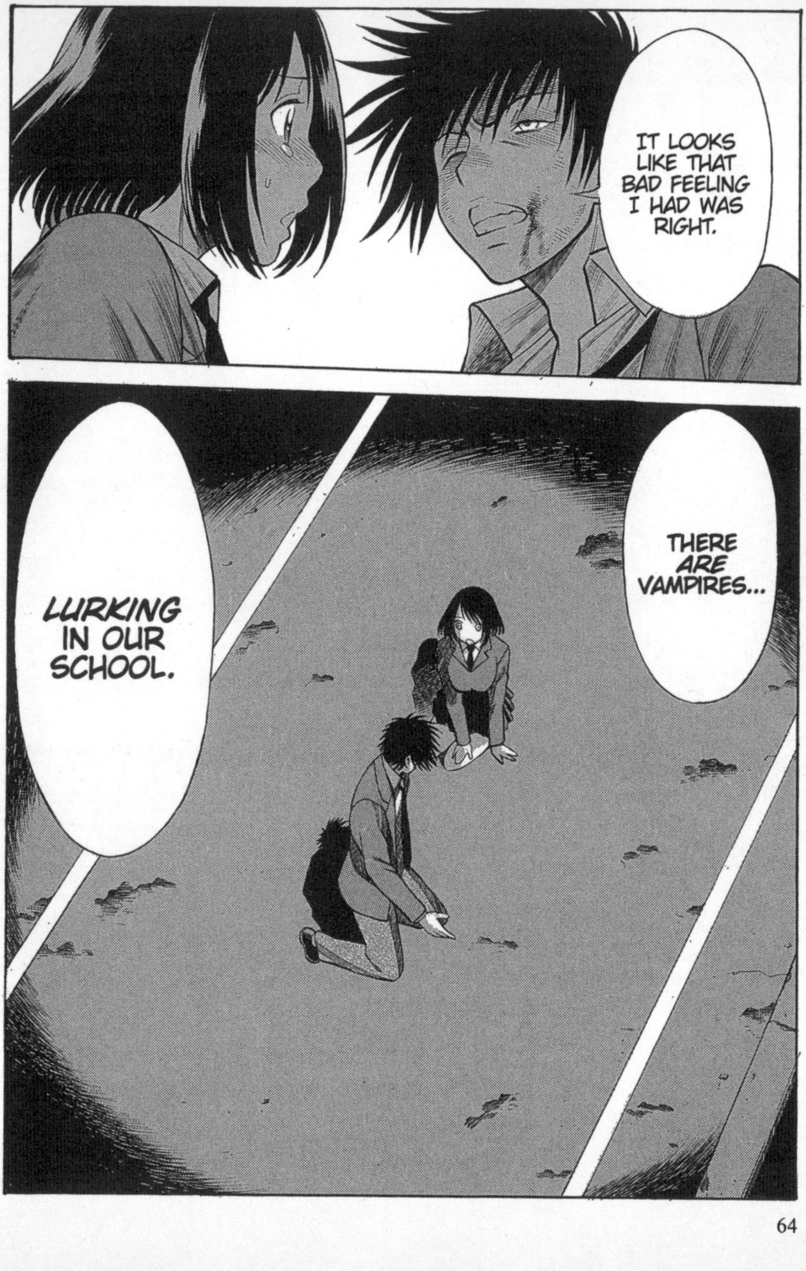
IT LOOKS LIKE THAT BAD FEELING I HAD WAS RIGHT.
THERE *ARE* VAMPIRES...
LURKING IN OUR SCHOOL.

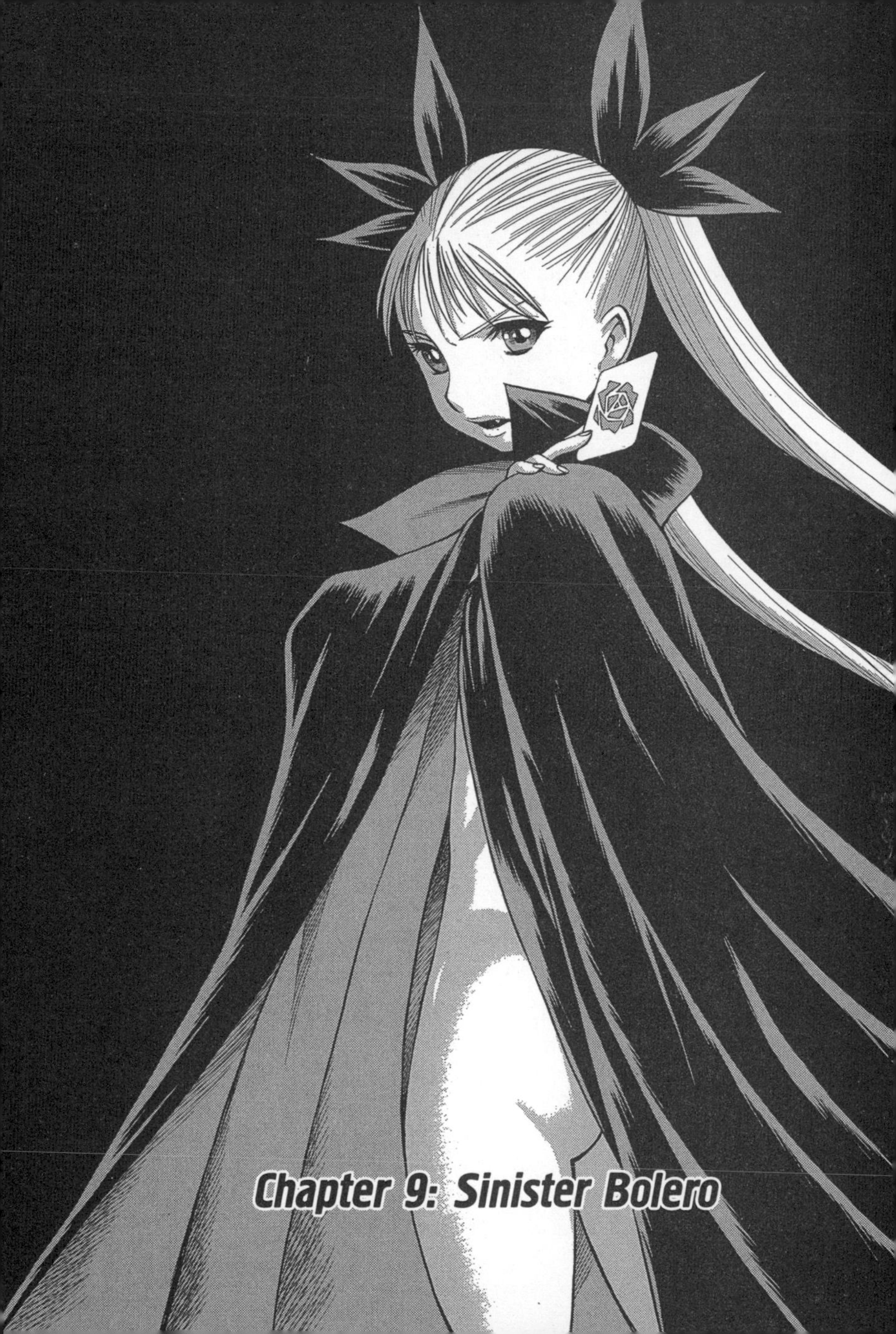

Chapter 9: Sinister Bolero

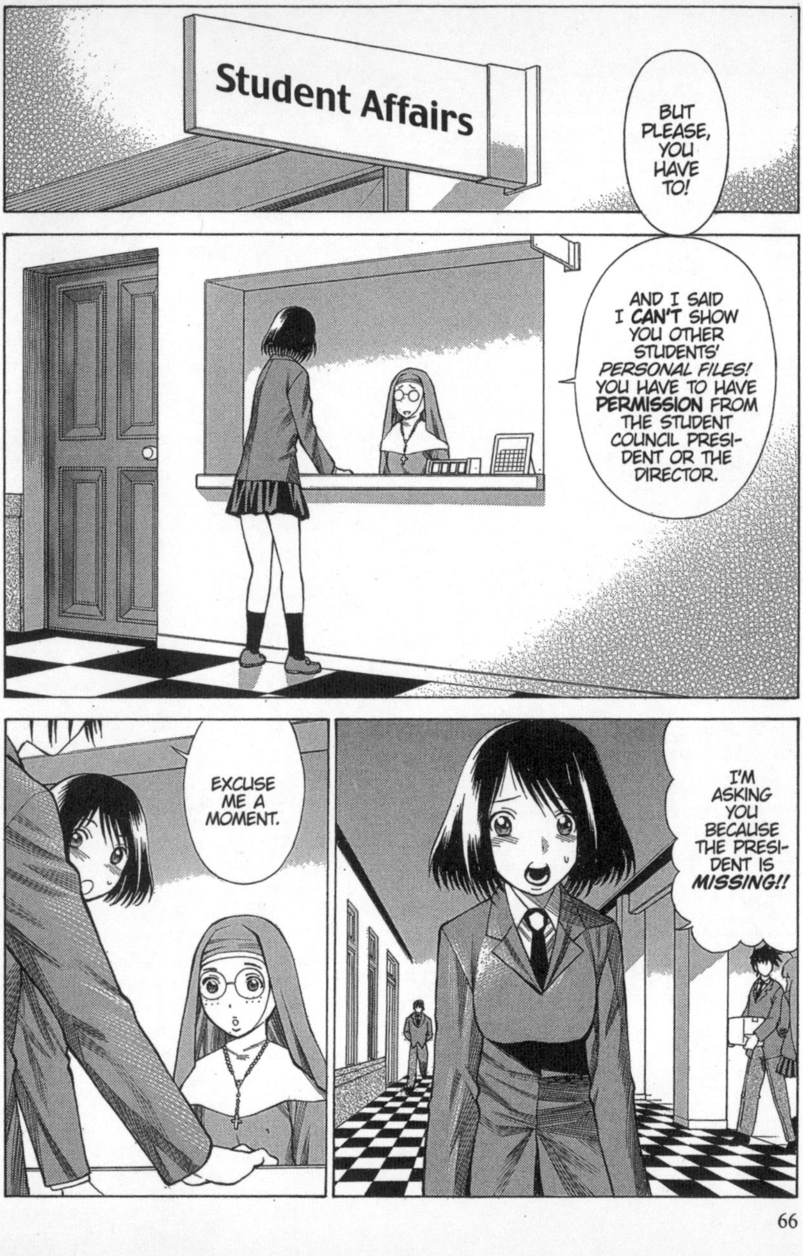
BUT PLEASE, YOU HAVE TO!
Student Affairs
AND I SAID I **CAN'T** SHOW YOU OTHER STUDENTS' *PERSONAL FILES!* YOU HAVE TO HAVE **PERMISSION** FROM THE STUDENT COUNCIL PRESIDENT OR THE DIRECTOR.
I'M ASKING YOU BECAUSE THE PRESIDENT IS *MISSING!!*
EXCUSE ME A MOMENT.

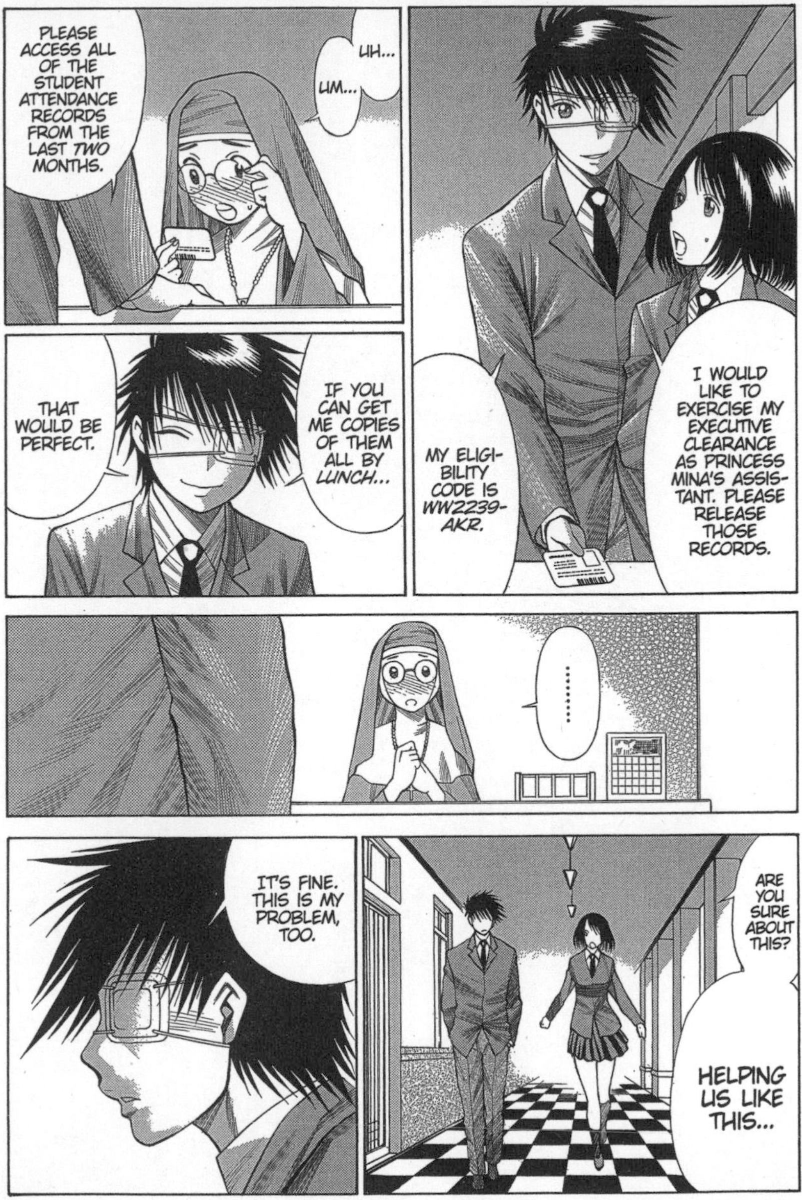
I WOULD LIKE TO EXERCISE MY EXECUTIVE CLEARANCE AS PRINCESS MINA'S ASSISTANT. PLEASE RELEASE THOSE RECORDS.
MY ELIGIBILITY CODE IS WW2239-AKR.
UH...
UM...
PLEASE ACCESS ALL OF THE STUDENT ATTENDANCE RECORDS FROM THE LAST *TWO* MONTHS.
IF YOU CAN GET ME COPIES OF THEM ALL BY *LUNCH*...
THAT WOULD BE PERFECT.
....
ARE YOU SURE ABOUT THIS?
HELPING US LIKE THIS...
IT'S FINE. THIS IS MY PROBLEM, TOO.

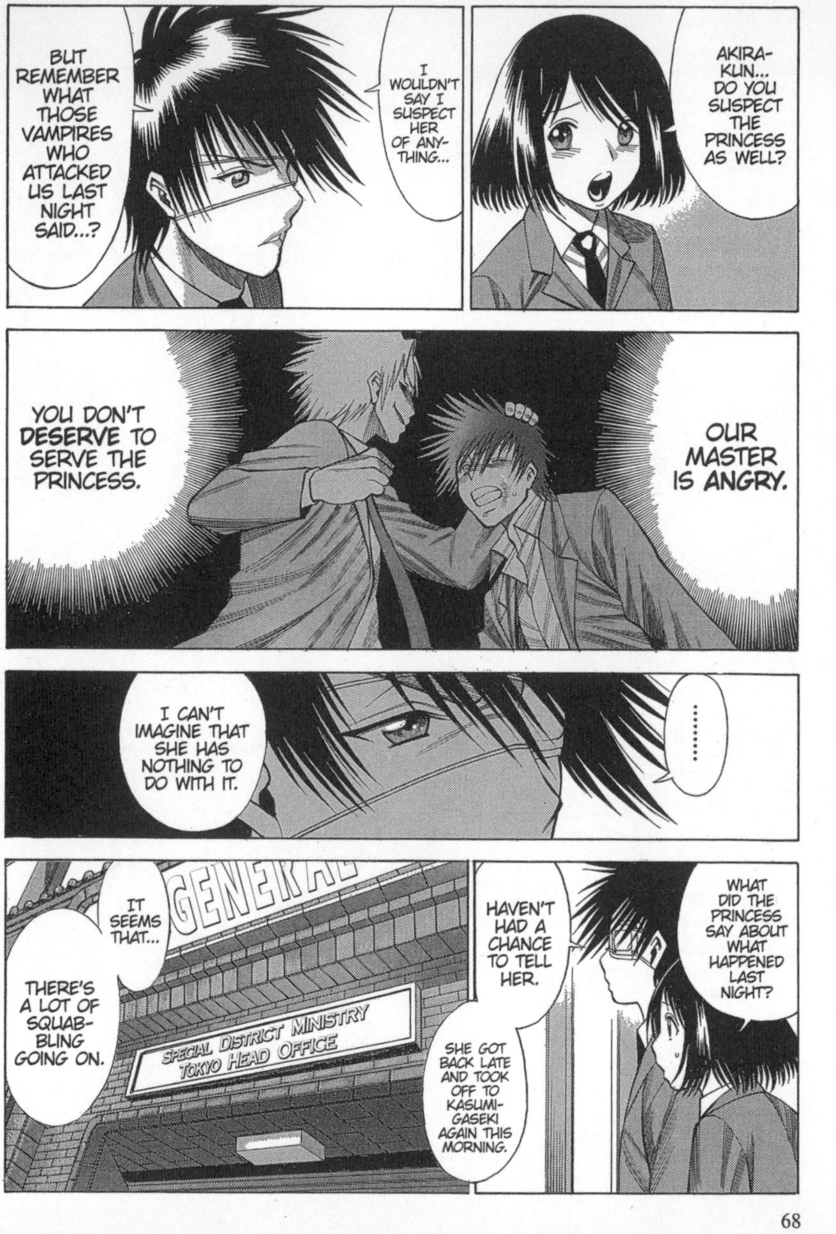
AKIRA-KUN... DO YOU SUSPECT THE PRINCESS AS WELL?
I WOULDN'T SAY I SUSPECT HER OF ANY-THING...
BUT REMEMBER WHAT THOSE VAMPIRES WHO ATTACKED US LAST NIGHT SAID...?
OUR MASTER IS ANGRY.
YOU DON'T DESERVE TO SERVE THE PRINCESS.
....
I CAN'T IMAGINE THAT SHE HAS NOTHING TO DO WITH IT.
WHAT DID THE PRINCESS SAY ABOUT WHAT HAPPENED LAST NIGHT?
HAVEN'T HAD A CHANCE TO TELL HER.
SHE GOT BACK LATE AND TOOK OFF TO KASUMI-GASEKI AGAIN THIS MORNING.
IT SEEMS THAT...
THERE'S A LOT OF SQUAB-BLING GOING ON.
SPECIAL DISTRICT MINISTRY
TOKYO HEAD OFFICE

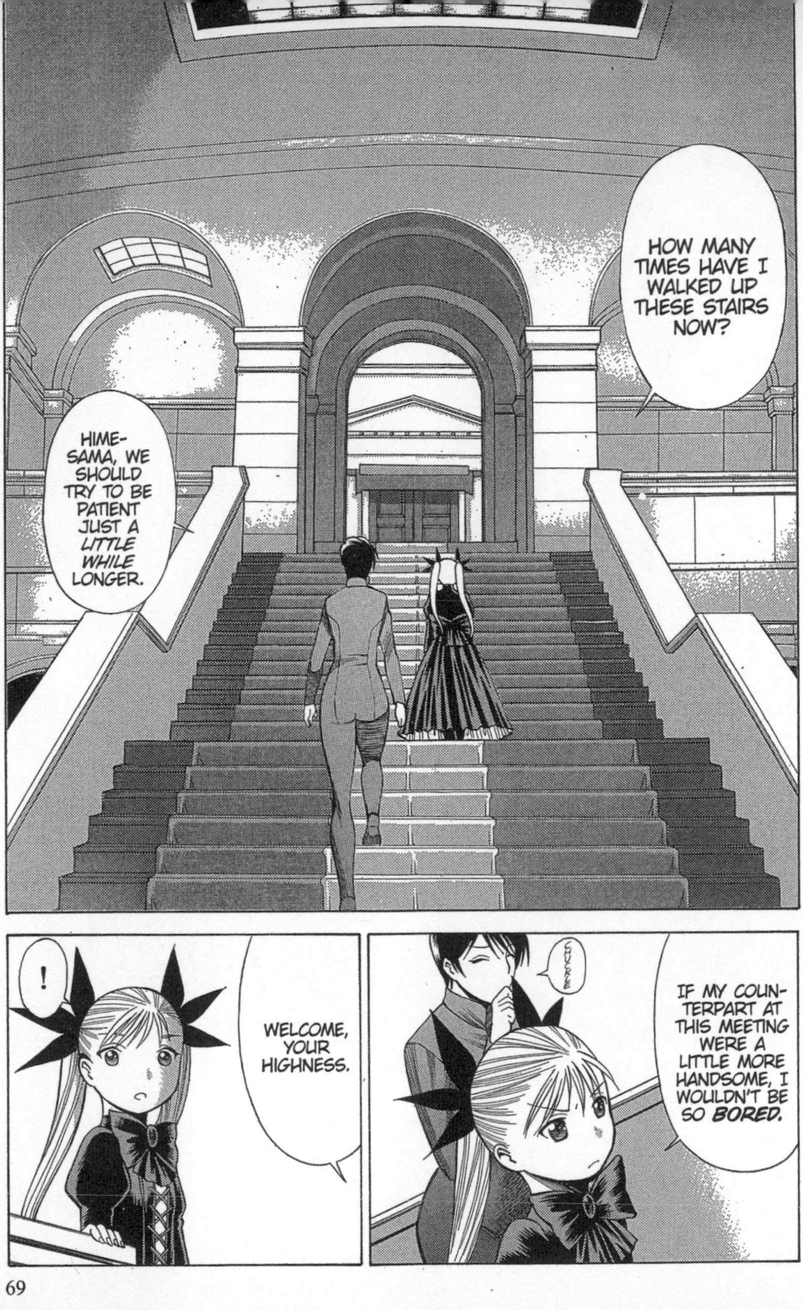
HOW MANY TIMES HAVE I WALKED UP THESE STAIRS NOW?
HIME-SAMA, WE SHOULD TRY TO BE PATIENT JUST A *LITTLE WHILE* LONGER.
IF MY COUNTERPART AT THIS MEETING WERE A LITTLE MORE HANDSOME, I WOULDN'T BE SO ***BORED.***
CHUCKLE
WELCOME, YOUR HIGHNESS.
!

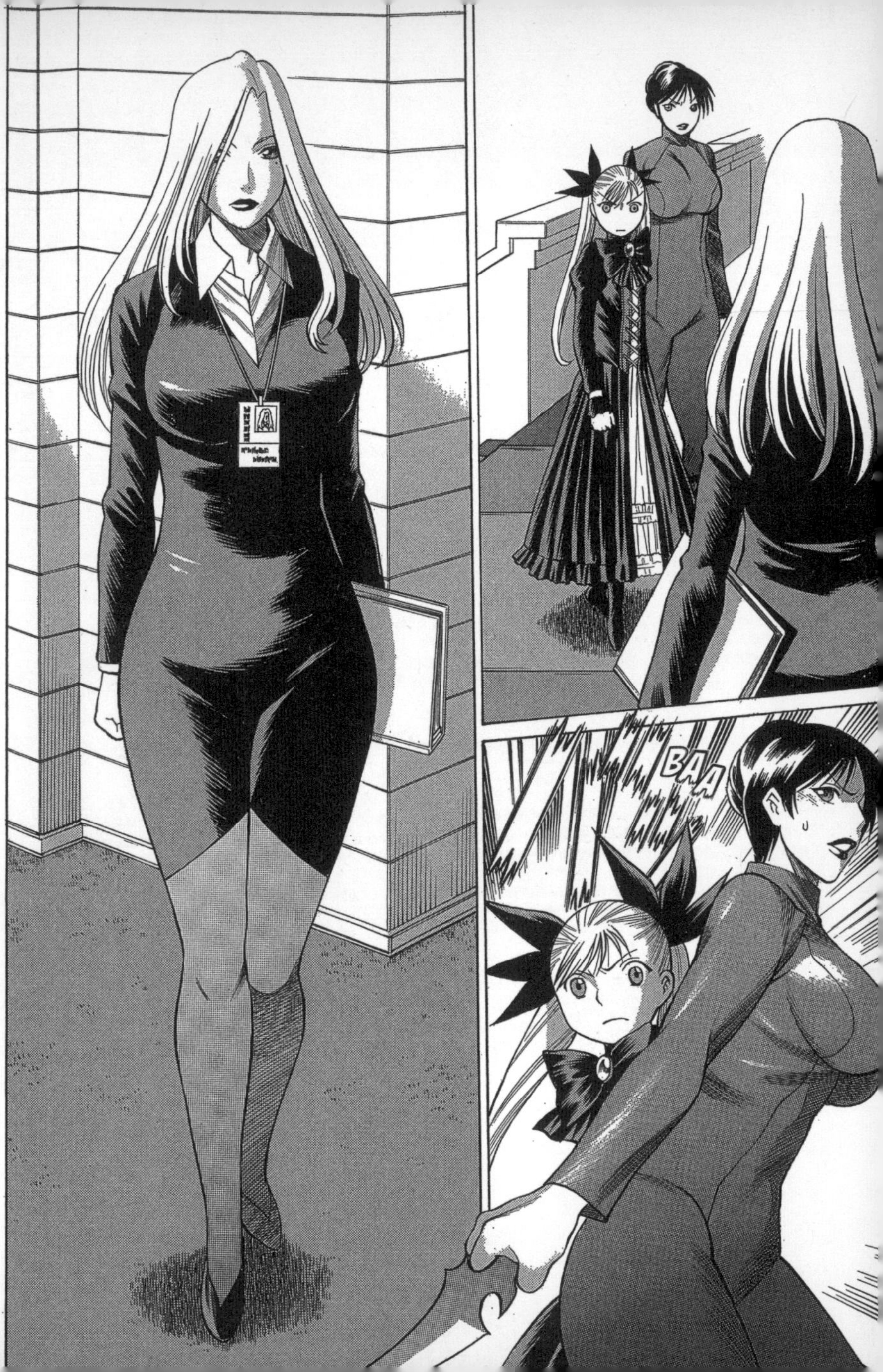
BAA

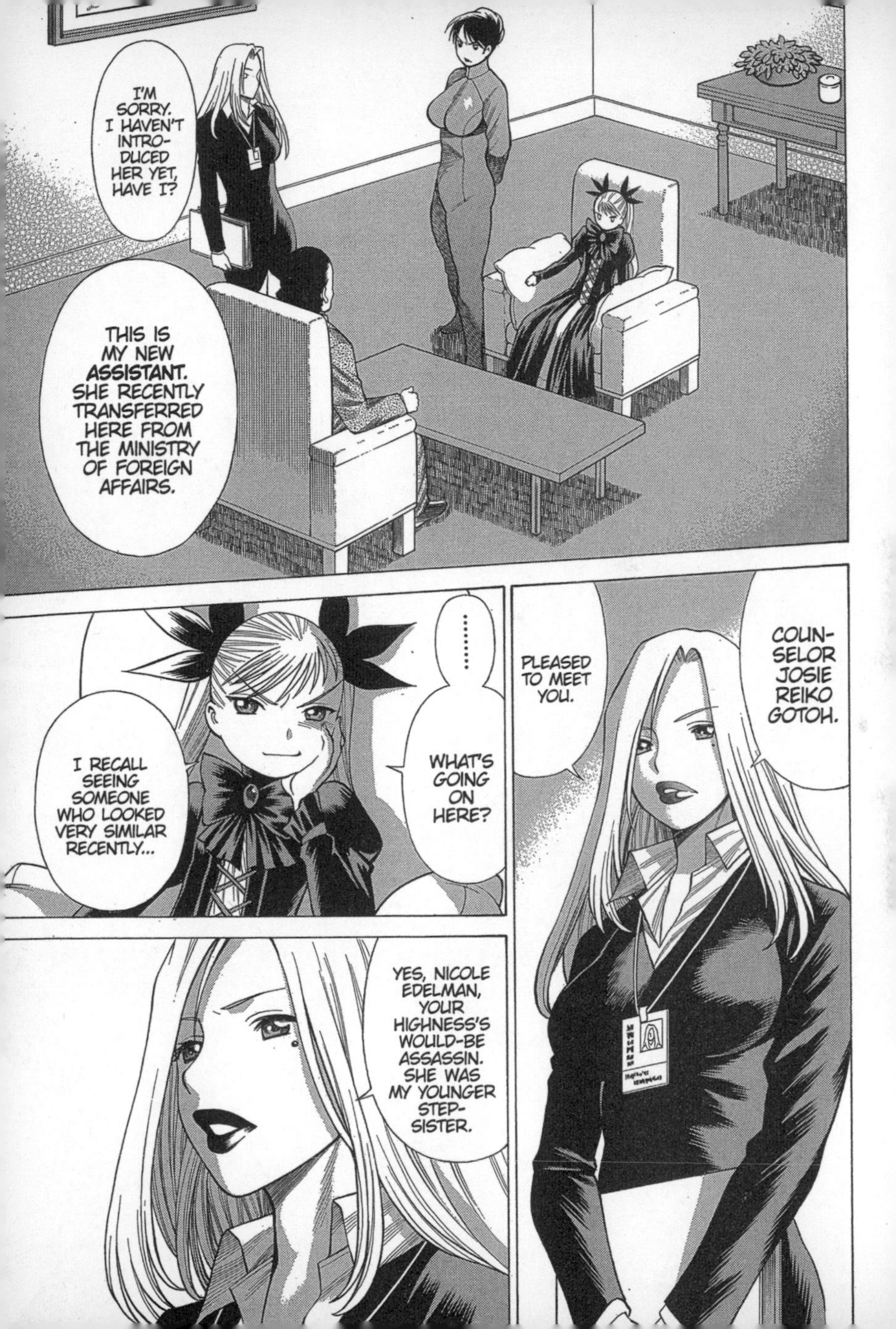
I'M SORRY. I HAVEN'T INTRO-DUCED HER YET, HAVE I?
THIS IS MY NEW ASSISTANT. SHE RECENTLY TRANSFERRED HERE FROM THE MINISTRY OF FOREIGN AFFAIRS.
COUN-SELOR JOSIE REIKO GOTOH.
PLEASED TO MEET YOU.
....
WHAT'S GOING ON HERE?
I RECALL SEEING SOMEONE WHO LOOKED VERY SIMILAR RECENTLY...
YES, NICOLE EDELMAN, YOUR HIGHNESS'S WOULD-BE ASSASSIN. SHE WAS MY YOUNGER STEP-SISTER.

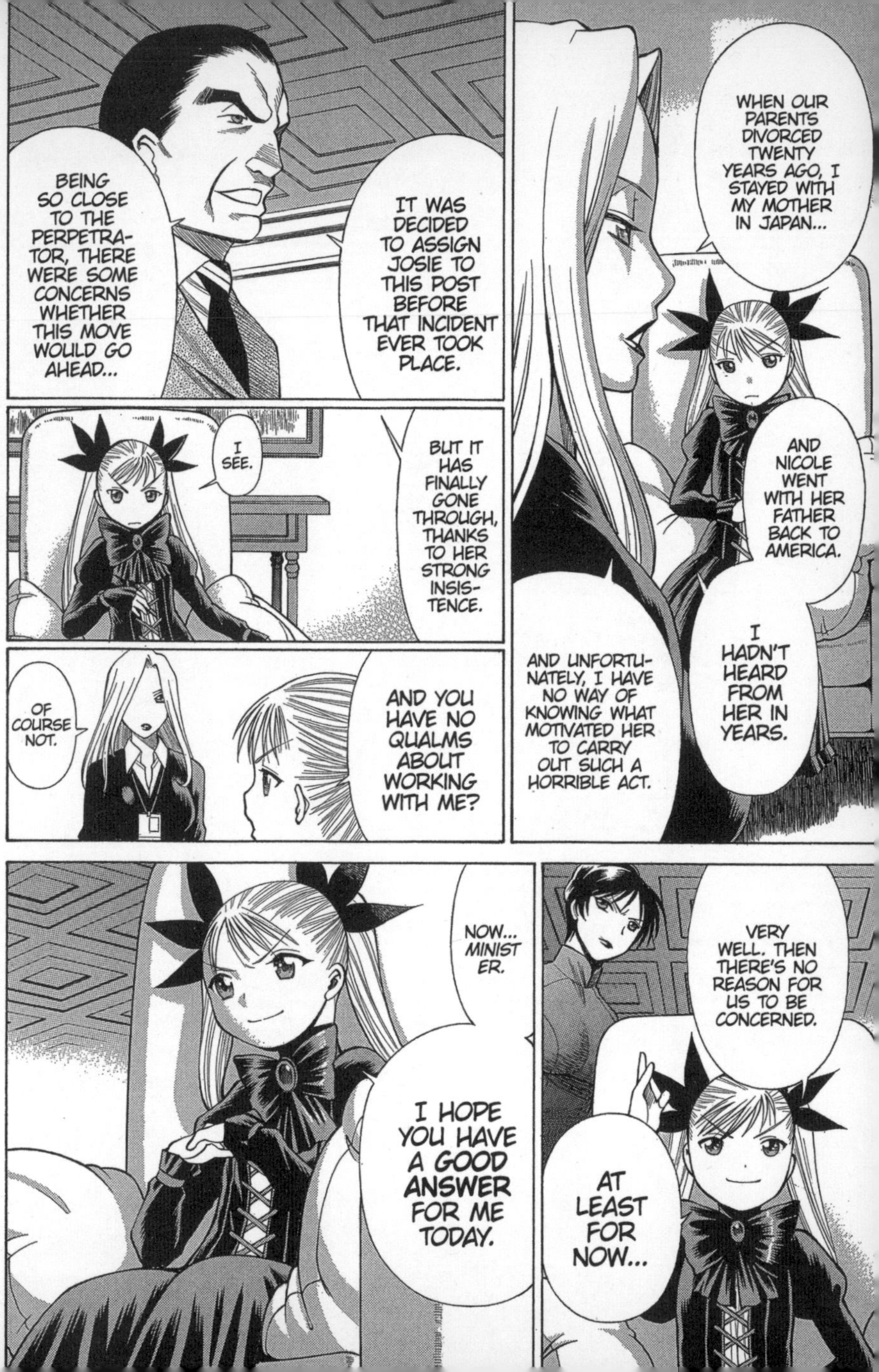
WHEN OUR PARENTS DIVORCED TWENTY YEARS AGO, I STAYED WITH MY MOTHER IN JAPAN...
AND NICOLE WENT WITH HER FATHER BACK TO AMERICA.
I HADN'T HEARD FROM HER IN YEARS.
AND UNFORTUNATELY, I HAVE NO WAY OF KNOWING WHAT MOTIVATED HER TO CARRY OUT SUCH A HORRIBLE ACT.
IT WAS DECIDED TO ASSIGN JOSIE TO THIS POST BEFORE THAT INCIDENT EVER TOOK PLACE.
BEING SO CLOSE TO THE PERPETRATOR, THERE WERE SOME CONCERNS WHETHER THIS MOVE WOULD GO AHEAD...
BUT IT HAS FINALLY GONE THROUGH, THANKS TO HER STRONG INSISTENCE.
I SEE.
AND YOU HAVE NO QUALMS ABOUT WORKING WITH ME?
OF COURSE NOT.
VERY WELL. THEN THERE'S NO REASON FOR US TO BE CONCERNED.
AT LEAST FOR NOW...
NOW... MINISTER.
I HOPE YOU HAVE A **GOOD ANSWER** FOR ME TODAY.

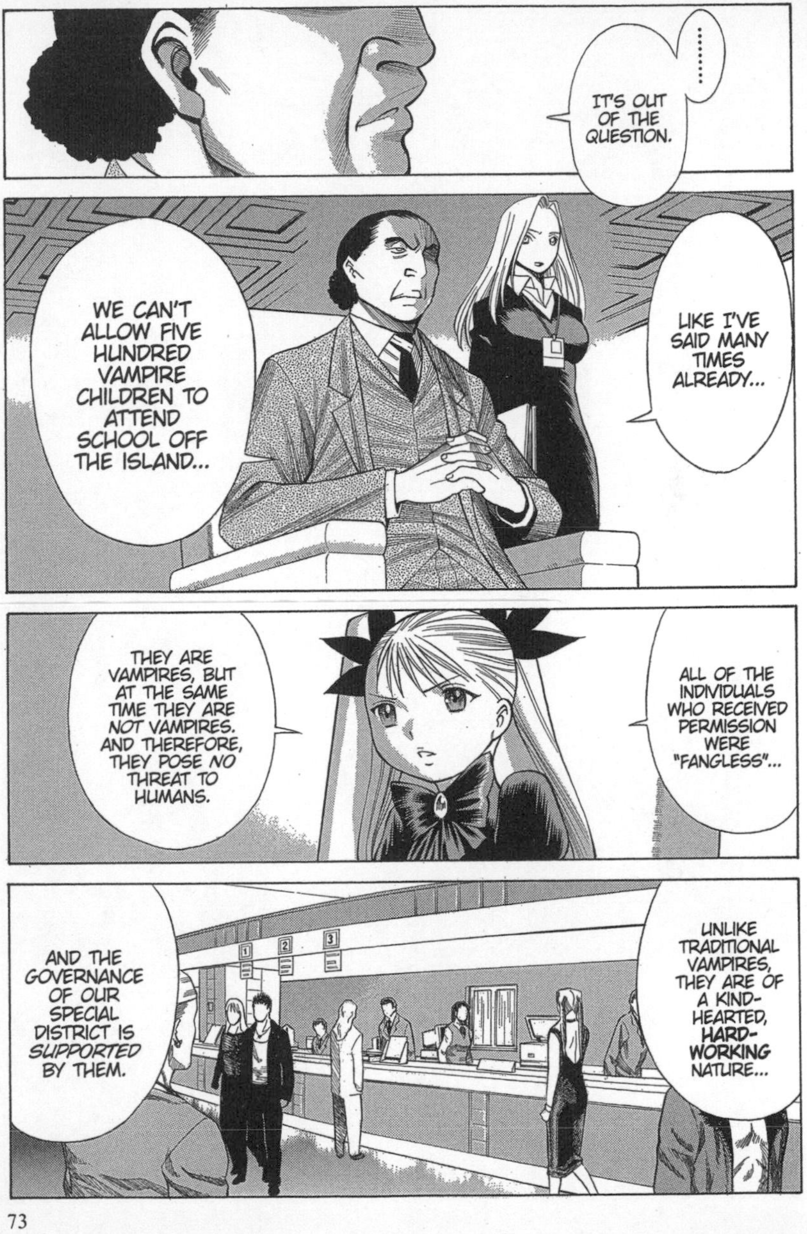
......
IT'S OUT OF THE QUESTION.
LIKE I'VE SAID MANY TIMES ALREADY...
WE CAN'T ALLOW FIVE HUNDRED VAMPIRE CHILDREN TO ATTEND SCHOOL OFF THE ISLAND...
ALL OF THE INDIVIDUALS WHO RECEIVED PERMISSION WERE "FANGLESS"...
THEY ARE VAMPIRES, BUT AT THE SAME TIME THEY ARE *NOT* VAMPIRES. AND THEREFORE, THEY POSE *NO* THREAT TO HUMANS.
UNLIKE TRADITIONAL VAMPIRES, THEY ARE OF A KIND-HEARTED, **HARD-WORKING** NATURE...
AND THE GOVERNANCE OF OUR SPECIAL DISTRICT IS *SUPPORTED* BY THEM.

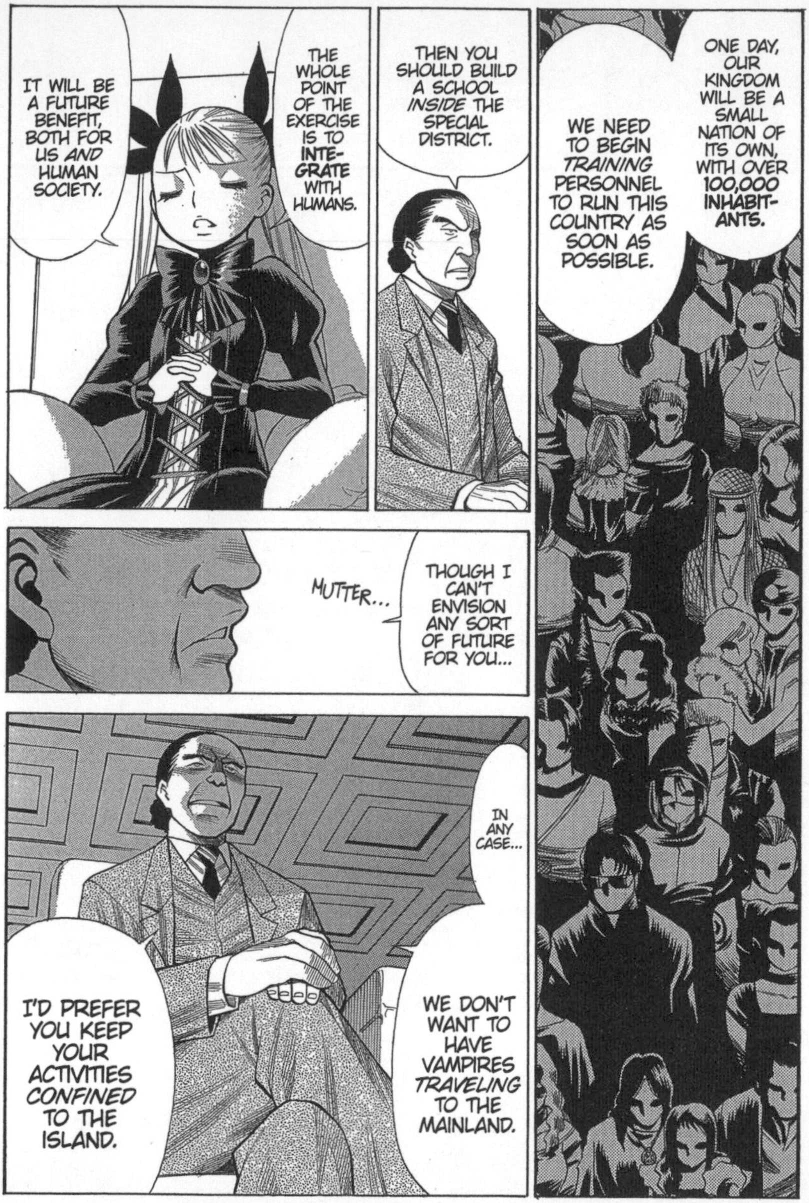

ONE DAY, OUR KINGDOM WILL BE A SMALL NATION OF ITS OWN, WITH OVER **100,000 INHABIT-ANTS.**
WE NEED TO BEGIN *TRAINING* PERSONNEL TO RUN THIS COUNTRY AS SOON AS POSSIBLE.
THEN YOU SHOULD BUILD A SCHOOL *INSIDE* THE SPECIAL DISTRICT.
THE WHOLE POINT OF THE EXERCISE IS TO **INTE-GRATE** WITH HUMANS.
IT WILL BE A FUTURE BENEFIT, BOTH FOR US *AND* HUMAN SOCIETY.
THOUGH I CAN'T ENVISION ANY SORT OF FUTURE FOR YOU...
MUTTER...
IN ANY CASE...
WE DON'T WANT TO HAVE VAMPIRES *TRAVELING* TO THE MAINLAND.
I'D PREFER YOU KEEP YOUR ACTIVITIES *CONFINED* TO THE ISLAND.

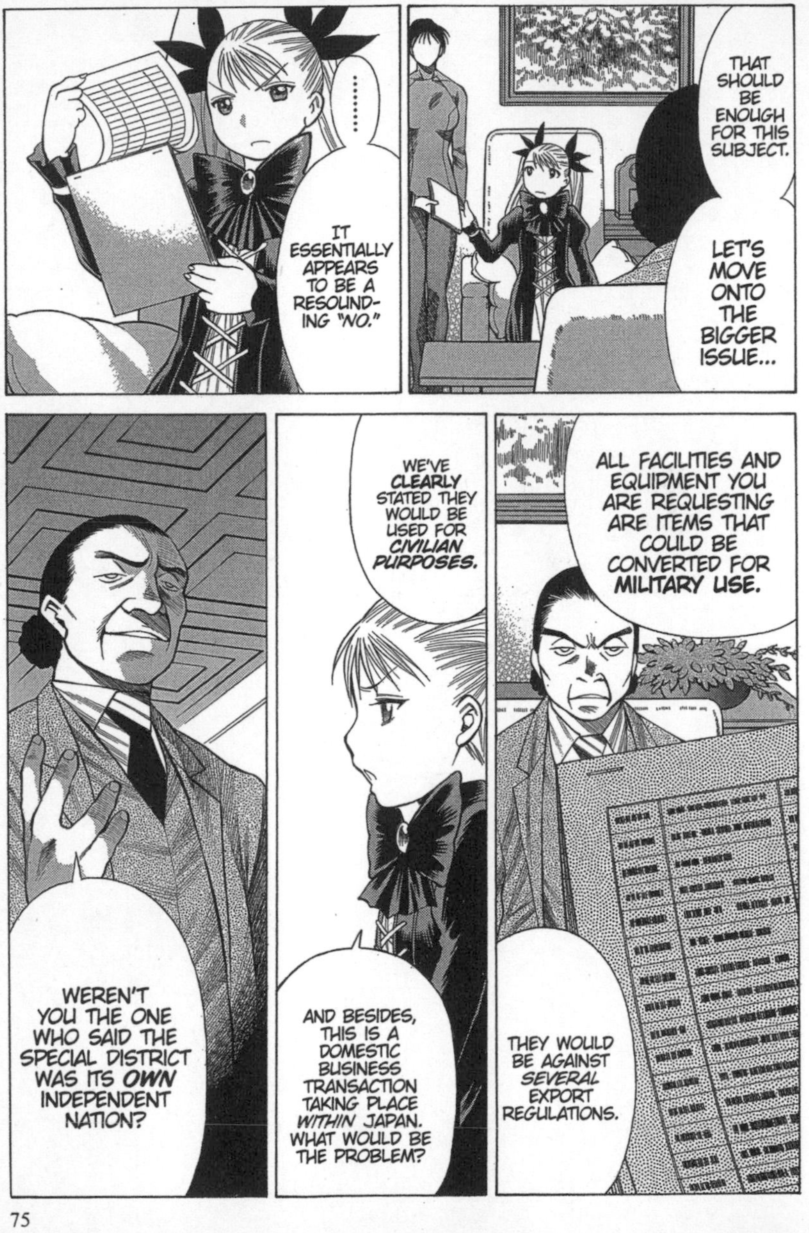
THAT SHOULD BE ENOUGH FOR THIS SUBJECT.
LET'S MOVE ONTO THE BIGGER ISSUE...
......
IT ESSENTIALLY APPEARS TO BE A RESOUNDING "NO."
ALL FACILITIES AND EQUIPMENT YOU ARE REQUESTING ARE ITEMS THAT COULD BE CONVERTED FOR MILITARY USE.
THEY WOULD BE AGAINST SEVERAL EXPORT REGULATIONS.
WE'VE CLEARLY STATED THEY WOULD BE USED FOR CIVILIAN PURPOSES.
AND BESIDES, THIS IS A DOMESTIC BUSINESS TRANSACTION TAKING PLACE WITHIN JAPAN. WHAT WOULD BE THE PROBLEM?
WEREN'T YOU THE ONE WHO SAID THE SPECIAL DISTRICT WAS ITS OWN INDEPENDENT NATION?

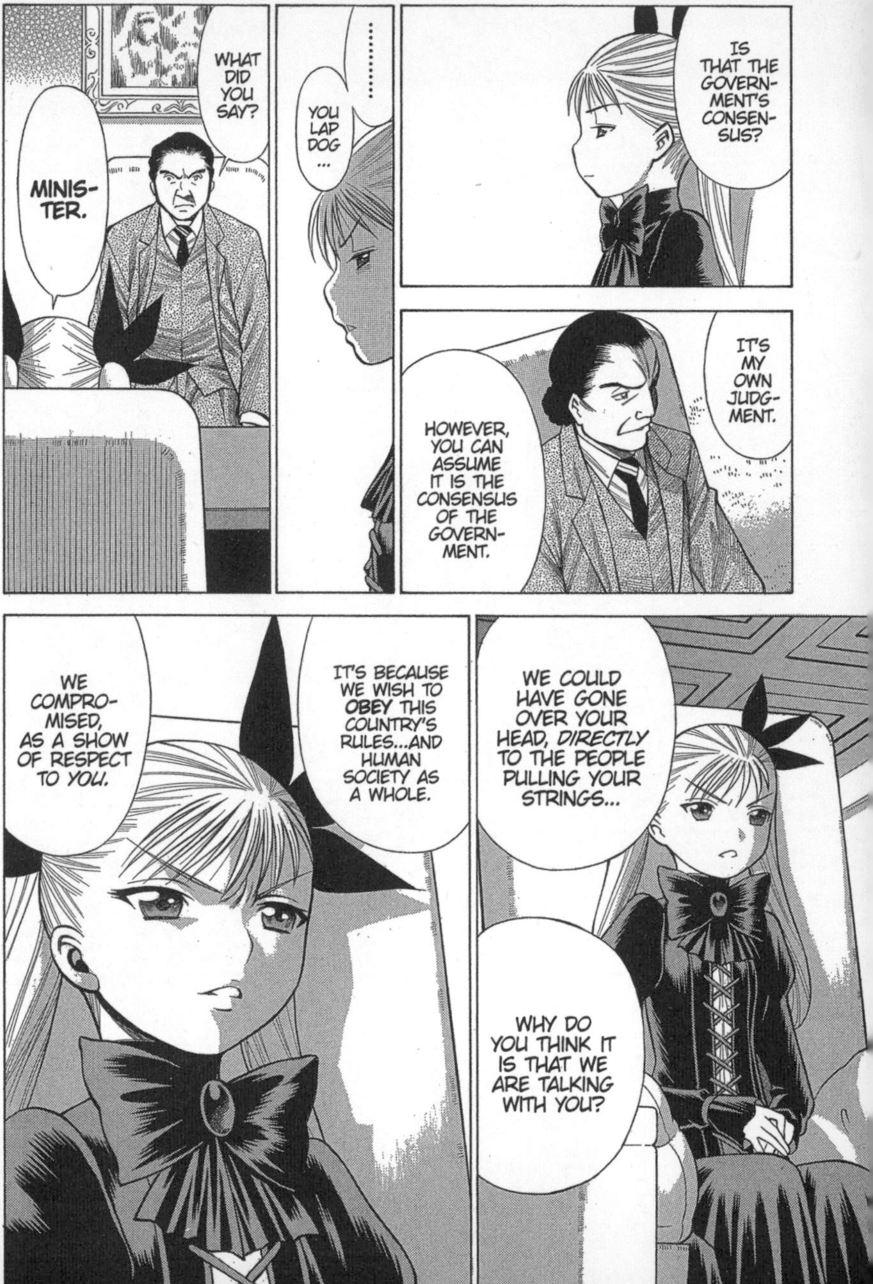
IS THAT THE GOVERN-MENT'S CONSEN-SUS?
IT'S MY OWN JUDG-MENT.
HOWEVER, YOU CAN ASSUME IT IS THE CONSENSUS OF THE GOVERN-MENT.
......
YOU LAP DOG ...
WHAT DID YOU SAY?
MINIS-TER.
WE COULD HAVE GONE OVER YOUR HEAD, *DIRECTLY* TO THE PEOPLE PULLING YOUR STRINGS...
WHY DO YOU THINK IT IS THAT WE ARE TALKING WITH YOU?
IT'S BECAUSE WE WISH TO **OBEY** THIS COUNTRY'S RULES...AND HUMAN SOCIETY AS A WHOLE.
WE COMPRO-MISED, AS A SHOW OF RESPECT TO *YOU*.

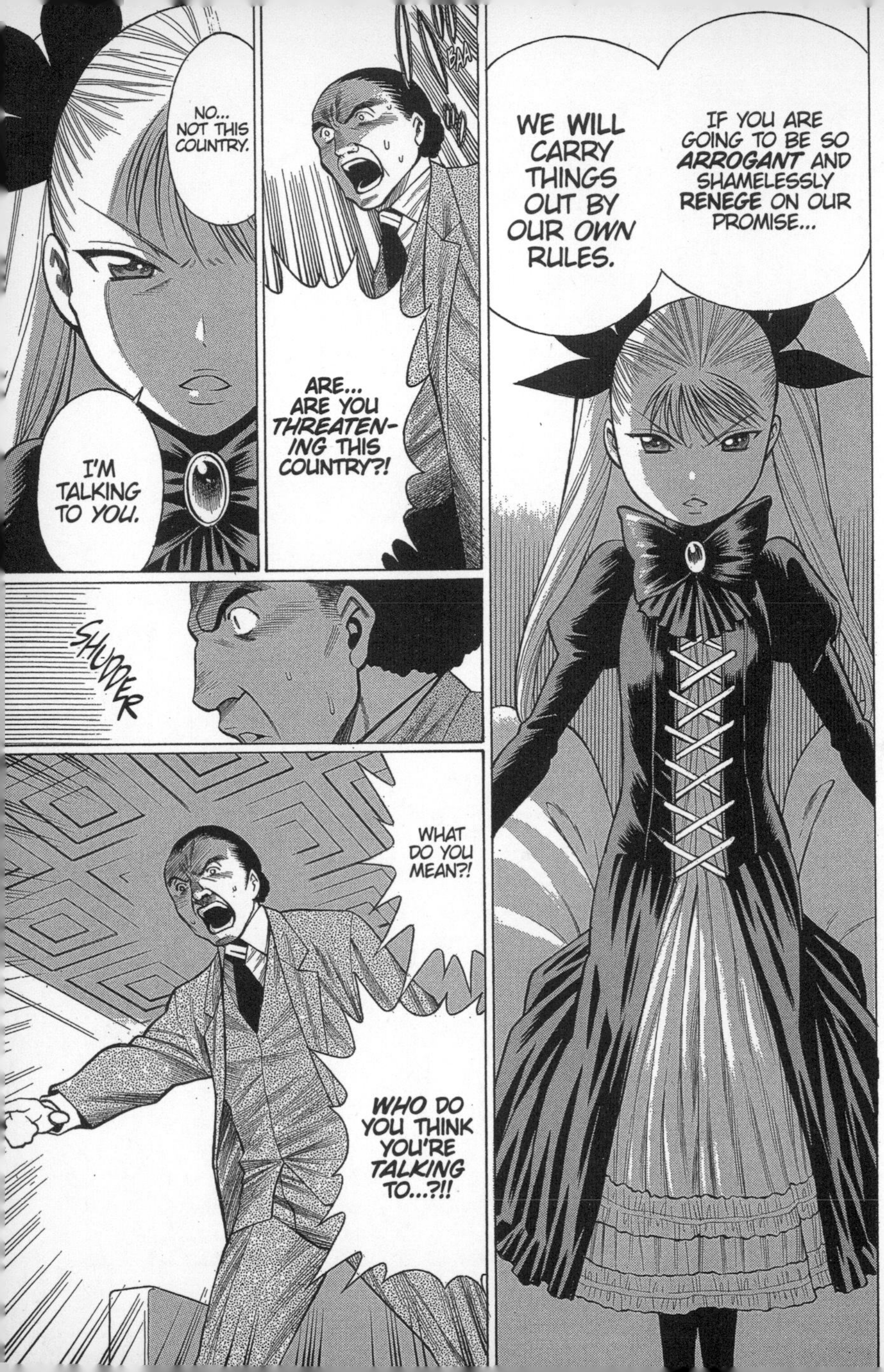
IF YOU ARE GOING TO BE SO *ARROGANT* AND SHAMELESSLY RENEGE ON OUR PROMISE...
WE WILL CARRY THINGS OUT BY OUR *OWN* RULES.
BAA
ARE... ARE YOU *THREATENING* THIS COUNTRY?!
NO... NOT THIS COUNTRY.
I'M TALKING TO *YOU*.
SHUDDER
WHAT DO YOU MEAN?!
WHO DO YOU THINK YOU'RE *TALKING* TO...?!!

I'M SORRY. PLEASE EXCUSE US A MOMENT...

MINISTER. PLEASE.

WHO DO YOU THINK YOU ARE, YOU LITTLE *BITCH!!*

·······

THAT'S IT THEN.

AS YOU WISH.

ALPHONSE...

DO IT.

VERA.

78

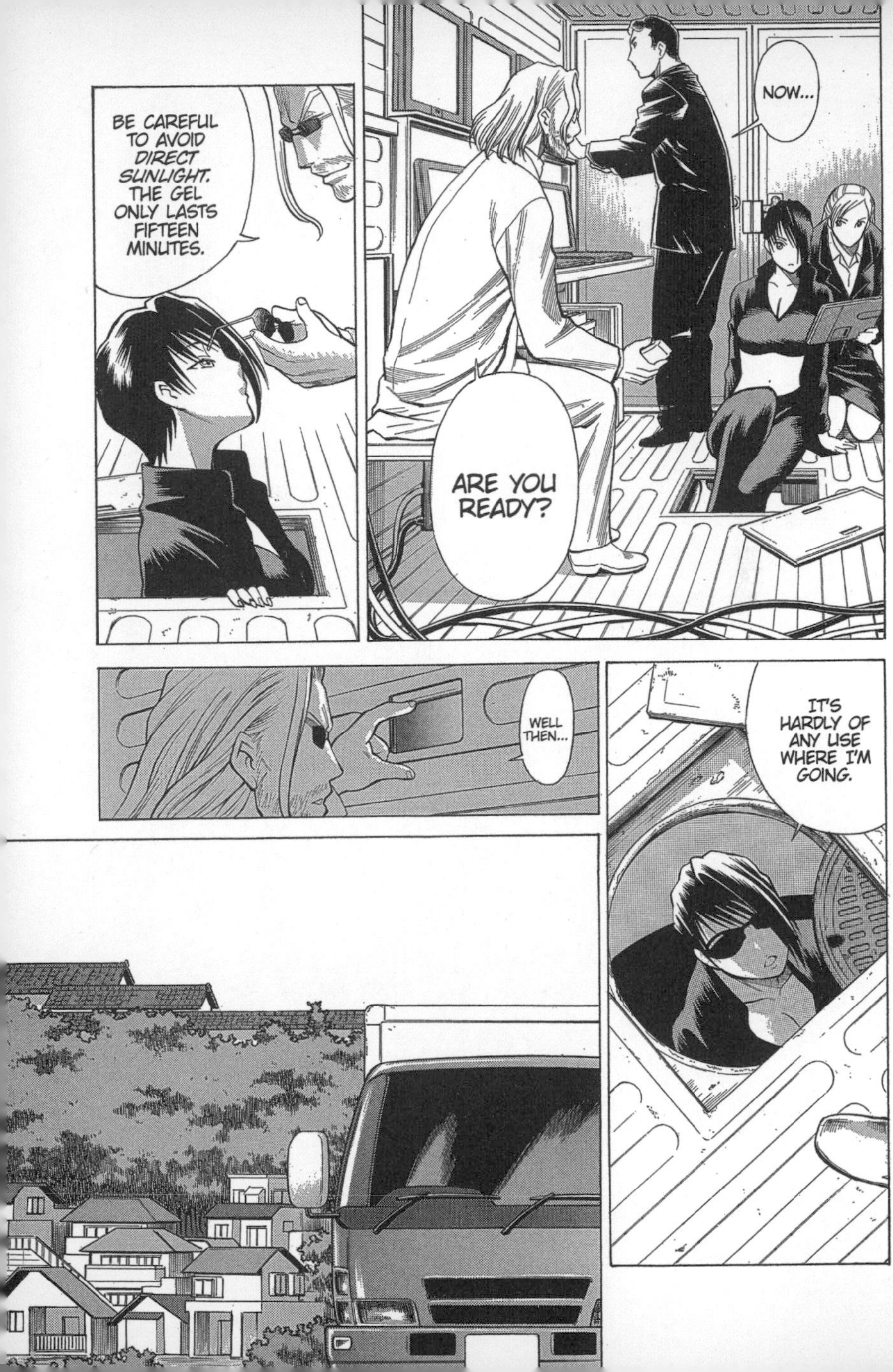
NOW...
ARE YOU READY?
BE CAREFUL TO AVOID DIRECT SUNLIGHT. THE GEL ONLY LASTS FIFTEEN MINUTES.
IT'S HARDLY OF ANY USE WHERE I'M GOING.
WELL THEN...

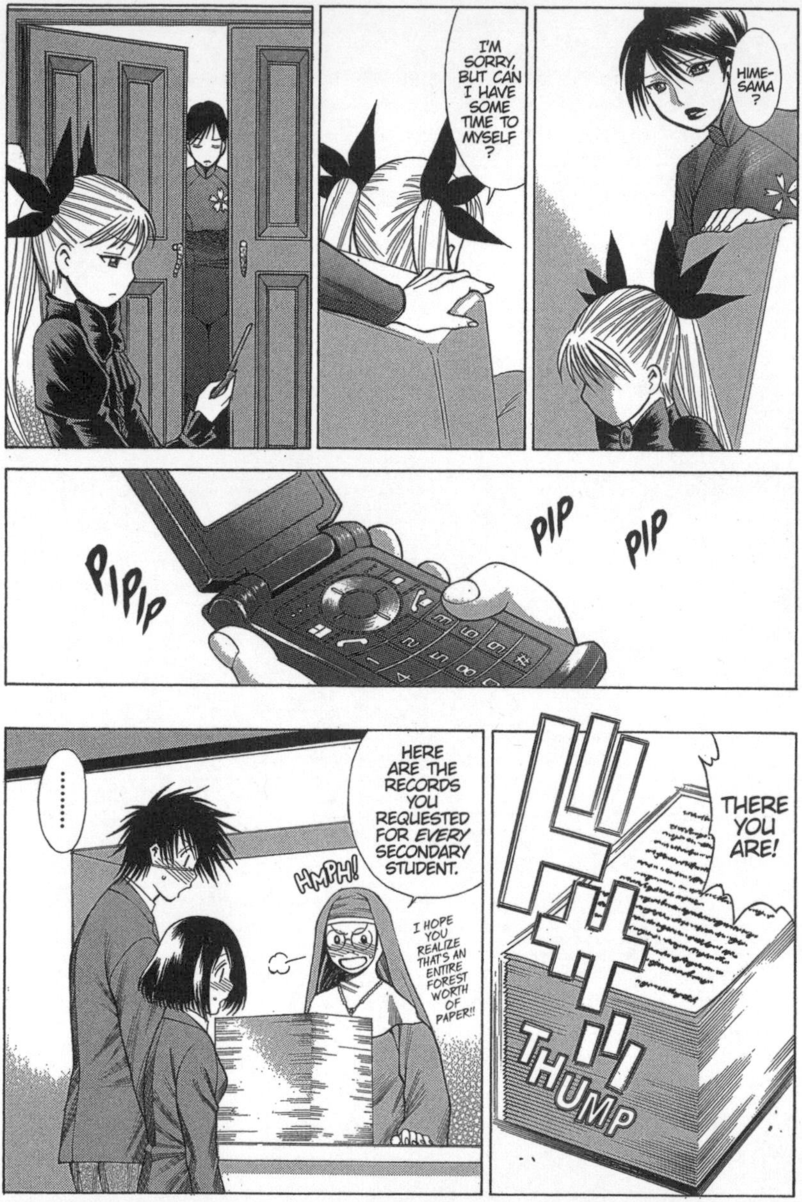
HIME-SAMA?
I'M SORRY, BUT CAN I HAVE SOME TIME TO MYSELF?
PIP
PIP
PIPIP
THERE YOU ARE!
THUMP
HERE ARE THE RECORDS YOU REQUESTED FOR *EVERY* SECONDARY STUDENT.
HMPH!
I HOPE YOU REALIZE THAT'S AN ENTIRE FOREST WORTH OF PAPER!!
....

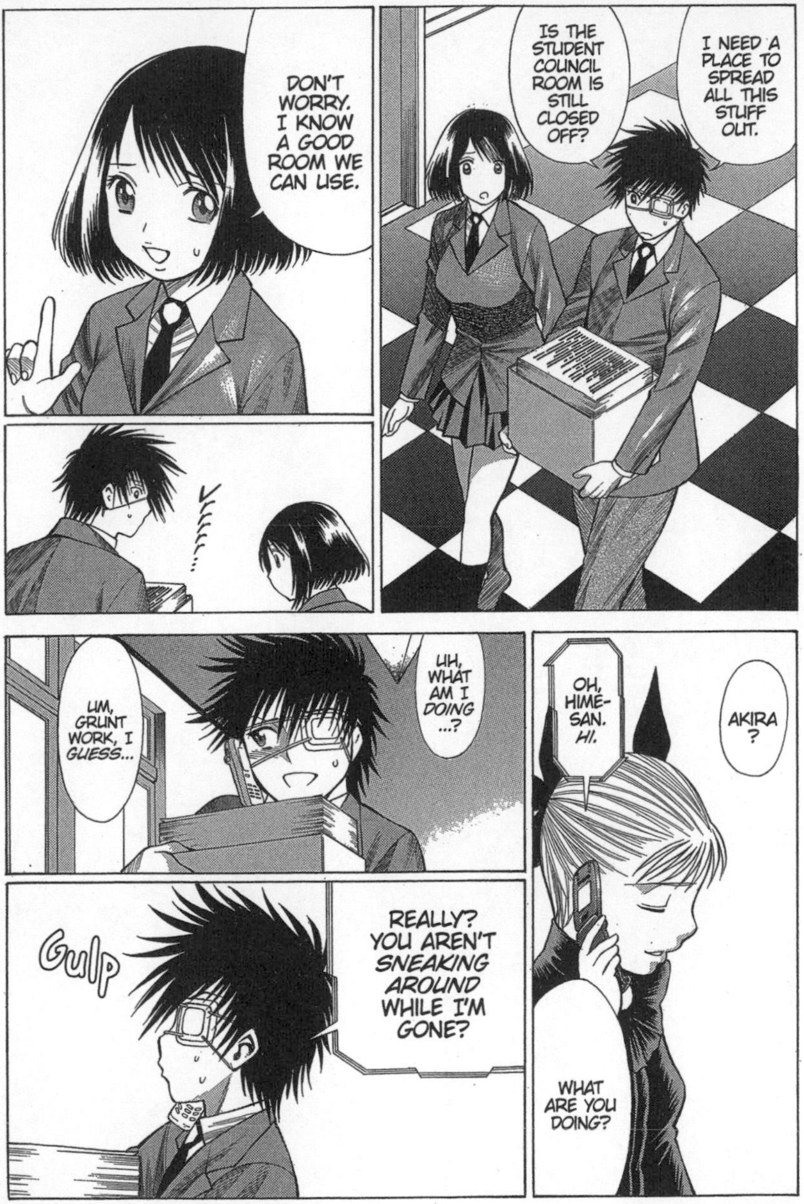
I NEED A PLACE TO SPREAD ALL THIS STUFF OUT.
IS THE STUDENT COUNCIL ROOM IS STILL CLOSED OFF?
DON'T WORRY. I KNOW A GOOD ROOM WE CAN USE.
AKIRA?
OH, HIME-SAN. HI.
WHAT ARE YOU DOING?
UH, WHAT AM I *DOING* ...?
UM, GRUNT WORK, I *GUESS*...
REALLY? YOU AREN'T *SNEAKING AROUND* WHILE I'M GONE?
Gulp

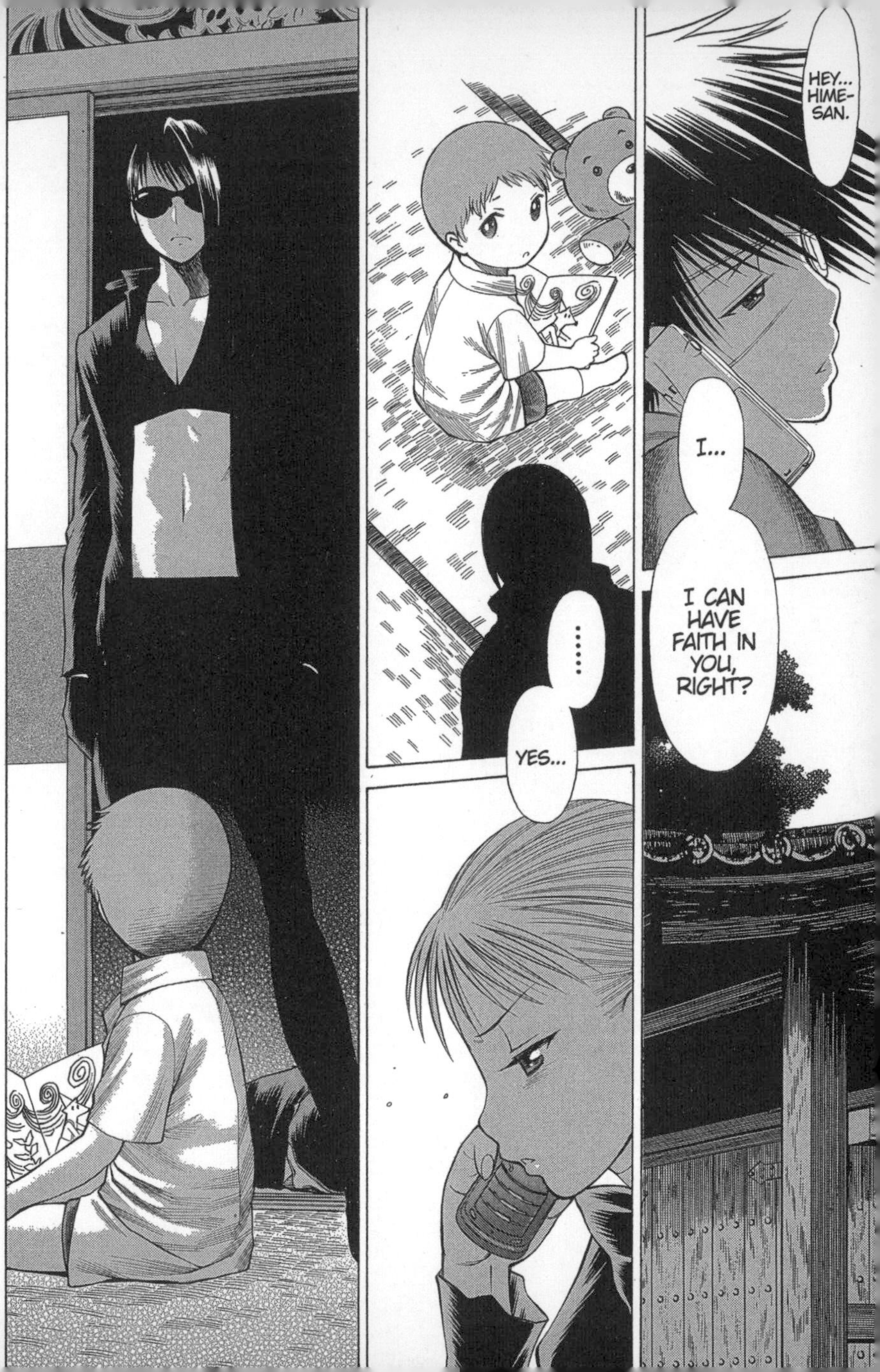
HEY... HIME-SAN.
I...
I CAN HAVE FAITH IN YOU, RIGHT?
......
YES...

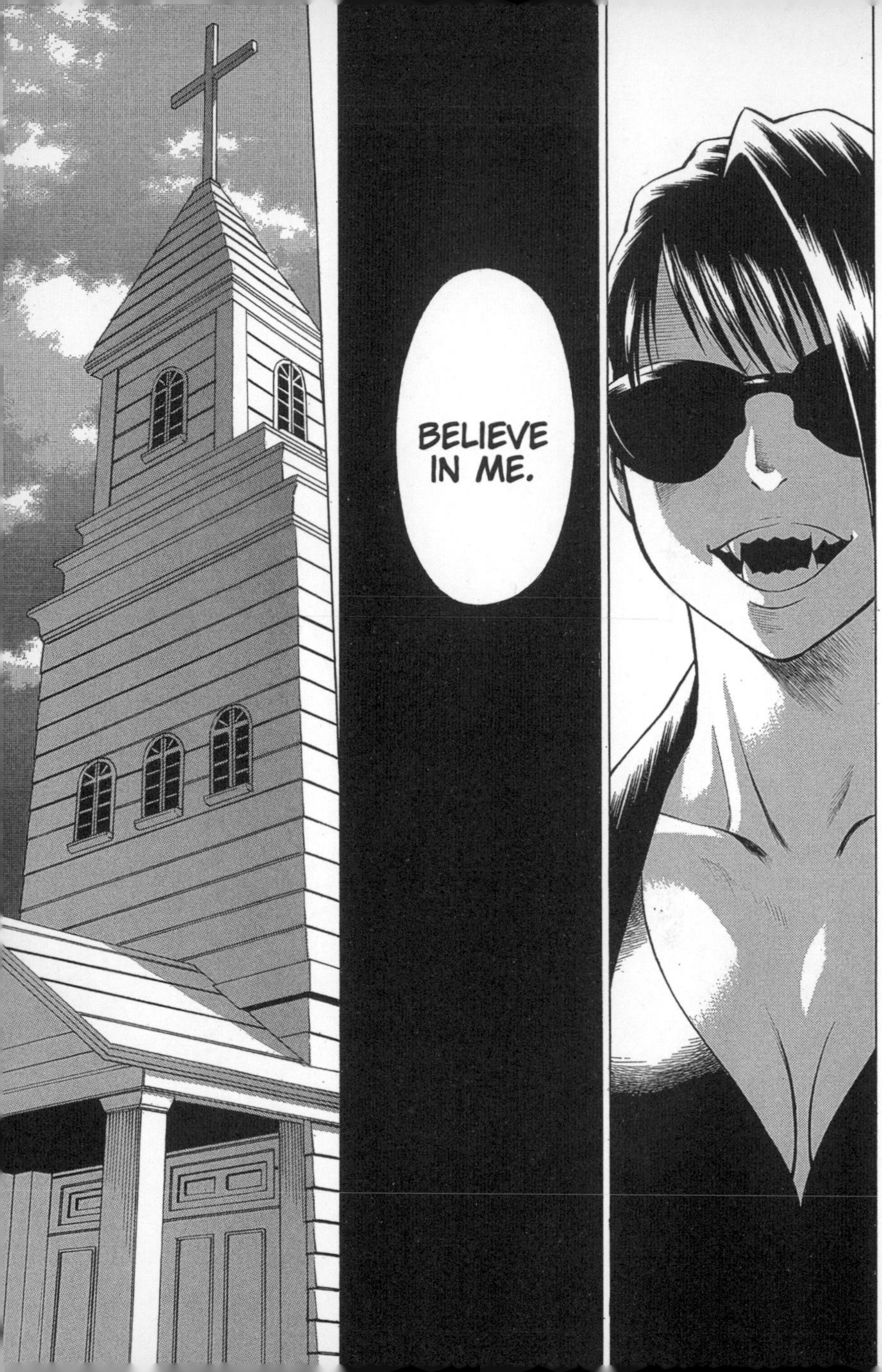
BELIEVE IN ME.

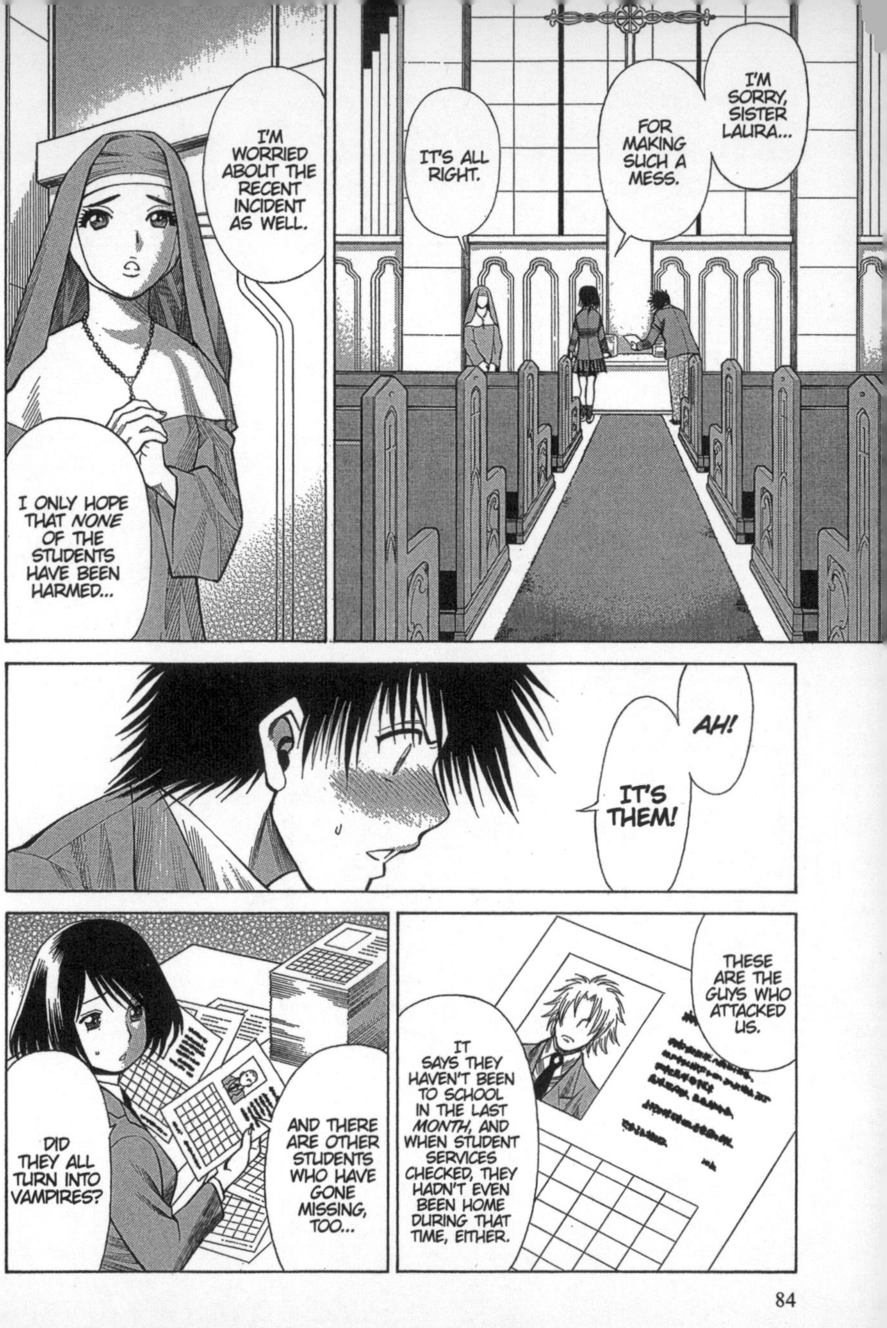
I'M SORRY, SISTER LAURA...
FOR MAKING SUCH A MESS.
IT'S ALL RIGHT.
I'M WORRIED ABOUT THE RECENT INCIDENT AS WELL.
I ONLY HOPE THAT *NONE* OF THE STUDENTS HAVE BEEN HARMED...
AH!
IT'S THEM!
THESE ARE THE GUYS WHO ATTACKED US.
IT SAYS THEY HAVEN'T BEEN TO SCHOOL IN THE LAST *MONTH*, AND WHEN STUDENT SERVICES CHECKED, THEY HADN'T EVEN BEEN HOME DURING THAT TIME, EITHER.
AND THERE ARE OTHER STUDENTS WHO HAVE GONE MISSING, TOO...
DID THEY ALL TURN INTO VAMPIRES?

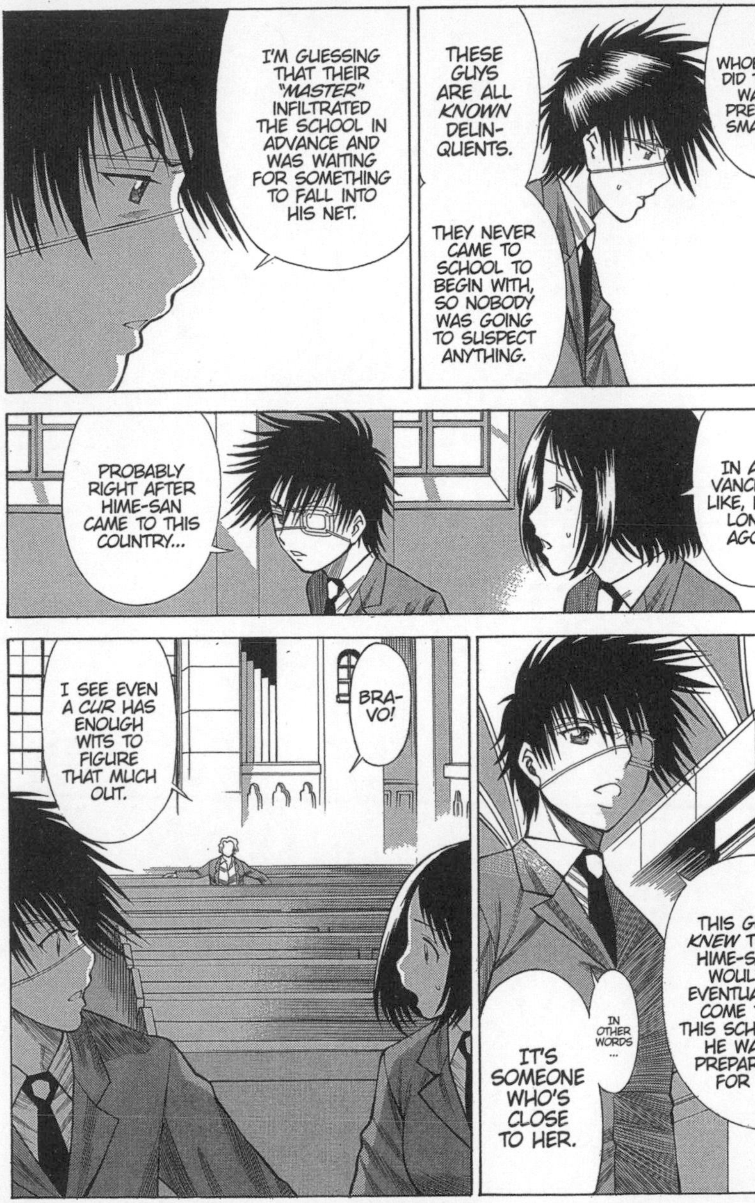
WHOEVER DID THIS WAS PRETTY SMART.
THESE GUYS ARE ALL *KNOWN* DELINQUENTS.
THEY NEVER CAME TO SCHOOL TO BEGIN WITH, SO NOBODY WAS GOING TO SUSPECT ANYTHING.
I'M GUESSING THAT THEIR *"MASTER"* INFILTRATED THE SCHOOL IN ADVANCE AND WAS WAITING FOR SOMETHING TO FALL INTO HIS NET.
IN ADVANCE...? LIKE, HOW LONG AGO?
PROBABLY RIGHT AFTER HIME-SAN CAME TO THIS COUNTRY...
THIS GUY *KNEW* THAT HIME-SAN WOULD EVENTUALLY COME TO THIS SCHOOL. HE WAS PREPARING FOR IT.
IN OTHER WORDS...
IT'S SOMEONE WHO'S CLOSE TO HER.
BRAVO!
I SEE EVEN A *CUR* HAS ENOUGH WITS TO FIGURE THAT MUCH OUT.

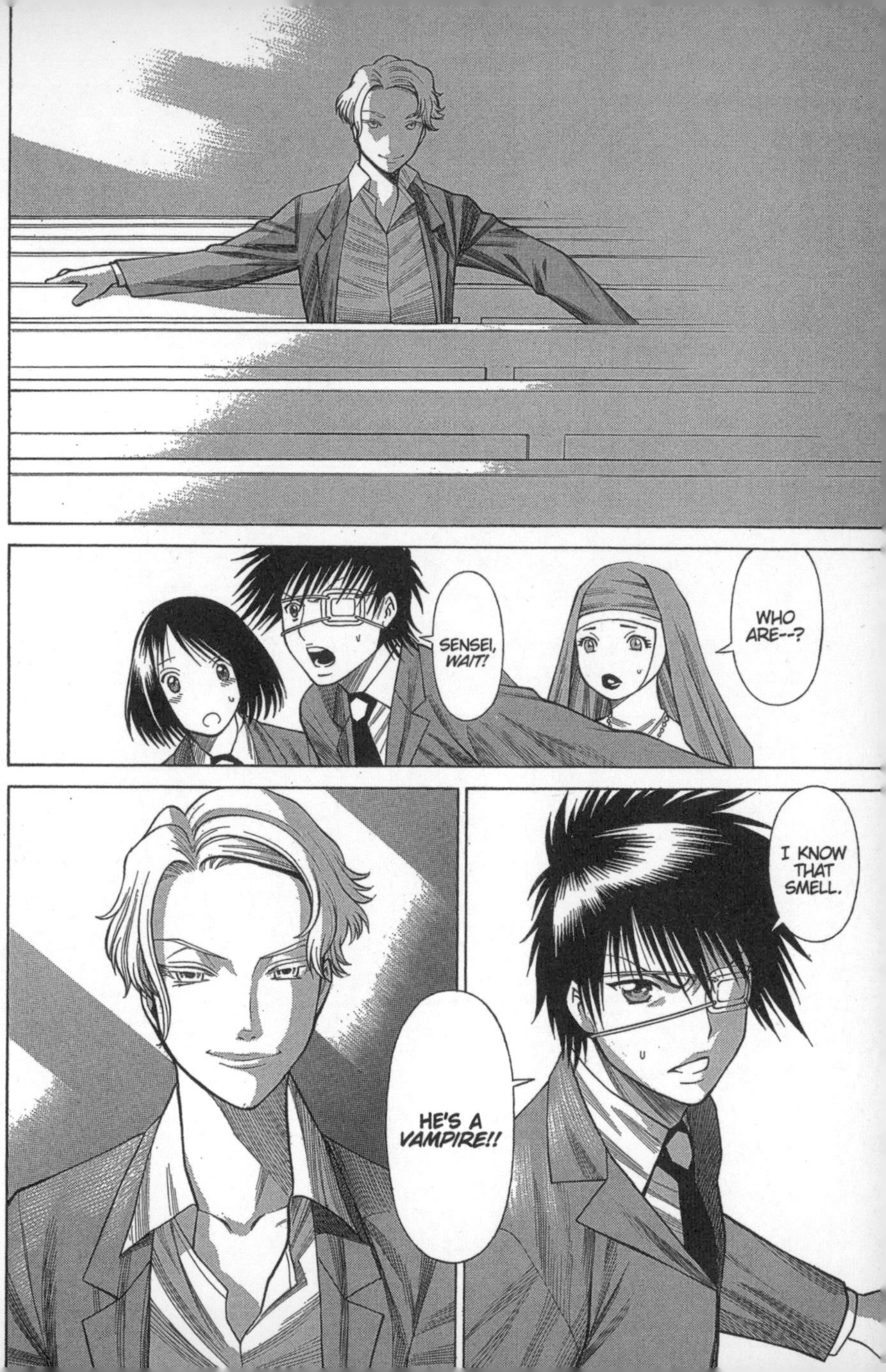
WHO ARE--?
SENSEI, WAIT!
I KNOW THAT SMELL.
HE'S A VAMPIRE!!

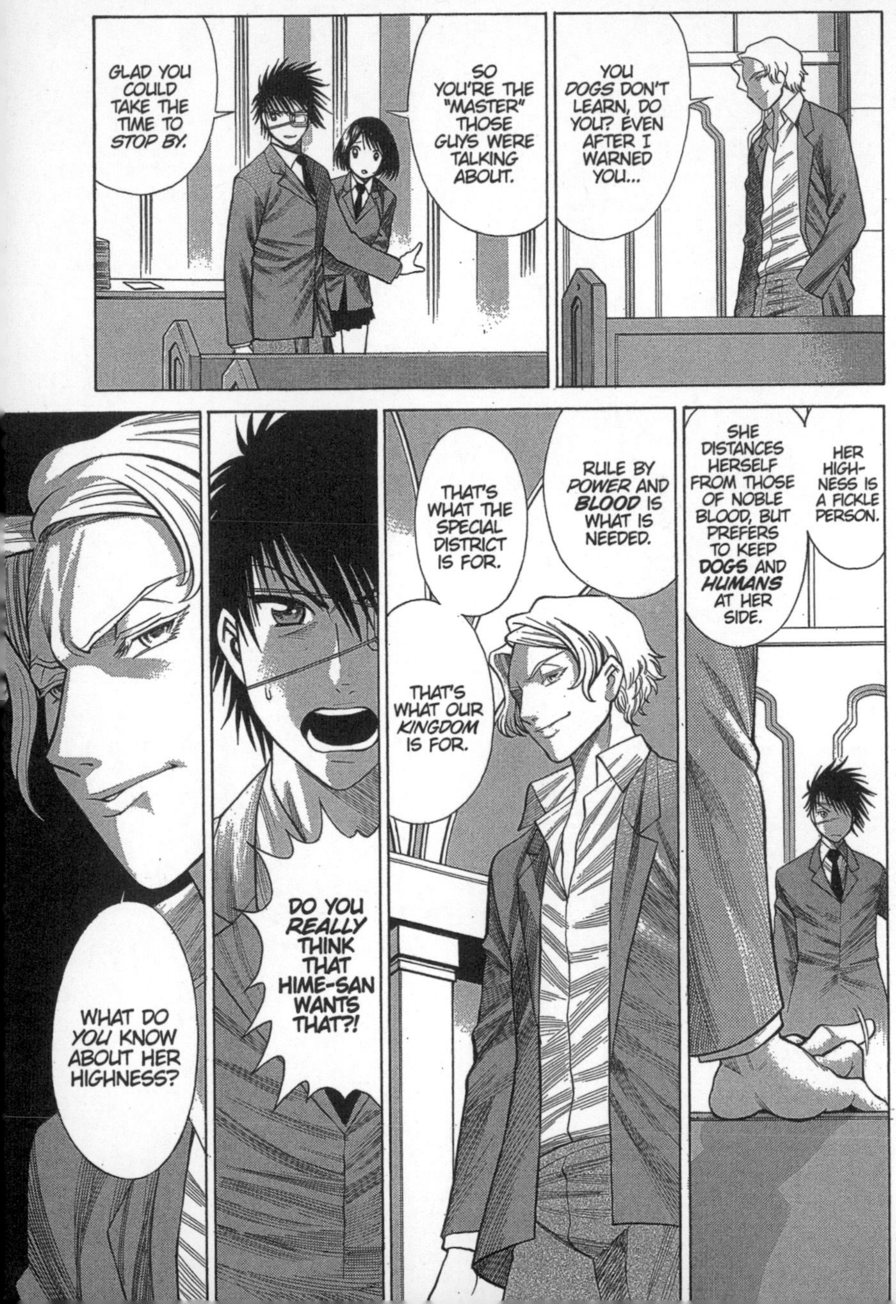
YOU DOGS DON'T LEARN, DO YOU? EVEN AFTER I WARNED YOU...
SO YOU'RE THE "MASTER" THOSE GUYS WERE TALKING ABOUT.
GLAD YOU COULD TAKE THE TIME TO STOP BY.
HER HIGHNESS IS A FICKLE PERSON.
SHE DISTANCES HERSELF FROM THOSE OF NOBLE BLOOD, BUT PREFERS TO KEEP DOGS AND HUMANS AT HER SIDE.
RULE BY POWER AND BLOOD IS WHAT IS NEEDED.
THAT'S WHAT THE SPECIAL DISTRICT IS FOR.
THAT'S WHAT OUR KINGDOM IS FOR.
DO YOU REALLY THINK THAT HIME-SAN WANTS THAT?!
WHAT DO YOU KNOW ABOUT HER HIGHNESS?

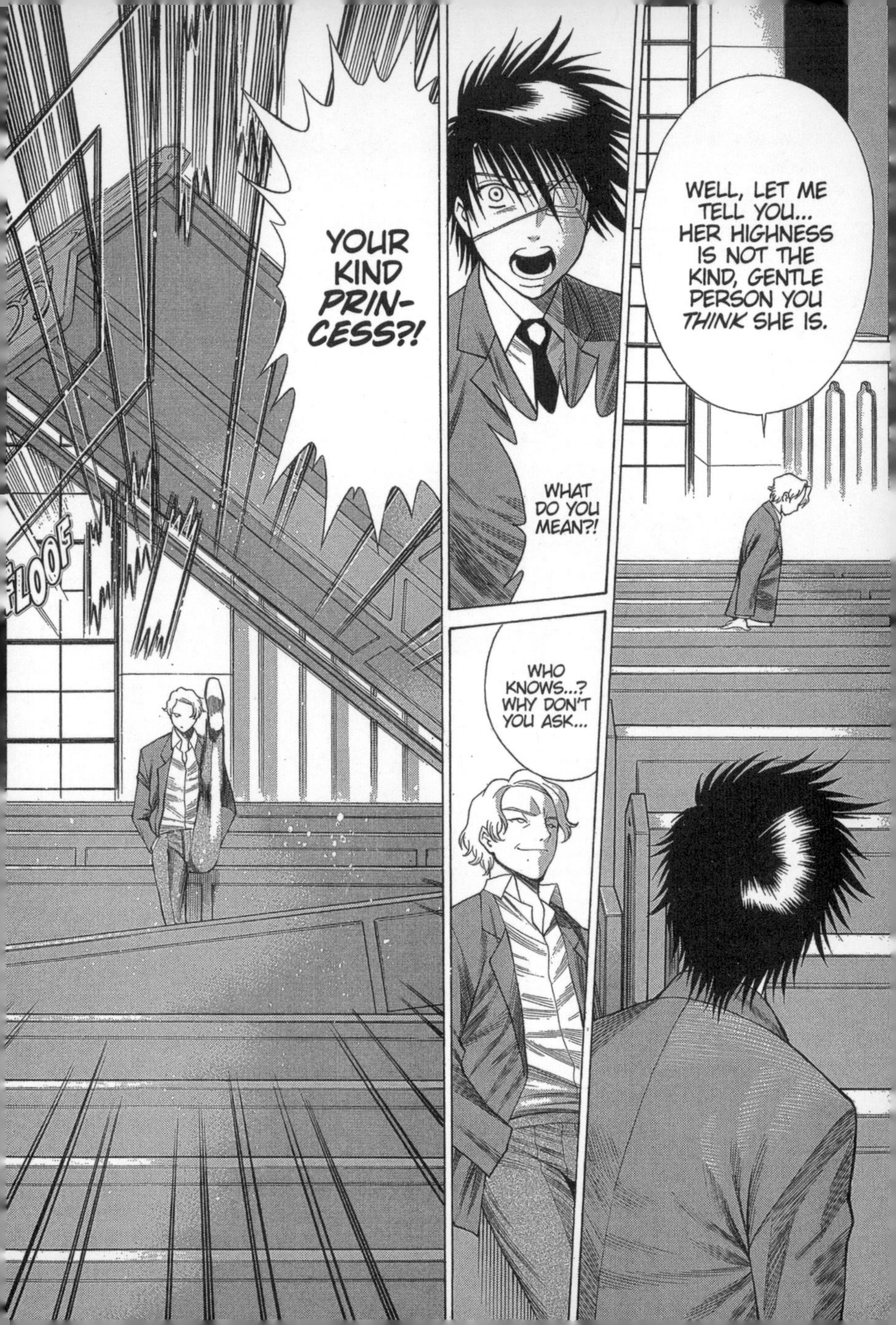
WELL, LET ME TELL YOU... HER HIGHNESS IS NOT THE KIND, GENTLE PERSON YOU *THINK* SHE IS.
WHAT DO YOU MEAN?!
WHO KNOWS...? WHY DON'T YOU ASK...
YOUR KIND *PRIN-CESS?!*
FLOOF

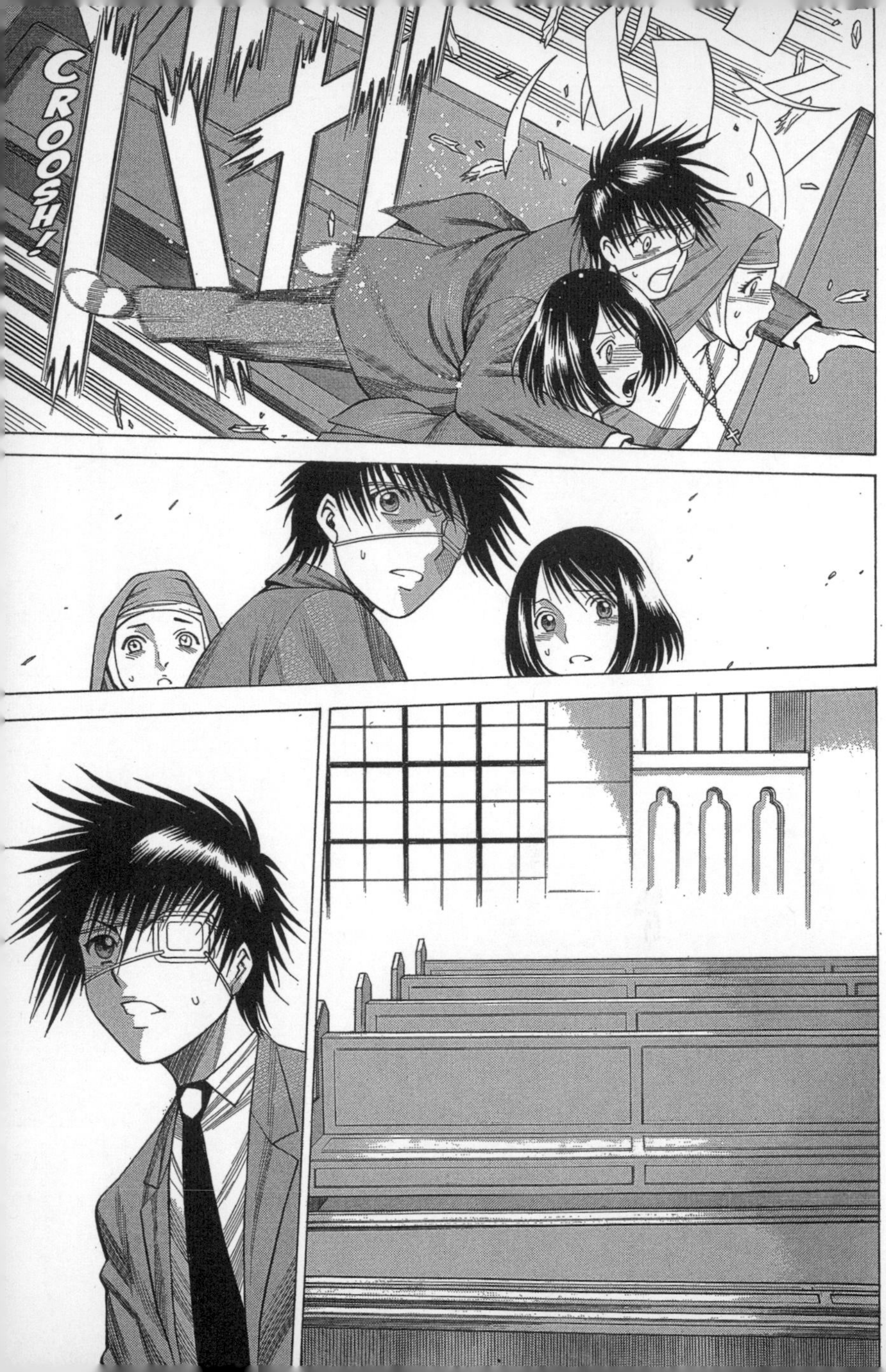
CROOSH!

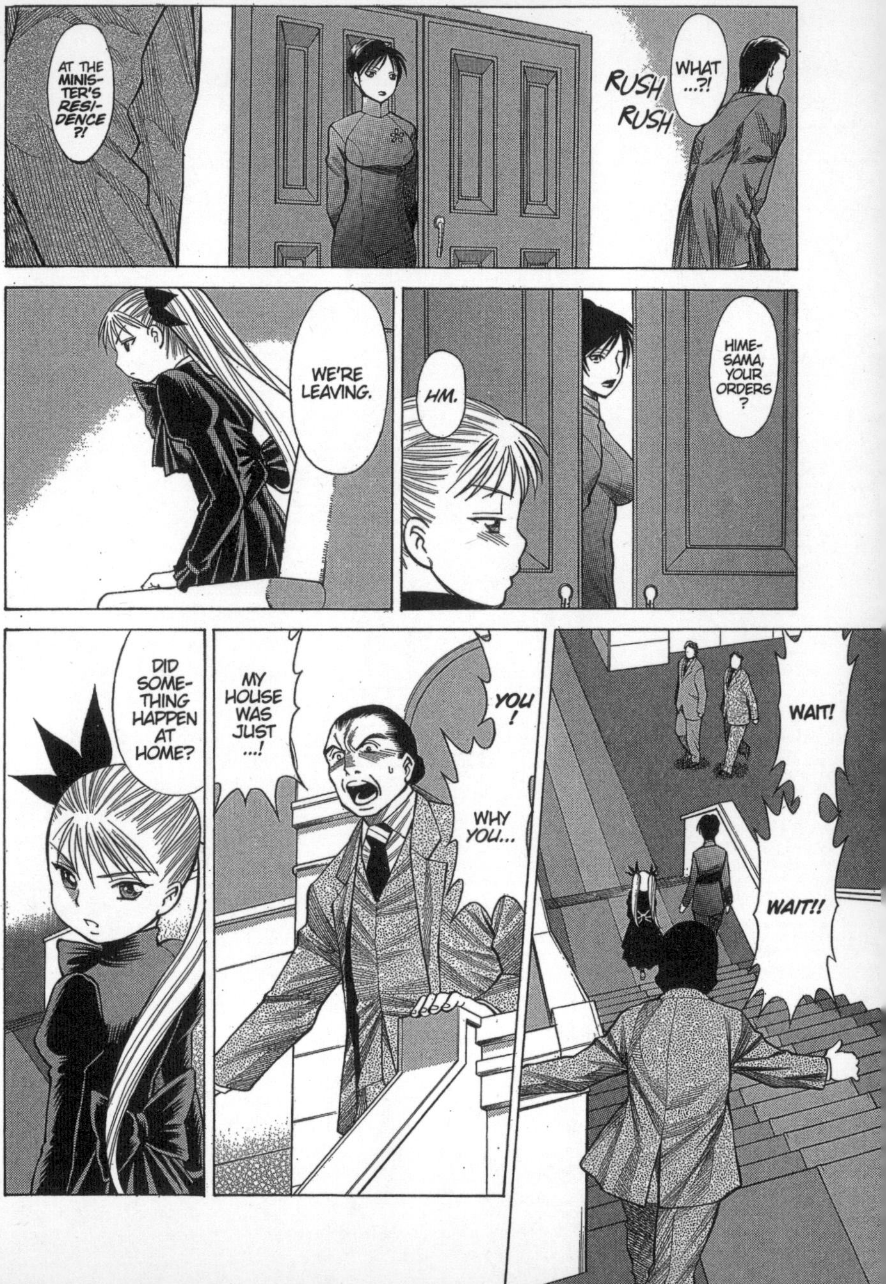
WHAT ...?!
RUSH
RUSH
AT THE MINISTER'S RESIDENCE?!
HIME-SAMA, YOUR ORDERS?
HM.
WE'RE LEAVING.
WAIT!
WAIT!!
YOU!
MY HOUSE WAS JUST ...!
WHY YOU...
DID SOMETHING HAPPEN AT HOME?

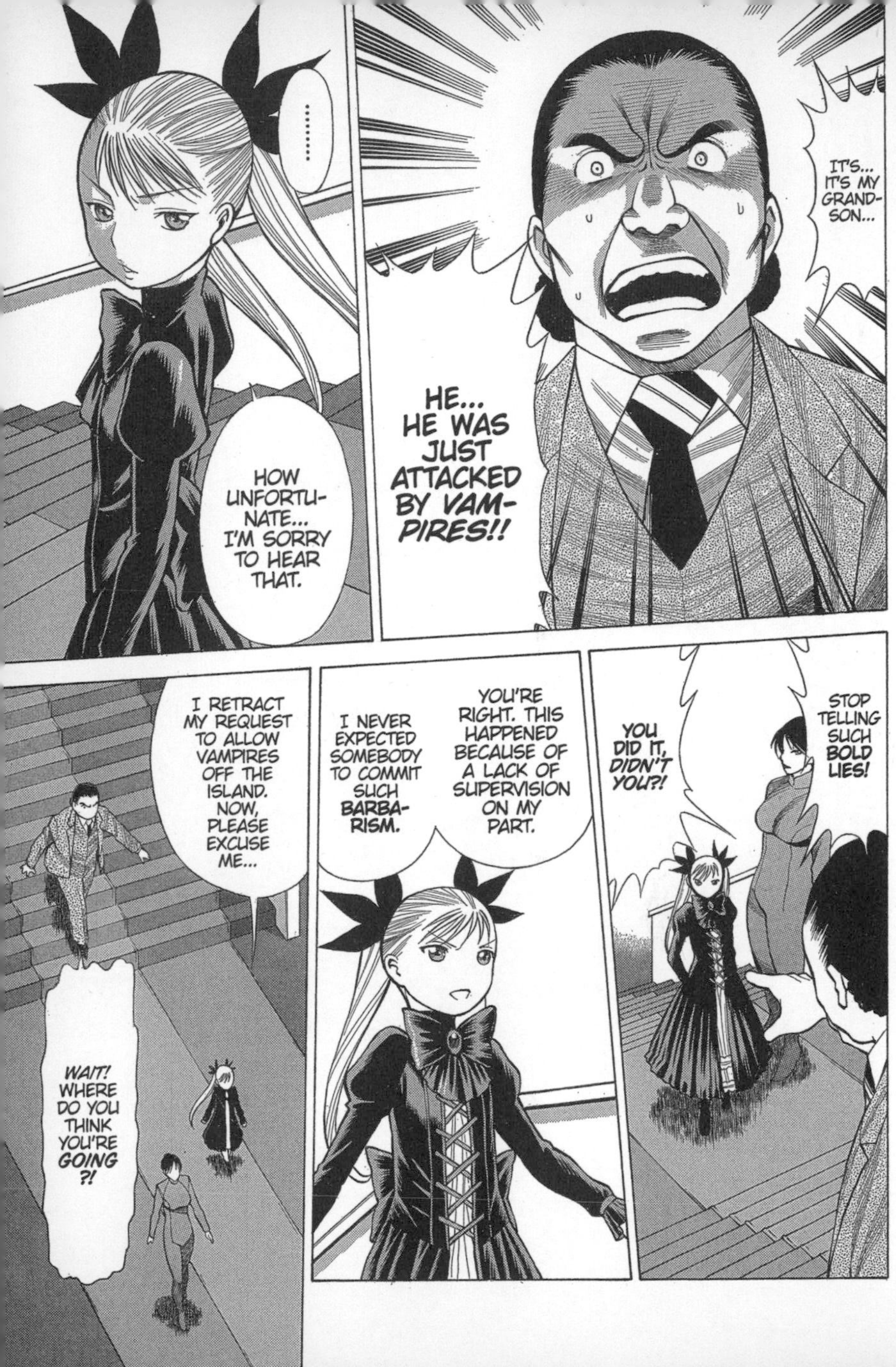
IT'S... IT'S MY GRANDSON...
HE... HE WAS JUST ATTACKED BY VAMPIRES!!
......
HOW UNFORTUNATE... I'M SORRY TO HEAR THAT.
STOP TELLING SUCH BOLD LIES!
YOU DID IT, DIDN'T YOU?!
YOU'RE RIGHT. THIS HAPPENED BECAUSE OF A LACK OF SUPERVISION ON MY PART.
I NEVER EXPECTED SOMEBODY TO COMMIT SUCH BARBARISM.
I RETRACT MY REQUEST TO ALLOW VAMPIRES OFF THE ISLAND. NOW, PLEASE EXCUSE ME...
WAIT! WHERE DO YOU THINK YOU'RE GOING?!

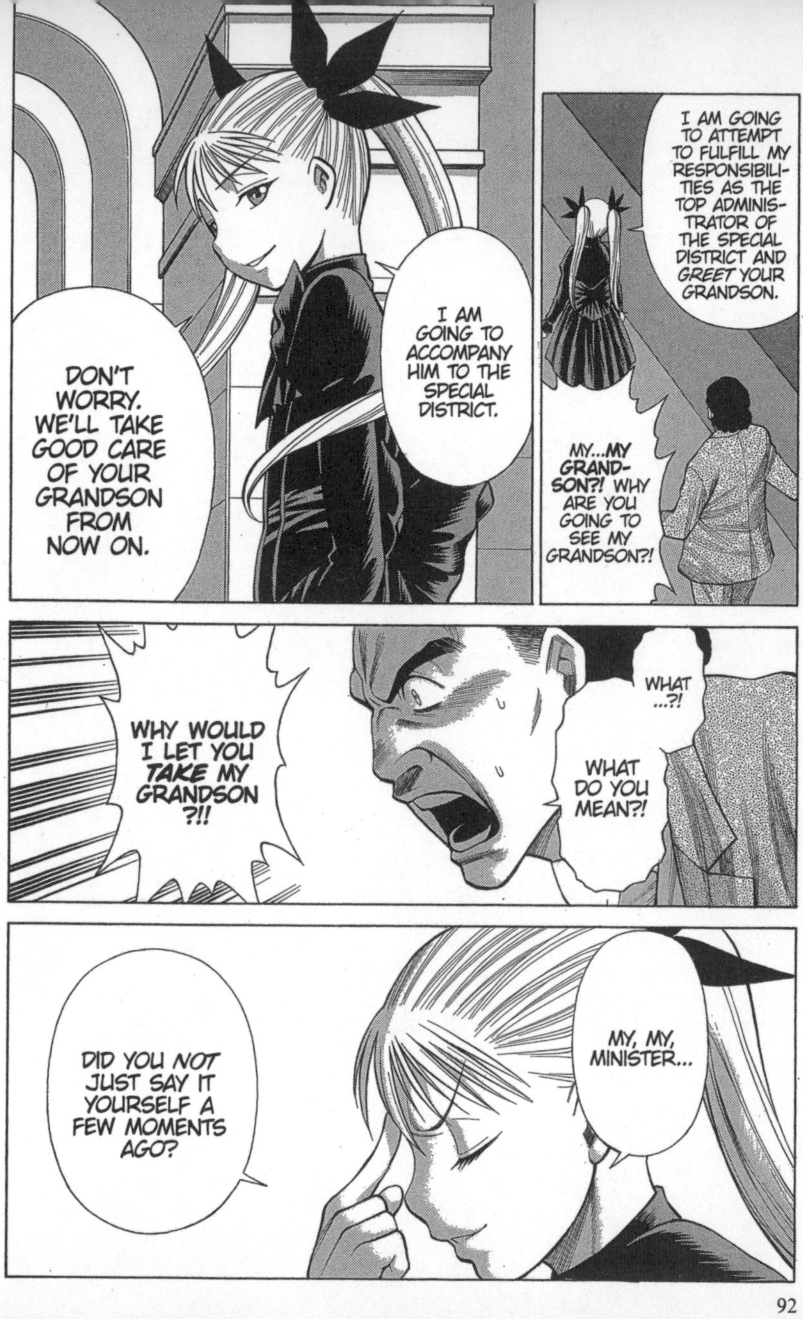
I AM GOING TO ATTEMPT TO FULFILL MY RESPONSIBILITIES AS THE TOP ADMINISTRATOR OF THE SPECIAL DISTRICT AND *GREET* YOUR GRANDSON.
MY...MY GRANDSON?! WHY ARE YOU GOING TO SEE MY GRANDSON?!
I AM GOING TO ACCOMPANY HIM TO THE SPECIAL DISTRICT.
DON'T WORRY. WE'LL TAKE GOOD CARE OF YOUR GRANDSON FROM NOW ON.
WHAT ...?!
WHAT DO YOU MEAN?!
WHY WOULD I LET YOU *TAKE* MY GRANDSON ?!!
MY, MY, MINISTER...
DID YOU *NOT* JUST SAY IT YOURSELF A FEW MOMENTS AGO?

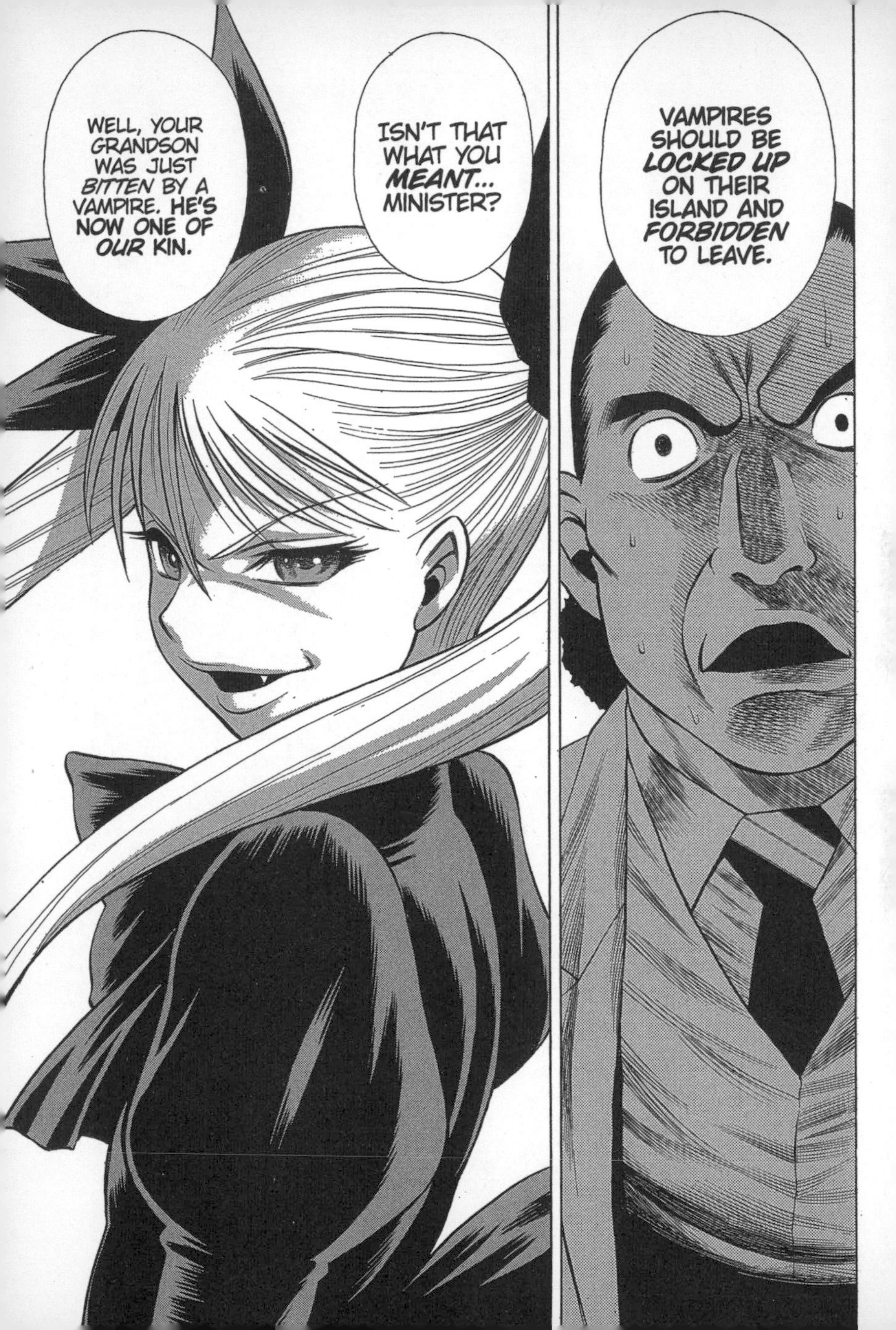
VAMPIRES SHOULD BE **LOCKED UP** ON THEIR ISLAND AND **FORBIDDEN** TO LEAVE.
WELL, YOUR GRANDSON WAS JUST *BITTEN* BY A VAMPIRE. HE'S NOW ONE OF **OUR** KIN.
ISN'T THAT WHAT YOU **MEANT...** MINISTER?

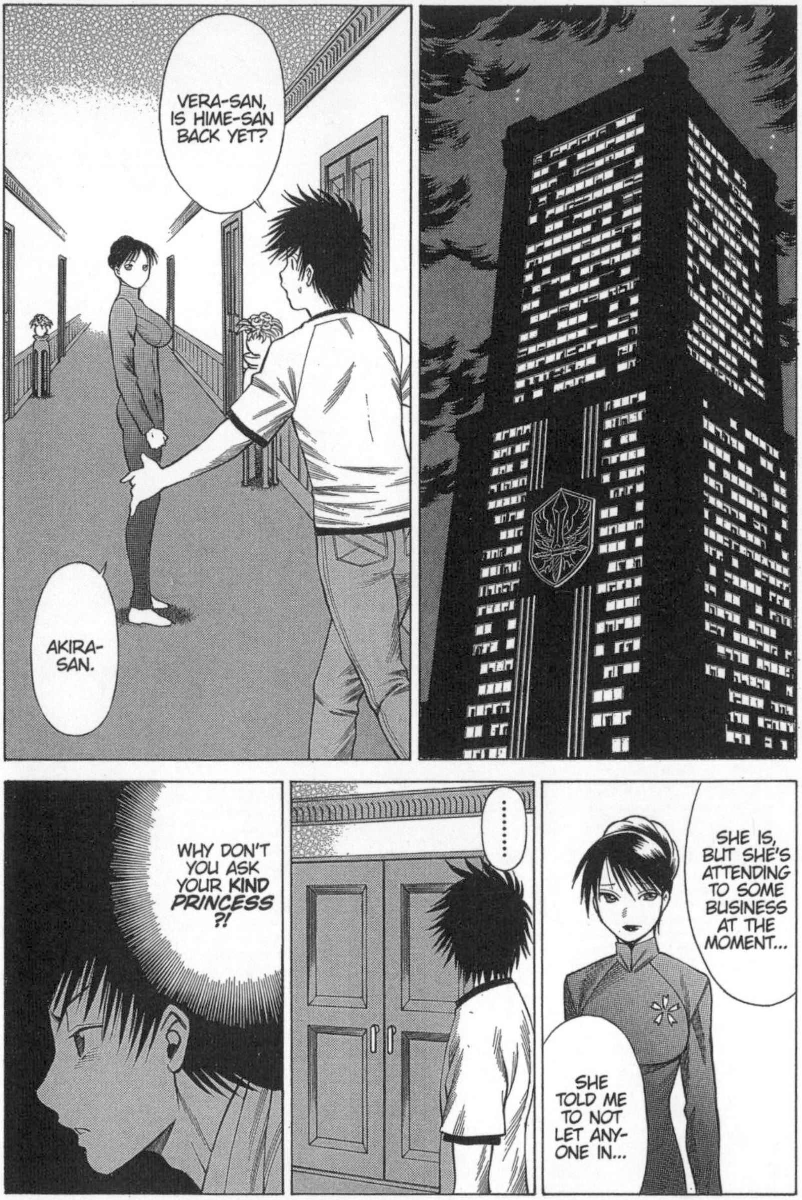
VERA-SAN, IS HIME-SAN BACK YET?
AKIRA-SAN.
SHE IS, BUT SHE'S ATTENDING TO SOME BUSINESS AT THE MOMENT...
SHE TOLD ME TO NOT LET ANY-ONE IN...
......
WHY DON'T YOU ASK YOUR **KIND *PRINCESS***?!

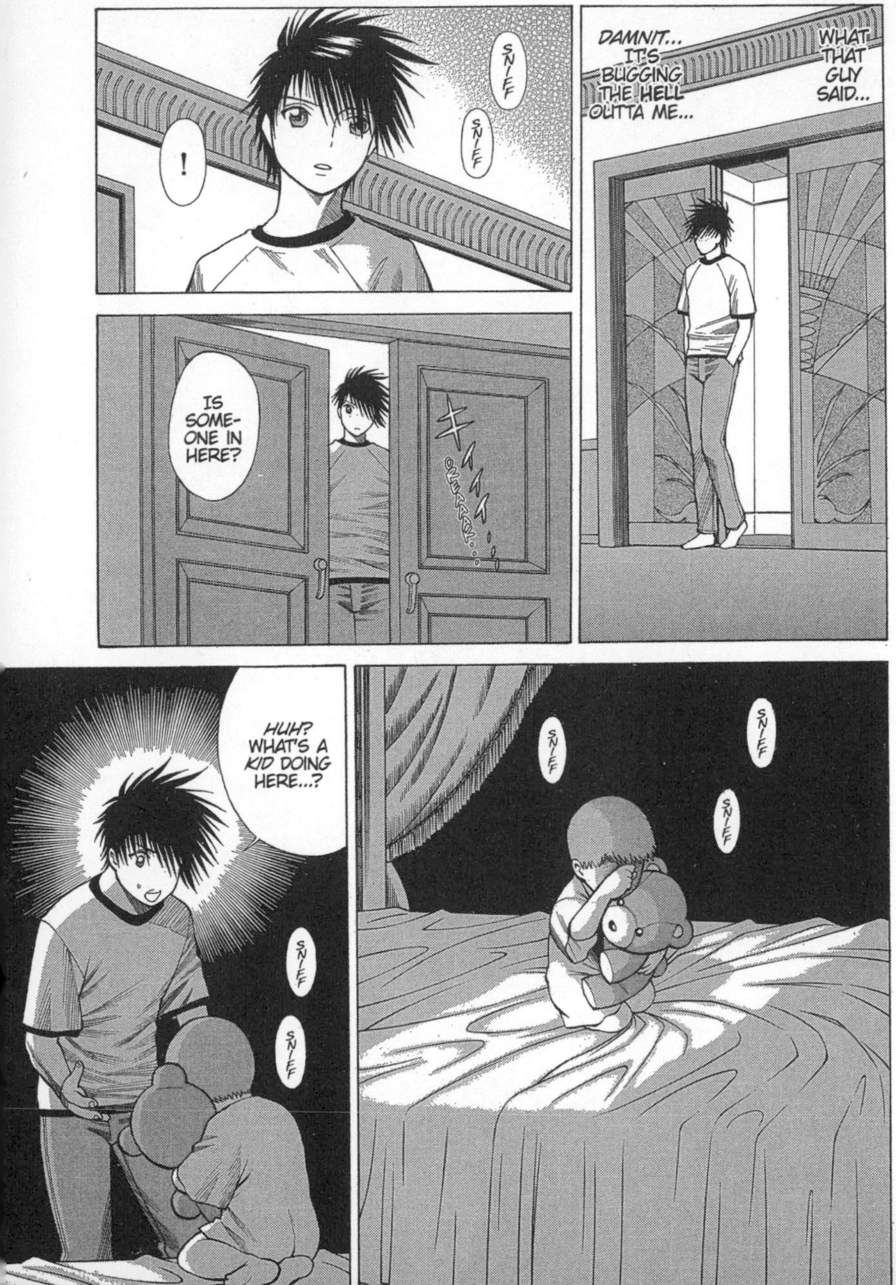
WHAT THAT GUY SAID...
DAMNIT... IT'S BUGGING THE HELL OUTTA ME...
SNIFF
SNIFF
!
キイイイ
CREAAAK...
IS SOME-ONE IN HERE?
SNIFF
SNIFF
SNIFF
HUH? WHAT'S A KID DOING HERE...?
SNIFF
SNIFF

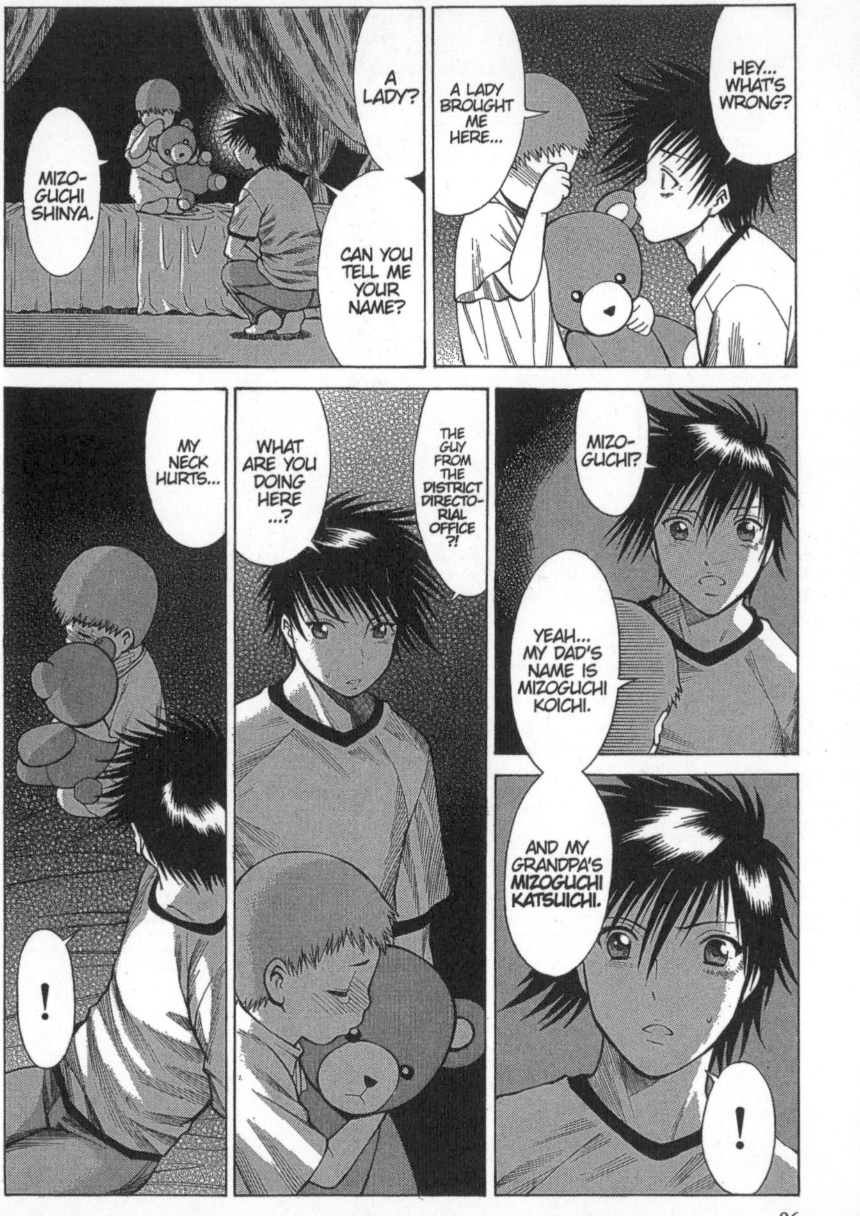
HEY... WHAT'S WRONG?
A LADY BROUGHT ME HERE...
A LADY?
CAN YOU TELL ME YOUR NAME?
MIZO-GUCHI SHINYA.
MIZO-GUCHI?
YEAH... MY DAD'S NAME IS MIZOGUCHI KOICHI.
AND MY GRANDPA'S MIZOGUCHI KATSUICHI.
!
THE GUY FROM THE DISTRICT DIRECTO-RIAL OFFICE ?!
WHAT ARE YOU DOING HERE ...?
MY NECK HURTS...
!

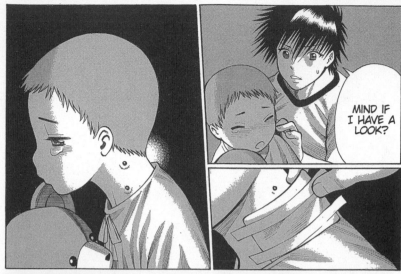

MIND IF I HAVE A LOOK?

•••••••

I WANT TO GO HOME...

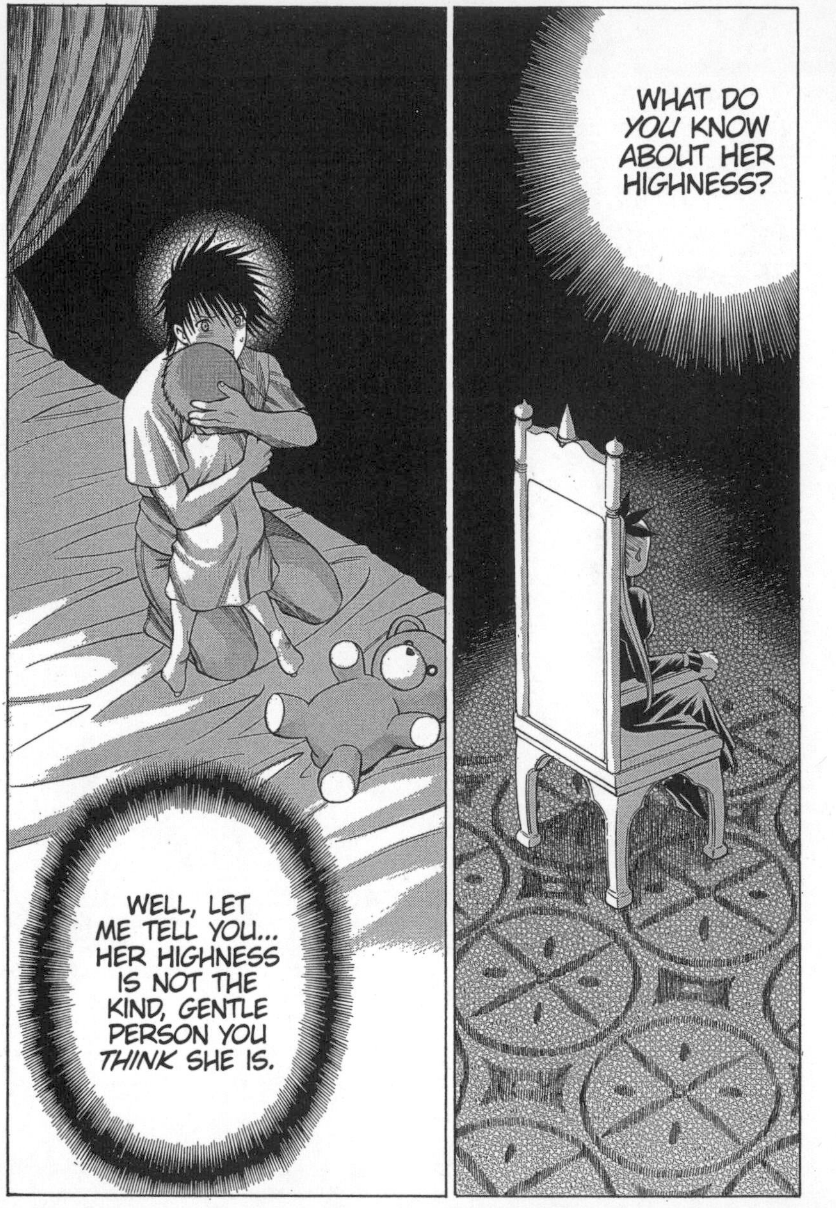
WHAT DO *YOU* KNOW ABOUT HER HIGHNESS?
WELL, LET ME TELL YOU... HER HIGHNESS IS NOT THE KIND, GENTLE PERSON YOU *THINK* SHE IS.

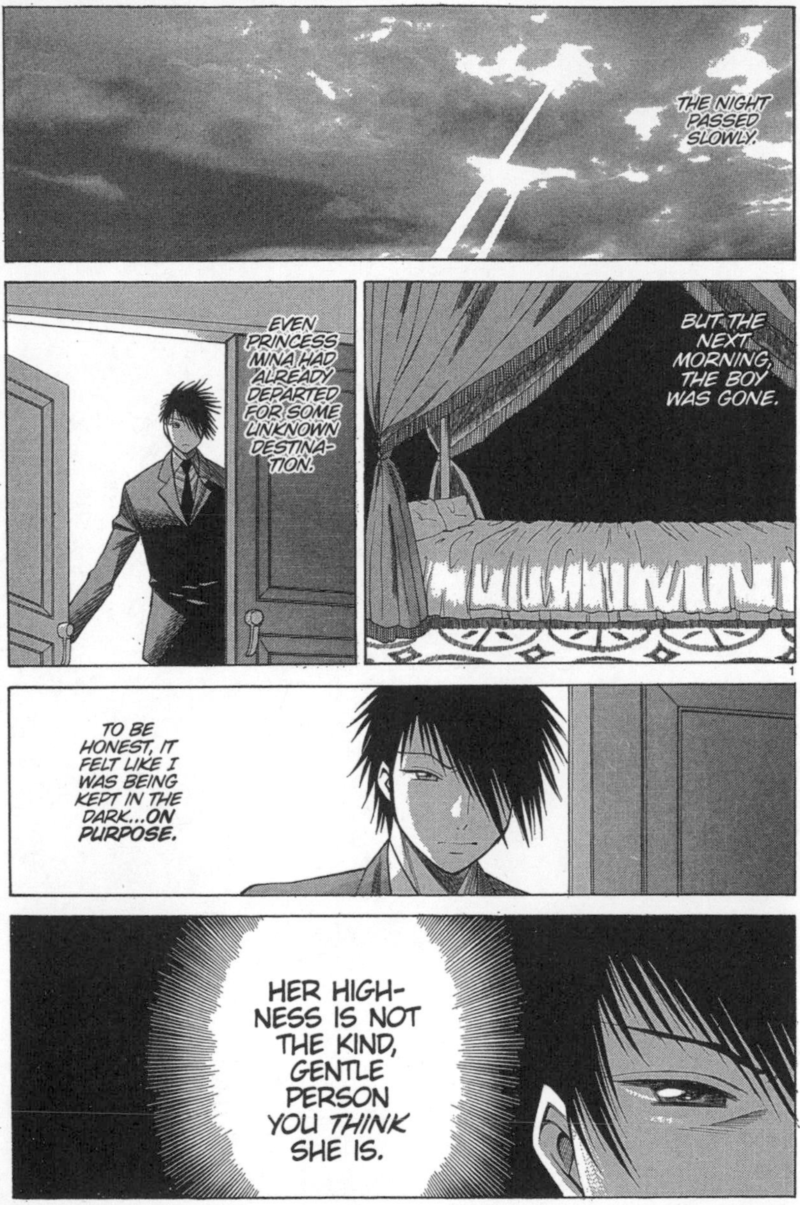
THE NIGHT PASSED SLOWLY.
BUT THE NEXT MORNING, THE BOY WAS GONE.
EVEN PRINCESS MINA HAD ALREADY DEPARTED FOR SOME UNKNOWN DESTINATION.
TO BE HONEST, IT FELT LIKE I WAS BEING KEPT IN THE DARK...ON **PURPOSE.**
HER HIGHNESS IS NOT THE KIND, GENTLE PERSON YOU *THINK* SHE IS.

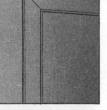

Chapter 10: I Can't See You

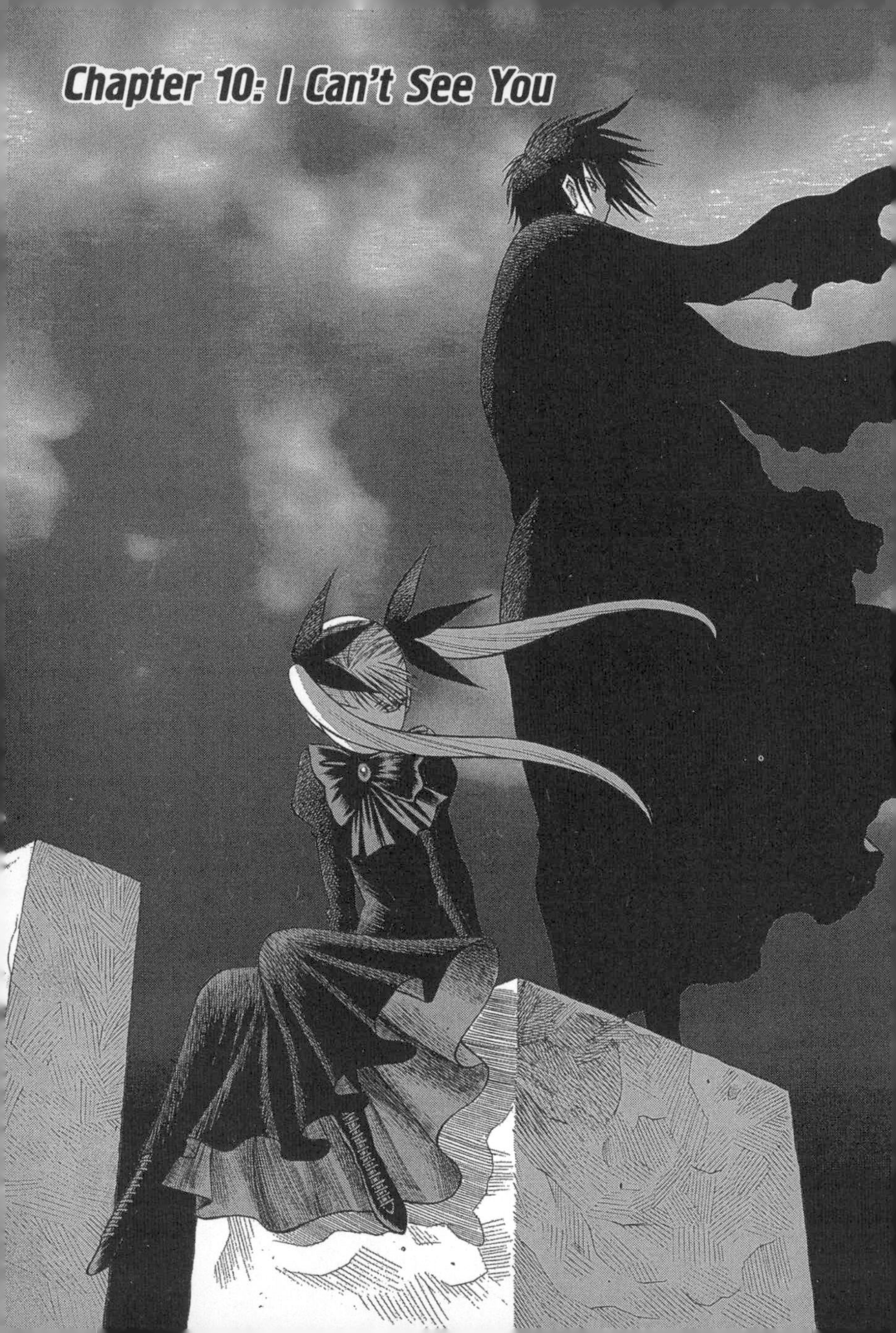

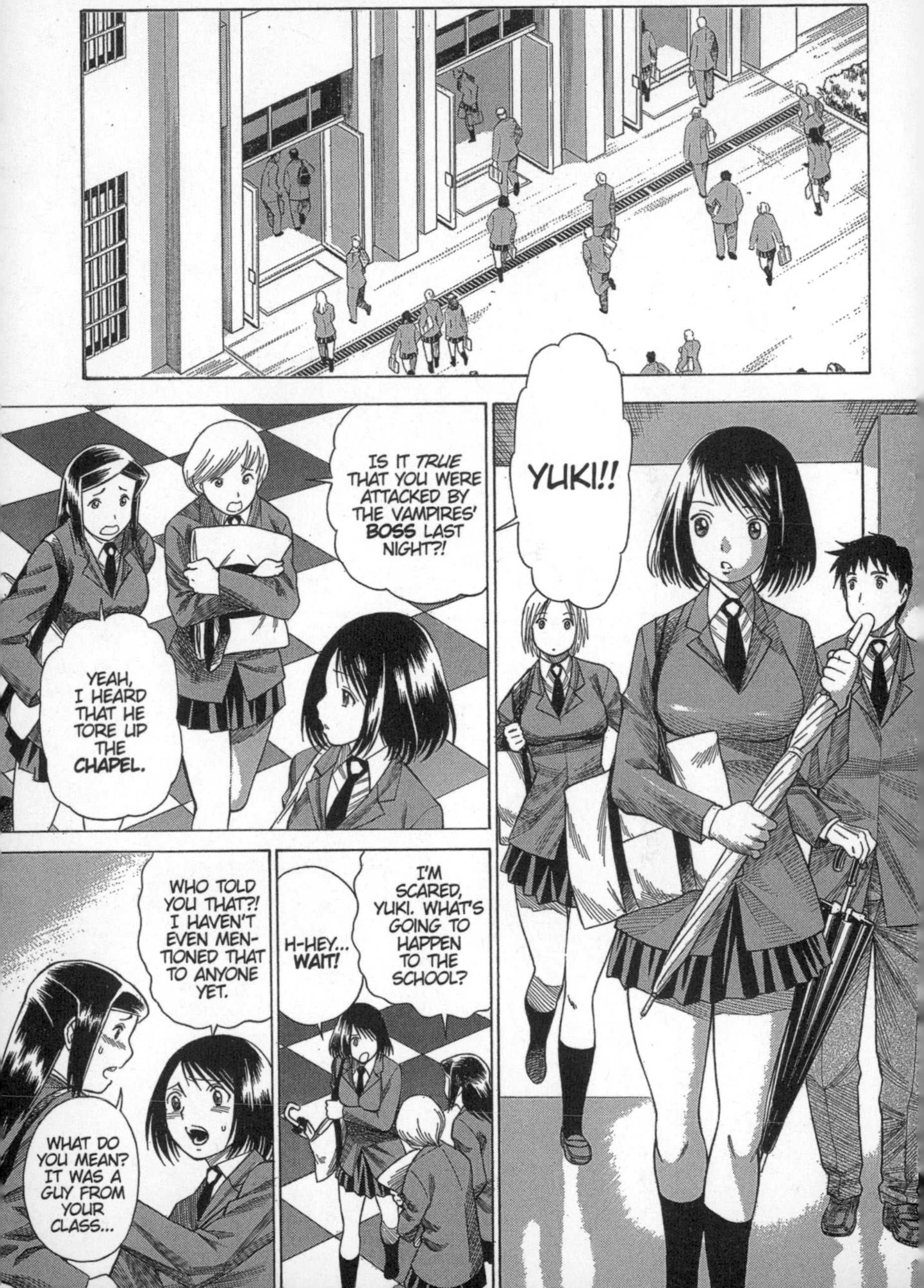
YUKI!!
IS IT *TRUE* THAT YOU WERE ATTACKED BY THE VAMPIRES' **BOSS** LAST NIGHT?!
YEAH, I HEARD THAT HE TORE UP THE **CHAPEL**.
I'M SCARED, YUKI. WHAT'S GOING TO HAPPEN TO THE SCHOOL?
H-HEY... **WAIT!**
WHO TOLD YOU THAT?! I HAVEN'T EVEN MEN-TIONED THAT TO ANYONE YET.
WHAT DO YOU MEAN? IT WAS A GUY FROM YOUR CLASS...

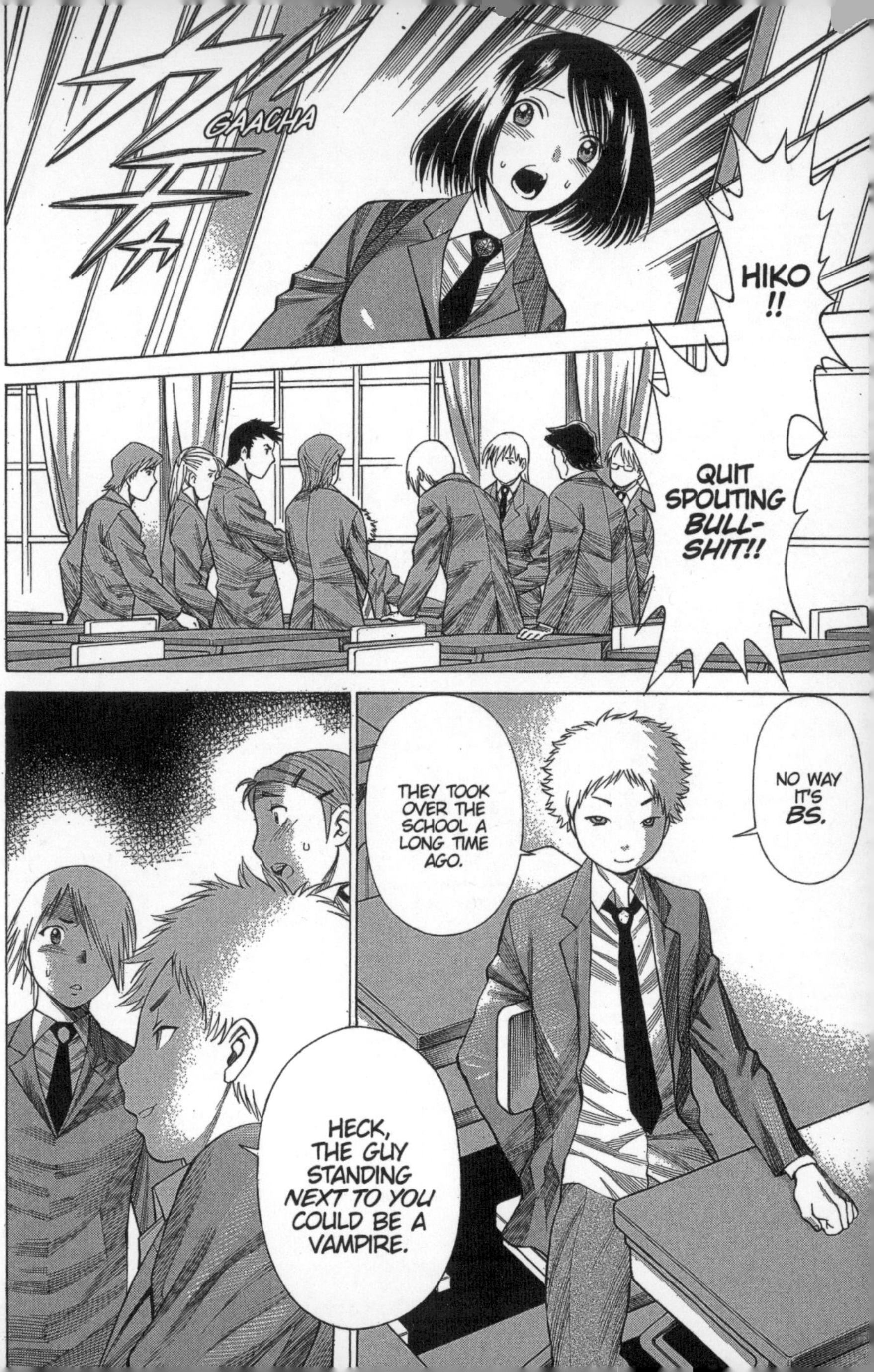
HIKO!! QUIT SPOUTING BULL-SHIT!!
GAACHA
NO WAY IT'S BS.
THEY TOOK OVER THE SCHOOL A LONG TIME AGO.
HECK, THE GUY STANDING NEXT TO YOU COULD BE A VAMPIRE.

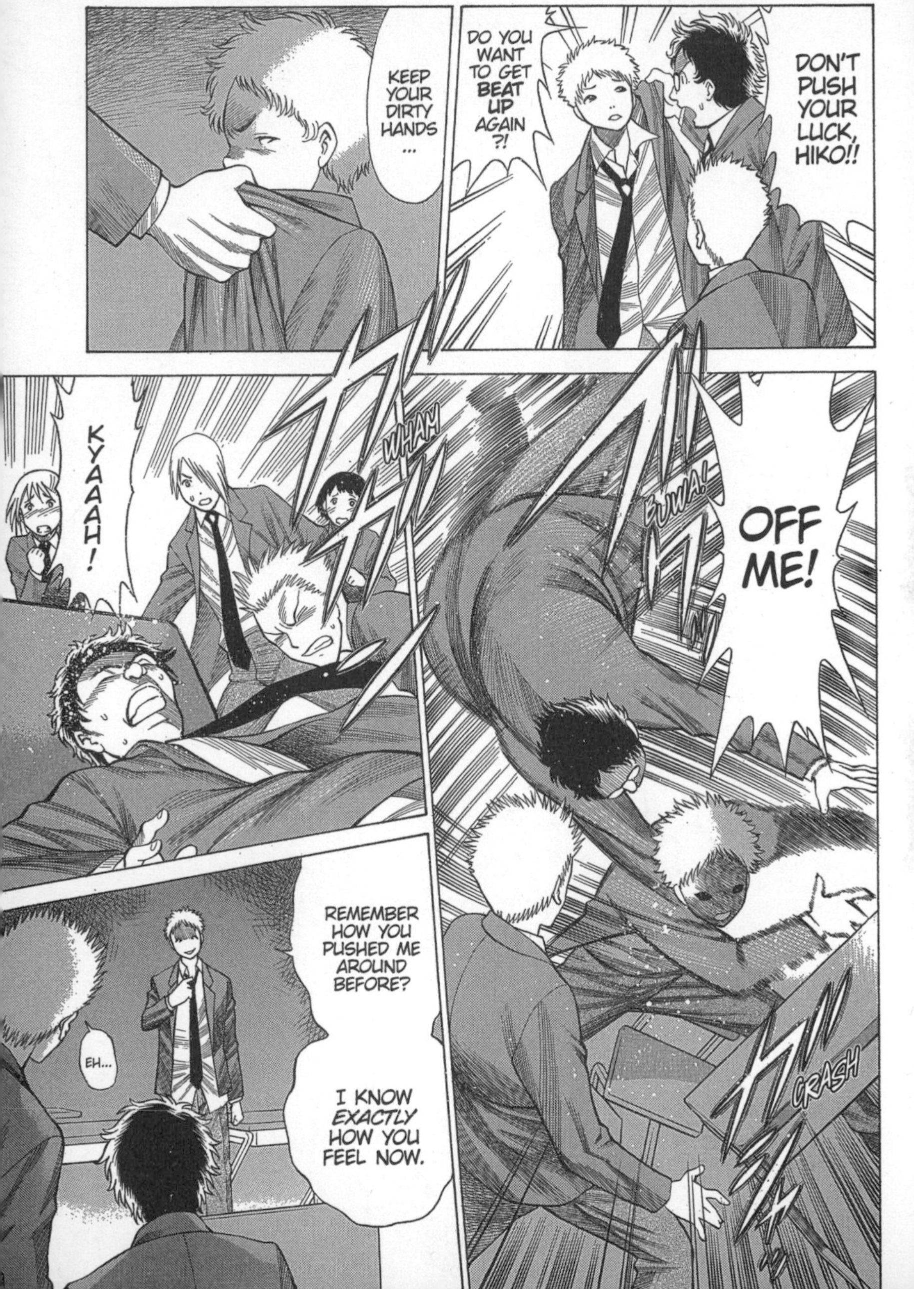
DON'T PUSH YOUR LUCK, HIKO!!
DO YOU WANT TO GET BEAT UP AGAIN?!
KEEP YOUR DIRTY HANDS ...
OFF ME!
BUWA!
WHAM
CRASH
KYAAAH!
REMEMBER HOW YOU PUSHED ME AROUND BEFORE?
I KNOW *EXACTLY* HOW YOU FEEL NOW.
EH...

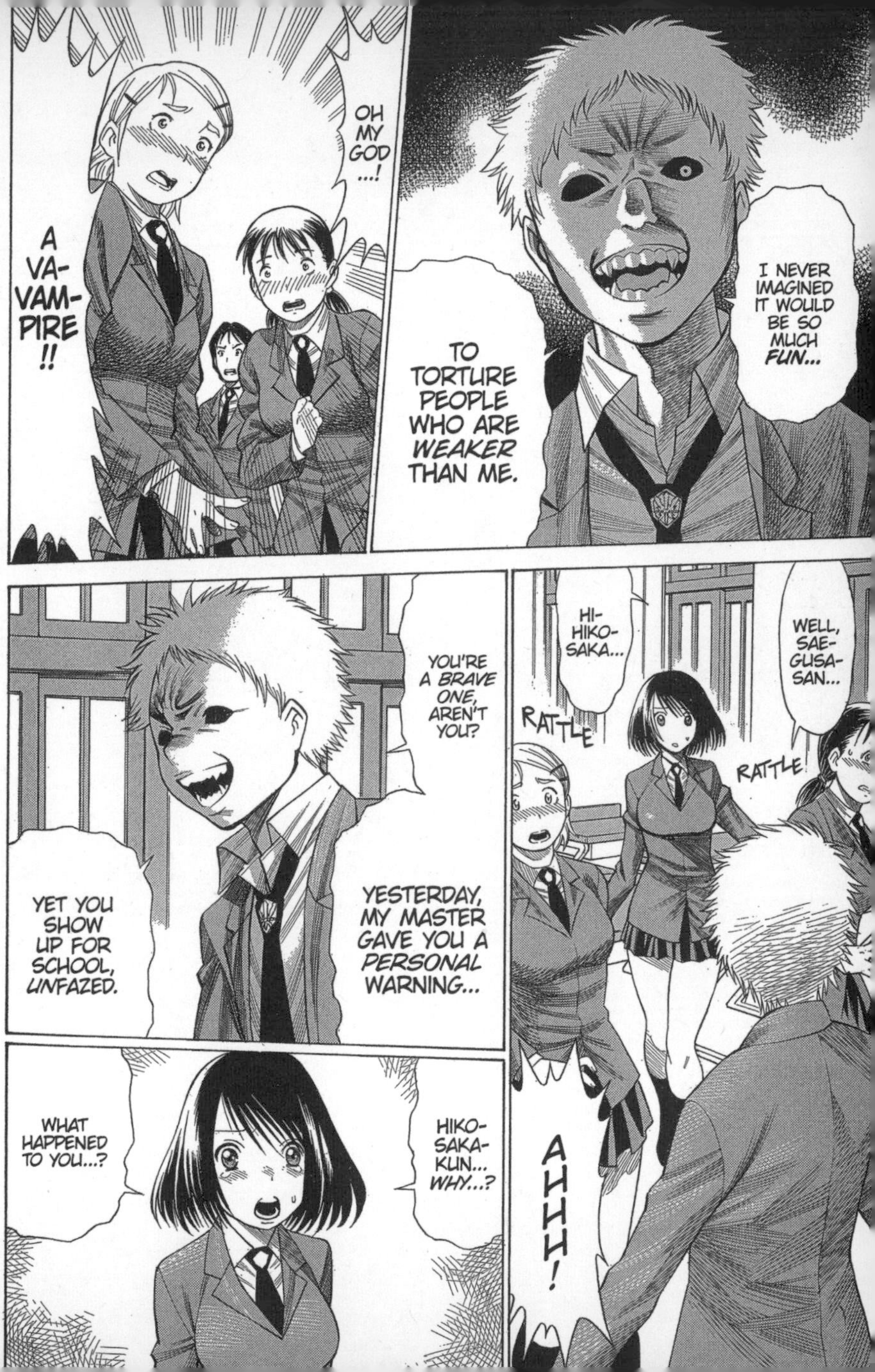
I NEVER IMAGINED IT WOULD BE SO MUCH *FUN*...
TO TORTURE PEOPLE WHO ARE *WEAKER* THAN ME.
OH MY GOD ...!
A VA-VAMPIRE !!
WELL, SAEGUSA-SAN...
HI-HIKOSAKA...
RATTLE
RATTLE
AHHH!
YOU'RE A *BRAVE* ONE, AREN'T YOU?
YESTERDAY, MY MASTER GAVE YOU A *PERSONAL* WARNING...
YET YOU SHOW UP FOR SCHOOL, *UNFAZED*.
HIKOSAKA-KUN... *WHY*...?
WHAT HAPPENED TO YOU...?

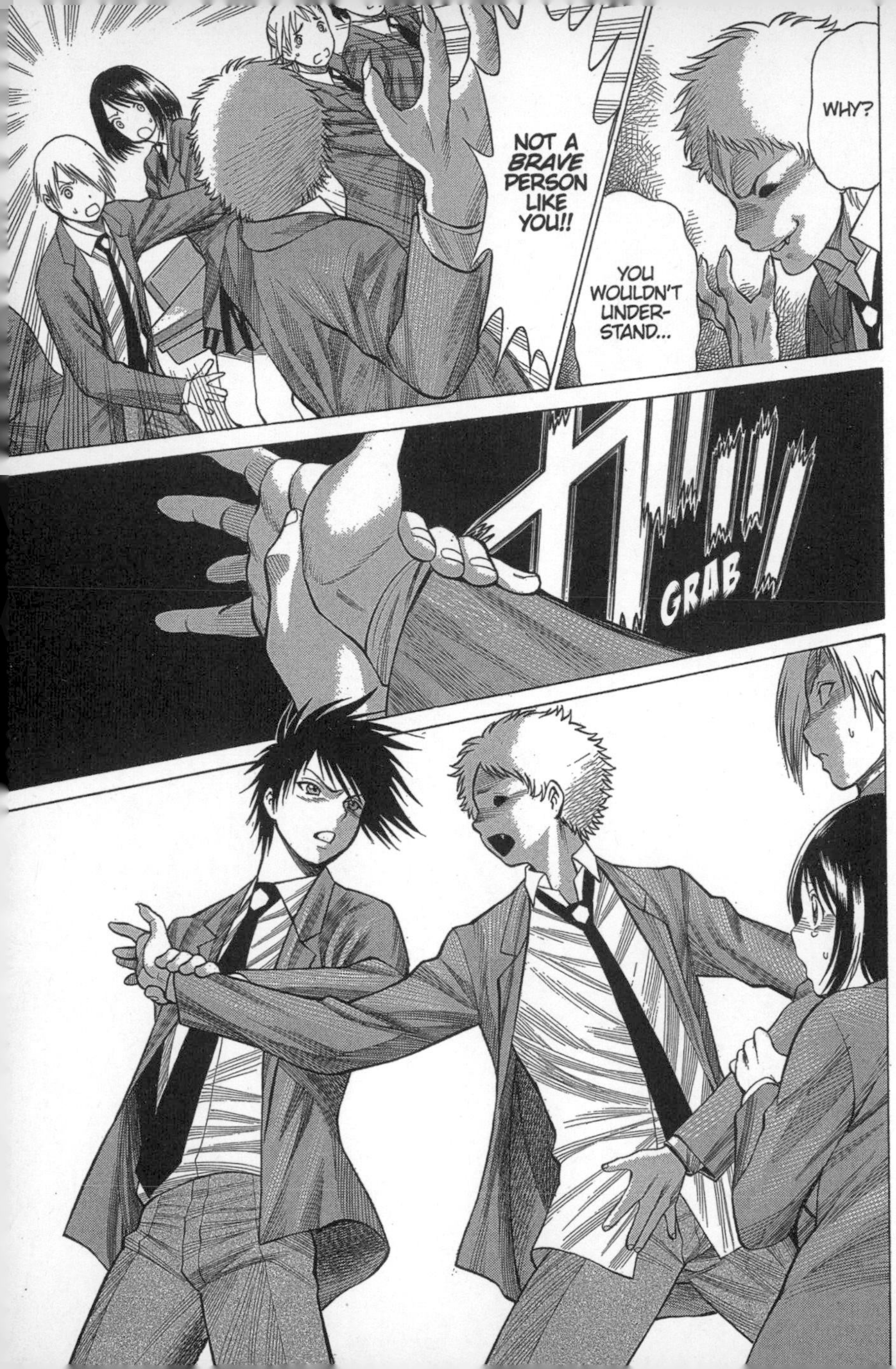
WHY?
YOU WOULDN'T UNDER-STAND...
NOT A *BRAVE* PERSON LIKE YOU!!
GRAB

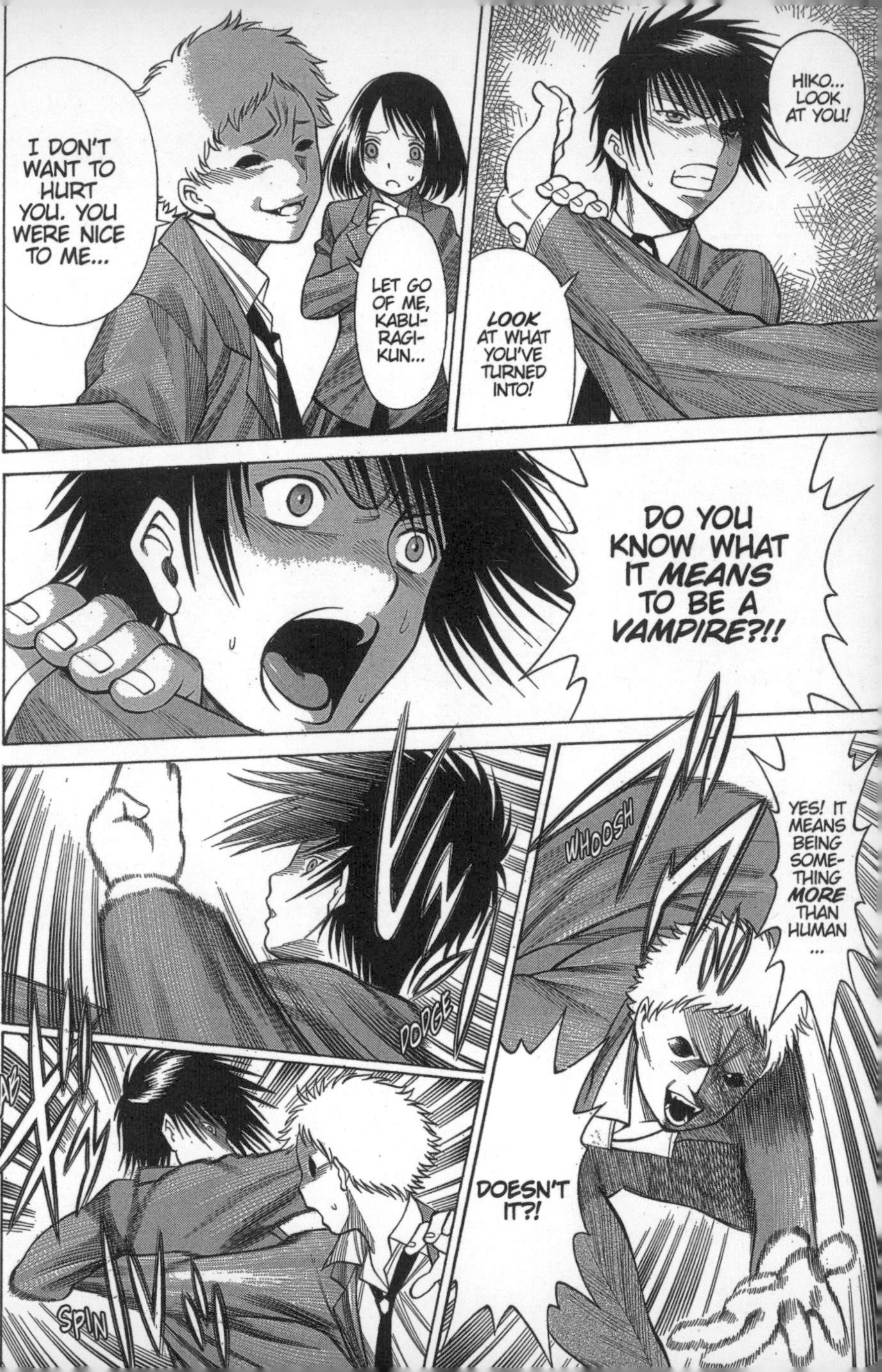
HIKO... LOOK AT YOU!
LOOK AT WHAT YOU'VE TURNED INTO!
LET GO OF ME, KABURAGI-KUN...
I DON'T WANT TO HURT YOU. YOU WERE NICE TO ME...
DO YOU KNOW WHAT IT MEANS TO BE A VAMPIRE?!!
YES! IT MEANS BEING SOMETHING MORE THAN HUMAN...
WHOOSH
DODGE
DOESN'T IT?!
GRAB
SPIN

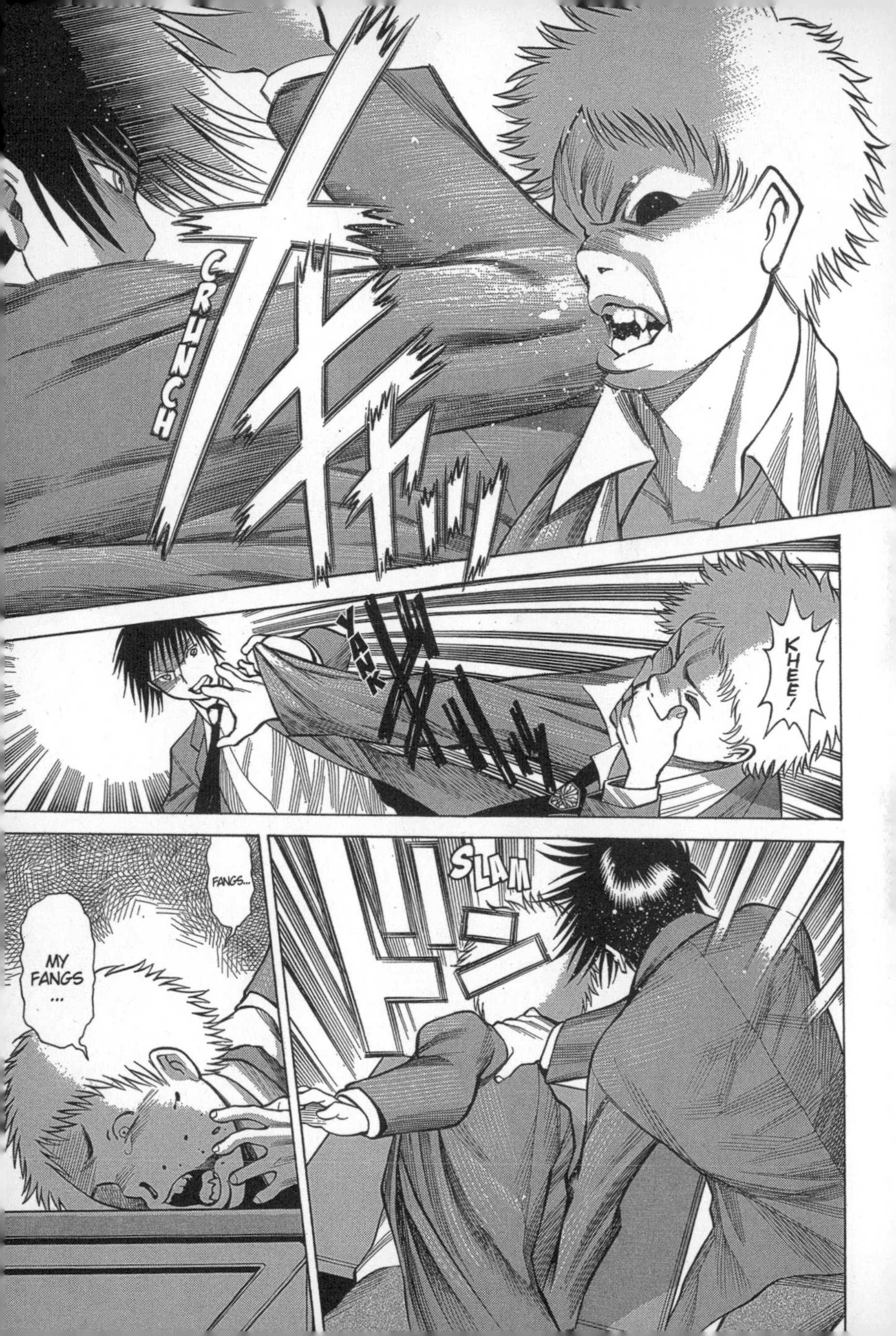
CRUNCH
KHEE!
YANK
SLAM
FANGS...
MY FANGS ...

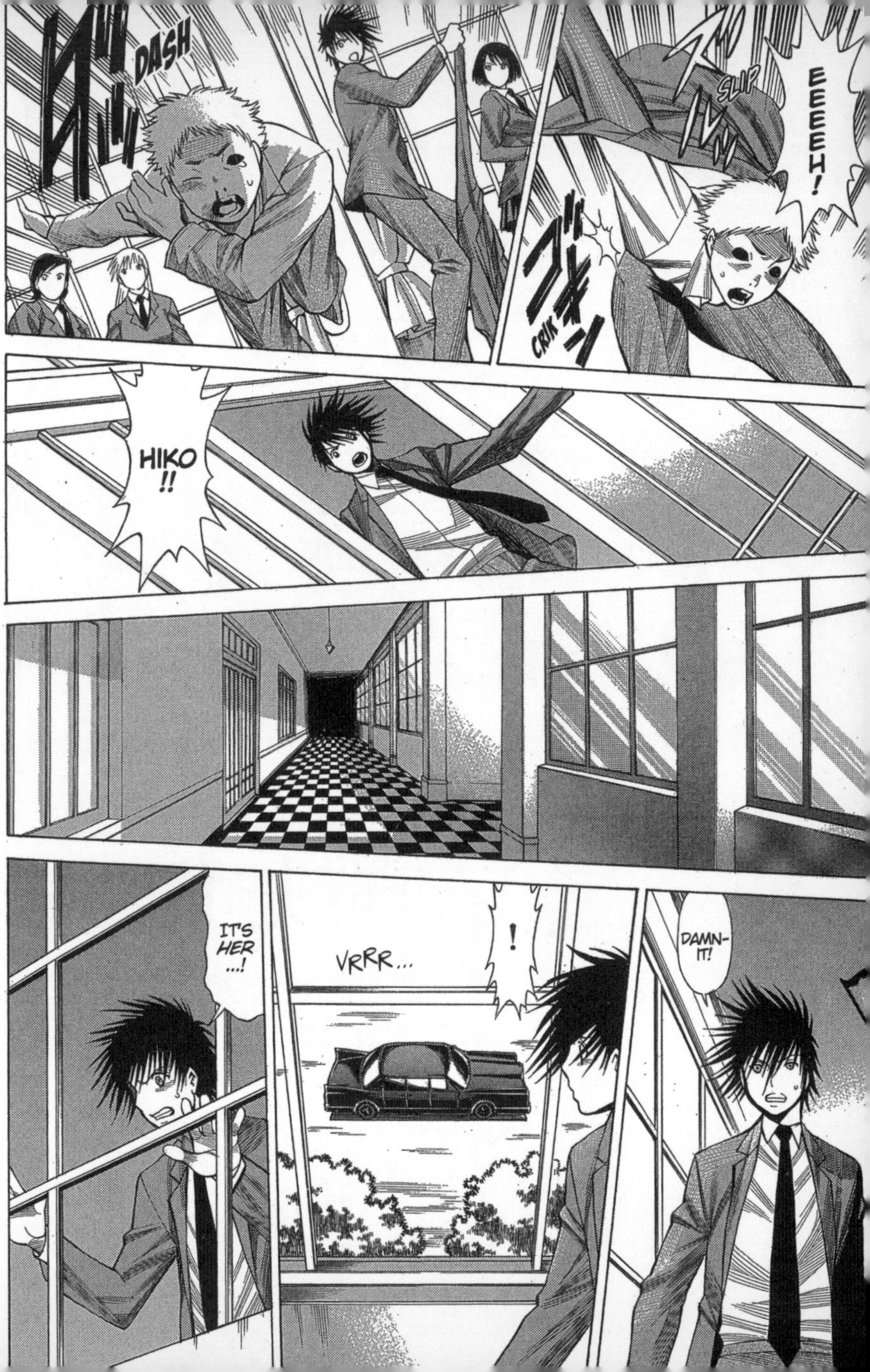
EEEEEH!
SLIP
CRIK
DASH
HIKO !!
DAMN-IT!
!
VRRR...
IT'S HER ...!

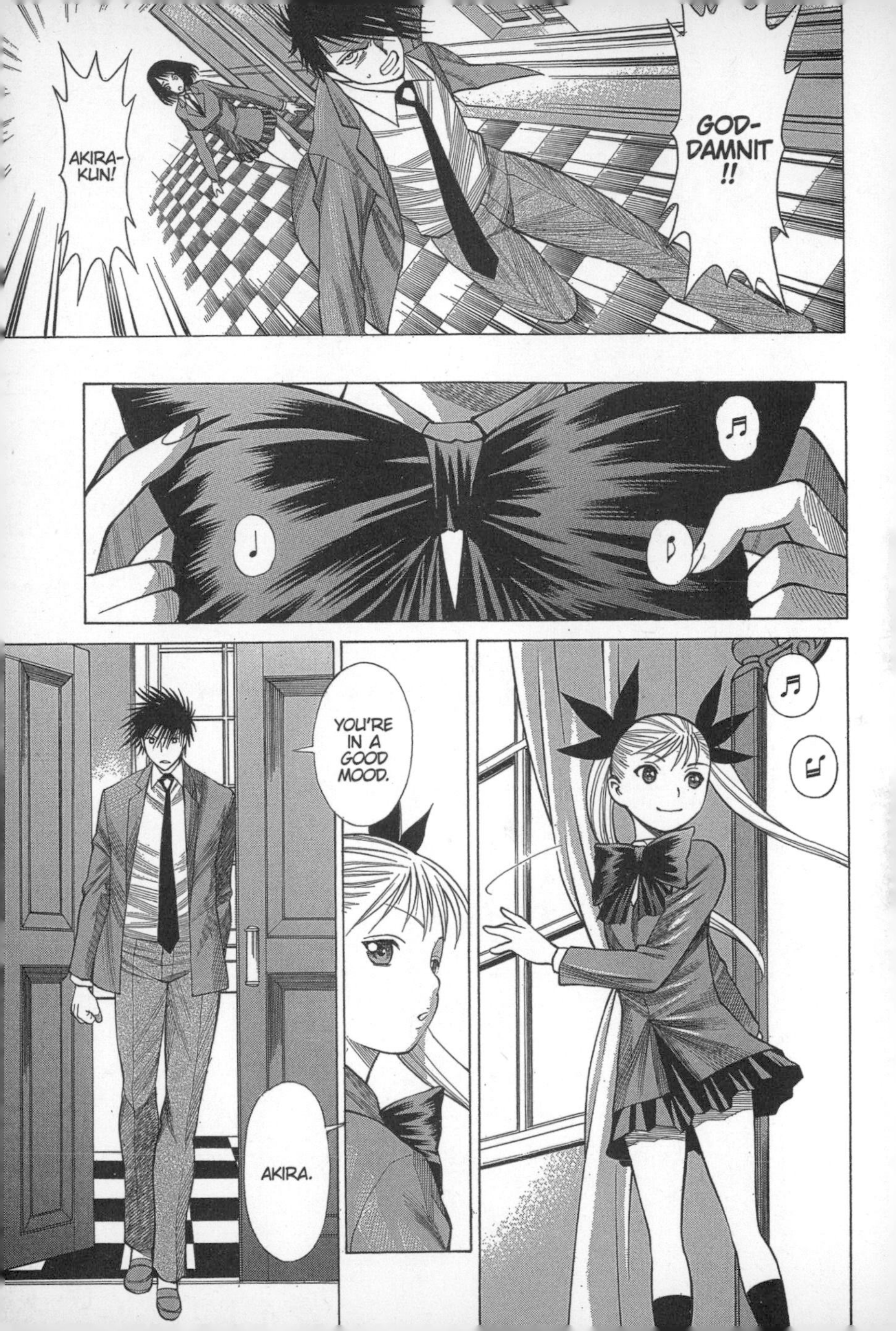
GOD-DAMNIT !!
AKIRA-KUN!
YOU'RE IN A GOOD MOOD.
AKIRA.

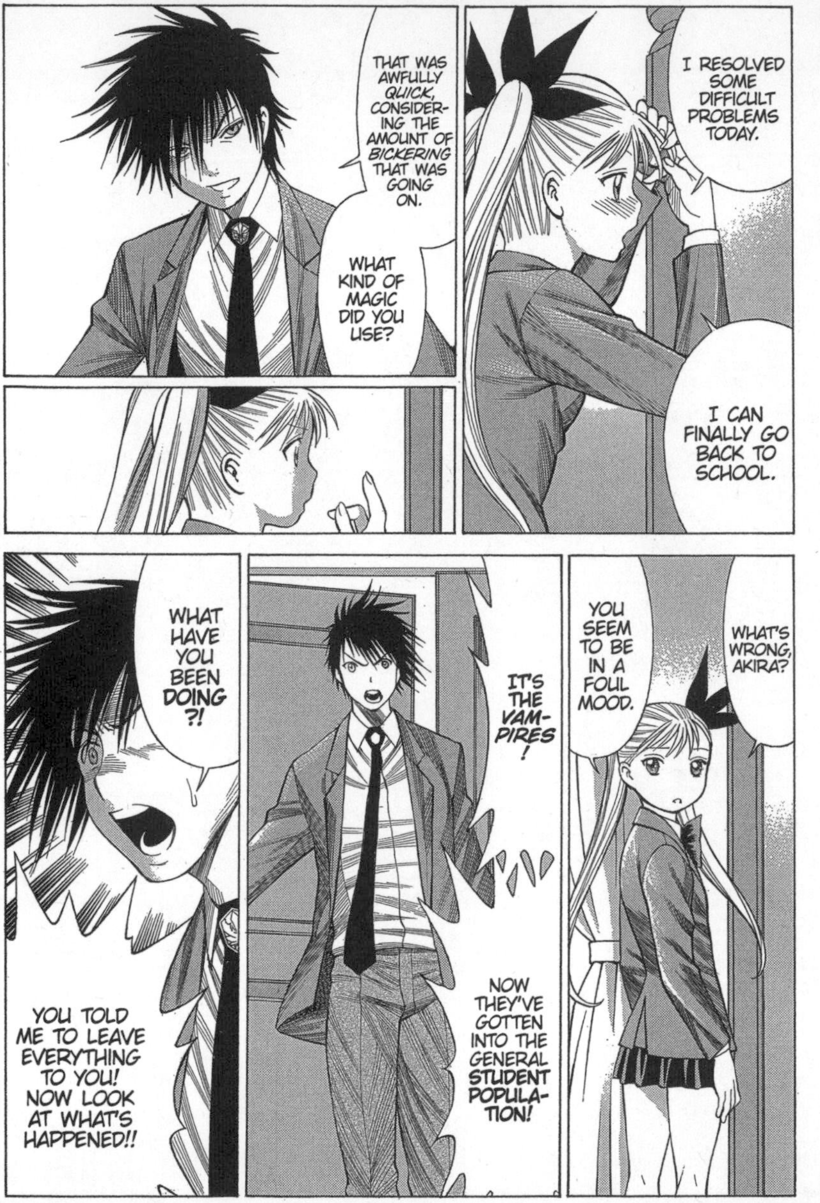
I RESOLVED SOME DIFFICULT PROBLEMS TODAY.
I CAN FINALLY GO BACK TO SCHOOL.
THAT WAS AWFULLY *QUICK*, CONSIDERING THE AMOUNT OF *BICKERING* THAT WAS GOING ON.
WHAT KIND OF MAGIC DID YOU USE?
WHAT'S WRONG, AKIRA?
YOU SEEM TO BE IN A FOUL MOOD.
IT'S THE *VAMPIRES*!
NOW THEY'VE GOTTEN INTO THE GENERAL **STUDENT POPULATION**!
WHAT HAVE YOU BEEN **DOING**?!
YOU TOLD ME TO LEAVE EVERYTHING TO YOU! NOW LOOK AT WHAT'S HAPPENED!!

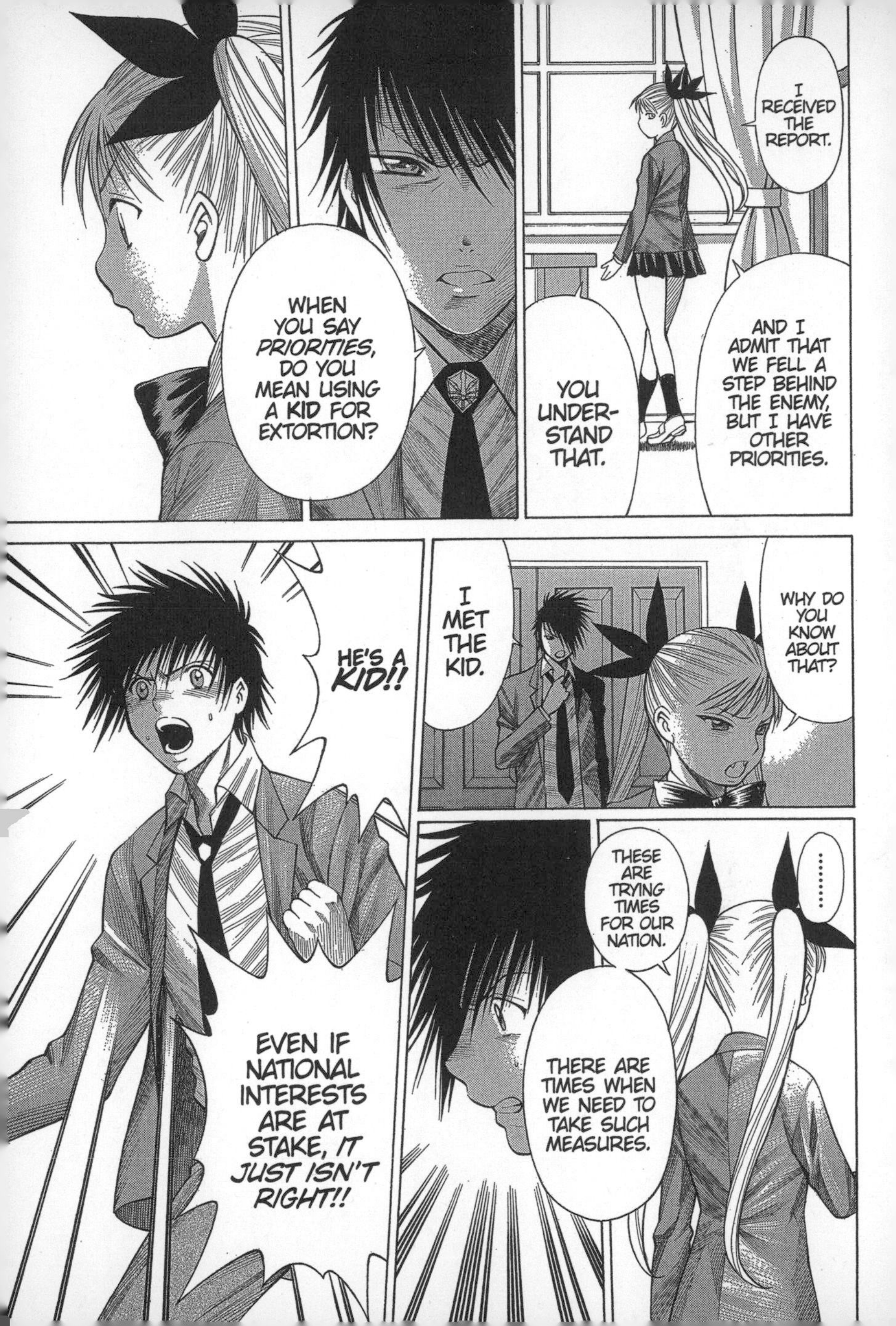
I RECEIVED THE REPORT.
AND I ADMIT THAT WE FELL A STEP BEHIND THE ENEMY, BUT I HAVE OTHER PRIORITIES.
YOU UNDER-STAND THAT.
WHEN YOU SAY PRIORITIES, DO YOU MEAN USING A KID FOR EXTORTION?
WHY DO YOU KNOW ABOUT THAT?
I MET THE KID.
......
THESE ARE TRYING TIMES FOR OUR NATION.
THERE ARE TIMES WHEN WE NEED TO TAKE SUCH MEASURES.
HE'S A KID!!
EVEN IF NATIONAL INTERESTS ARE AT STAKE, IT JUST ISN'T RIGHT!!

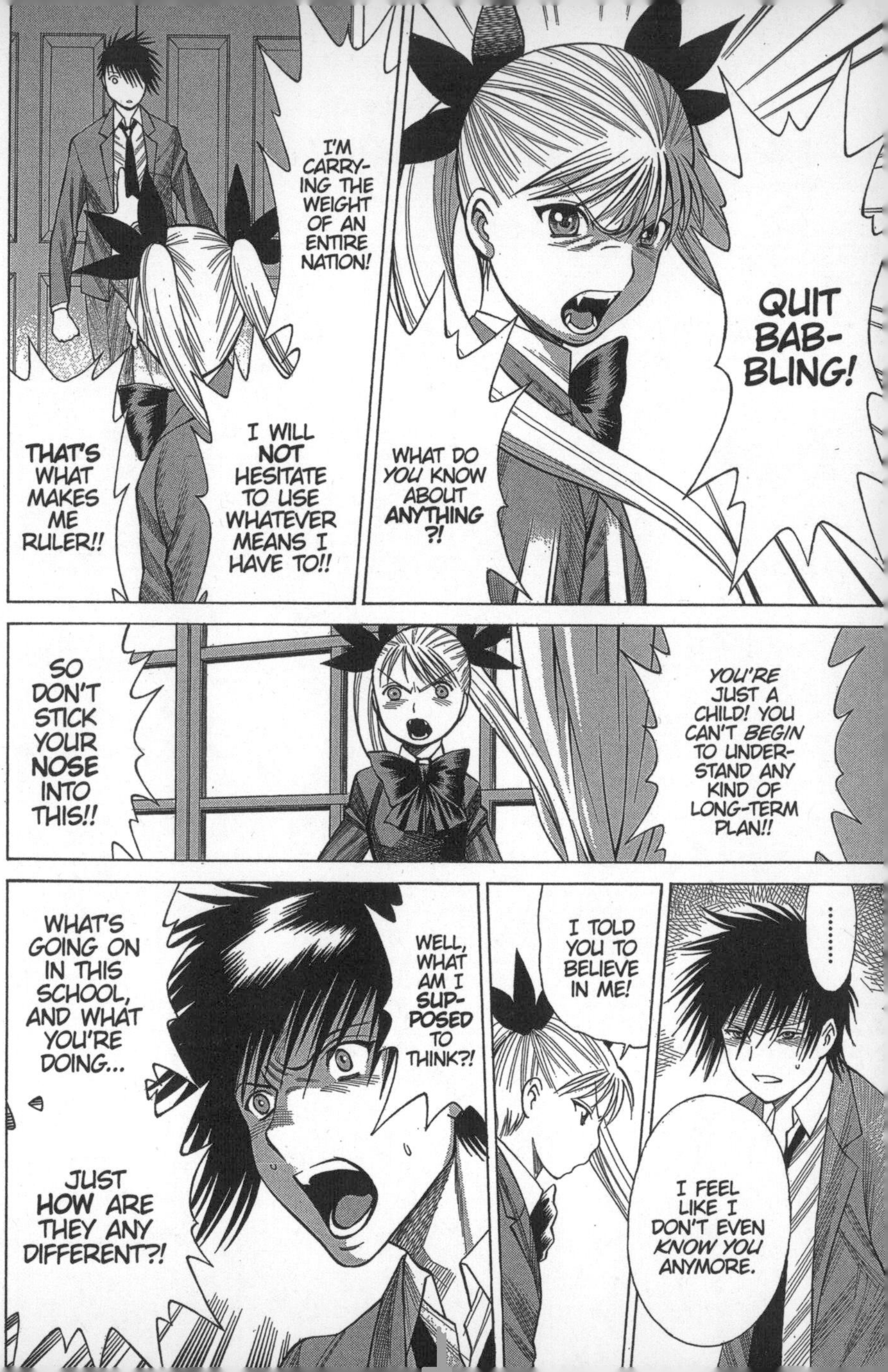
QUIT BABBLING!
WHAT DO YOU KNOW ABOUT ANYTHING?!
I'M CARRYING THE WEIGHT OF AN ENTIRE NATION!
I WILL NOT HESITATE TO USE WHATEVER MEANS I HAVE TO!!
THAT'S WHAT MAKES ME RULER!!
YOU'RE JUST A CHILD! YOU CAN'T BEGIN TO UNDERSTAND ANY KIND OF LONG-TERM PLAN!!
SO DON'T STICK YOUR NOSE INTO THIS!!
......
I TOLD YOU TO BELIEVE IN ME!
I FEEL LIKE I DON'T EVEN KNOW YOU ANYMORE.
WELL, WHAT AM I SUPPOSED TO THINK?!
WHAT'S GOING ON IN THIS SCHOOL, AND WHAT YOU'RE DOING...
JUST HOW ARE THEY ANY DIFFERENT?!

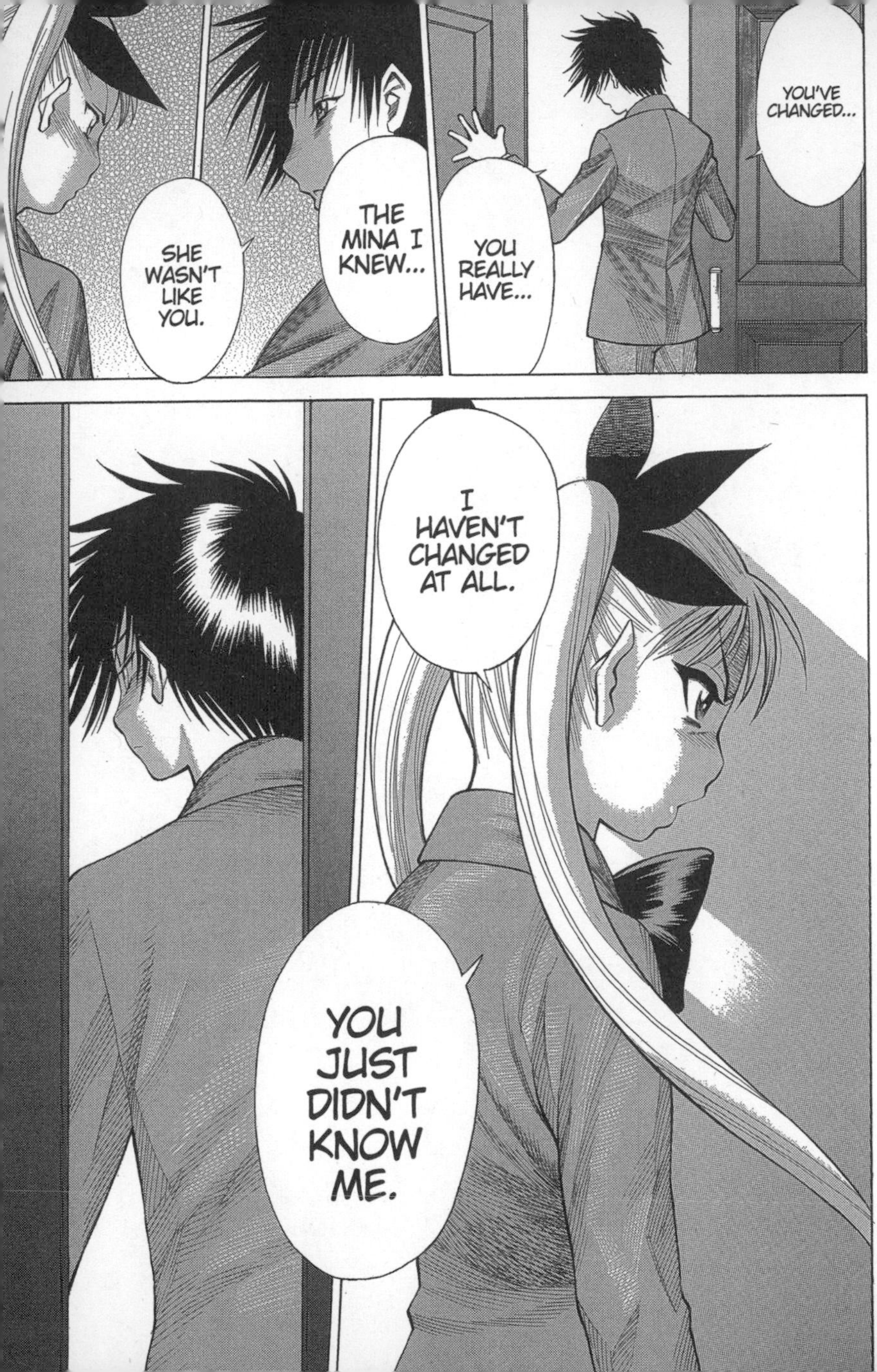
YOU'VE CHANGED...
YOU REALLY HAVE...
THE MINA I KNEW...
SHE WASN'T LIKE YOU.
I HAVEN'T CHANGED AT ALL.
YOU JUST DIDN'T KNOW ME.

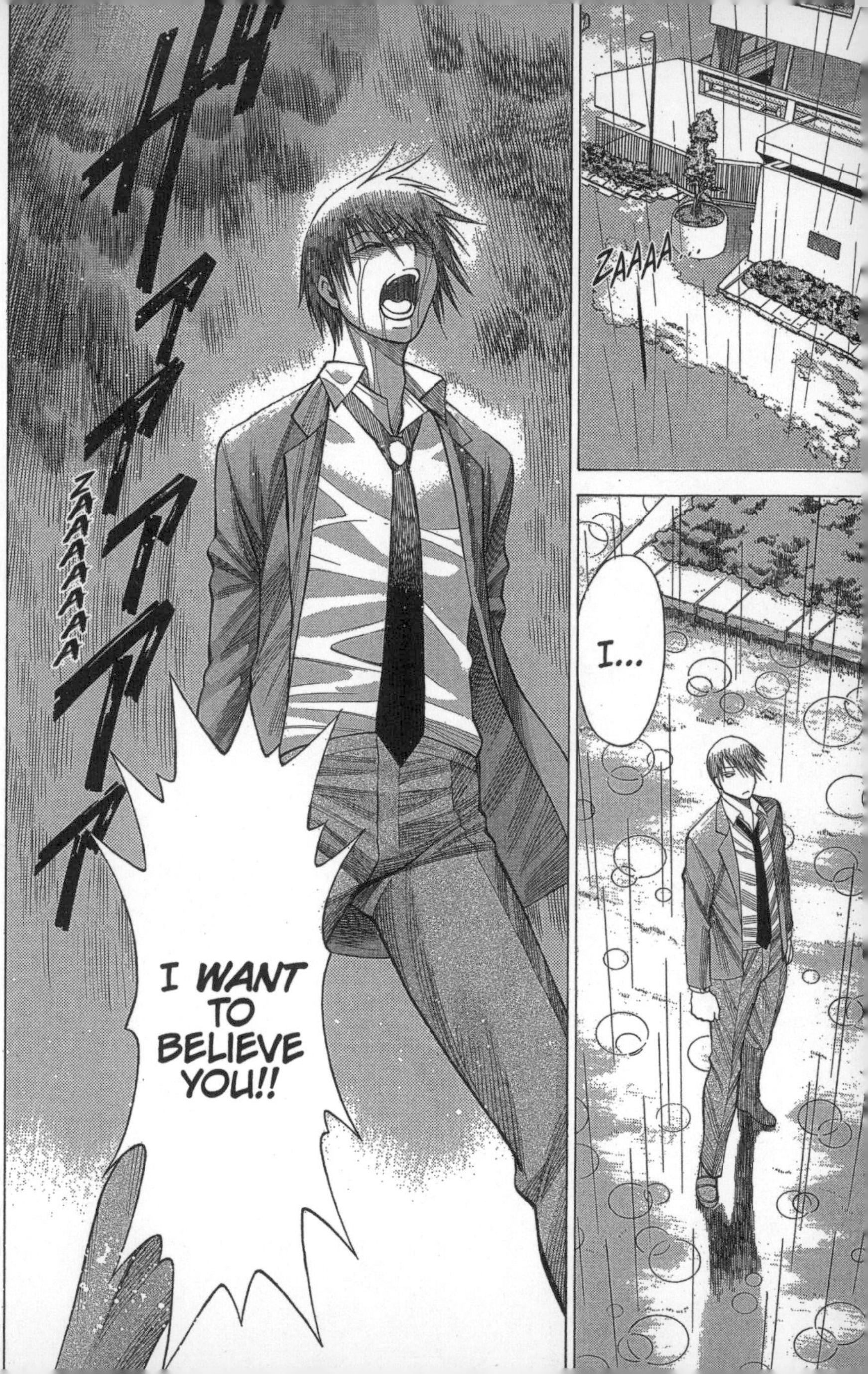
ZAAAA...
I...
ZAAAAAAAA
I WANT TO BELIEVE YOU!!

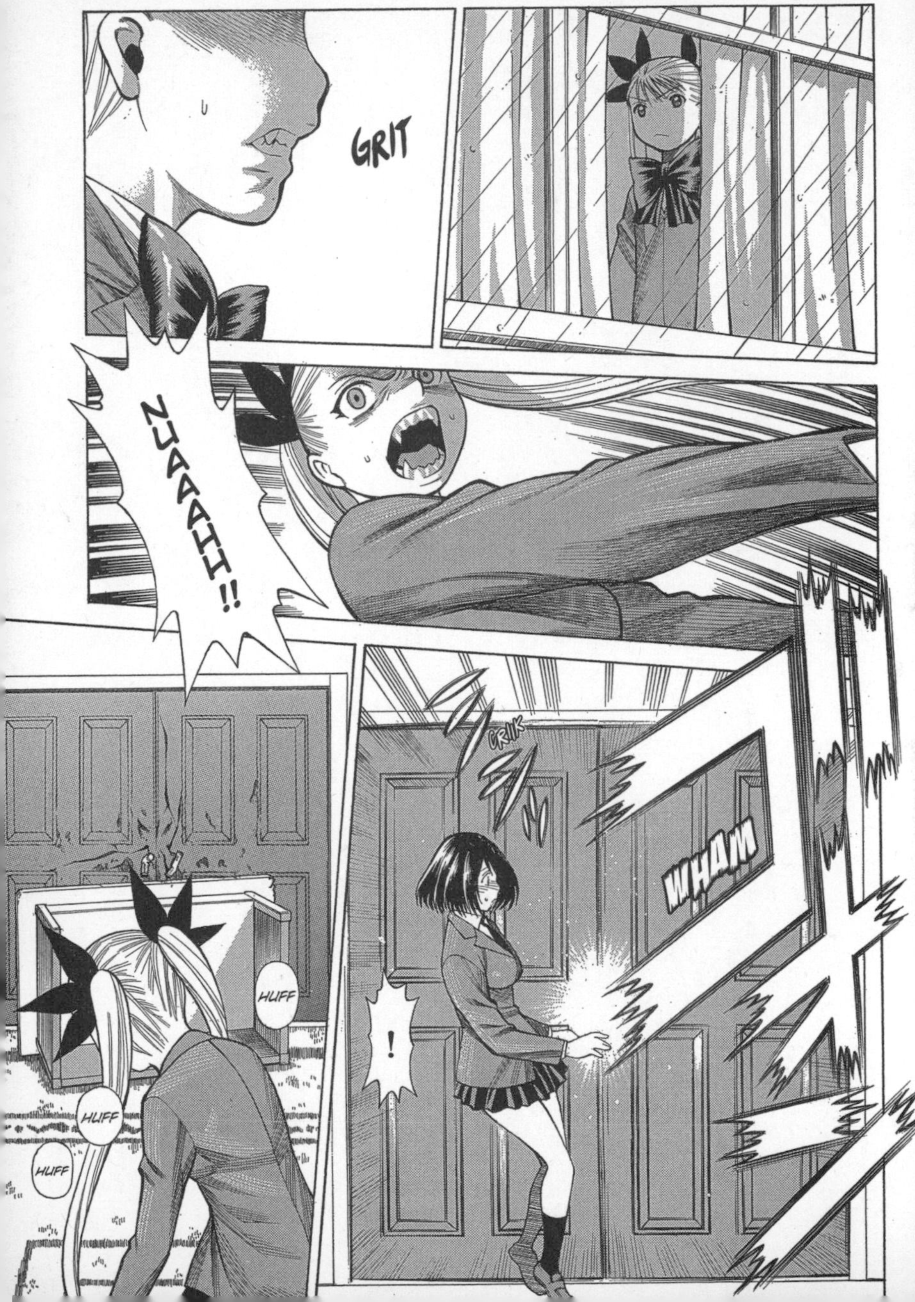
GRIT
NUAAAHH!!
CRIIK
WHAM
!
HUFF
HUFF
HUFF

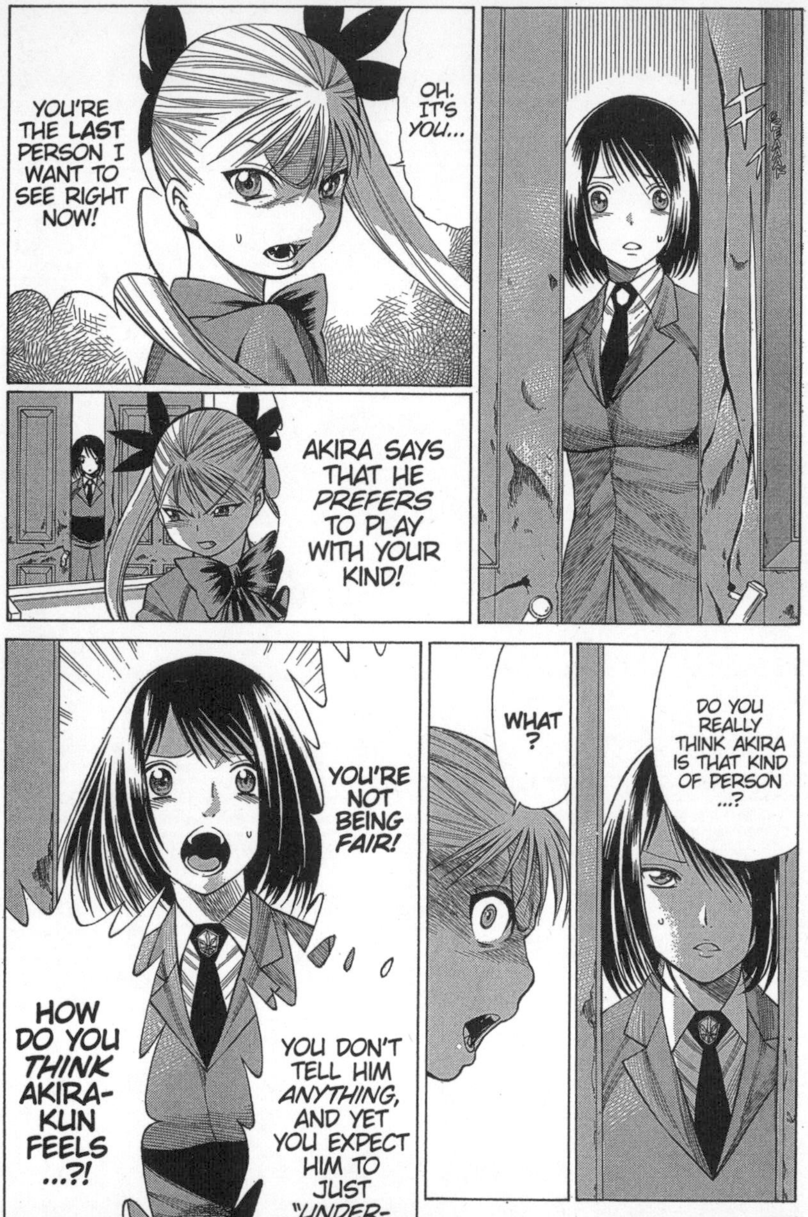
OH. IT'S YOU...
YOU'RE THE LAST PERSON I WANT TO SEE RIGHT NOW!
AKIRA SAYS THAT HE PREFERS TO PLAY WITH YOUR KIND!
DO YOU REALLY THINK AKIRA IS THAT KIND OF PERSON ...?
WHAT ?
YOU'RE NOT BEING FAIR!
YOU DON'T TELL HIM ANYTHING, AND YET YOU EXPECT HIM TO JUST "UNDER-STAND"?!
HOW DO YOU THINK AKIRA-KUN FEELS ...?!

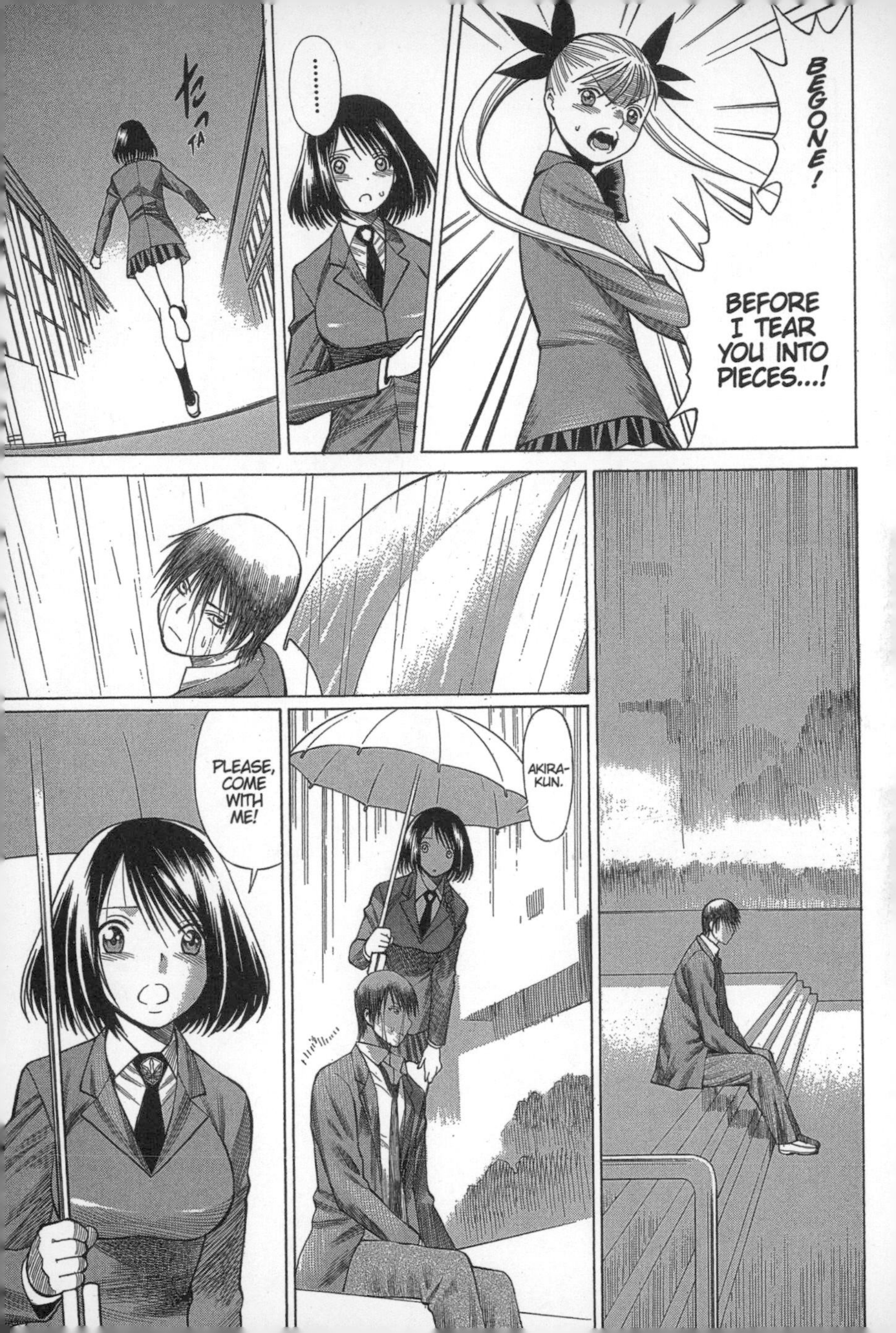
BEGONE!
BEFORE I TEAR YOU INTO PIECES...!
......
TA
AKIRA-KUN.
PLEASE, COME WITH ME!

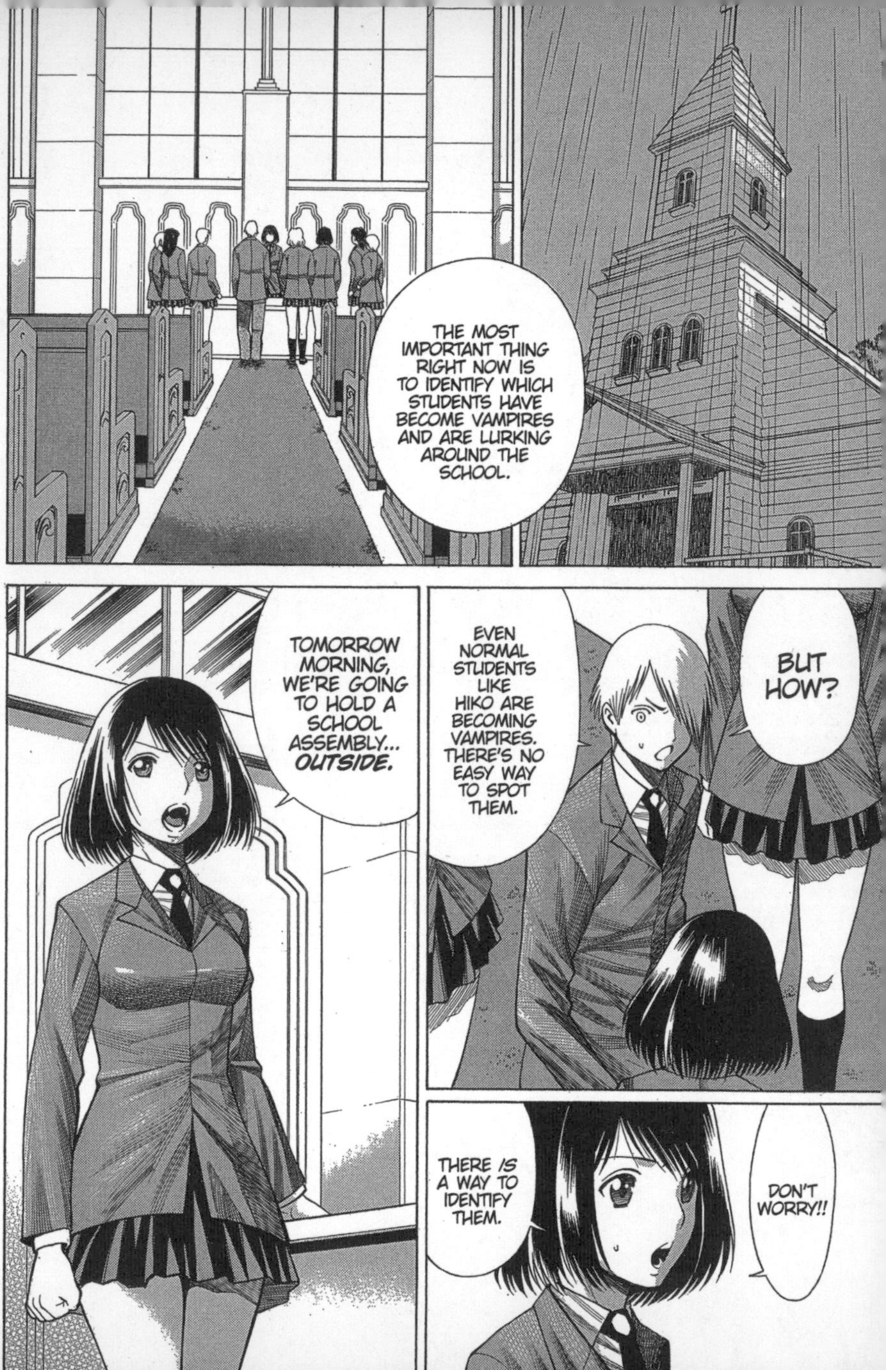
THE MOST IMPORTANT THING RIGHT NOW IS TO IDENTIFY WHICH STUDENTS HAVE BECOME VAMPIRES AND ARE LURKING AROUND THE SCHOOL.
BUT HOW?
EVEN NORMAL STUDENTS LIKE HIKO ARE BECOMING VAMPIRES. THERE'S NO EASY WAY TO SPOT THEM.
DON'T WORRY!!
THERE *IS* A WAY TO IDENTIFY THEM.
TOMORROW MORNING, WE'RE GOING TO HOLD A SCHOOL ASSEMBLY... ***OUTSIDE.***

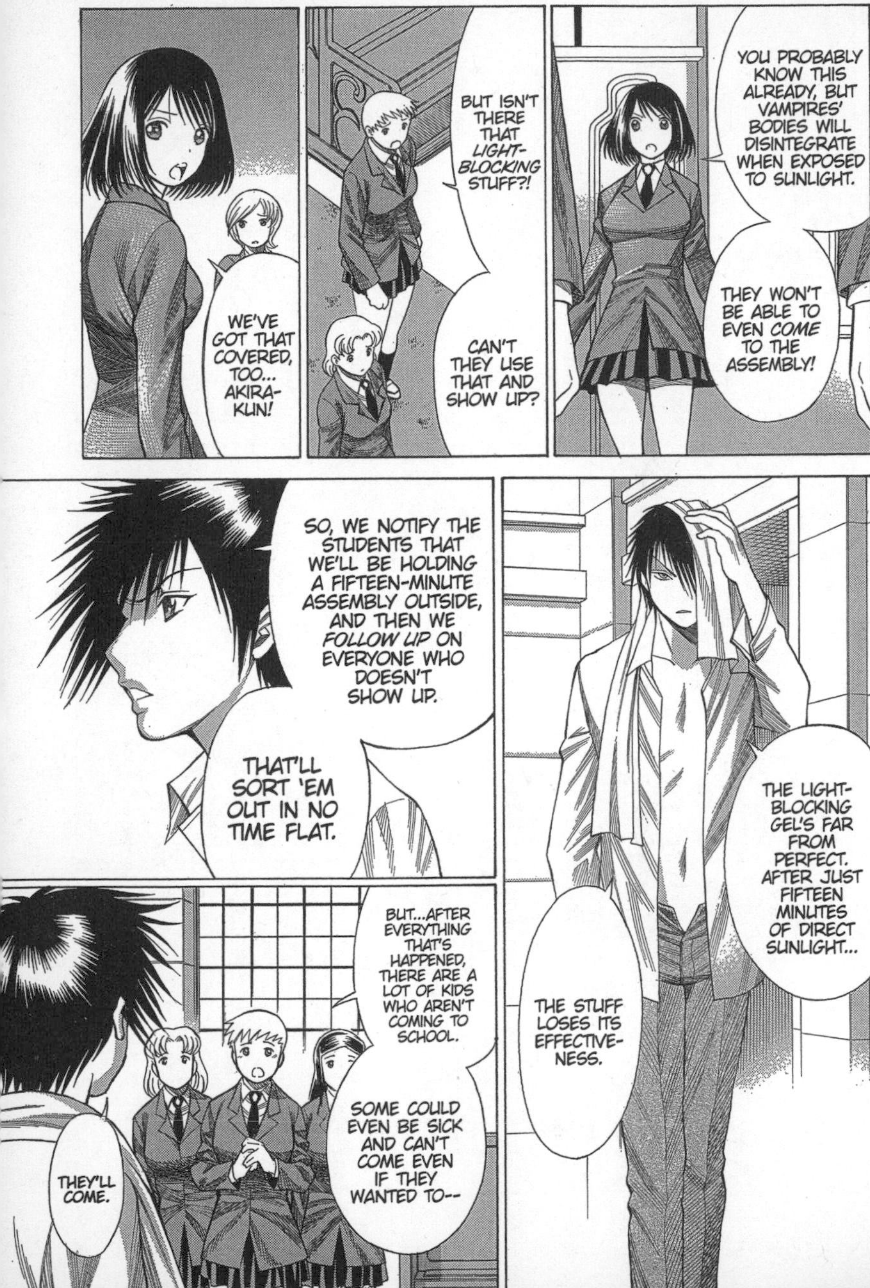
YOU PROBABLY KNOW THIS ALREADY, BUT VAMPIRES' BODIES WILL DISINTEGRATE WHEN EXPOSED TO SUNLIGHT.
THEY WON'T BE ABLE TO EVEN *COME* TO THE ASSEMBLY!
BUT ISN'T THERE THAT *LIGHT-BLOCKING* STUFF?!
CAN'T THEY USE THAT AND SHOW UP?
WE'VE GOT THAT COVERED, TOO... AKIRA-KUN!
THE LIGHT-BLOCKING GEL'S FAR FROM PERFECT. AFTER JUST FIFTEEN MINUTES OF DIRECT SUNLIGHT...
THE STUFF LOSES ITS EFFECTIVE-NESS.
SO, WE NOTIFY THE STUDENTS THAT WE'LL BE HOLDING A FIFTEEN-MINUTE ASSEMBLY OUTSIDE, AND THEN WE *FOLLOW UP* ON EVERYONE WHO DOESN'T SHOW UP.
THAT'LL SORT 'EM OUT IN NO TIME FLAT.
BUT...AFTER EVERYTHING THAT'S HAPPENED, THERE ARE A LOT OF KIDS WHO AREN'T COMING TO SCHOOL.
SOME COULD EVEN BE SICK AND CAN'T COME EVEN IF THEY WANTED TO--
THEY'LL COME.

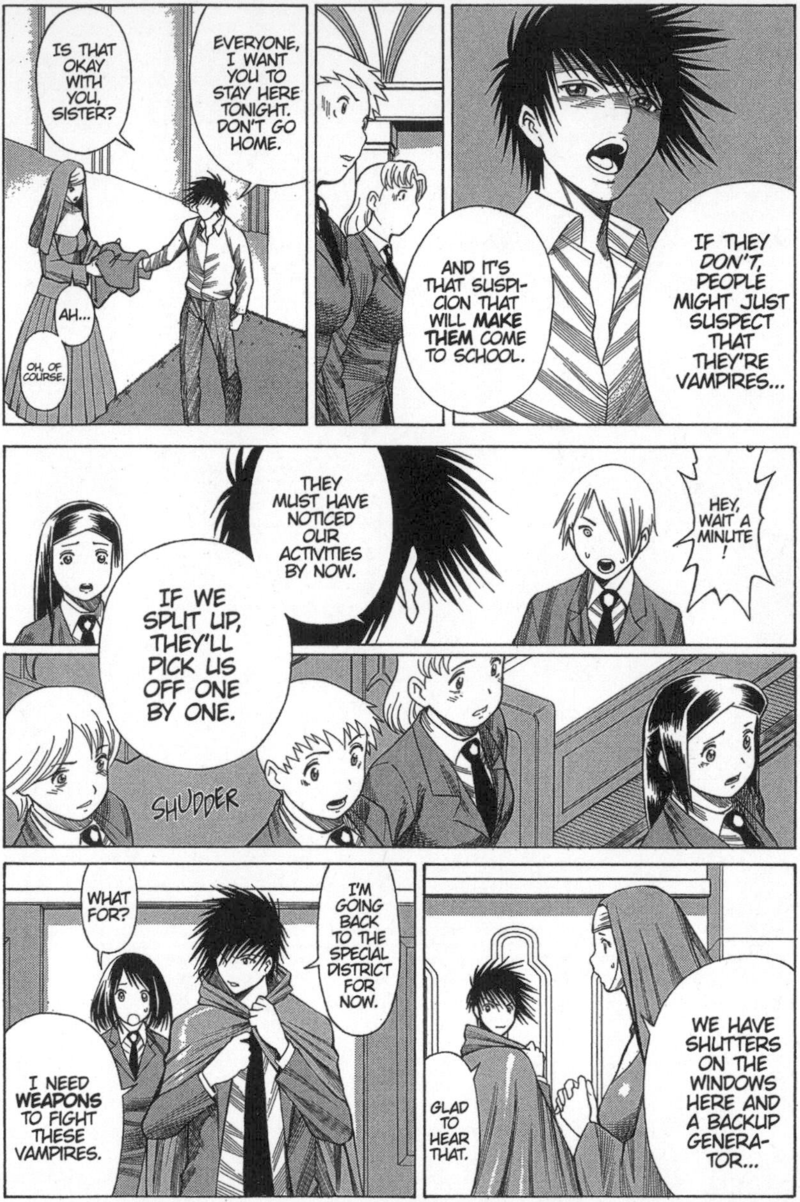
IF THEY DON'T, PEOPLE MIGHT JUST SUSPECT THAT THEY'RE VAMPIRES...
AND IT'S THAT SUSPICION THAT WILL MAKE THEM COME TO SCHOOL.
EVERYONE, I WANT YOU TO STAY HERE TONIGHT. DON'T GO HOME.
IS THAT OKAY WITH YOU, SISTER?
AH...
OH, OF COURSE.
HEY, WAIT A MINUTE!
THEY MUST HAVE NOTICED OUR ACTIVITIES BY NOW.
IF WE SPLIT UP, THEY'LL PICK US OFF ONE BY ONE.
SHUDDER
WE HAVE SHUTTERS ON THE WINDOWS HERE AND A BACKUP GENERATOR...
GLAD TO HEAR THAT.
I'M GOING BACK TO THE SPECIAL DISTRICT FOR NOW.
WHAT FOR?
I NEED WEAPONS TO FIGHT THESE VAMPIRES.

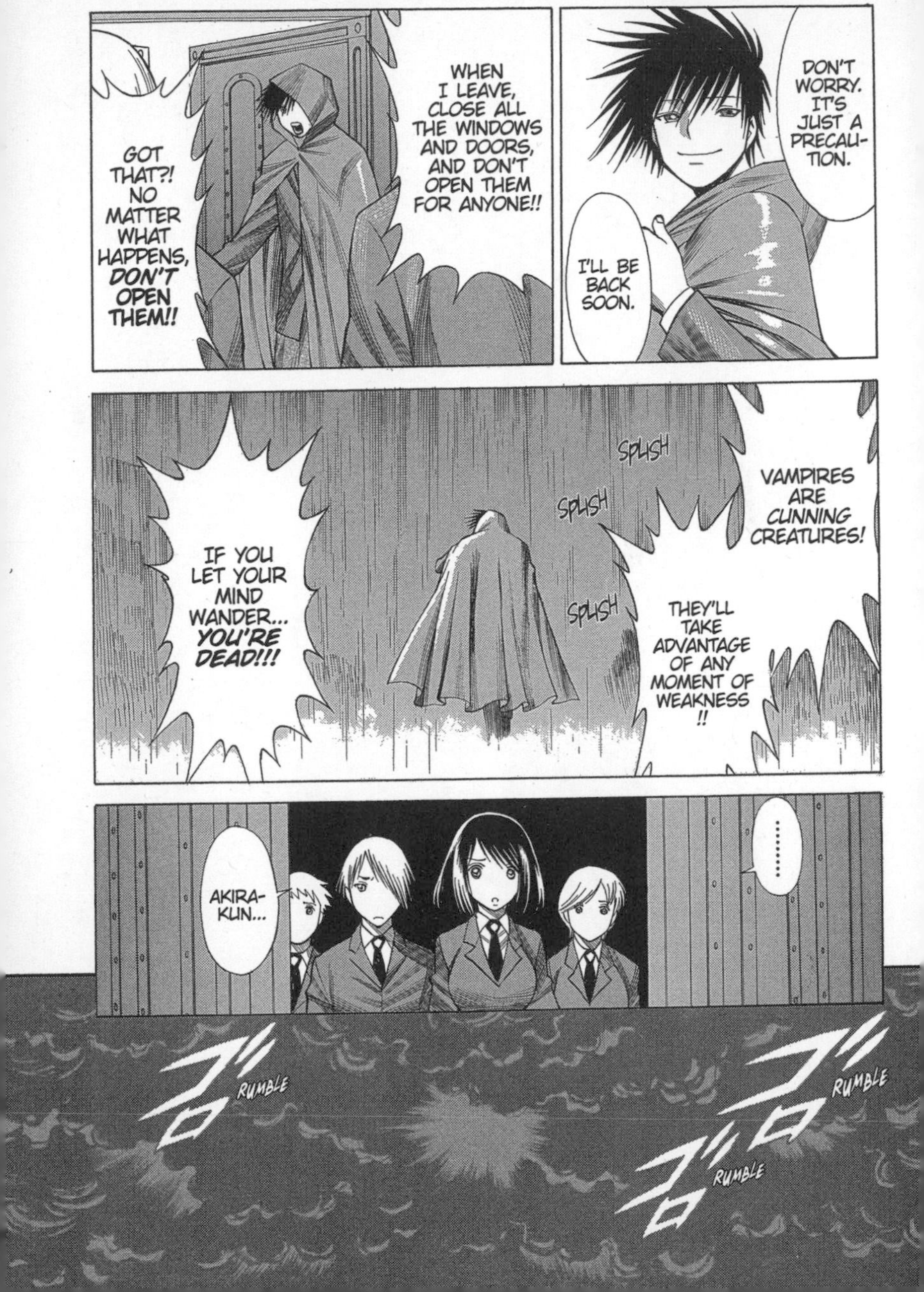
DON'T WORRY. IT'S JUST A PRECAUTION.
I'LL BE BACK SOON.
WHEN I LEAVE, CLOSE ALL THE WINDOWS AND DOORS, AND DON'T OPEN THEM FOR ANYONE!!
GOT THAT?! NO MATTER WHAT HAPPENS, ***DON'T* OPEN THEM!!**
VAMPIRES ARE CUNNING CREATURES!
THEY'LL TAKE ADVANTAGE OF ANY MOMENT OF WEAKNESS !!
SPLISH
SPLISH
SPLISH
IF YOU LET YOUR MIND WANDER... ***YOU'RE DEAD!!!***
....
AKIRA-KUN...
RUMBLE
RUMBLE
RUMBLE

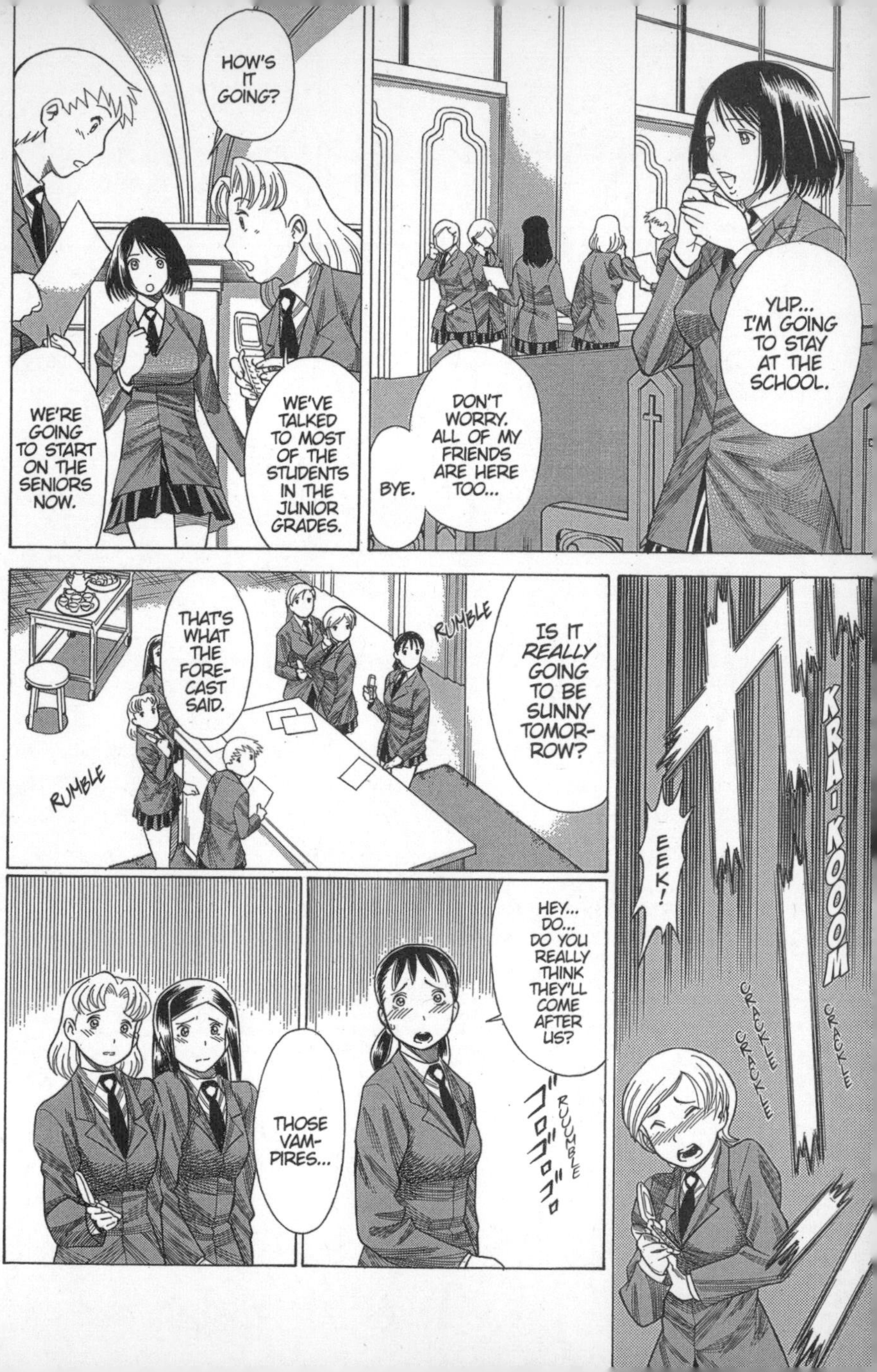
YUP... I'M GOING TO STAY AT THE SCHOOL.
DON'T WORRY. ALL OF MY FRIENDS ARE HERE TOO...
BYE.
HOW'S IT GOING?
WE'VE TALKED TO MOST OF THE STUDENTS IN THE JUNIOR GRADES.
WE'RE GOING TO START ON THE SENIORS NOW.
KRA-KOOOM
EEK!
CRACKLE
CRACKLE
CRACKLE
IS IT *REALLY* GOING TO BE SUNNY TOMORROW?
RUMBLE
THAT'S WHAT THE FORE-CAST SAID.
RUMBLE
HEY... DO... DO YOU REALLY THINK THEY'LL COME AFTER US?
RUUMBLE
THOSE VAM-PIRES...

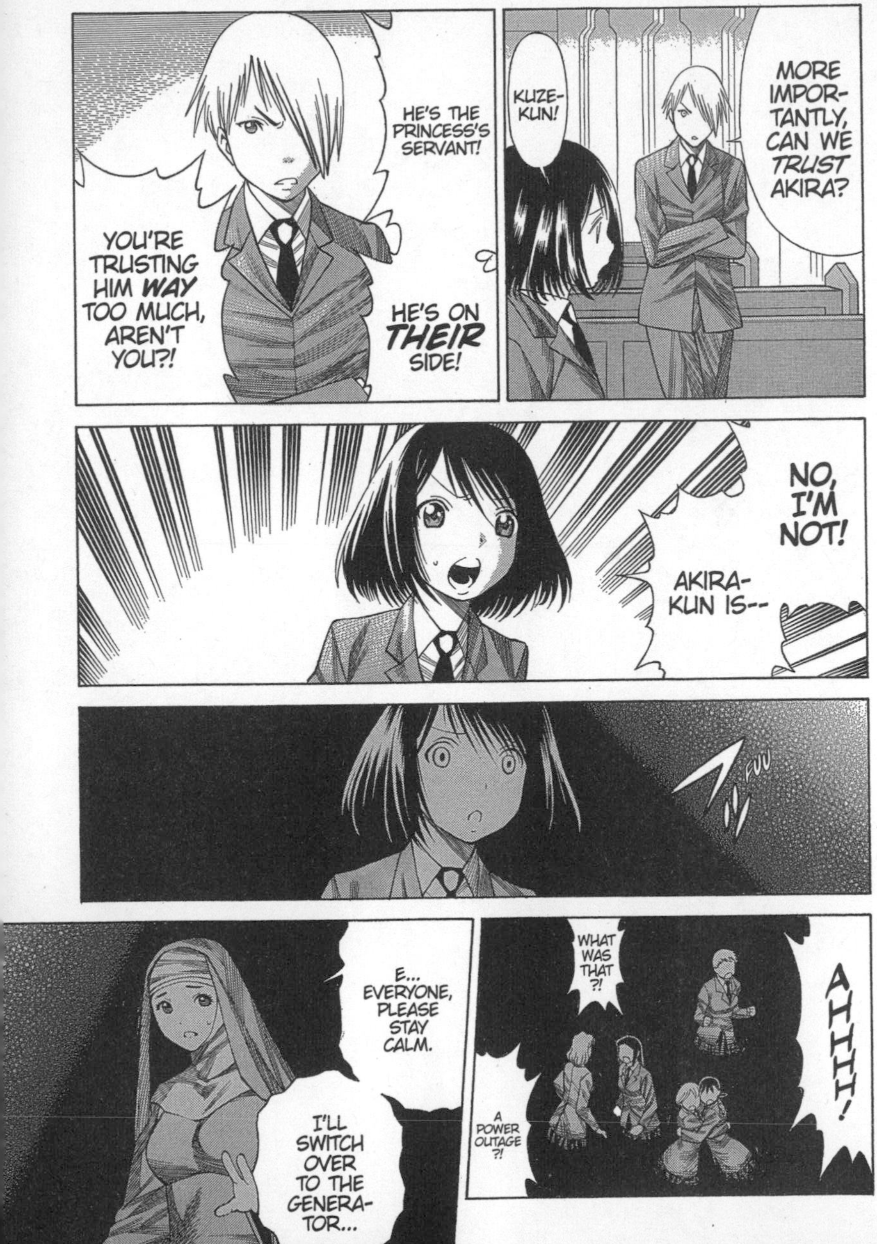
MORE IMPORTANTLY, CAN WE TRUST AKIRA?
KUZE-KUN!
HE'S THE PRINCESS'S SERVANT!
HE'S ON THEIR SIDE!
YOU'RE TRUSTING HIM WAY TOO MUCH, AREN'T YOU?!
NO, I'M NOT!
AKIRA-KUN IS--
FUU
AHHHH!
WHAT WAS THAT?!
A POWER OUTAGE?!
E... EVERYONE, PLEASE STAY CALM.
I'LL SWITCH OVER TO THE GENERATOR...

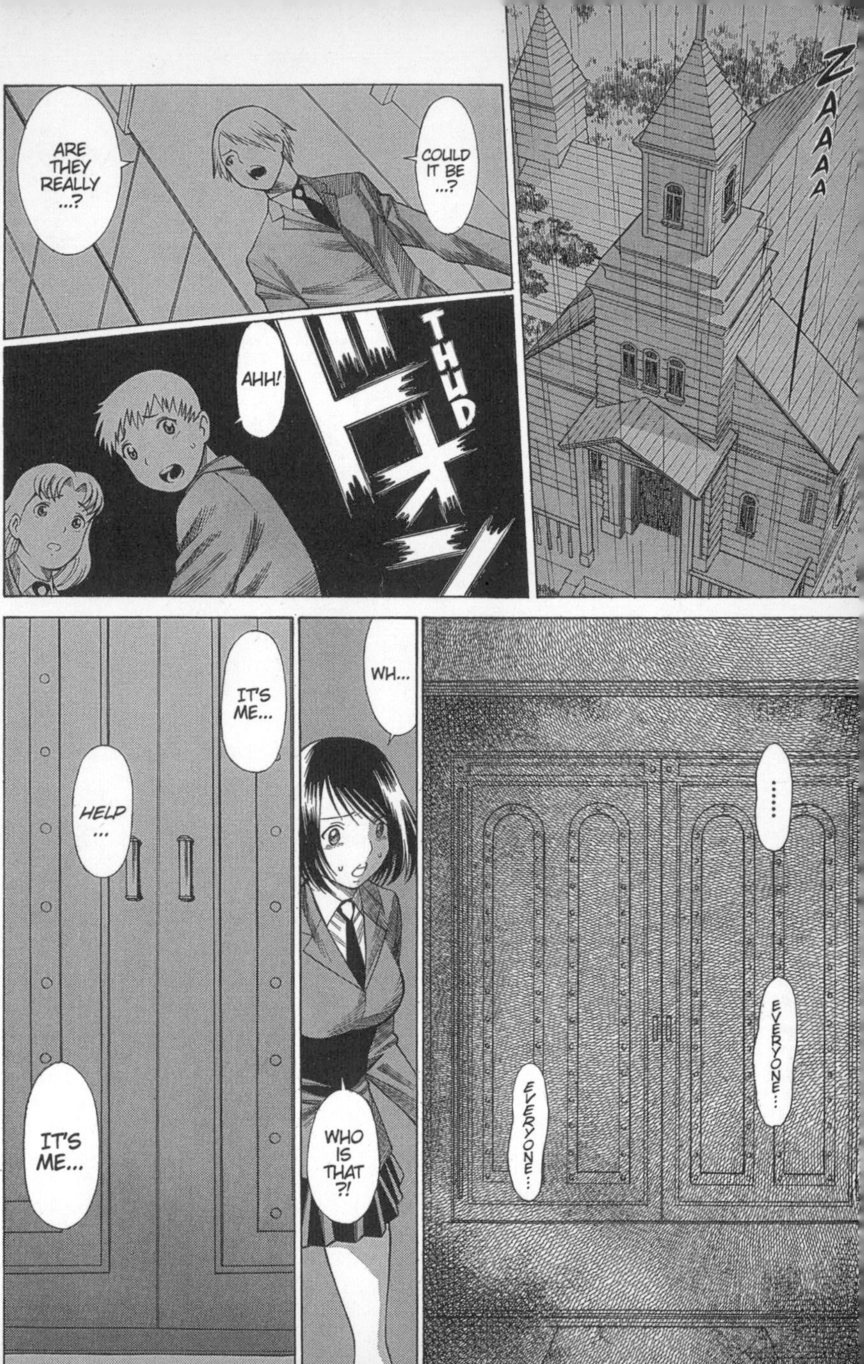
ZAAAA
COULD IT BE ...?
ARE THEY REALLY ...?
THUD
AHH!
......
EVERYONE...
EVERYONE...
WH...
WHO IS THAT ?!
IT'S ME...
HELP ...
IT'S ME...

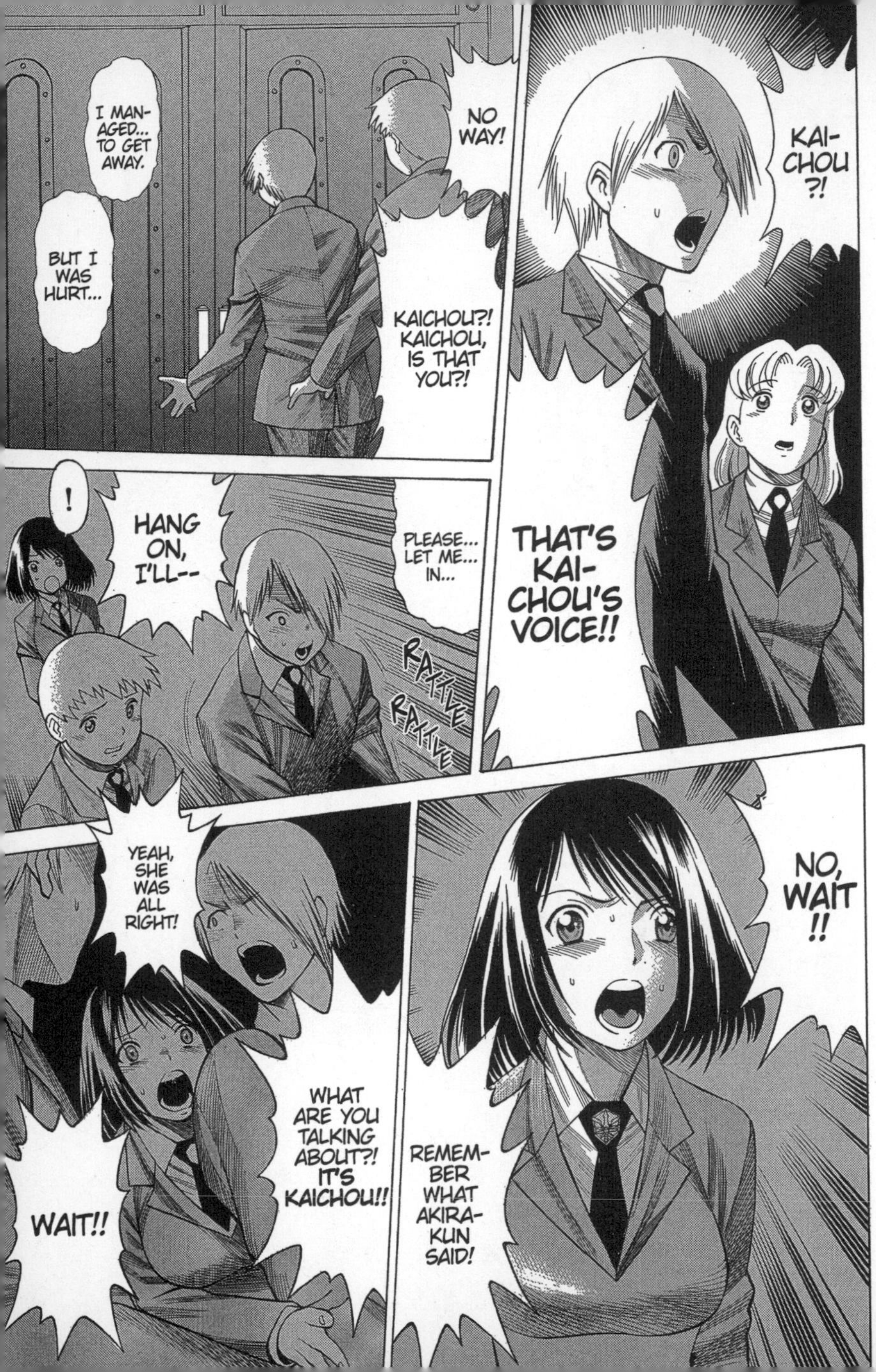
KAI-CHOU?!
THAT'S KAI-CHOU'S VOICE!!
NO WAY!
I MAN-AGED... TO GET AWAY.
BUT I WAS HURT...
KAICHOU?! KAICHOU, IS THAT YOU?!
PLEASE... LET ME... IN...
RATTLE RATTLE
HANG ON, I'LL--
!
NO, WAIT!!
REMEM-BER WHAT AKIRA-KUN SAID!
YEAH, SHE WAS ALL RIGHT!
WHAT ARE YOU TALKING ABOUT?! IT'S KAICHOU!!
WAIT!!

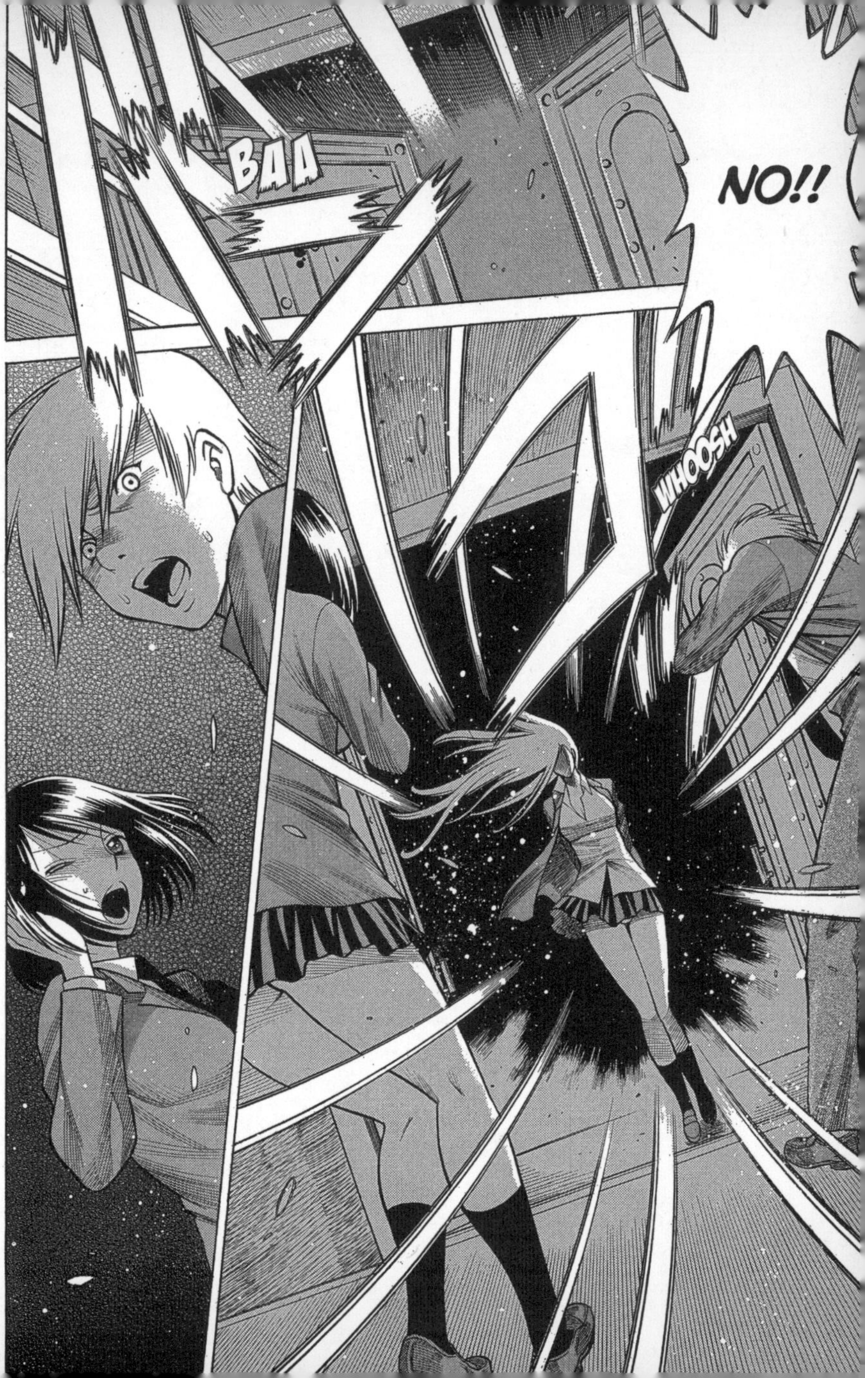
NO!!
BAA
WHOOSH

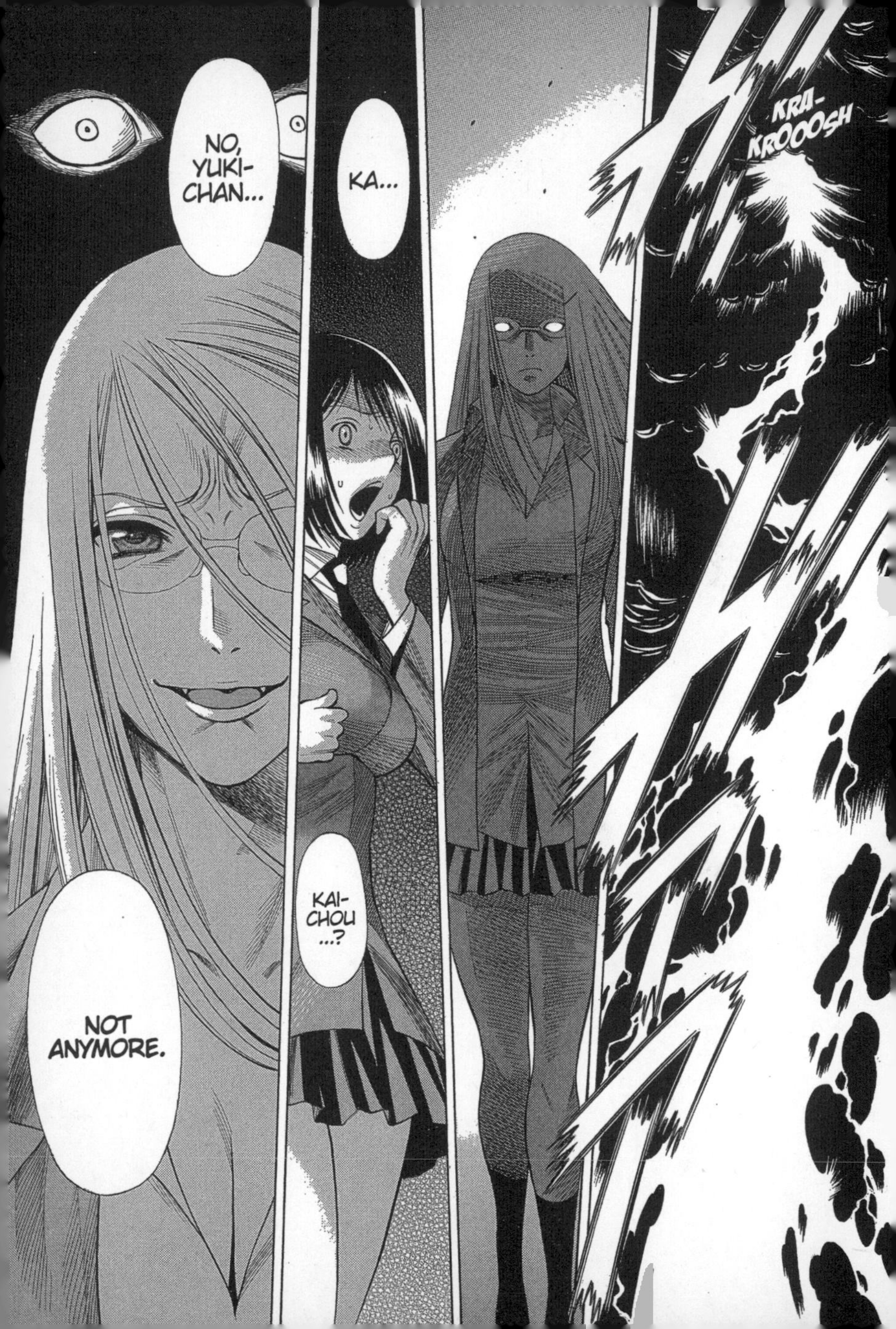
KRA-KROOOSH
KA...
KAI-CHOU ...?
NO, YUKI-CHAN...
NOT ANYMORE.

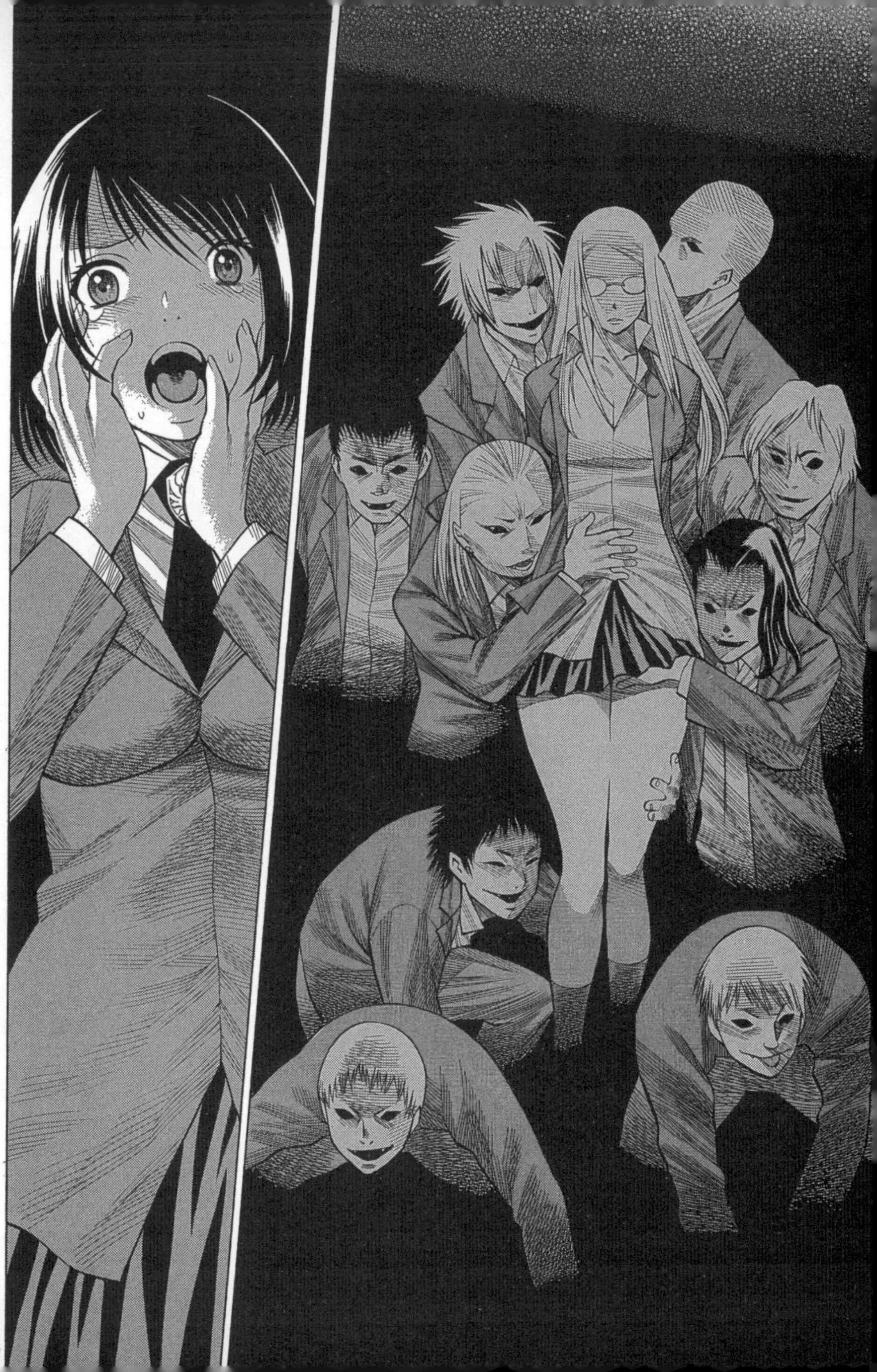

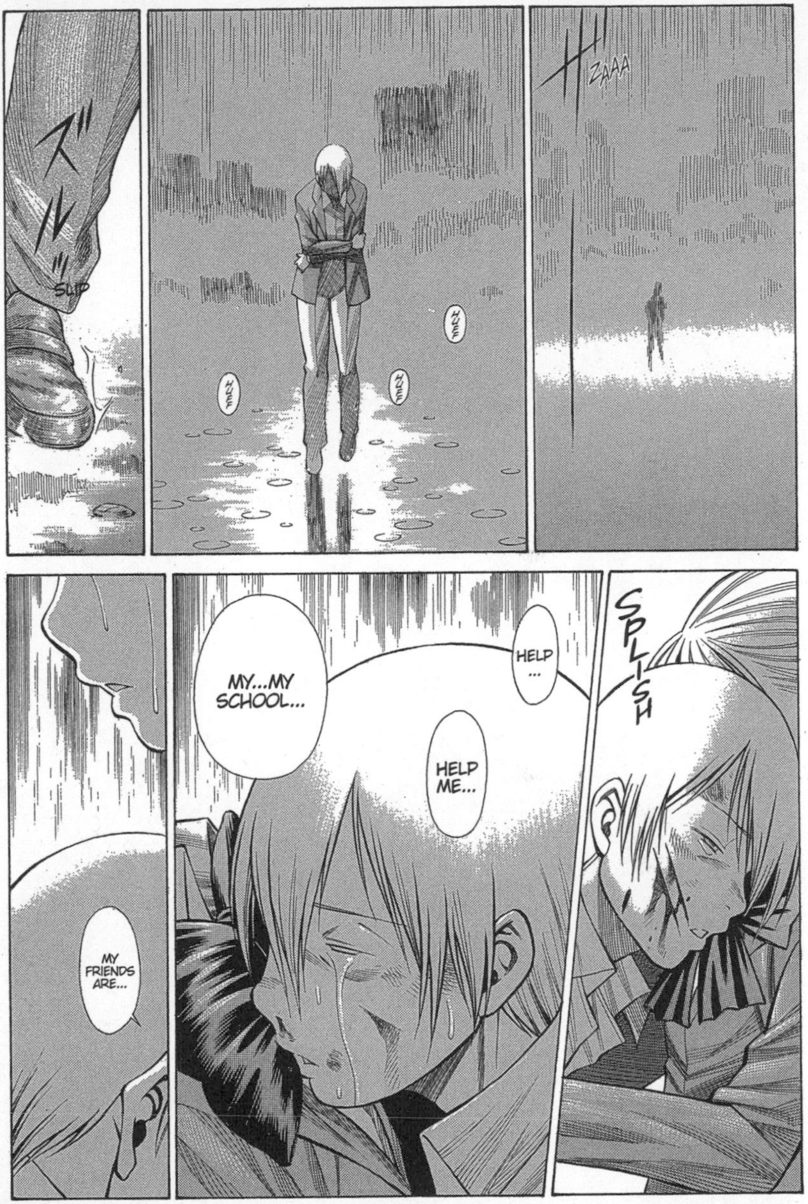
ZAAA
HUFF
HUFF
HUFF
ズルッ
SLIP
SPLISH
HELP ...
MY...MY SCHOOL...
HELP ME...
MY FRIENDS ARE...

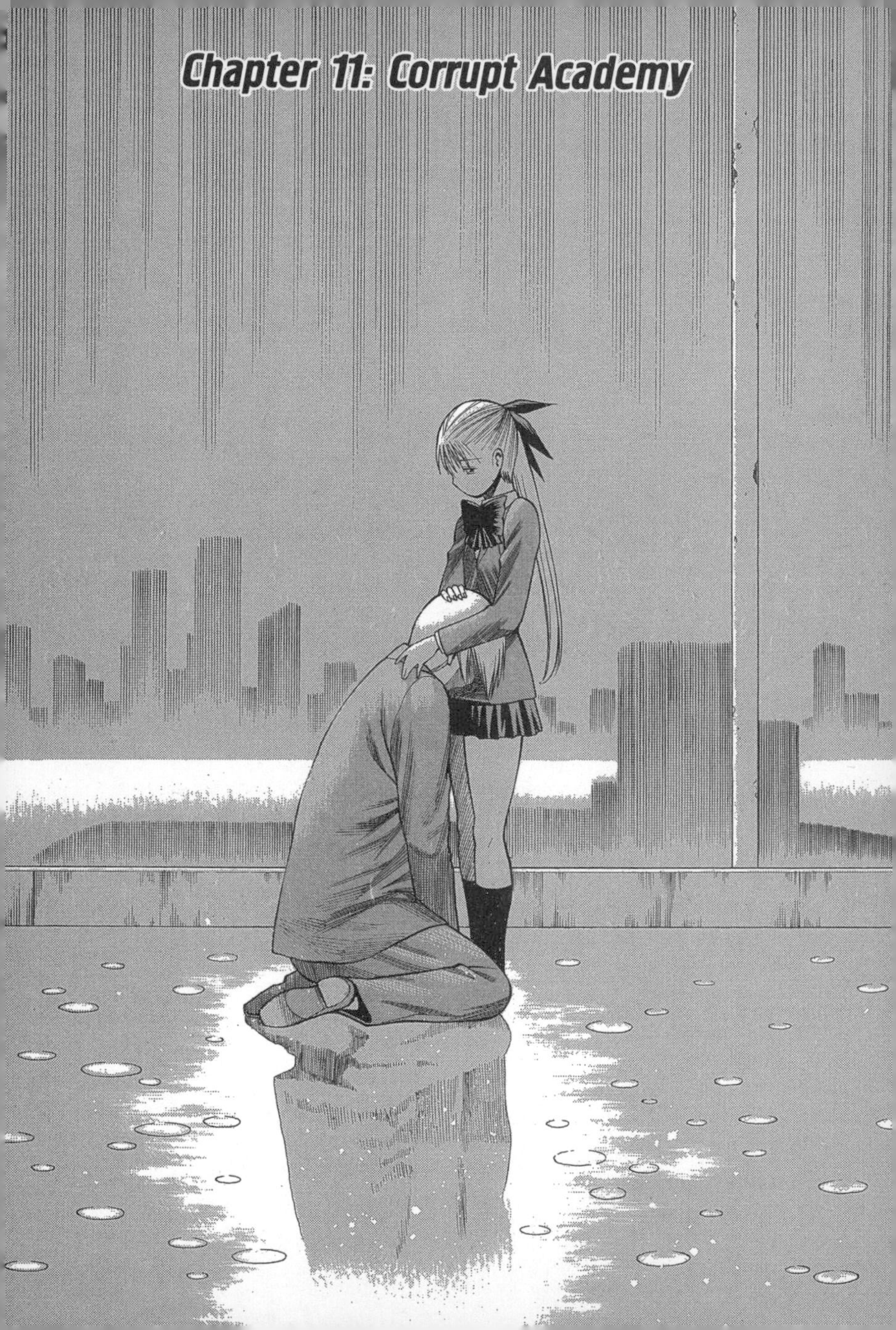
Chapter 11: Corrupt Academy

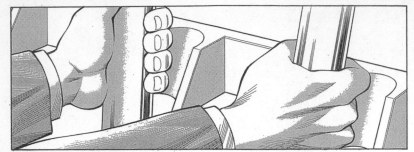

ARE YOU SURE YOU HAVE *TIME* TO BE HANGING AROUND HERE, YOUNG MAN?

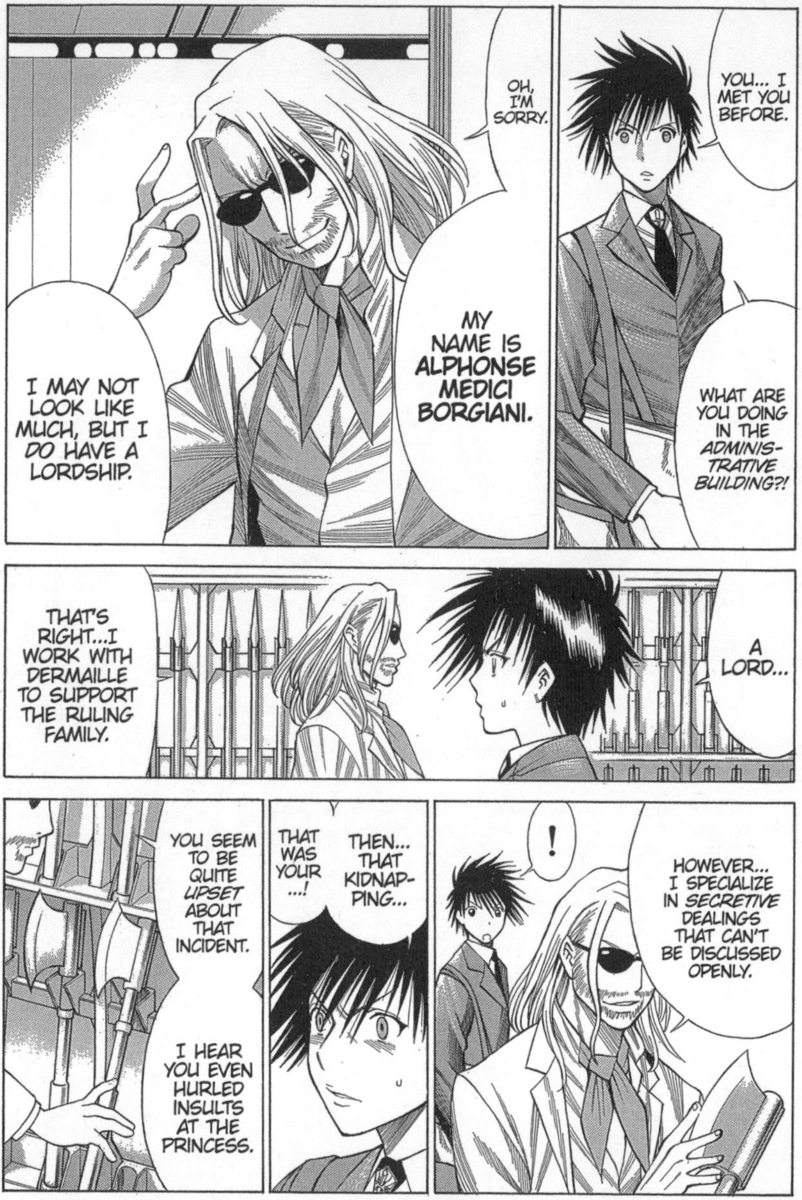
YOU... I MET YOU BEFORE.
WHAT ARE YOU DOING IN THE *ADMINISTRATIVE BUILDING?!*
OH, I'M SORRY.
MY NAME IS **ALPHONSE MEDICI BORGIANI.**
I MAY NOT LOOK LIKE MUCH, BUT I *DO* HAVE A LORDSHIP.
A LORD...
THAT'S RIGHT...I WORK WITH DERMAILLE TO SUPPORT THE RULING FAMILY.
HOWEVER... I SPECIALIZE IN *SECRETIVE* DEALINGS THAT CAN'T BE DISCUSSED OPENLY.
!
THEN... THAT KIDNAPPING...
THAT WAS YOUR ...!
YOU SEEM TO BE QUITE *UPSET* ABOUT THAT INCIDENT.
I HEAR YOU EVEN HURLED INSULTS AT THE PRINCESS.

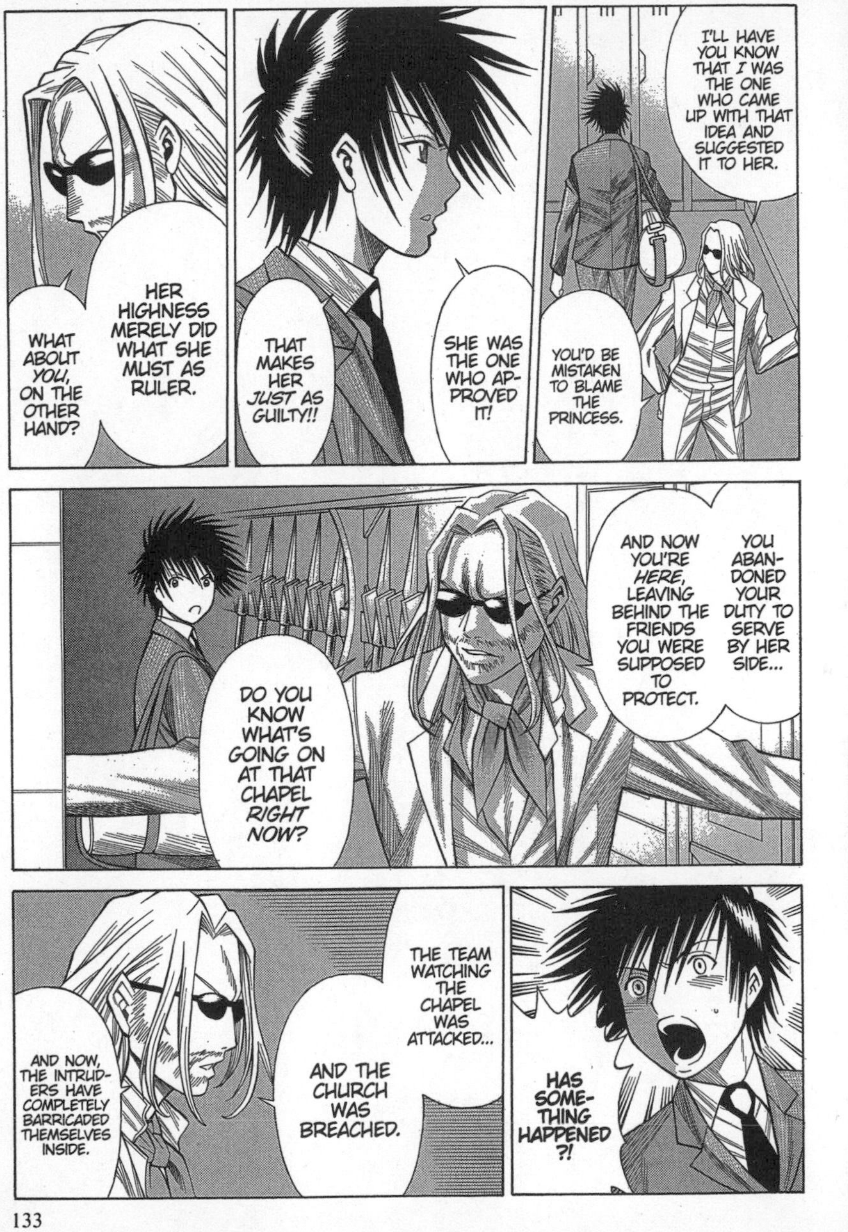
I'LL HAVE YOU KNOW THAT *I* WAS THE ONE WHO CAME UP WITH THAT IDEA AND SUGGESTED IT TO HER.
YOU'D BE MISTAKEN TO BLAME THE PRINCESS.
SHE WAS THE ONE WHO AP-PROVED IT!
THAT MAKES HER *JUST* AS GUILTY!!
HER HIGHNESS MERELY DID WHAT SHE MUST AS RULER.
WHAT ABOUT *YOU*, ON THE OTHER HAND?
YOU ABAN-DONED YOUR DUTY TO SERVE BY HER SIDE...
AND NOW YOU'RE *HERE*, LEAVING BEHIND THE FRIENDS YOU WERE SUPPOSED TO PROTECT.
DO YOU KNOW WHAT'S GOING ON AT THAT CHAPEL *RIGHT NOW*?
HAS SOME-THING HAPPENED ?!
THE TEAM WATCHING THE CHAPEL WAS ATTACKED...
AND THE CHURCH WAS BREACHED.
AND NOW, THE INTRUD-ERS HAVE COMPLETELY BARRICADED THEMSELVES INSIDE.

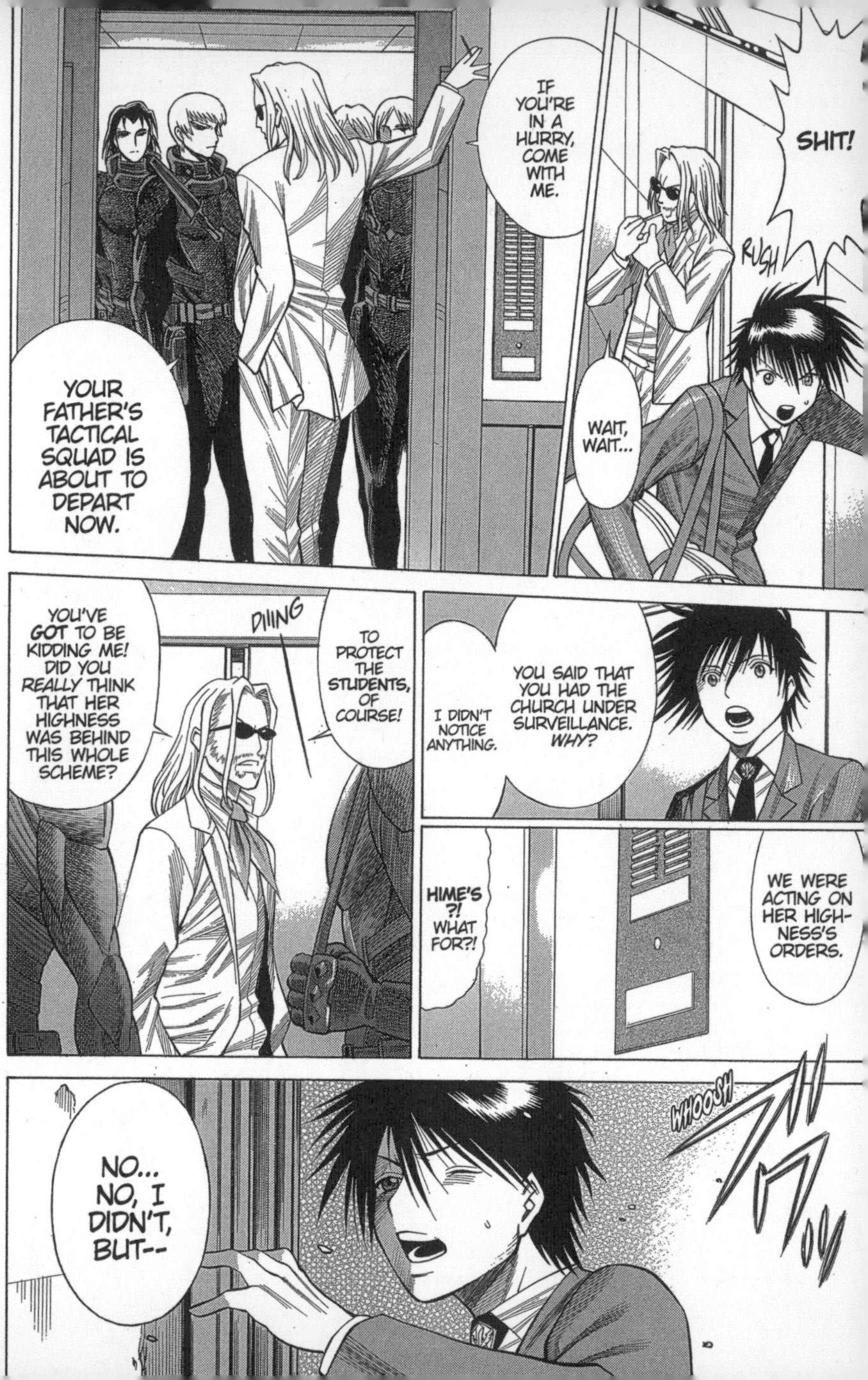
SHIT!
IF YOU'RE IN A HURRY, COME WITH ME.
RUSH
WAIT, WAIT...
YOUR FATHER'S TACTICAL SQUAD IS ABOUT TO DEPART NOW.
YOU SAID THAT YOU HAD THE CHURCH UNDER SURVEILLANCE. *WHY?*
I DIDN'T NOTICE ANYTHING.
WE WERE ACTING ON HER HIGHNESS'S ORDERS.
HIME'S?! WHAT FOR?!
TO PROTECT THE STUDENTS, OF COURSE!
DIIING
YOU'VE **GOT** TO BE KIDDING ME! DID YOU *REALLY* THINK THAT HER HIGHNESS WAS BEHIND THIS WHOLE SCHEME?
WHOOSH
NO... NO, I DIDN'T, BUT--

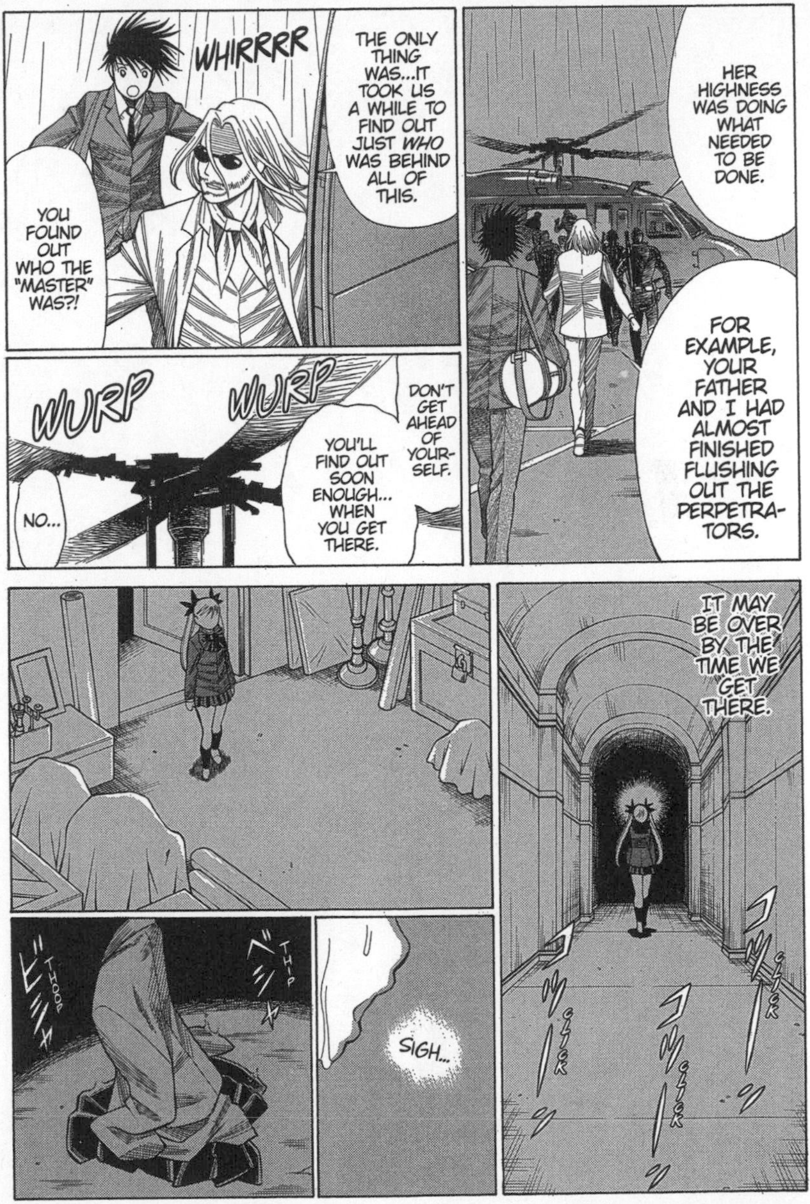
HER HIGHNESS WAS DOING WHAT NEEDED TO BE DONE.
FOR EXAMPLE, YOUR FATHER AND I HAD ALMOST FINISHED FLUSHING OUT THE PERPETRATORS.
THE ONLY THING WAS...IT TOOK US A WHILE TO FIND OUT JUST *WHO* WAS BEHIND ALL OF THIS.
WHIRRRR
YOU FOUND OUT WHO THE "MASTER" WAS?!
DON'T GET AHEAD OF YOURSELF.
YOU'LL FIND OUT SOON ENOUGH... WHEN YOU GET THERE.
WURP
WURP
NO...
IT MAY BE OVER BY THE TIME WE GET THERE.
CLICK
CLICK
CLICK
CLICK
SIGH...
THIP
THOOP

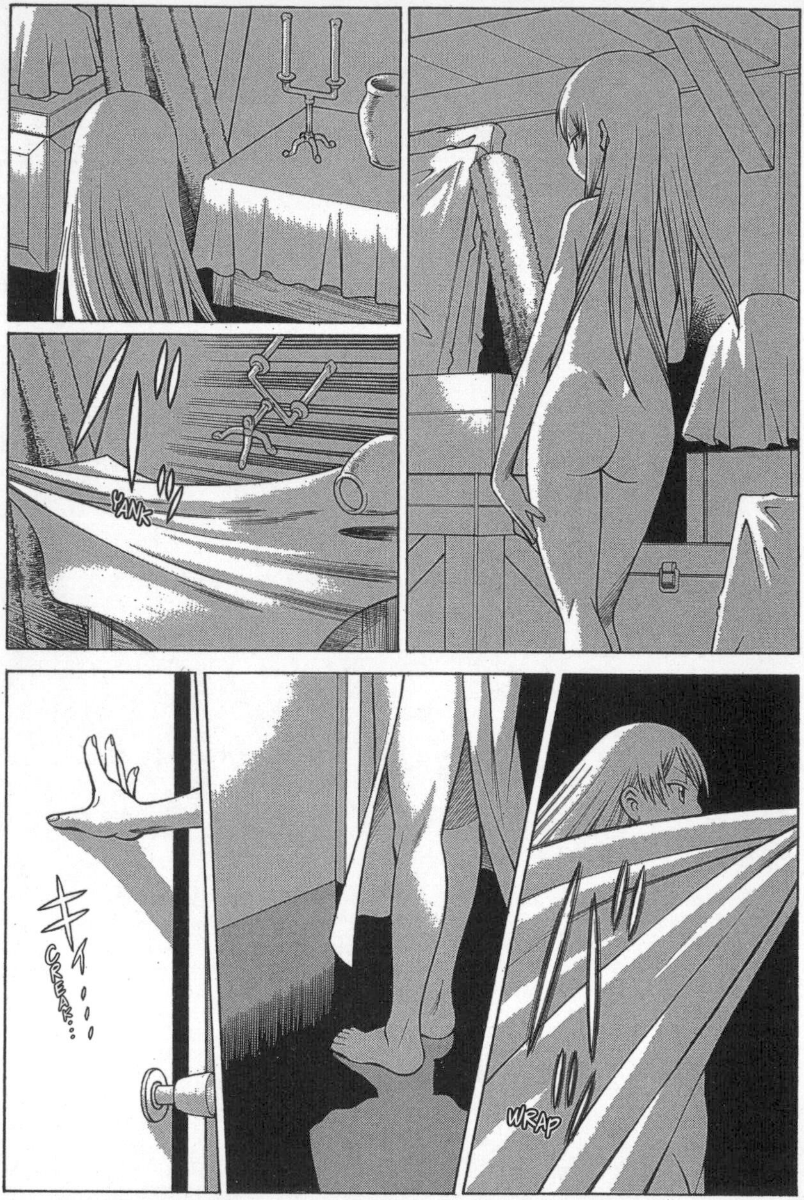
YANK
WRAP
キイ
CREAK...

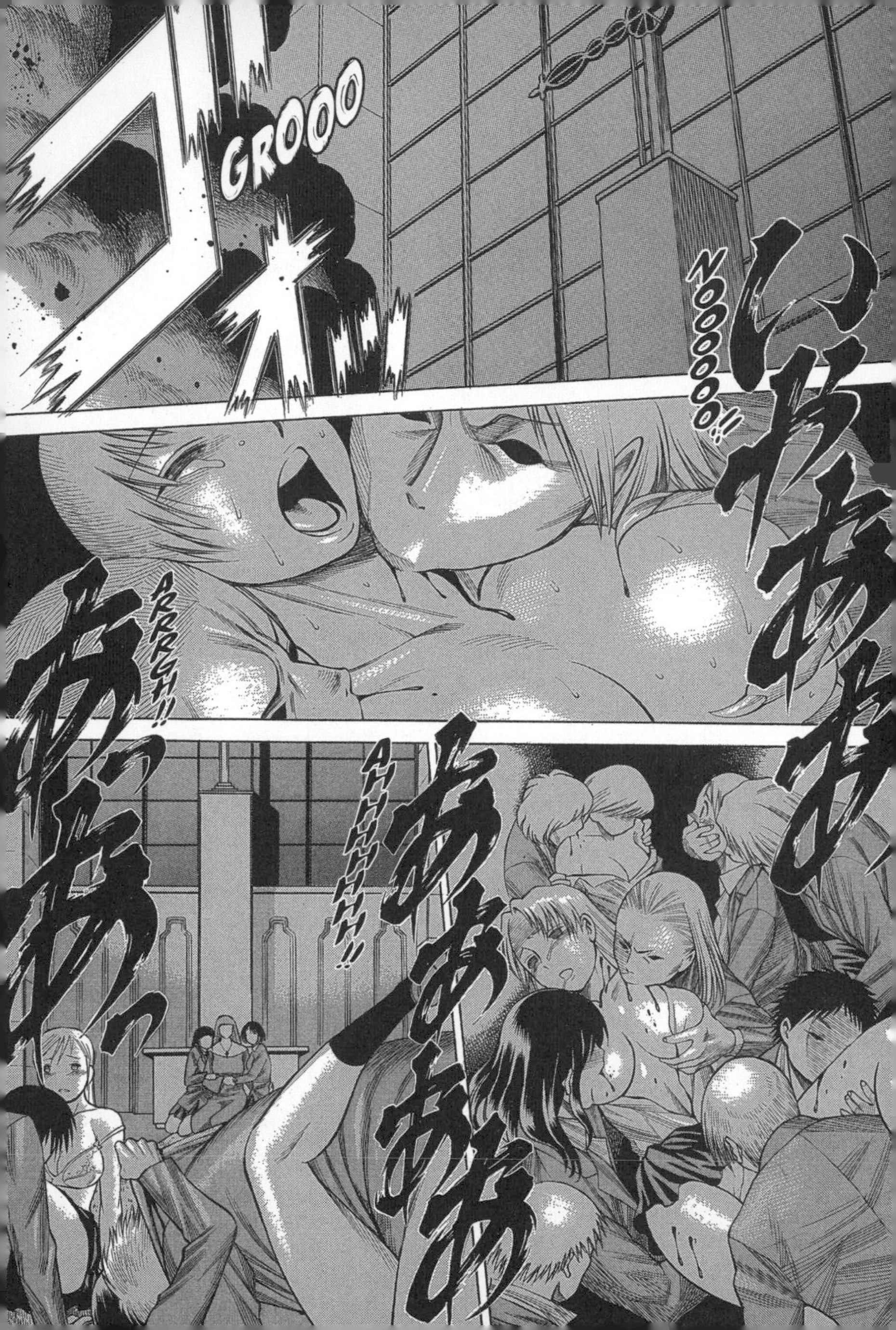
GROOO
NOOOOOOO!!
ARRRGH!!
AHHHHHHHH!!

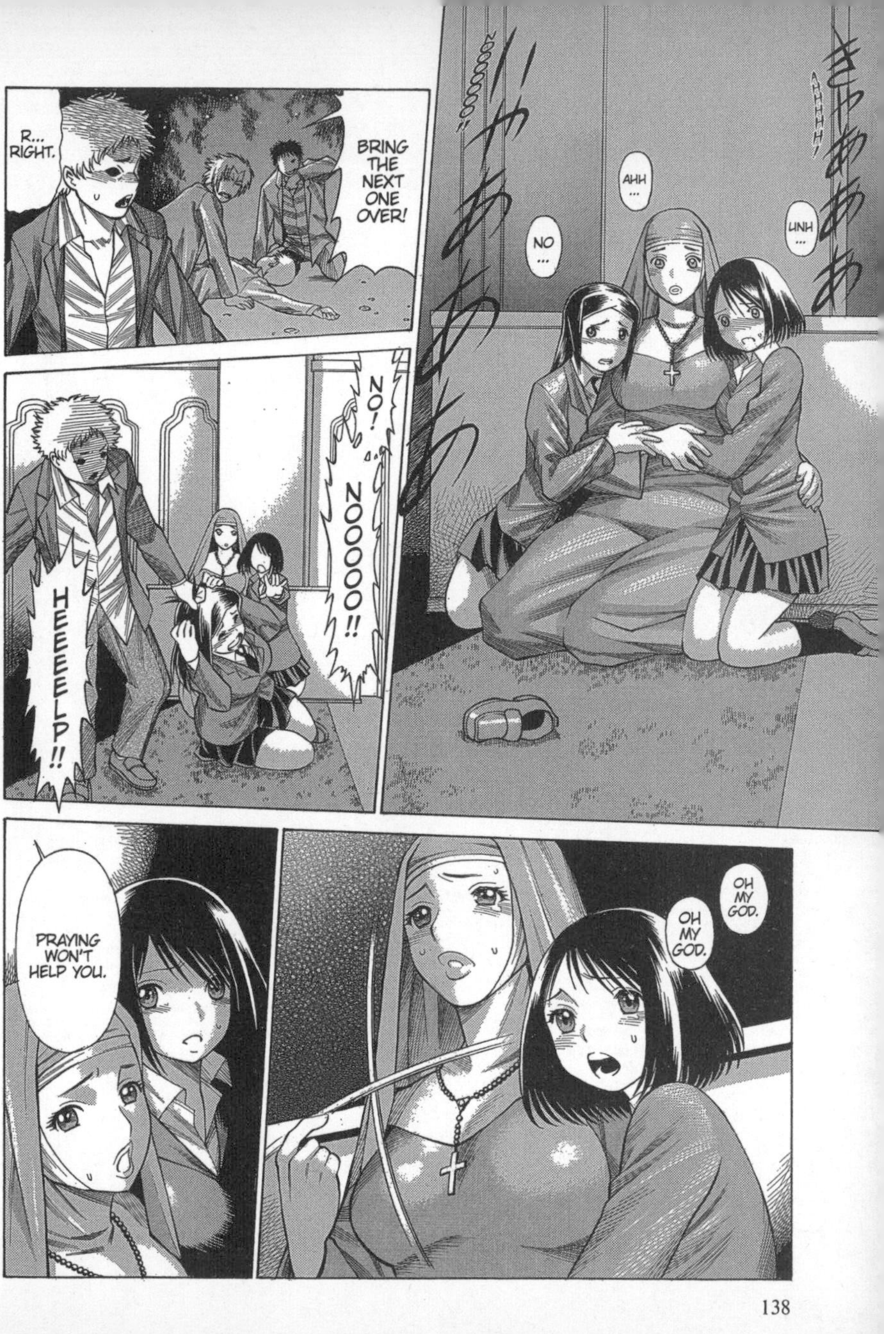
AHHHHH!
UNH ...
AHH ...
NO ...
NOOOOOOO!!
BRING THE NEXT ONE OVER!
R... RIGHT.
NO! NOOOOOO!!
HEEEELP!!
OH MY GOD.
OH MY GOD.
PRAYING WON'T HELP YOU.

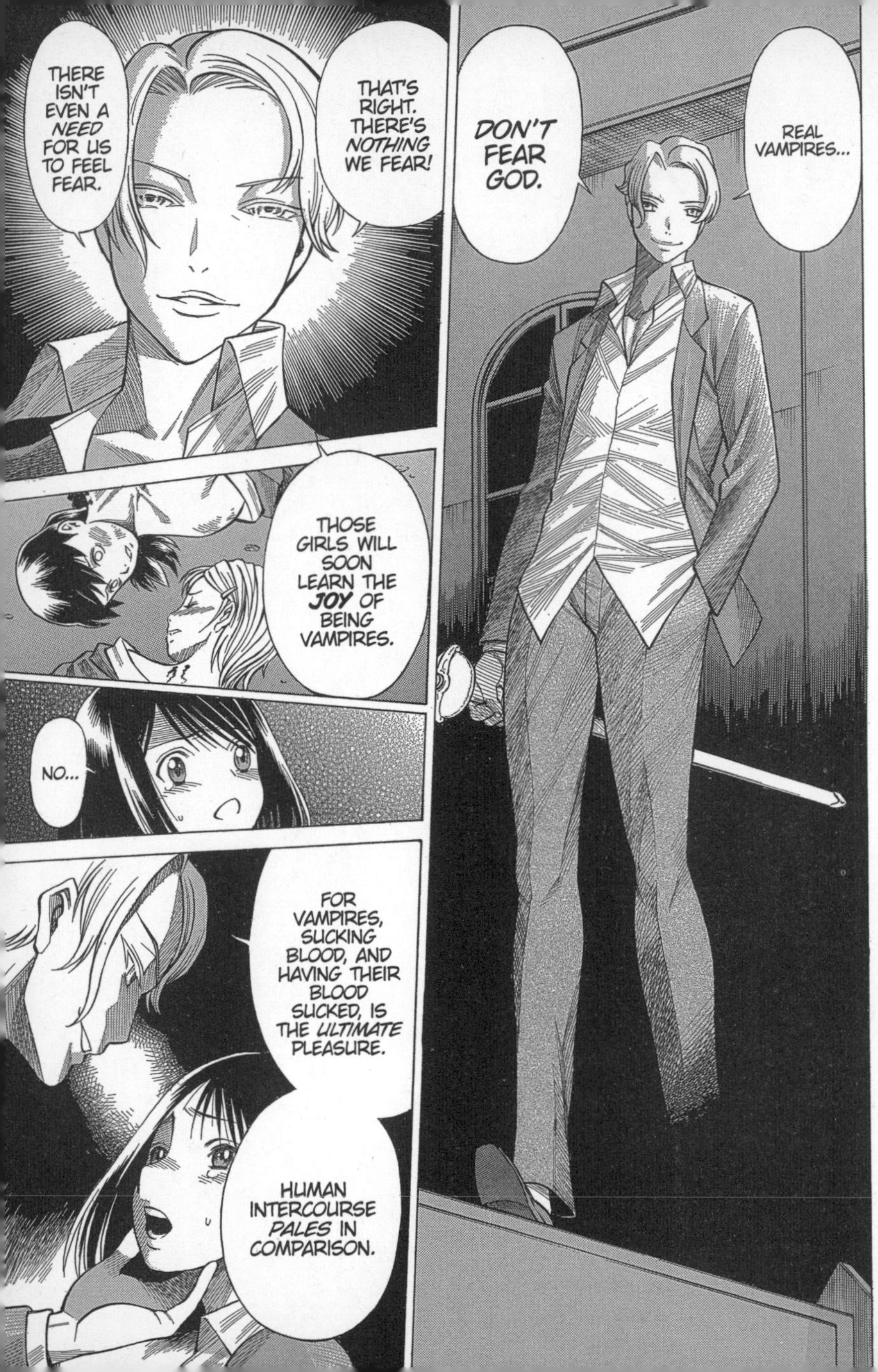
REAL VAMPIRES...
DON'T FEAR GOD.
THAT'S RIGHT. THERE'S *NOTHING* WE FEAR!
THERE ISN'T EVEN A *NEED* FOR US TO FEEL FEAR.
THOSE GIRLS WILL SOON LEARN THE **JOY** OF BEING VAMPIRES.
NO...
FOR VAMPIRES, SUCKING BLOOD, AND HAVING THEIR BLOOD SUCKED, IS THE *ULTIMATE* PLEASURE.
HUMAN INTERCOURSE *PALES* IN COMPARISON.

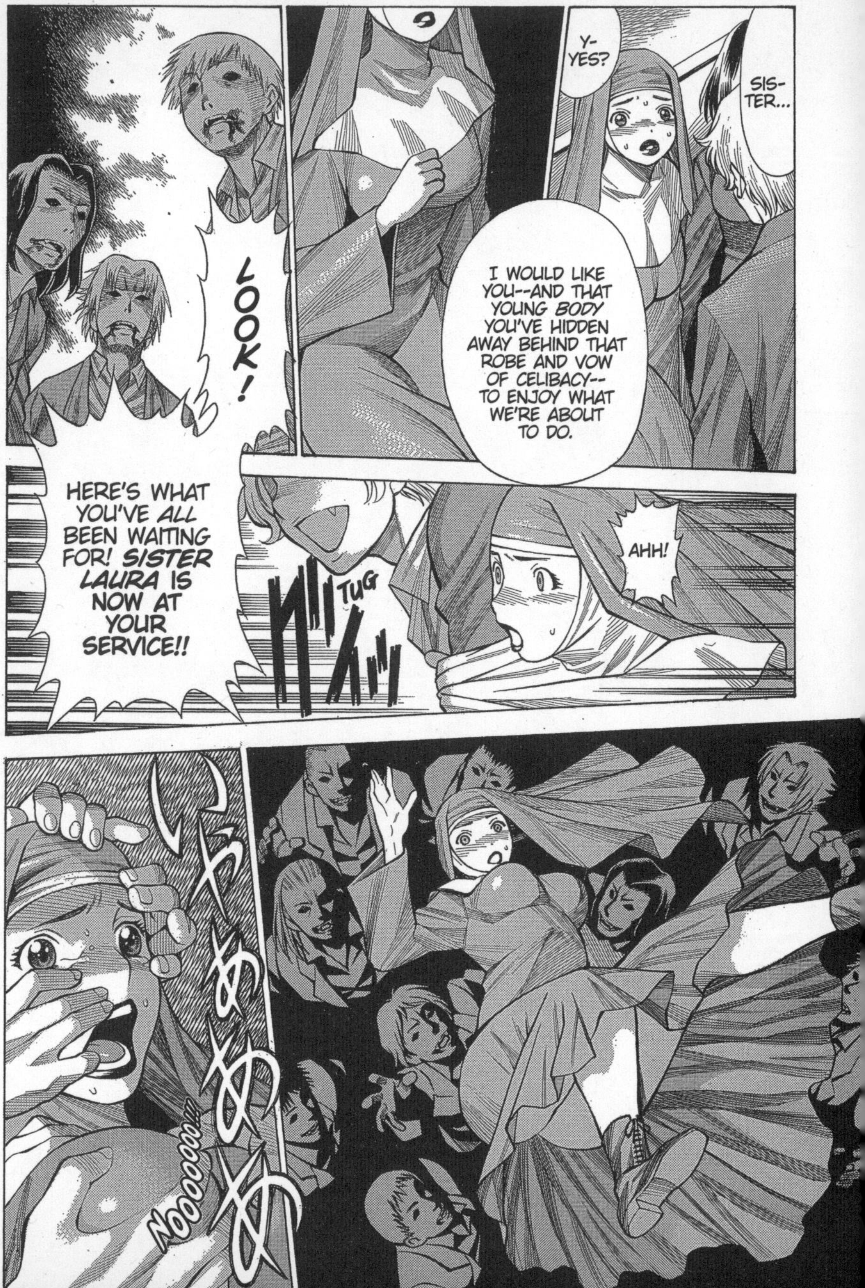
SIS-
TER...
Y-
YES?
I WOULD LIKE YOU--AND THAT YOUNG *BODY* YOU'VE HIDDEN AWAY BEHIND THAT ROBE AND VOW OF CELIBACY--TO ENJOY WHAT WE'RE ABOUT TO DO.
LOOK!
AHH!
TUG
HERE'S WHAT YOU'VE *ALL* BEEN WAITING FOR! *SISTER LAURA* IS NOW AT YOUR SERVICE!!
NOOOOOOO!!

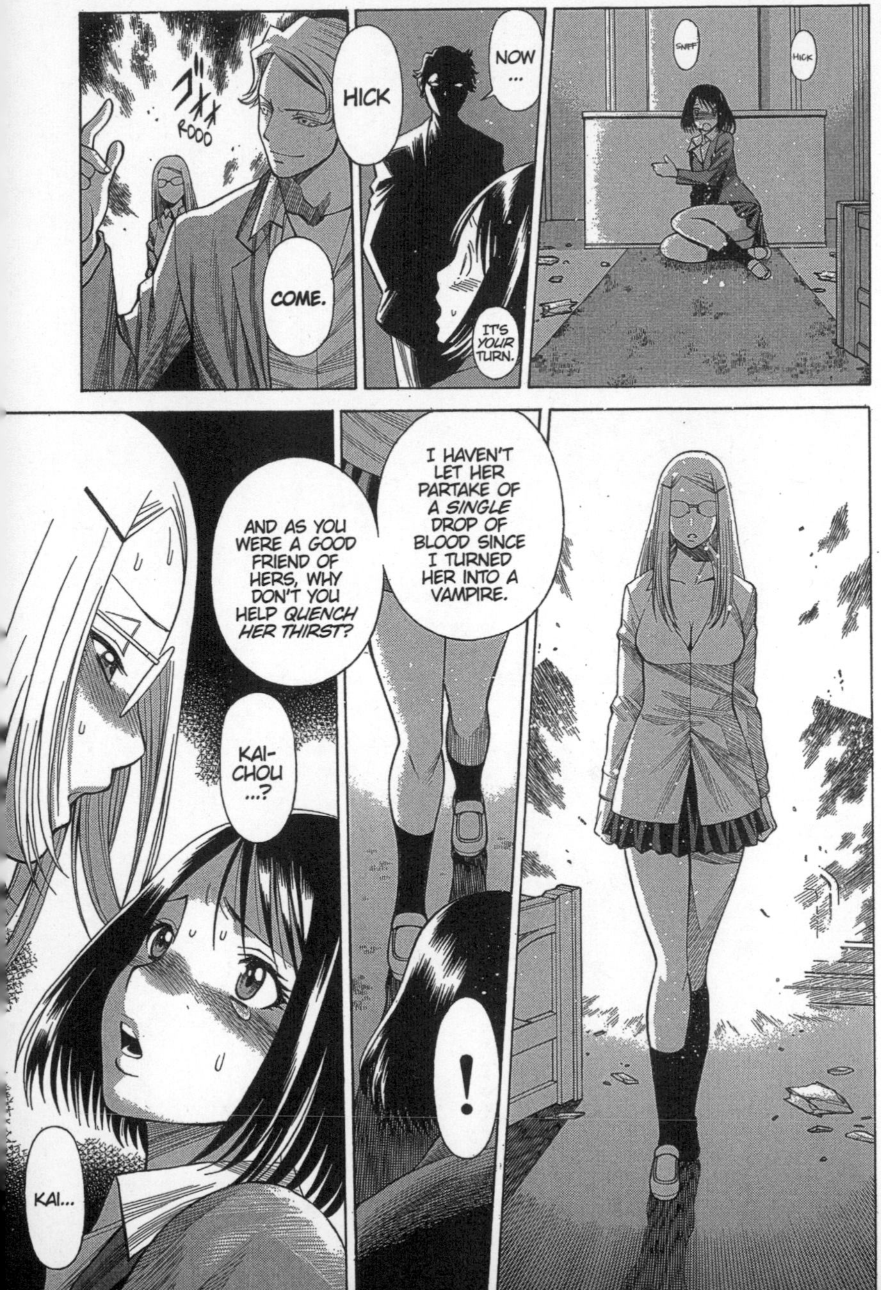
SNIFF
HICK
NOW...
HICK
IT'S YOUR TURN.
ゴオオ
ROOO
COME.
I HAVEN'T LET HER PARTAKE OF A *SINGLE* DROP OF BLOOD SINCE I TURNED HER INTO A VAMPIRE.
AND AS YOU WERE A GOOD FRIEND OF HERS, WHY DON'T YOU HELP *QUENCH HER THIRST*?
!
KAI-CHOU...?
KAI...

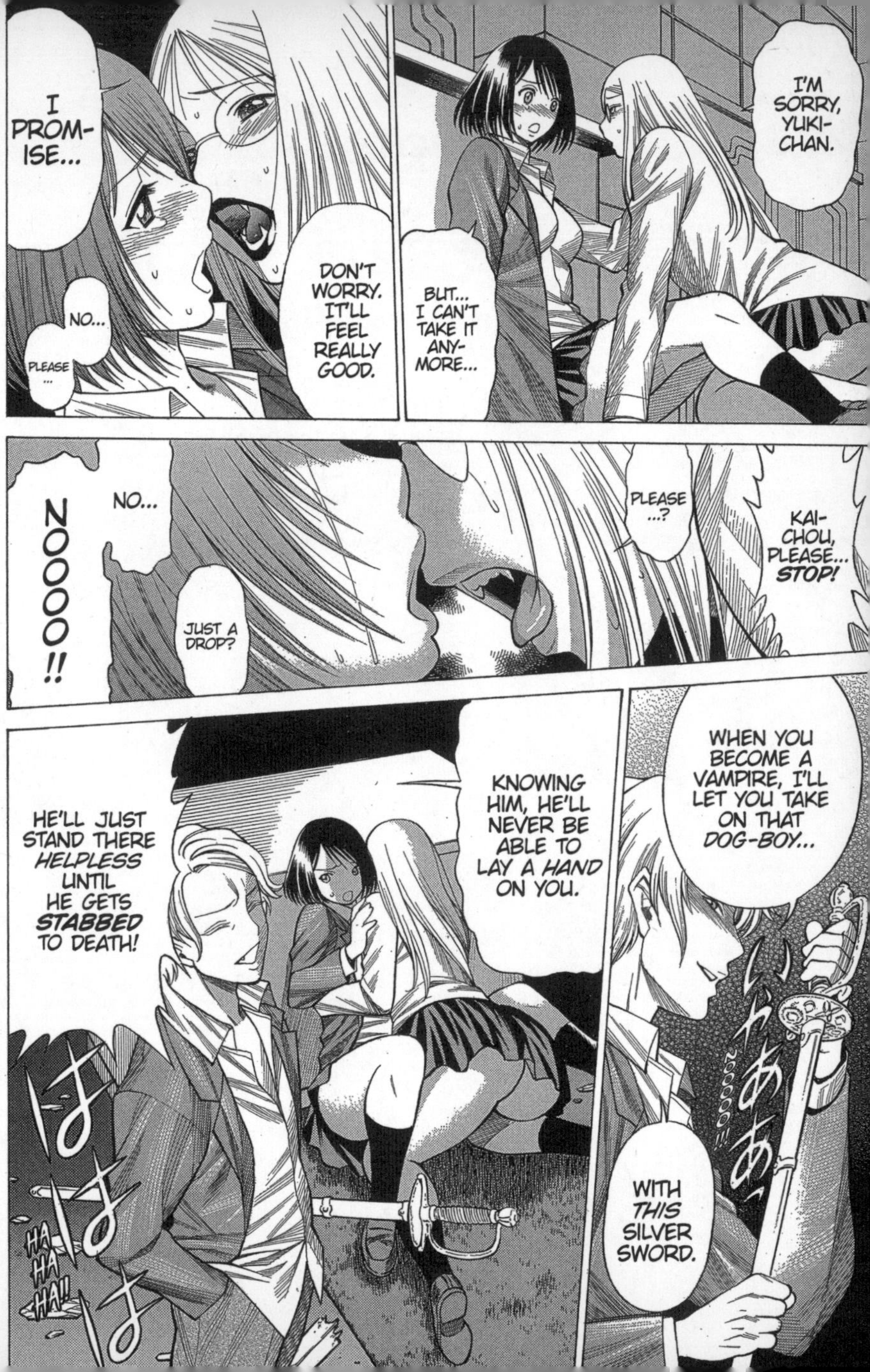
I'M SORRY, YUKI-CHAN.
BUT... I CAN'T TAKE IT ANYMORE...
DON'T WORRY. IT'LL FEEL REALLY GOOD.
I PROMISE...
NO...
PLEASE ...
KAI-CHOU, PLEASE... *STOP!*
PLEASE ...?
JUST A DROP?
NO...
NOOOOO!!
WHEN YOU BECOME A VAMPIRE, I'LL LET YOU TAKE ON THAT *DOG-BOY*...
NOOOOO!!
WITH *THIS* SILVER SWORD.
KNOWING HIM, HE'LL NEVER BE ABLE TO LAY A *HAND* ON YOU.
HE'LL JUST STAND THERE *HELPLESS* UNTIL HE GETS ***STABBED*** TO DEATH!
HA HA HA!!

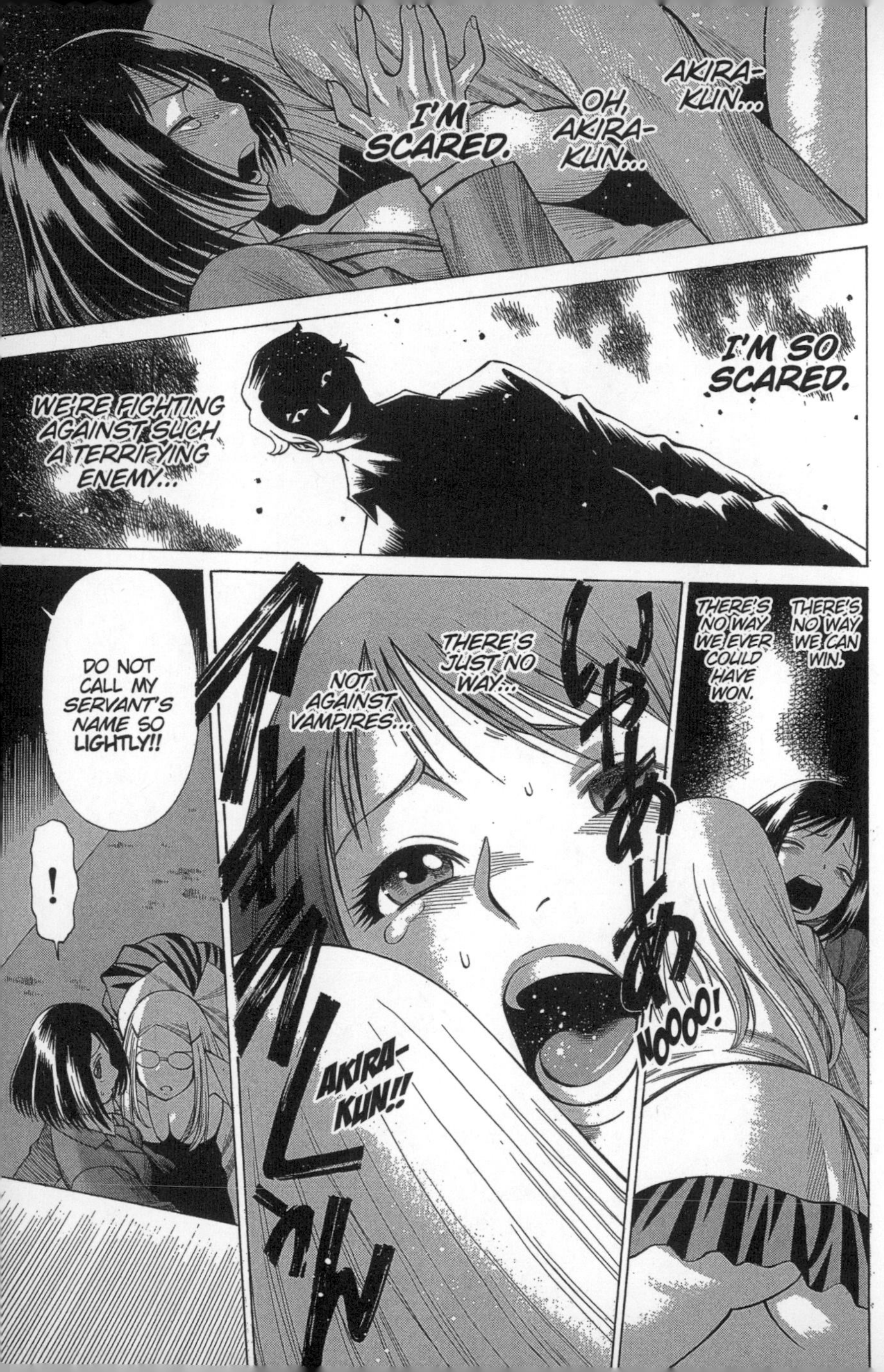
AKIRA-KUN...
OH, AKIRA-KUN...
I'M SCARED.
I'M SO SCARED.
WE'RE FIGHTING AGAINST SUCH A TERRIFYING ENEMY...
THERE'S NO WAY WE CAN WIN.
THERE'S NO WAY WE EVER COULD HAVE WON.
THERE'S JUST NO WAY...
NOT AGAINST VAMPIRES...
NOOOO!
AKIRA-KUN!!
DO NOT CALL MY SERVANT'S NAME SO LIGHTLY!!
!

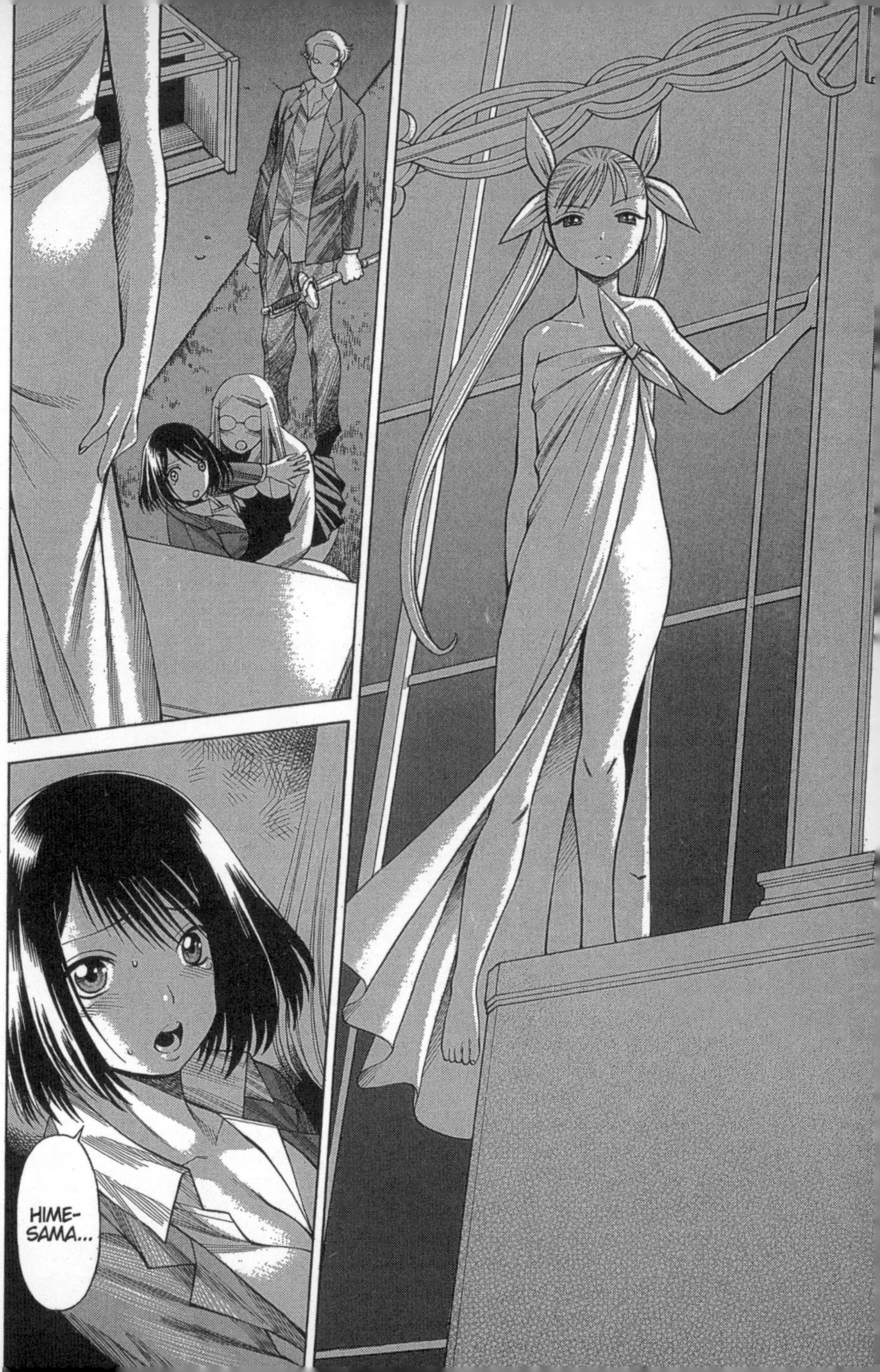
HIME-SAMA...

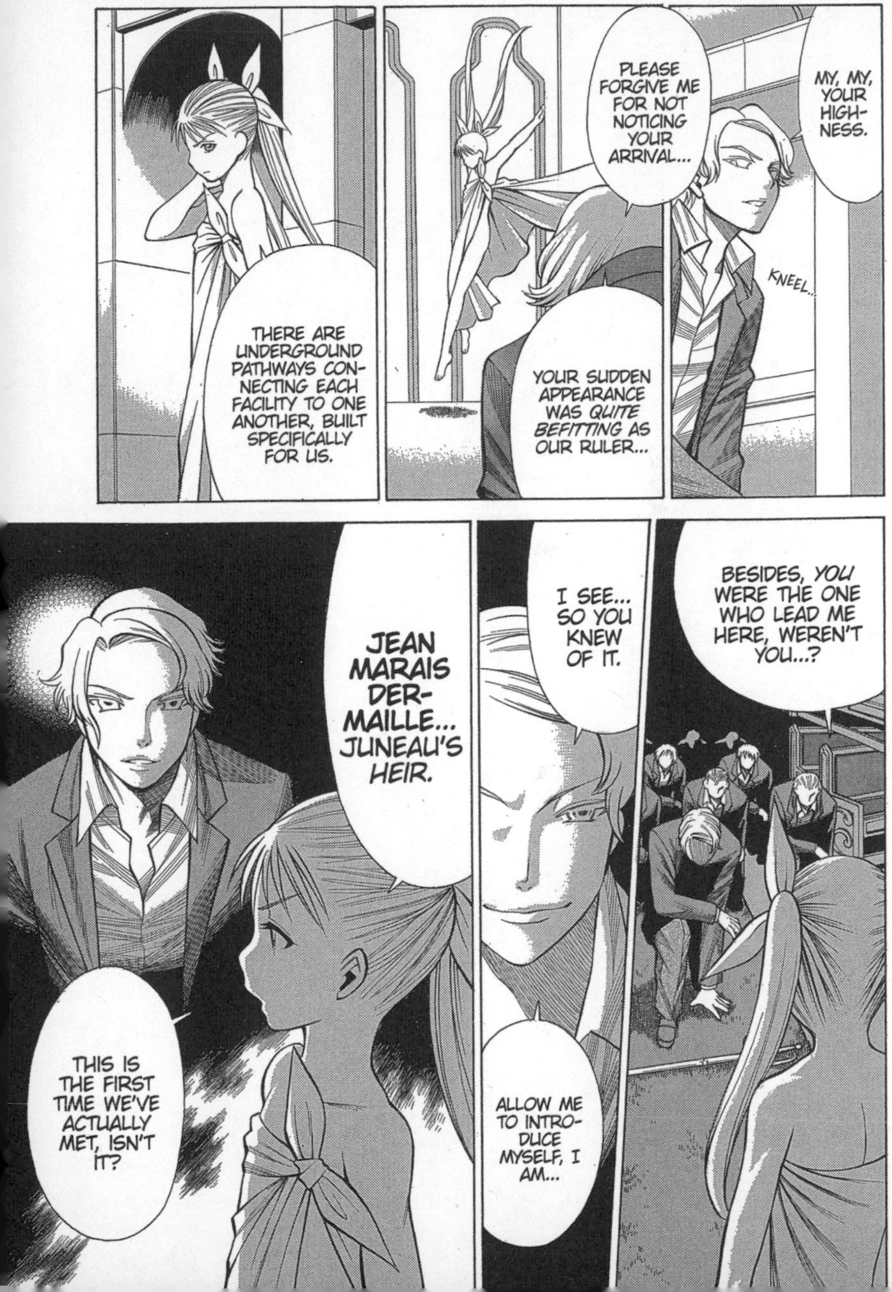
MY, MY, YOUR HIGH-NESS.
PLEASE FORGIVE ME FOR NOT NOTICING YOUR ARRIVAL...
KNEEL...
YOUR SUDDEN APPEARANCE WAS *QUITE BEFITTING* AS OUR RULER...
THERE ARE UNDERGROUND PATHWAYS CON-NECTING EACH FACILITY TO ONE ANOTHER, BUILT SPECIFICALLY FOR US.
BESIDES, *YOU* WERE THE ONE WHO LEAD ME HERE, WEREN'T YOU...?
I SEE... SO YOU KNEW OF IT.
ALLOW ME TO INTRO-DUCE MYSELF, I AM...
JEAN MARAIS DER-MAILLE... JUNEAU'S HEIR.
THIS IS THE FIRST TIME WE'VE ACTUALLY MET, ISN'T IT?

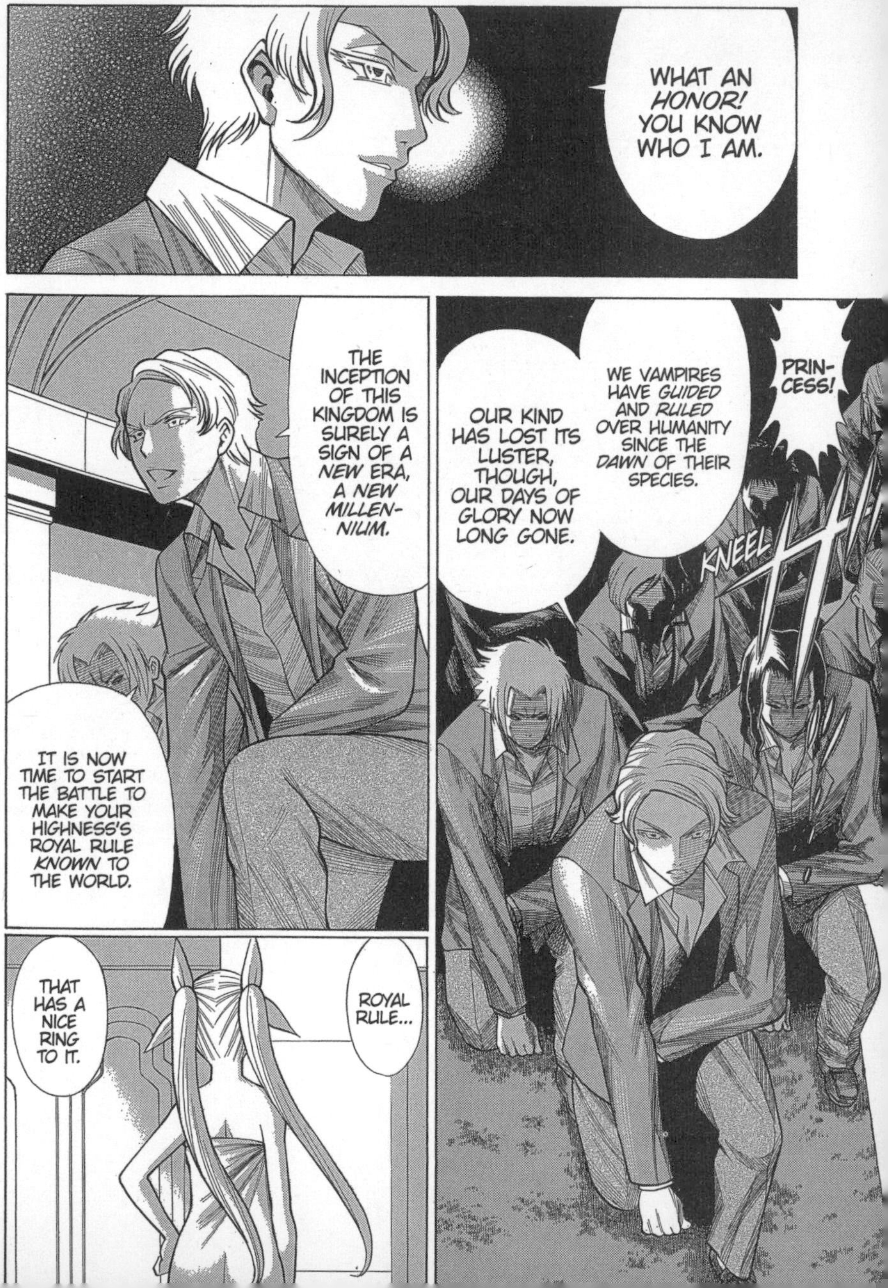
WHAT AN *HONOR!* YOU KNOW WHO I AM.
PRIN-CESS!
KNEEL
WE VAMPIRES HAVE *GUIDED* AND *RULED* OVER HUMANITY SINCE THE *DAWN* OF THEIR SPECIES.
OUR KIND HAS LOST ITS LUSTER, THOUGH, OUR DAYS OF GLORY NOW LONG GONE.
THE INCEPTION OF THIS KINGDOM IS SURELY A SIGN OF A *NEW* ERA, A *NEW MILLEN-NIUM.*
IT IS NOW TIME TO START THE BATTLE TO MAKE YOUR HIGHNESS'S ROYAL RULE *KNOWN* TO THE WORLD.
ROYAL RULE...
THAT HAS A NICE RING TO IT.

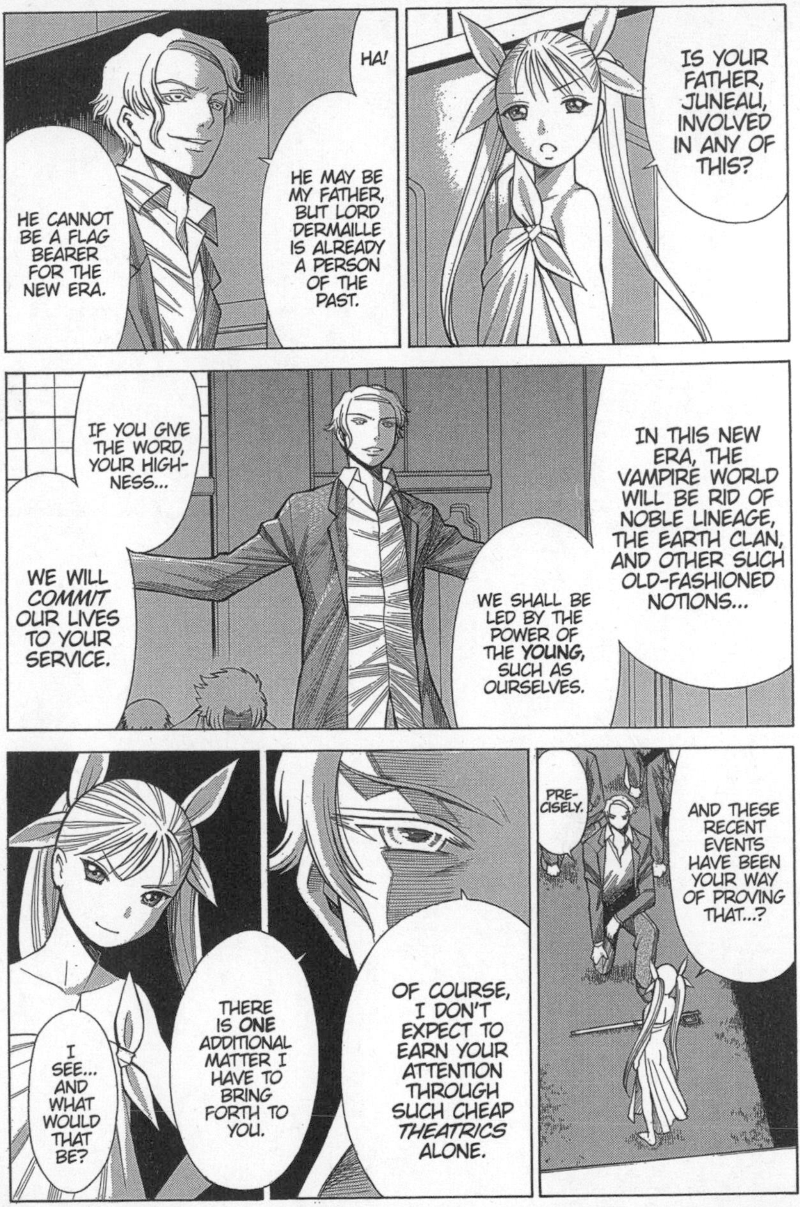
IS YOUR FATHER, JUNEAU, INVOLVED IN ANY OF THIS?
HA!
HE MAY BE MY FATHER, BUT LORD DERMAILLE IS ALREADY A PERSON OF THE PAST.
HE CANNOT BE A FLAG BEARER FOR THE NEW ERA.
IN THIS NEW ERA, THE VAMPIRE WORLD WILL BE RID OF NOBLE LINEAGE, THE EARTH CLAN, AND OTHER SUCH OLD-FASHIONED NOTIONS...
WE SHALL BE LED BY THE POWER OF THE **YOUNG**, SUCH AS OURSELVES.
IF YOU GIVE THE WORD, YOUR HIGHNESS...
WE WILL *COMMIT* OUR LIVES TO YOUR SERVICE.
AND THESE RECENT EVENTS HAVE BEEN YOUR WAY OF PROVING THAT...?
PRECISELY.
OF COURSE, I DON'T EXPECT TO EARN YOUR ATTENTION THROUGH SUCH CHEAP *THEATRICS* ALONE.
THERE IS **ONE** ADDITIONAL MATTER I HAVE TO BRING FORTH TO YOU.
I SEE... AND WHAT WOULD THAT BE?

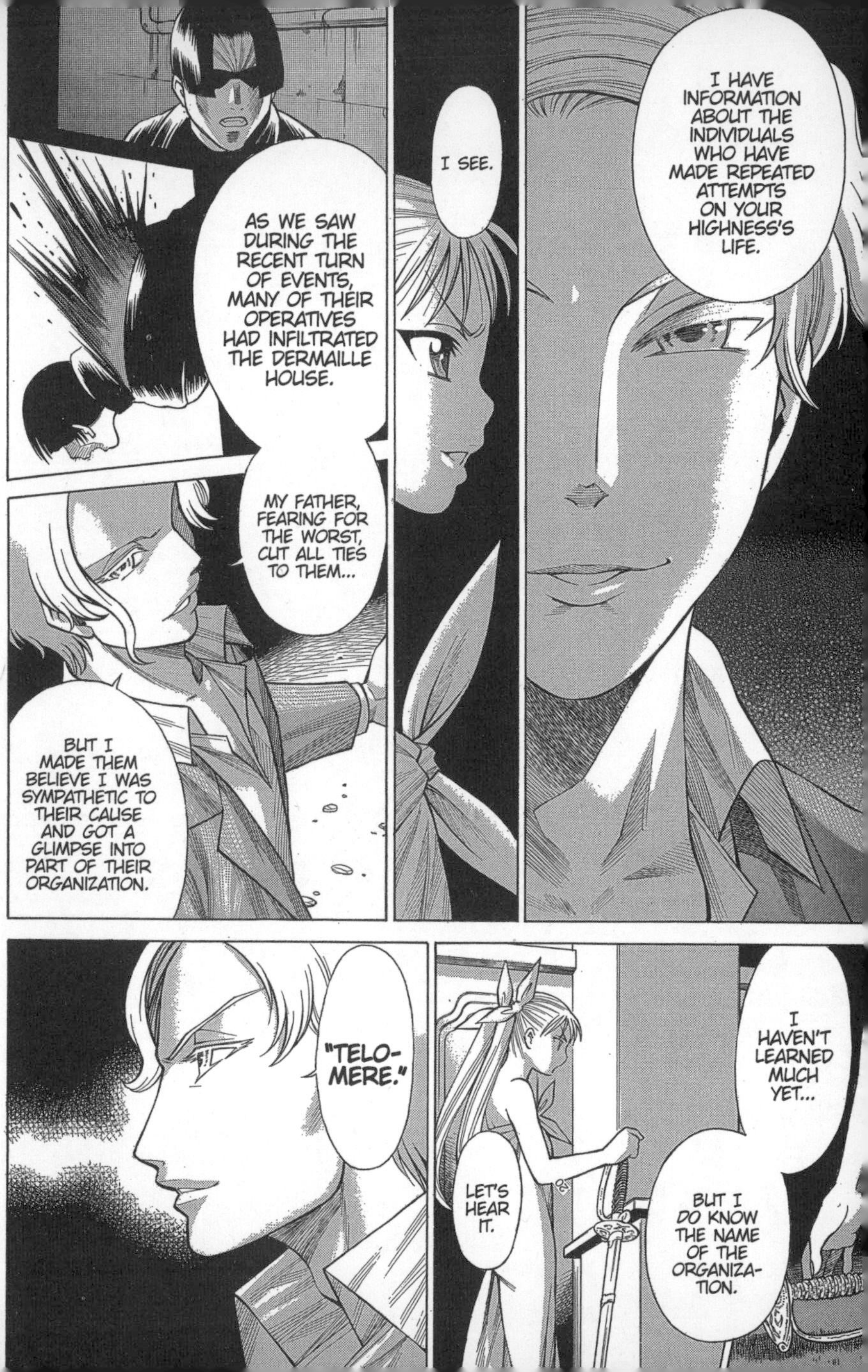
I HAVE INFORMATION ABOUT THE INDIVIDUALS WHO HAVE MADE REPEATED ATTEMPTS ON YOUR HIGHNESS'S LIFE.
I SEE.
AS WE SAW DURING THE RECENT TURN OF EVENTS, MANY OF THEIR OPERATIVES HAD INFILTRATED THE DERMAILLE HOUSE.
MY FATHER, FEARING FOR THE WORST, CUT ALL TIES TO THEM...
BUT I MADE THEM BELIEVE I WAS SYMPATHETIC TO THEIR CAUSE AND GOT A GLIMPSE INTO PART OF THEIR ORGANIZATION.
I HAVEN'T LEARNED MUCH YET...
BUT I DO KNOW THE NAME OF THE ORGANIZATION.
LET'S HEAR IT.
"TELOMERE."

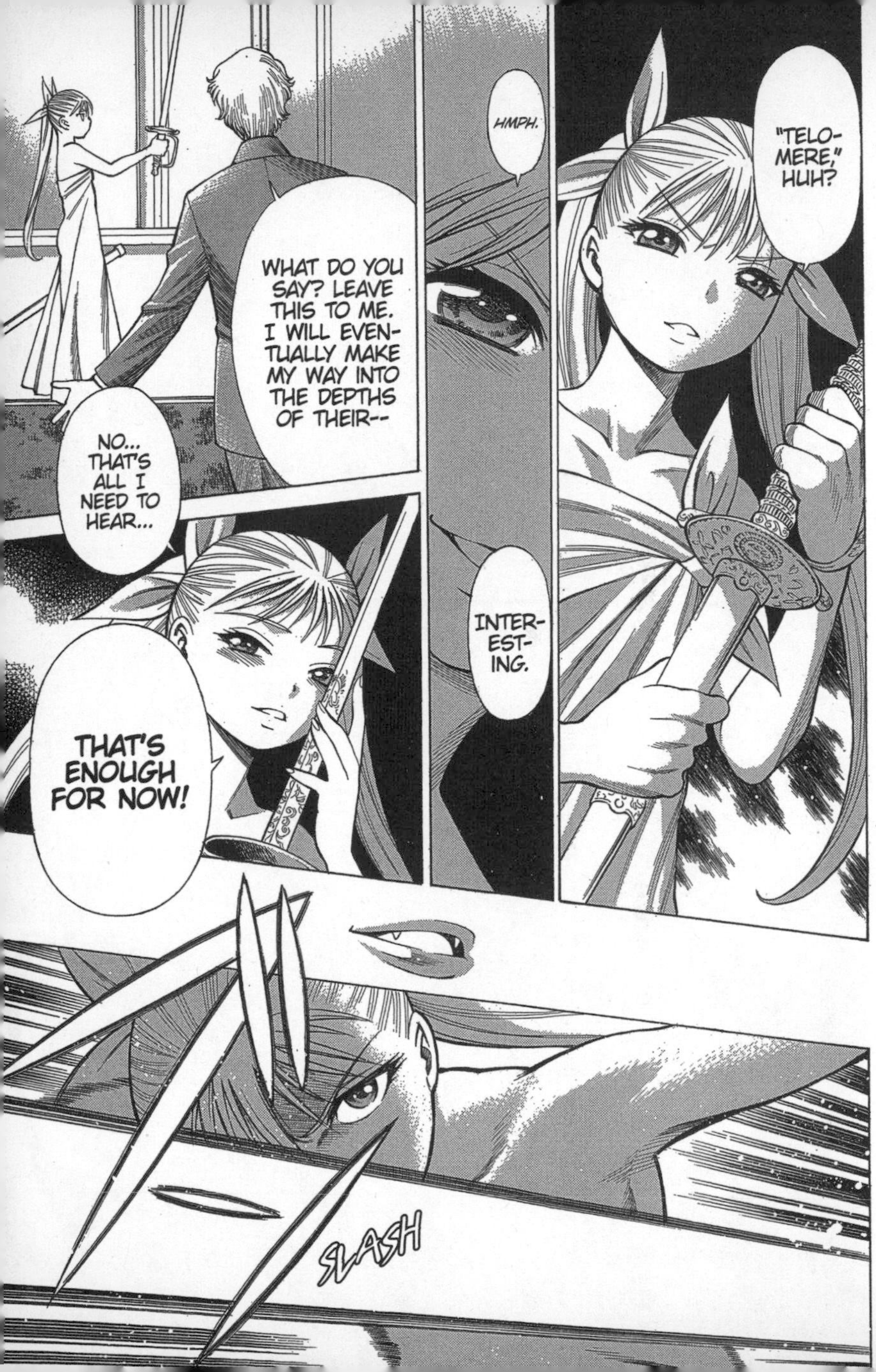
"TELO-MERE," HUH?
HMPH.
INTER-EST-ING.
WHAT DO YOU SAY? LEAVE THIS TO ME. I WILL EVEN-TUALLY MAKE MY WAY INTO THE DEPTHS OF THEIR--
NO... THAT'S ALL I NEED TO HEAR...
THAT'S ENOUGH FOR NOW!
SLASH

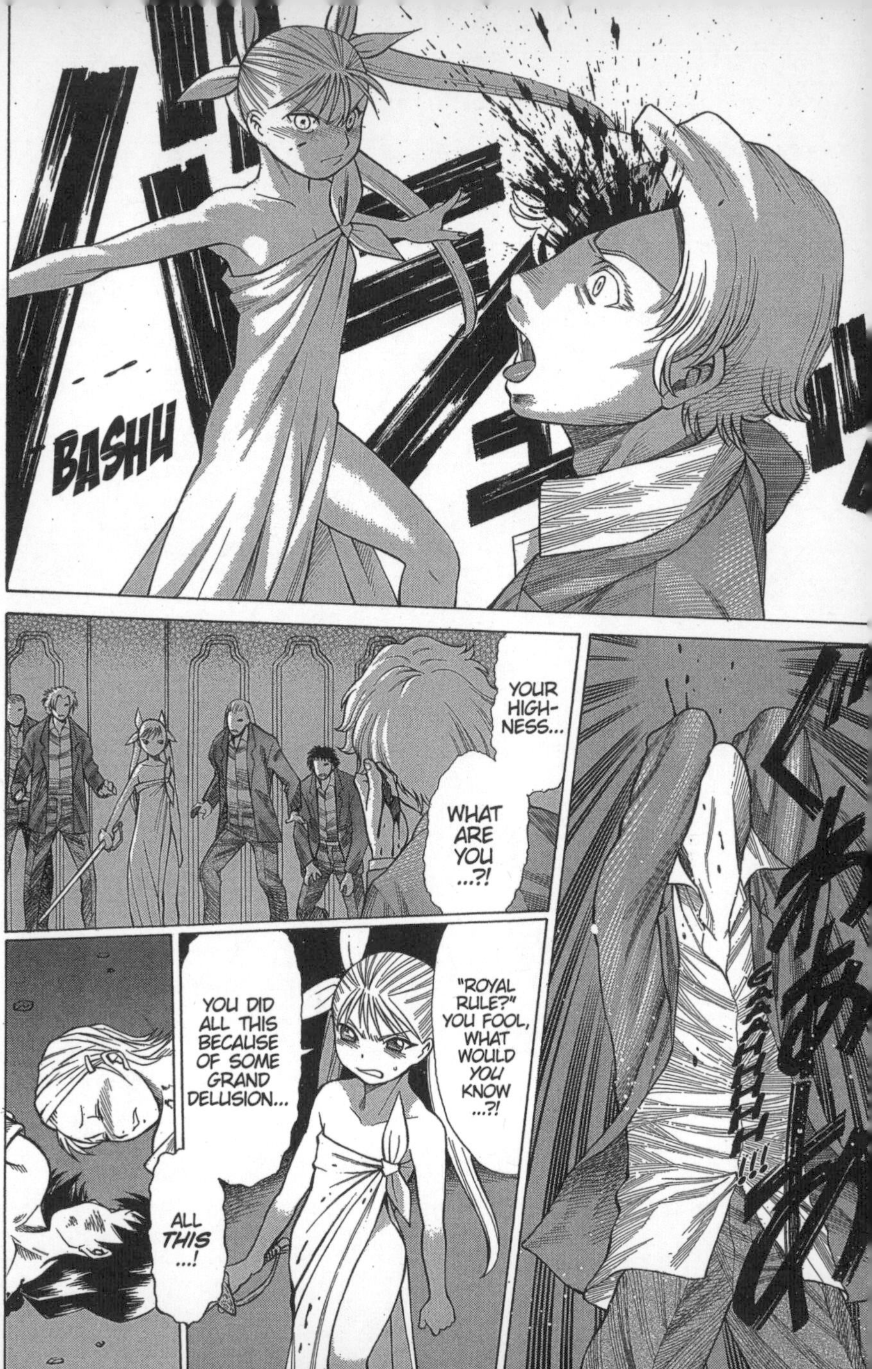
BASHU
GAAHHHH!!!
YOUR HIGHNESS...
WHAT ARE YOU ...?!
"ROYAL RULE?" YOU FOOL, WHAT WOULD YOU KNOW ...?!
YOU DID ALL THIS BECAUSE OF SOME GRAND DELUSION...
ALL THIS ...!

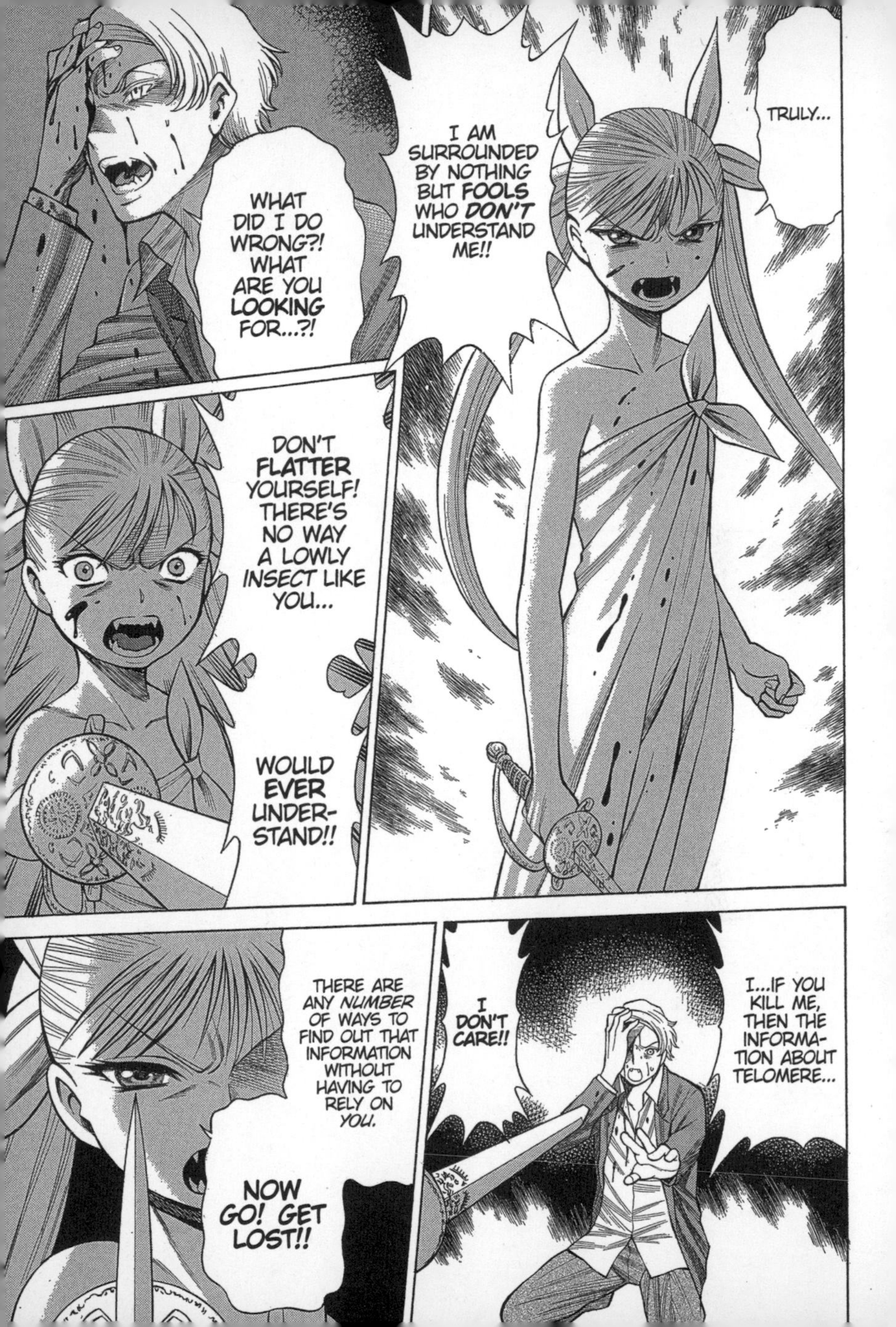
TRULY...
I AM SURROUNDED BY NOTHING BUT FOOLS WHO DON'T UNDERSTAND ME!!
WHAT DID I DO WRONG?! WHAT ARE YOU LOOKING FOR...?!
DON'T FLATTER YOURSELF! THERE'S NO WAY A LOWLY INSECT LIKE YOU...
WOULD EVER UNDER-STAND!!
I...IF YOU KILL ME, THEN THE INFORMA-TION ABOUT TELOMERE...
I DON'T CARE!!
THERE ARE ANY NUMBER OF WAYS TO FIND OUT THAT INFORMATION WITHOUT HAVING TO RELY ON YOU.
NOW GO! GET LOST!!

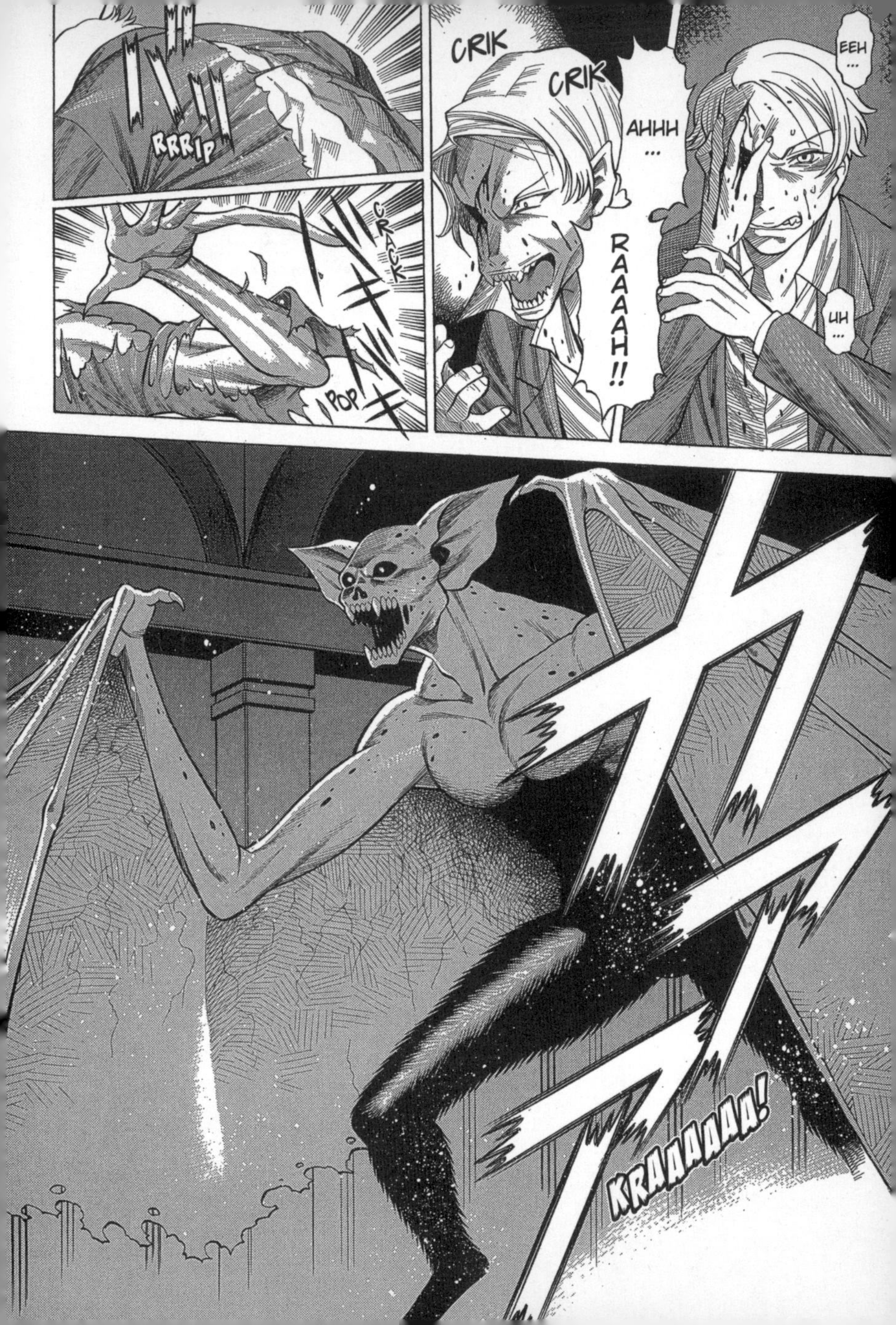
EEH...
UH...
CRIK
CRIK
AHHH...
RAAAAAH!!
RRRIP
CRACK
POP
KRAAAAAA!

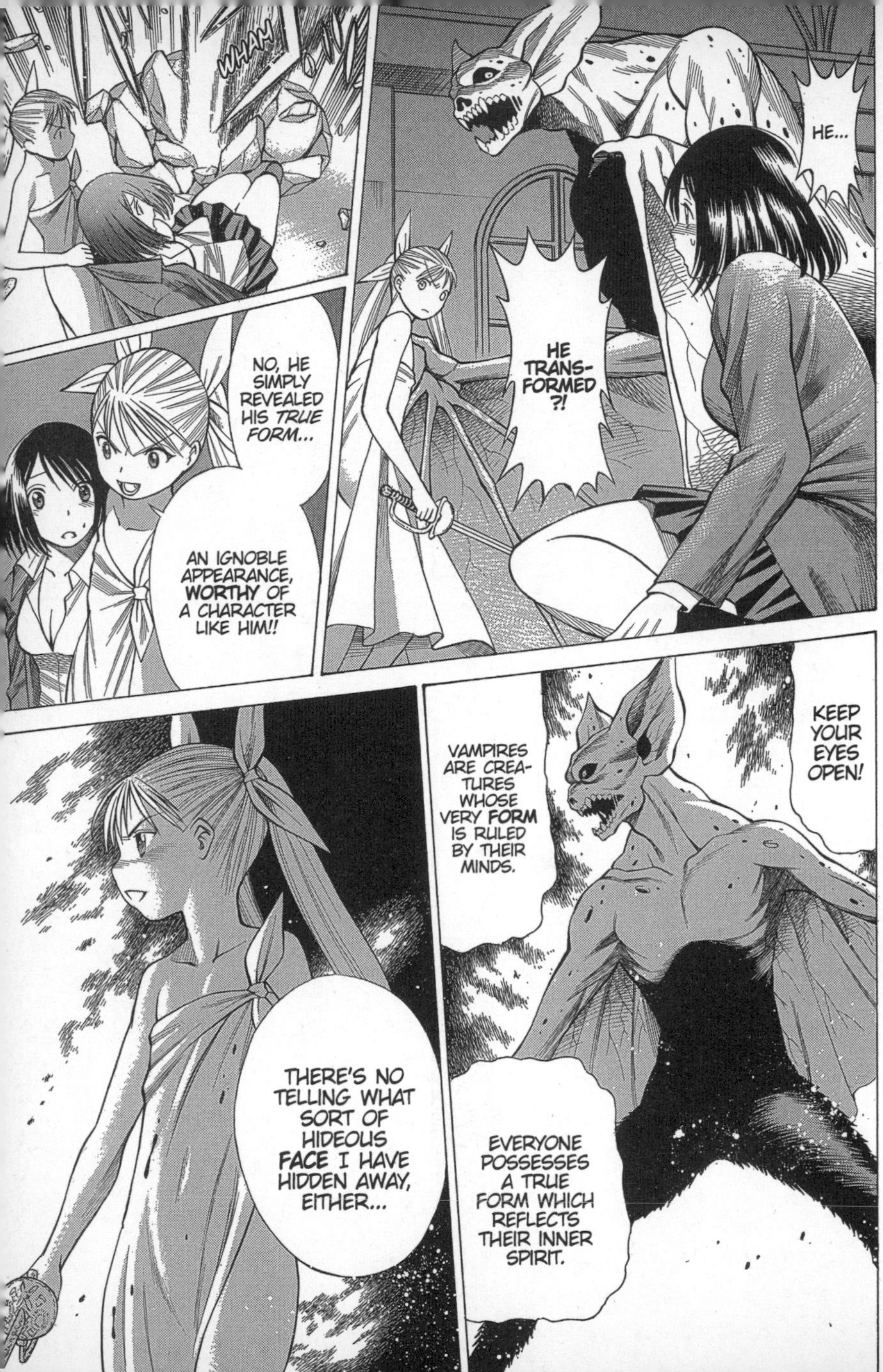
HE...
HE TRANSFORMED?!
WHAM
NO, HE SIMPLY REVEALED HIS *TRUE FORM*...
AN IGNOBLE APPEARANCE, **WORTHY** OF A CHARACTER LIKE HIM!!
KEEP YOUR EYES OPEN!
VAMPIRES ARE CREATURES WHOSE VERY **FORM** IS RULED BY THEIR MINDS.
EVERYONE POSSESSES A TRUE FORM WHICH REFLECTS THEIR INNER SPIRIT.
THERE'S NO TELLING WHAT SORT OF HIDEOUS **FACE** I HAVE HIDDEN AWAY, EITHER...

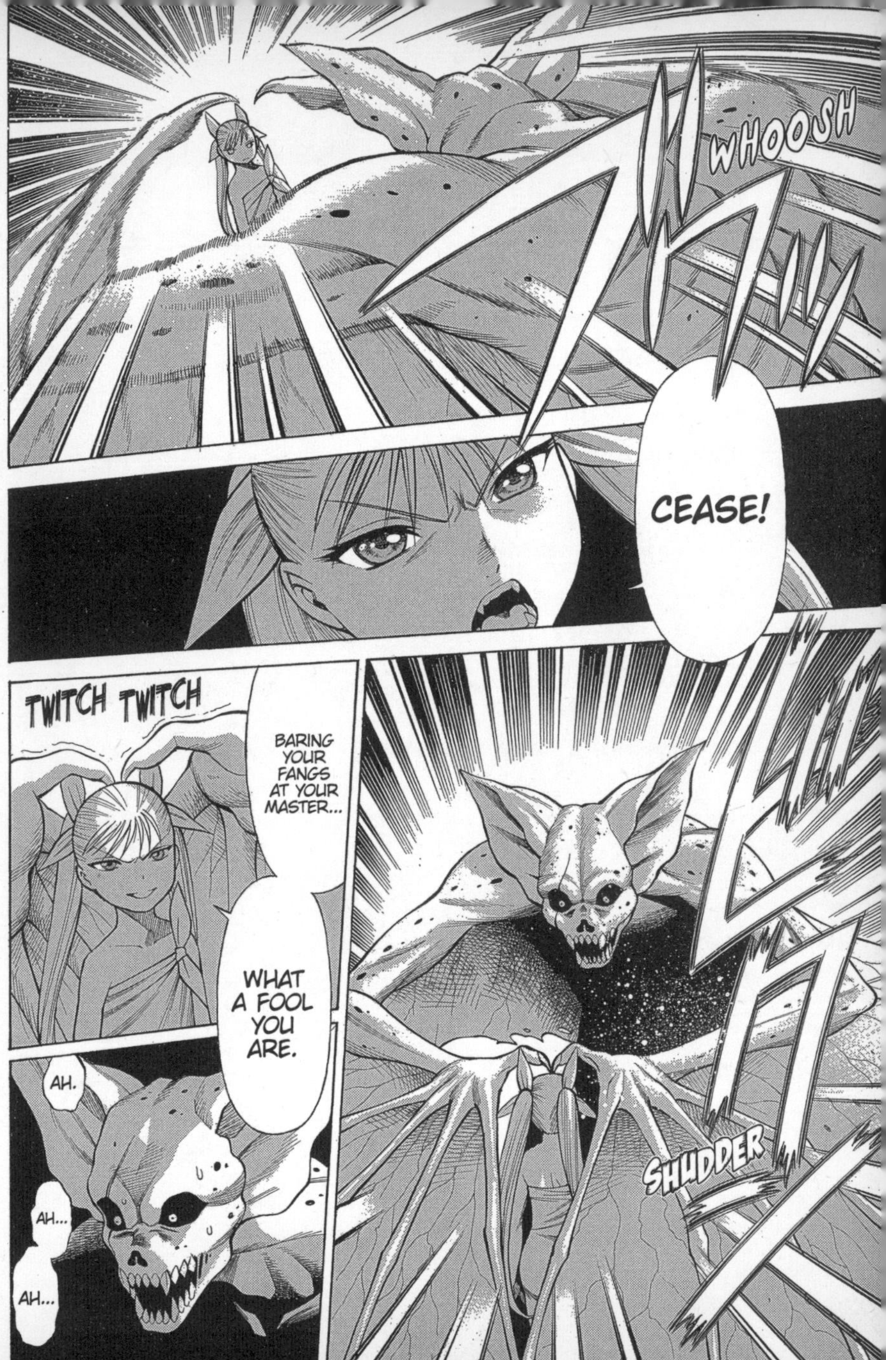
WHOOSH
CEASE!
SHUDDER
TWITCH TWITCH
BARING YOUR FANGS AT YOUR MASTER...
WHAT A FOOL YOU ARE.
AH.
AH...
AH...

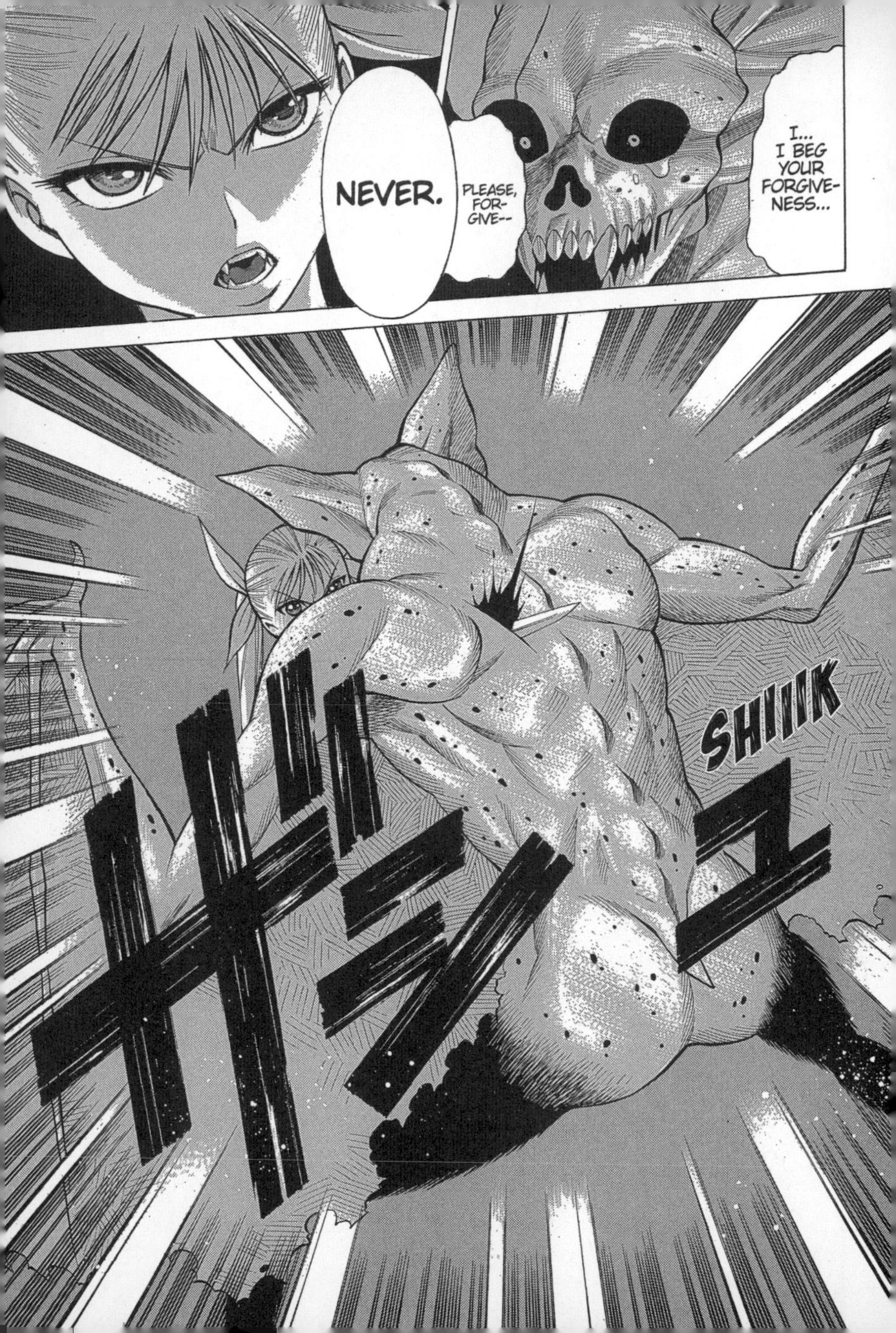
I... I BEG YOUR FORGIVENESS...
PLEASE, FORGIVE--
NEVER.
SHIIIK

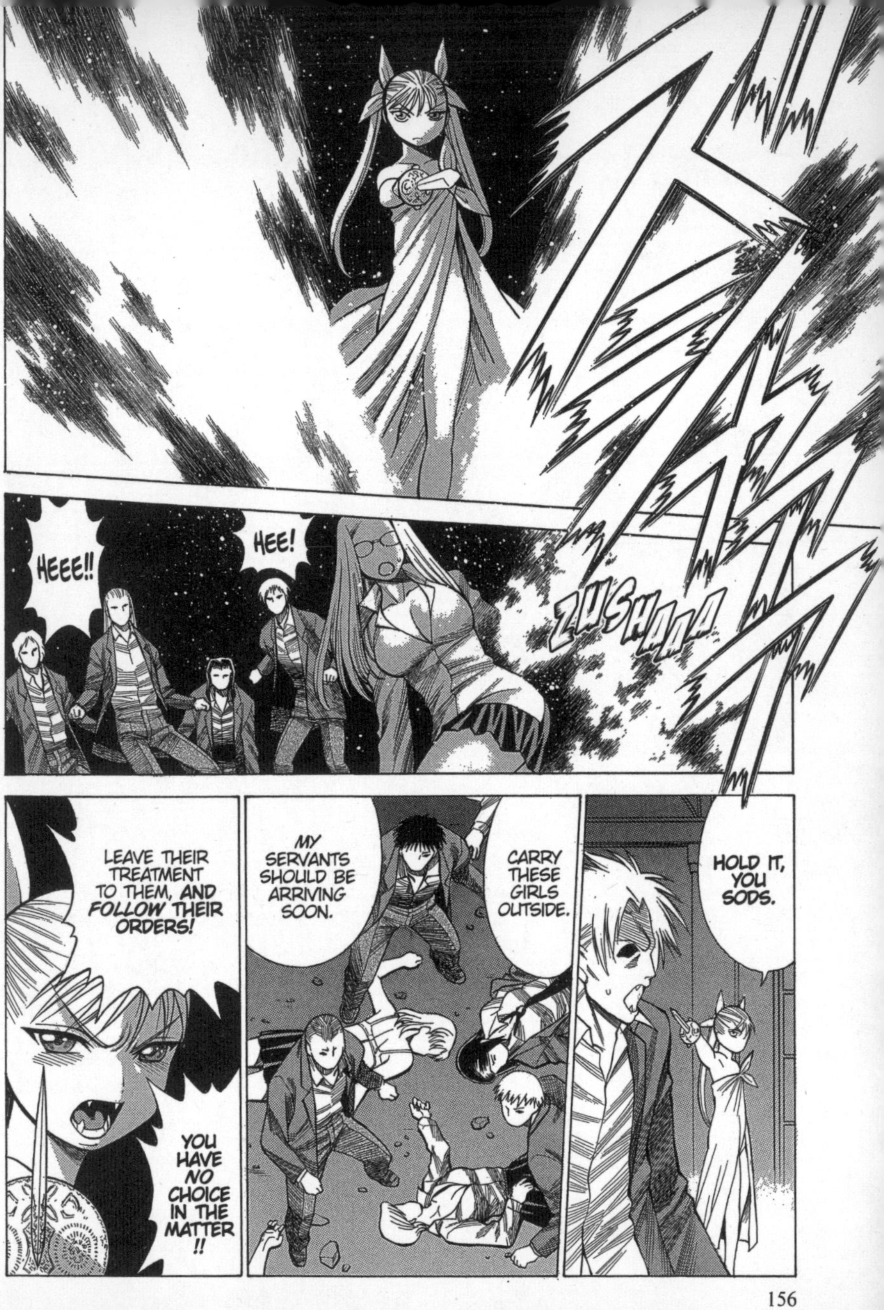
ZUSHAAA
HEE!
HEEE!!
HOLD IT, YOU SODS.
CARRY THESE GIRLS OUTSIDE.
MY SERVANTS SHOULD BE ARRIVING SOON.
LEAVE THEIR TREATMENT TO THEM, AND FOLLOW THEIR ORDERS!
YOU HAVE NO CHOICE IN THE MATTER!!

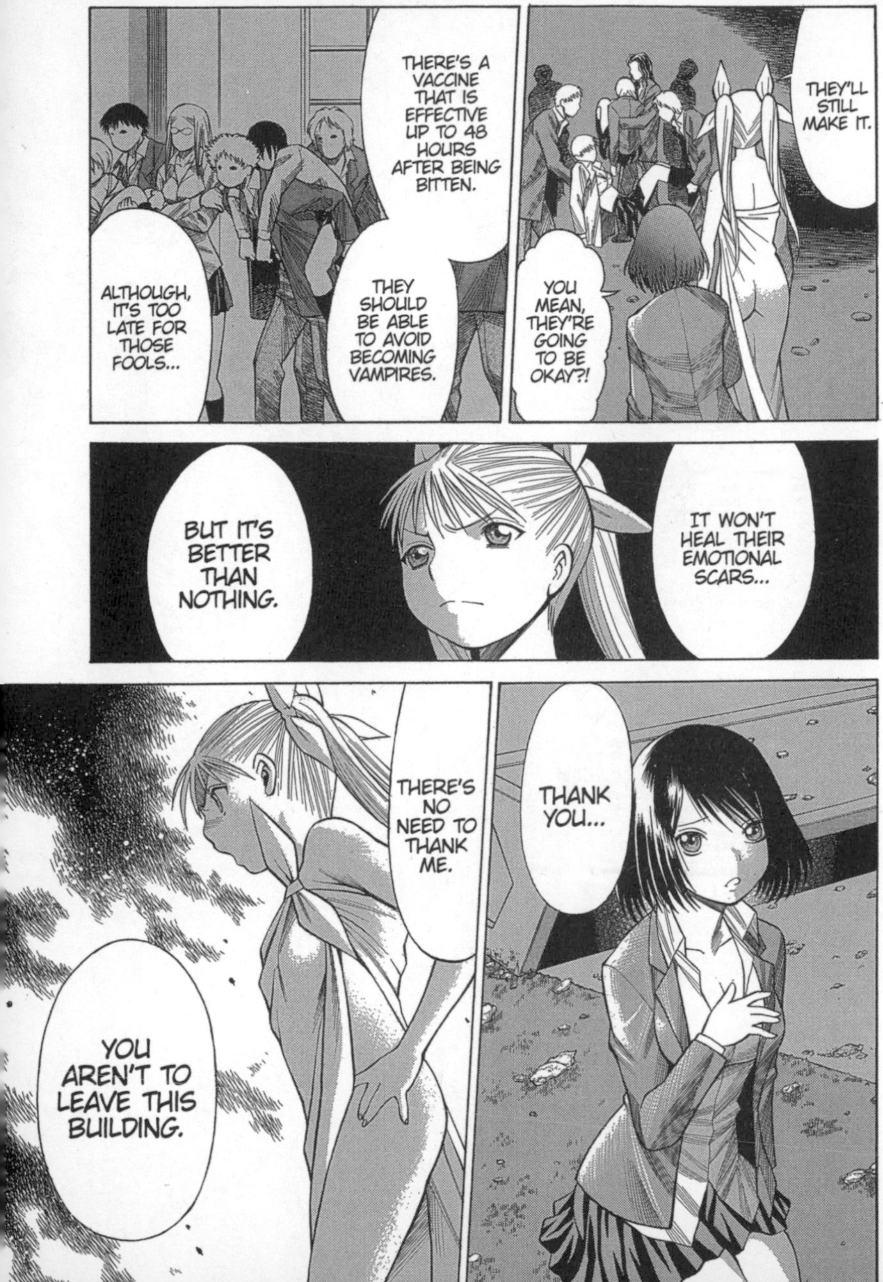
THEY'LL STILL MAKE IT.
YOU MEAN, THEY'RE GOING TO BE OKAY?!
THERE'S A VACCINE THAT IS EFFECTIVE UP TO 48 HOURS AFTER BEING BITTEN.
THEY SHOULD BE ABLE TO AVOID BECOMING VAMPIRES.
ALTHOUGH, IT'S TOO LATE FOR THOSE FOOLS...
IT WON'T HEAL THEIR EMOTIONAL SCARS...
BUT IT'S BETTER THAN NOTHING.
THANK YOU...
THERE'S NO NEED TO THANK ME.
YOU AREN'T TO LEAVE THIS BUILDING.

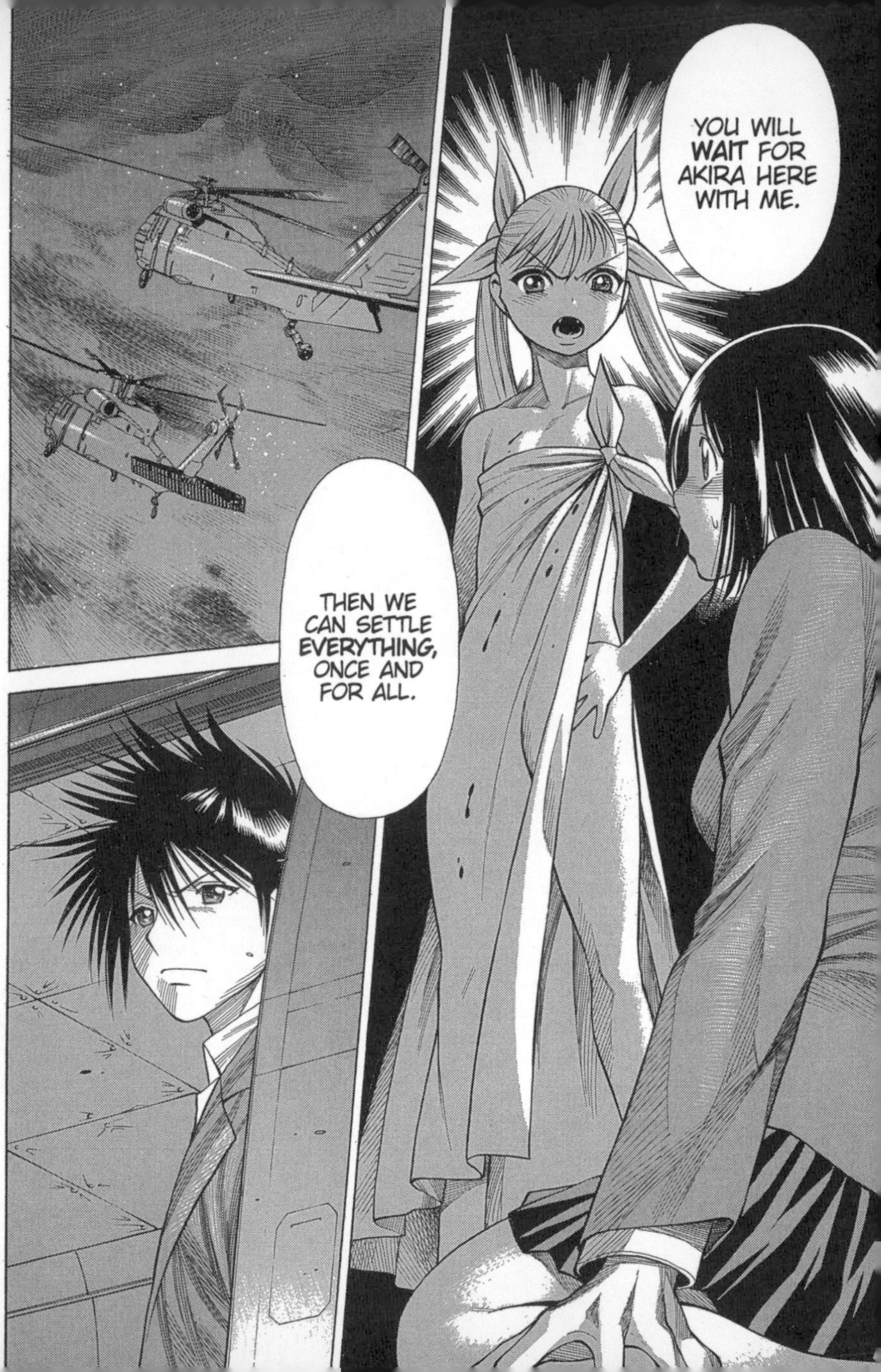
YOU WILL WAIT FOR AKIRA HERE WITH ME.
THEN WE CAN SETTLE EVERYTHING, ONCE AND FOR ALL.

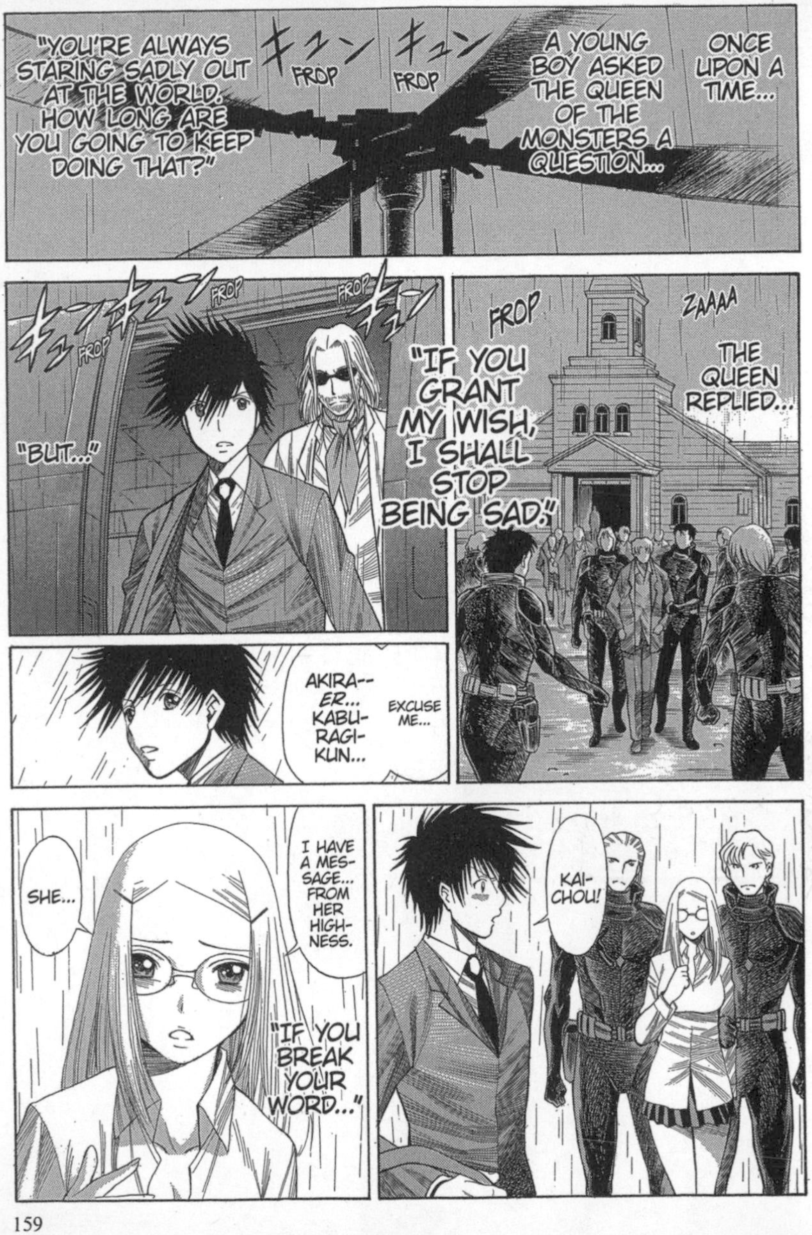
ONCE UPON A TIME...
A YOUNG BOY ASKED THE QUEEN OF THE MONSTERS A QUESTION...
キュン
FROP
キュン
FROP
"YOU'RE ALWAYS STARING SADLY OUT AT THE WORLD. HOW LONG ARE YOU GOING TO KEEP DOING THAT?"
ZAAAA
THE QUEEN REPLIED...
FROP
"IF YOU GRANT MY WISH, I SHALL STOP BEING SAD."
FROP
FROP
FROP
"BUT..."
EXCUSE ME...
AKIRA-- ER... KABURAGI-KUN...
KAICHOU!
I HAVE A MESSAGE... FROM HER HIGHNESS.
SHE...
"IF YOU BREAK YOUR WORD..."

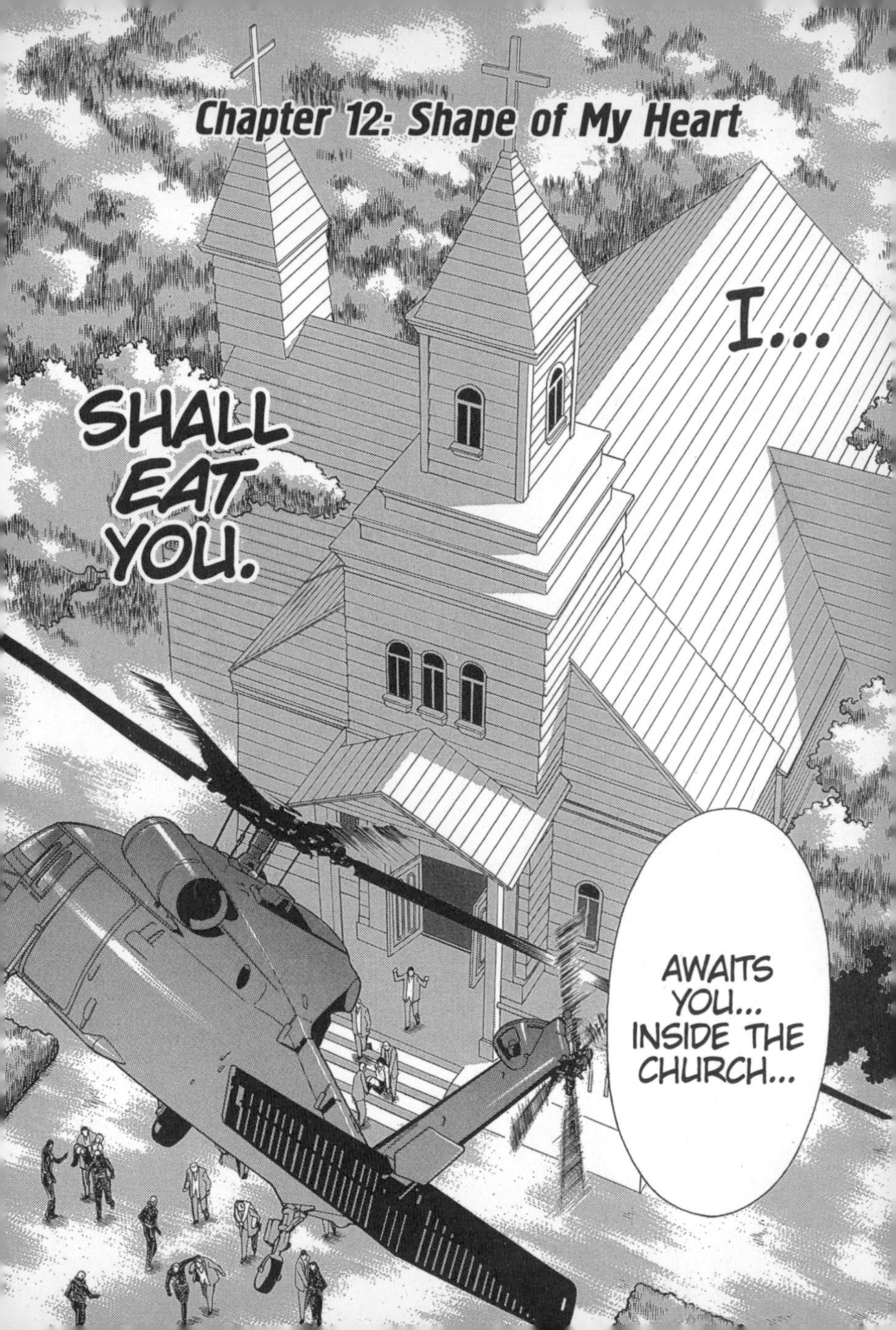
Chapter 12: Shape of My Heart
I...
SHALL EAT YOU.
AWAITS YOU... INSIDE THE CHURCH...

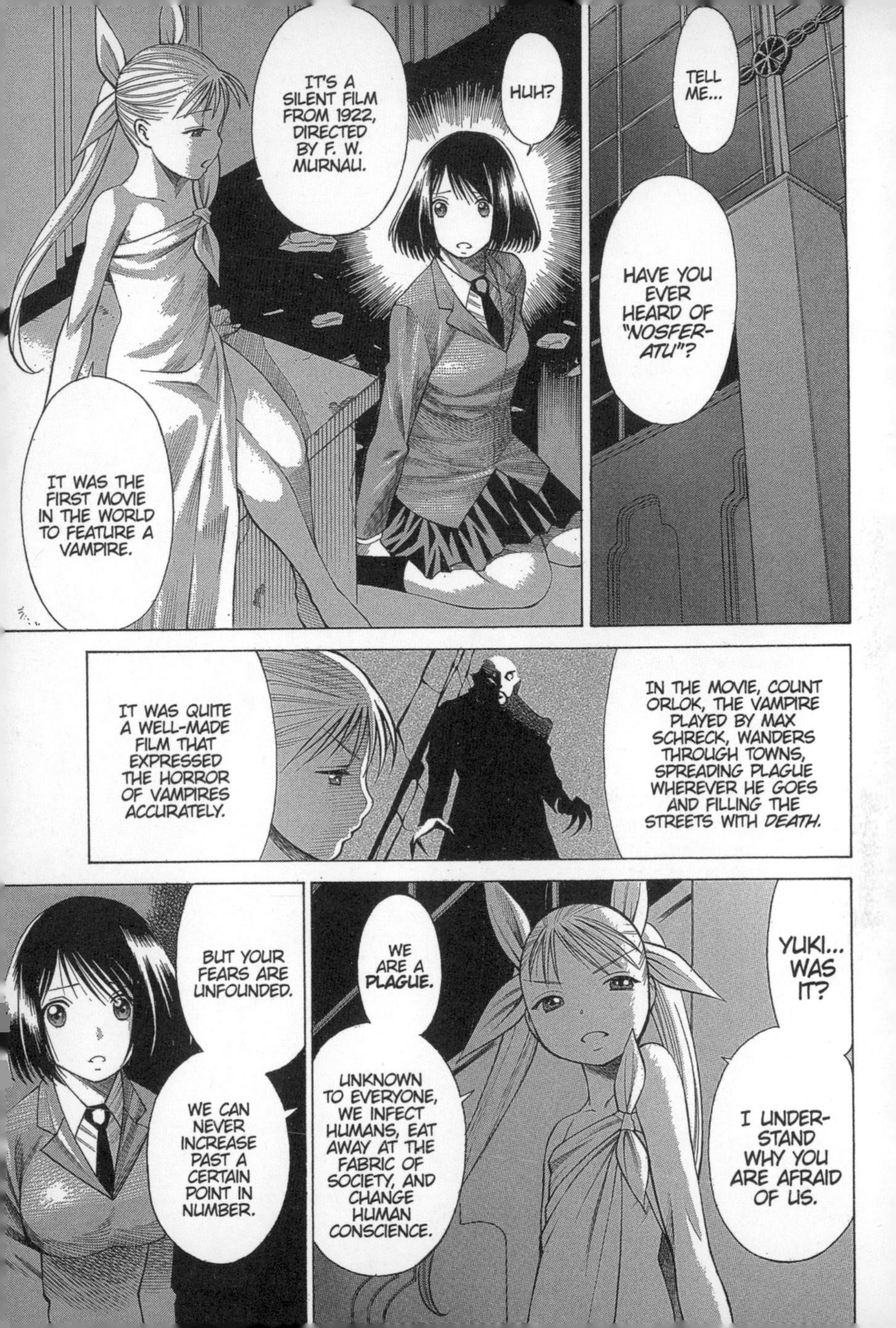
TELL ME...
HAVE YOU EVER HEARD OF *"NOSFERATU"*?
HUH?
IT'S A SILENT FILM FROM 1922, DIRECTED BY F. W. MURNAU.
IT WAS THE FIRST MOVIE IN THE WORLD TO FEATURE A VAMPIRE.
IN THE MOVIE, COUNT ORLOK, THE VAMPIRE PLAYED BY MAX SCHRECK, WANDERS THROUGH TOWNS, SPREADING PLAGUE WHEREVER HE GOES AND FILLING THE STREETS WITH *DEATH.*
IT WAS QUITE A WELL-MADE FILM THAT EXPRESSED THE HORROR OF VAMPIRES ACCURATELY.
YUKI... WAS IT?
I UNDERSTAND WHY YOU ARE AFRAID OF US.
WE ARE A **PLAGUE.**
UNKNOWN TO EVERYONE, WE INFECT HUMANS, EAT AWAY AT THE FABRIC OF SOCIETY, AND CHANGE HUMAN CONSCIENCE.
BUT YOUR FEARS ARE UNFOUNDED.
WE CAN NEVER INCREASE PAST A CERTAIN POINT IN NUMBER.

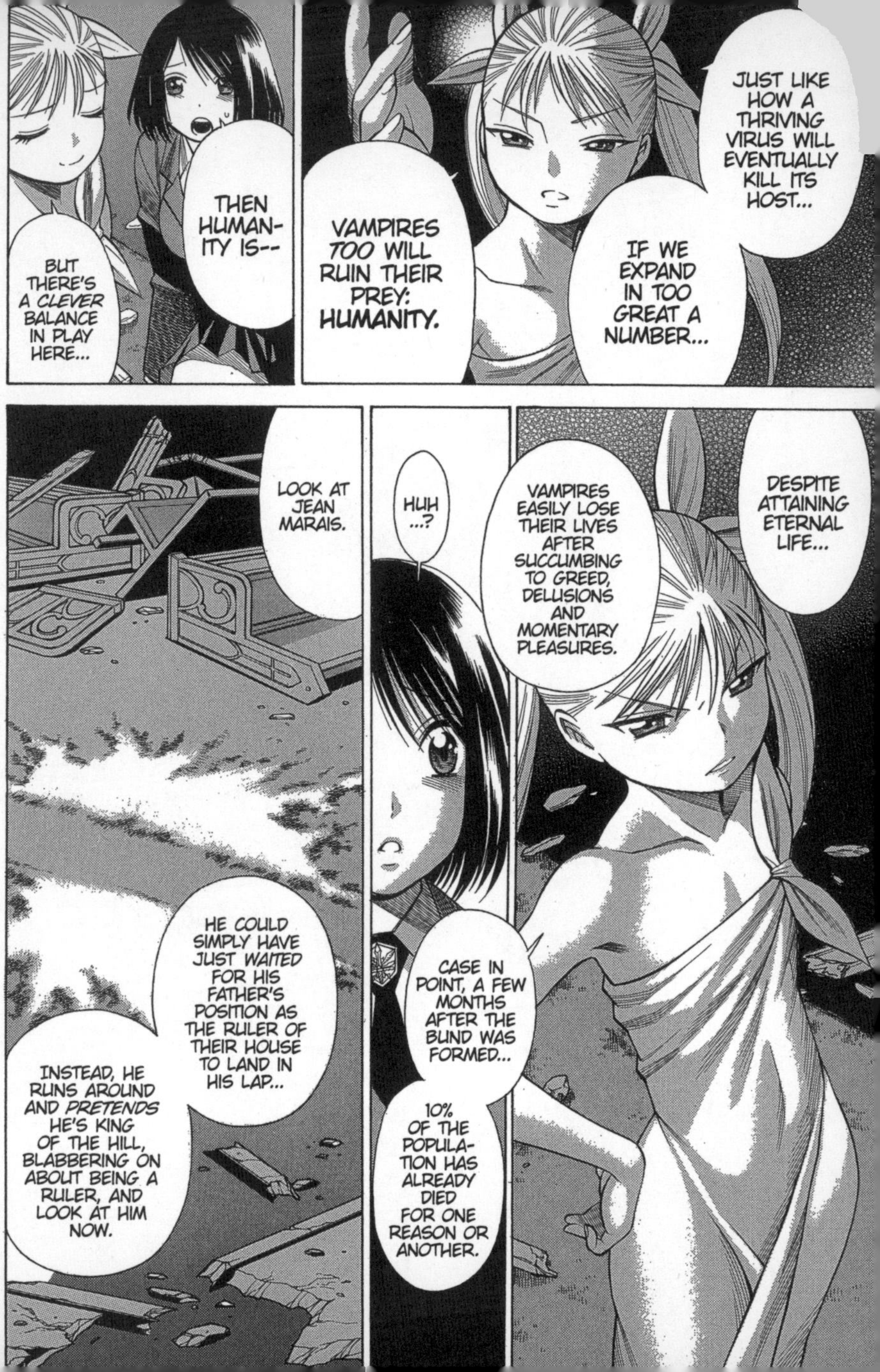
JUST LIKE HOW A THRIVING VIRUS WILL EVENTUALLY KILL ITS HOST...
IF WE EXPAND IN TOO GREAT A NUMBER...
VAMPIRES *TOO* WILL RUIN THEIR PREY: **HUMANITY.**
THEN HUMANITY IS--
BUT THERE'S A *CLEVER* BALANCE IN PLAY HERE...
DESPITE ATTAINING ETERNAL LIFE...
VAMPIRES EASILY LOSE THEIR LIVES AFTER SUCCUMBING TO GREED, DELUSIONS AND MOMENTARY PLEASURES.
HUH ...?
CASE IN POINT, A FEW MONTHS AFTER THE BUND WAS FORMED...
10% OF THE POPULATION HAS ALREADY DIED FOR ONE REASON OR ANOTHER.
LOOK AT JEAN MARAIS.
HE COULD SIMPLY HAVE JUST *WAITED* FOR HIS FATHER'S POSITION AS THE RULER OF THEIR HOUSE TO LAND IN HIS LAP...
INSTEAD, HE RUNS AROUND AND *PRETENDS* HE'S KING OF THE HILL, BLABBERING ON ABOUT BEING A RULER, AND LOOK AT HIM NOW.

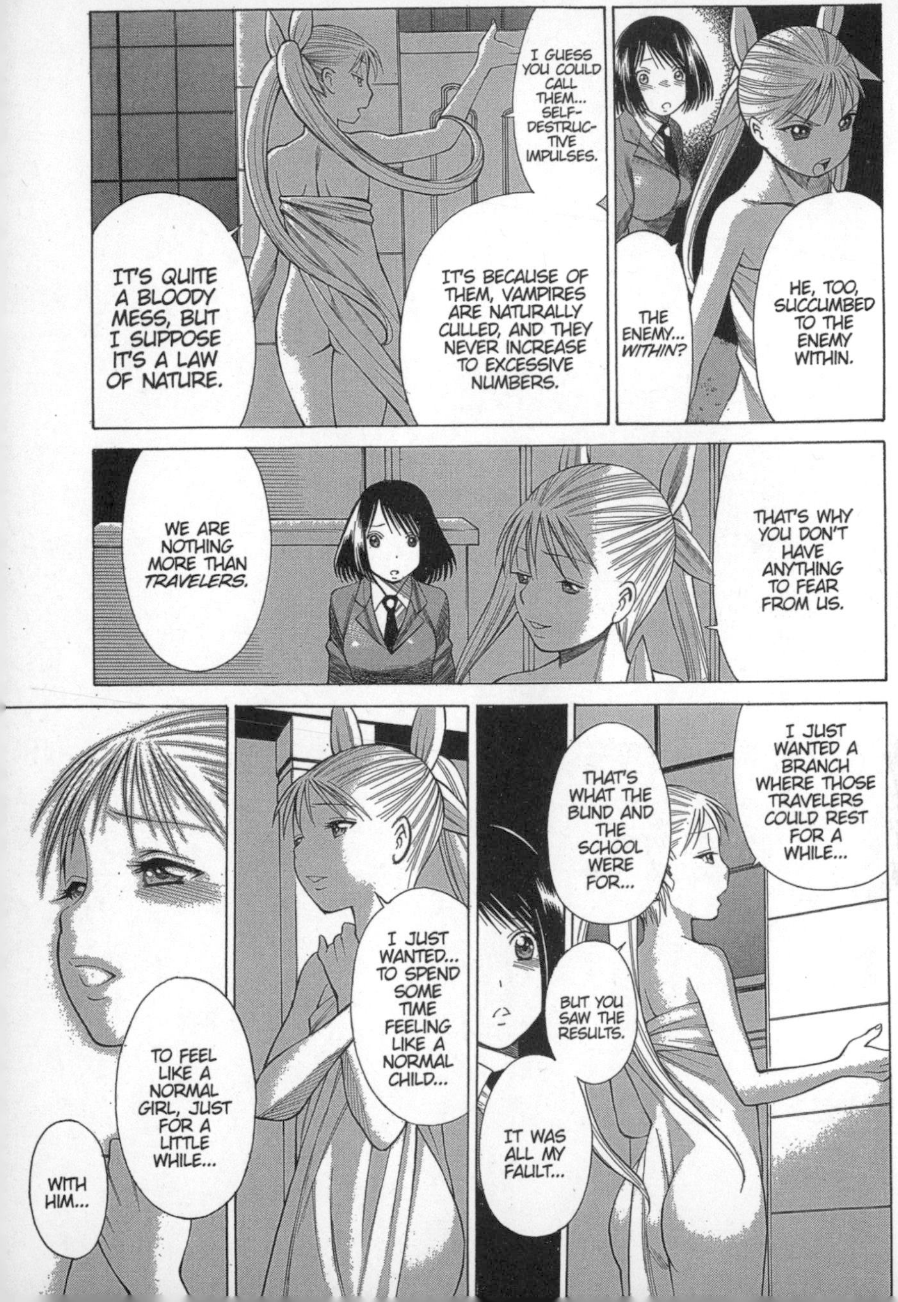
HE, TOO, SUCCUMBED TO THE ENEMY WITHIN.
THE ENEMY... *WITHIN*?
I GUESS YOU COULD CALL THEM... SELF-DESTRUCTIVE IMPULSES.
IT'S BECAUSE OF THEM, VAMPIRES ARE NATURALLY CULLED, AND THEY NEVER INCREASE TO EXCESSIVE NUMBERS.
IT'S QUITE A BLOODY MESS, BUT I SUPPOSE IT'S A LAW OF NATURE.
THAT'S WHY YOU DON'T HAVE ANYTHING TO FEAR FROM US.
WE ARE NOTHING MORE THAN *TRAVELERS*.
I JUST WANTED A BRANCH WHERE THOSE TRAVELERS COULD REST FOR A WHILE...
THAT'S WHAT THE BUND AND THE SCHOOL WERE FOR...
BUT YOU SAW THE RESULTS.
IT WAS ALL MY FAULT...
I JUST WANTED... TO SPEND SOME TIME FEELING LIKE A NORMAL CHILD...
TO FEEL LIKE A NORMAL GIRL, JUST FOR A LITTLE WHILE...
WITH HIM...

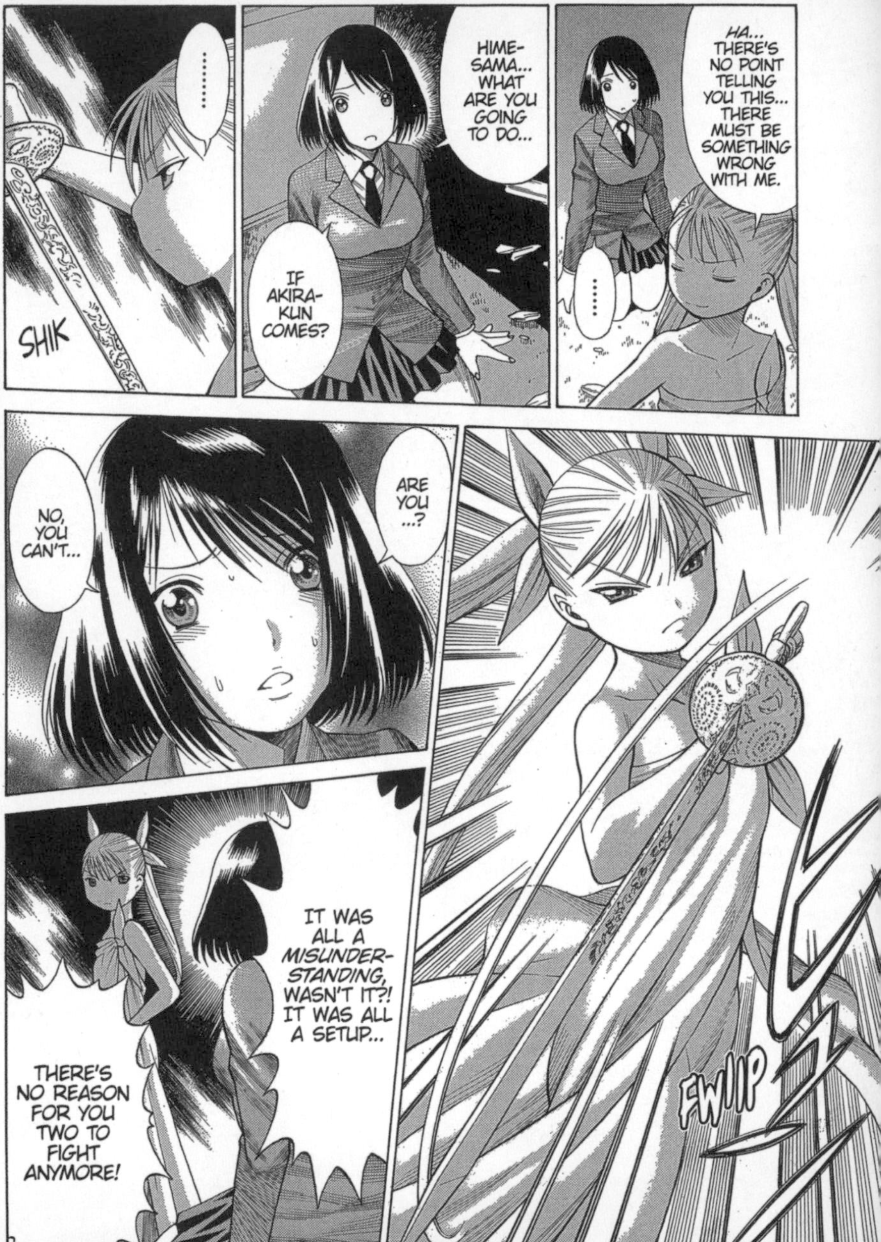
HA... THERE'S NO POINT TELLING YOU THIS... THERE MUST BE SOMETHING WRONG WITH ME.
......
HIME-SAMA... WHAT ARE YOU GOING TO DO...
IF AKIRA-KUN COMES?
......
SHIK
FWIP
ARE YOU ...?
NO, YOU CAN'T...
IT WAS ALL A *MISUNDERSTANDING,* WASN'T IT?! IT WAS ALL A SETUP...
THERE'S NO REASON FOR YOU TWO TO FIGHT ANYMORE!

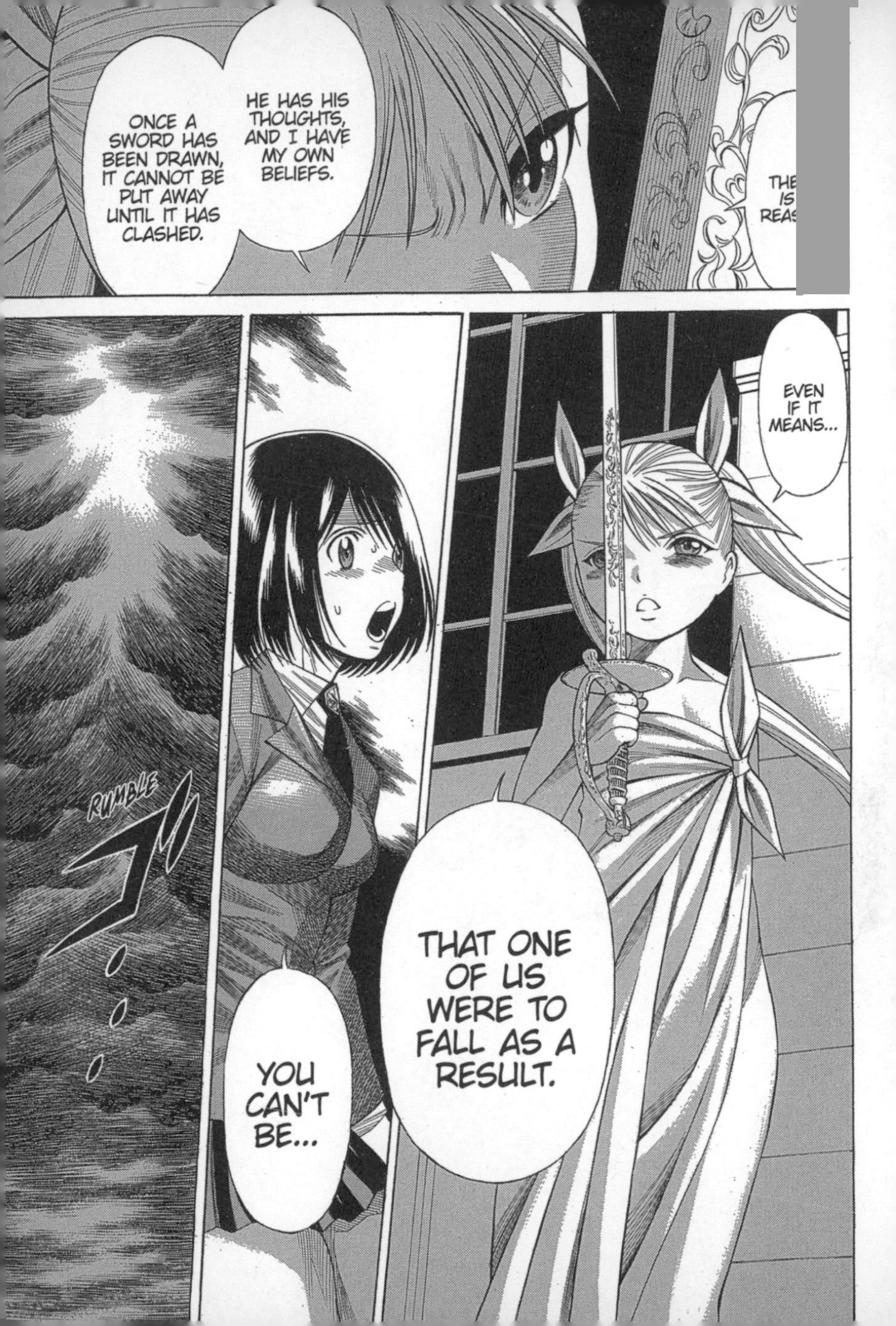
HE HAS HIS THOUGHTS, AND I HAVE MY OWN BELIEFS.
ONCE A SWORD HAS BEEN DRAWN, IT CANNOT BE PUT AWAY UNTIL IT HAS CLASHED.
EVEN IF IT MEANS...
THAT ONE OF US WERE TO FALL AS A RESULT.
YOU CAN'T BE...
RUMBLE

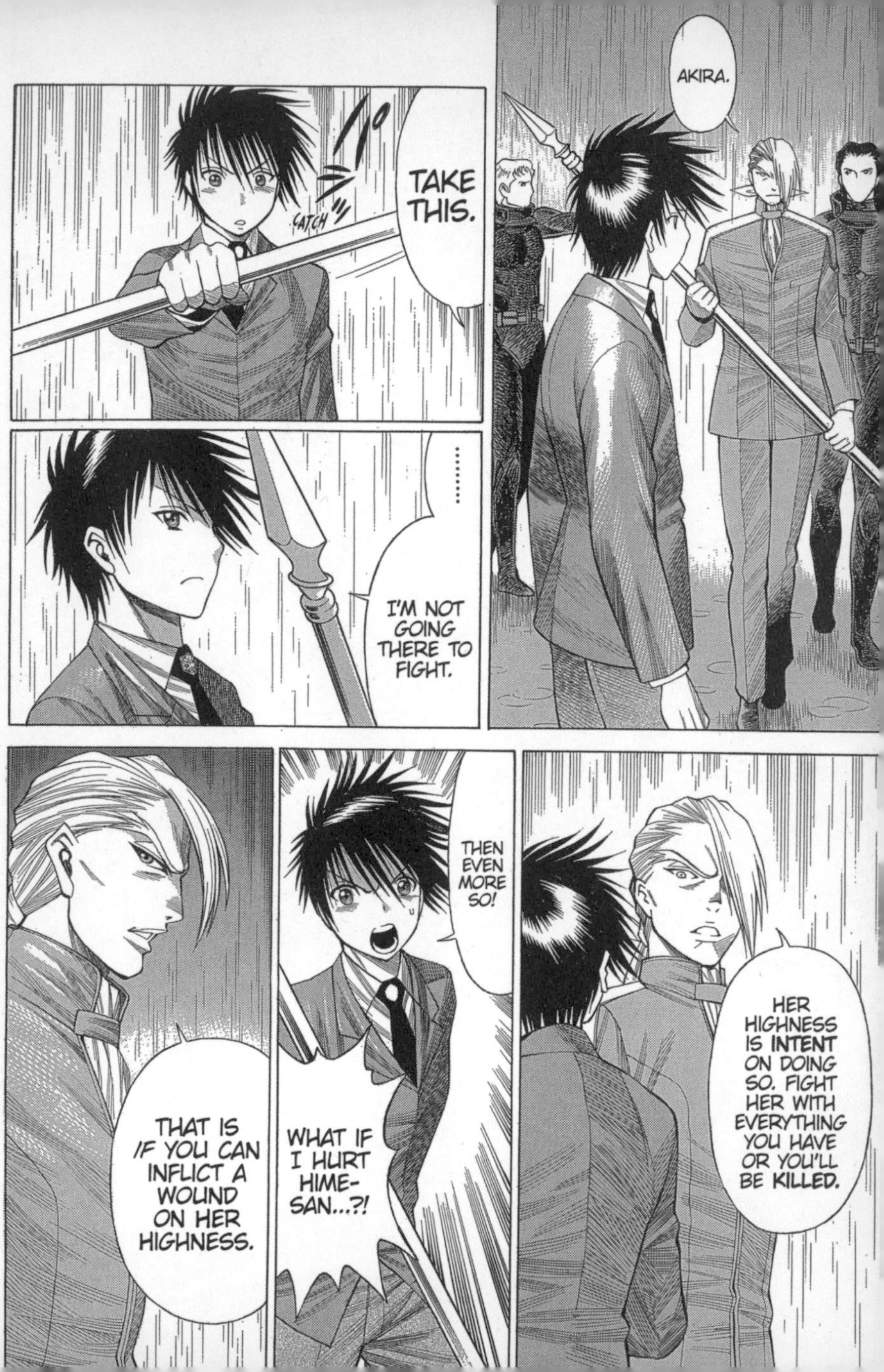
AKIRA.
TAKE THIS.
CATCH
....
I'M NOT GOING THERE TO FIGHT.
HER HIGHNESS IS **INTENT** ON DOING SO. FIGHT HER WITH EVERYTHING YOU HAVE OR YOU'LL BE **KILLED.**
THEN EVEN MORE SO!
WHAT IF I HURT HIME-SAN...?!
THAT IS IF YOU CAN INFLICT A WOUND ON HER HIGHNESS.

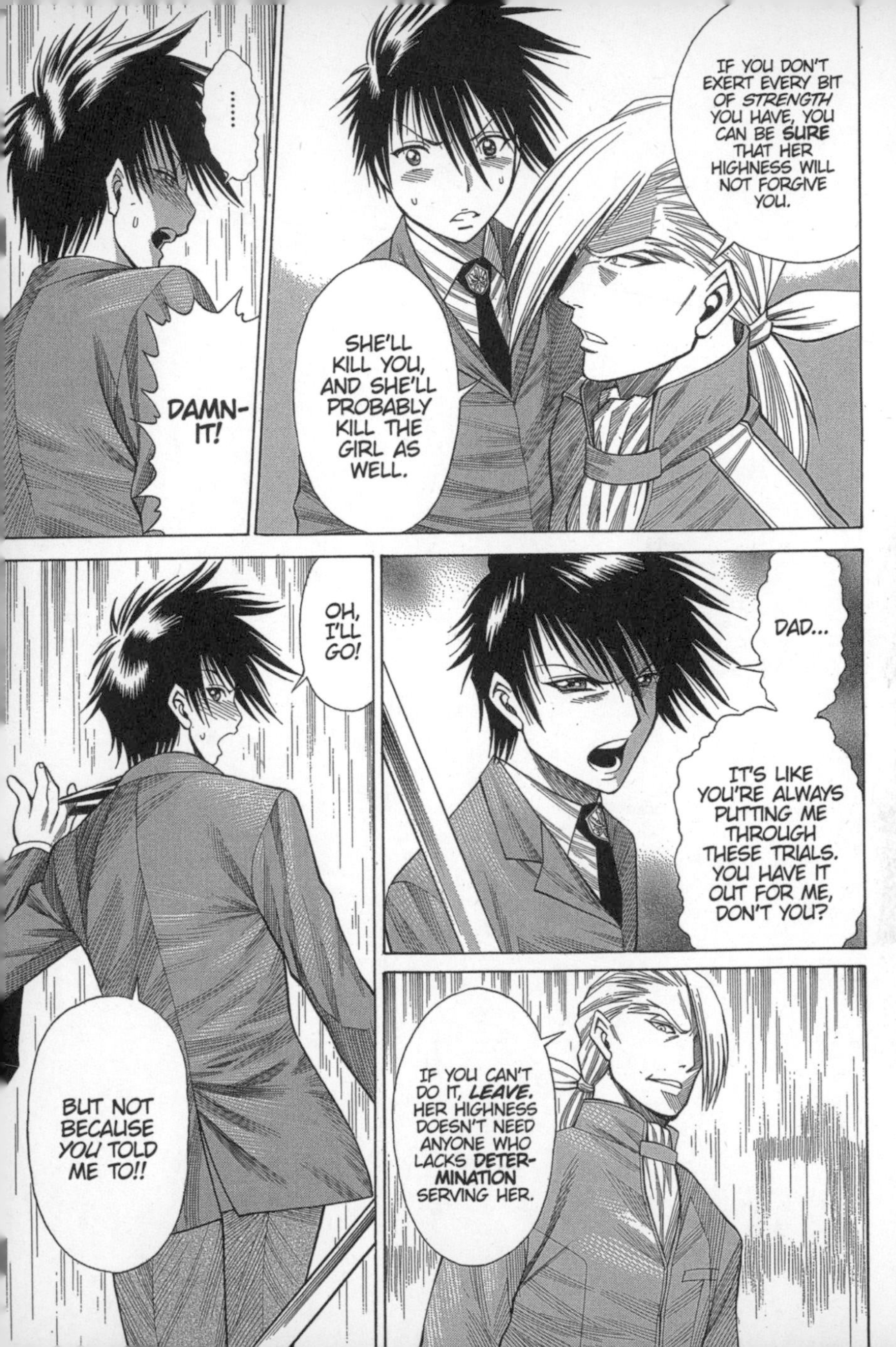
IF YOU DON'T EXERT EVERY BIT OF *STRENGTH* YOU HAVE, YOU CAN BE **SURE** THAT HER HIGHNESS WILL NOT FORGIVE YOU.
SHE'LL KILL YOU, AND SHE'LL PROBABLY KILL THE GIRL AS WELL.
......
DAMN-IT!
DAD...
IT'S LIKE YOU'RE ALWAYS PUTTING ME THROUGH THESE TRIALS. YOU HAVE IT OUT FOR ME, DON'T YOU?
IF YOU CAN'T DO IT, ***LEAVE.*** HER HIGHNESS DOESN'T NEED ANYONE WHO LACKS **DETER-MINATION** SERVING HER.
OH, I'LL GO!
BUT NOT BECAUSE *YOU* TOLD ME TO!!

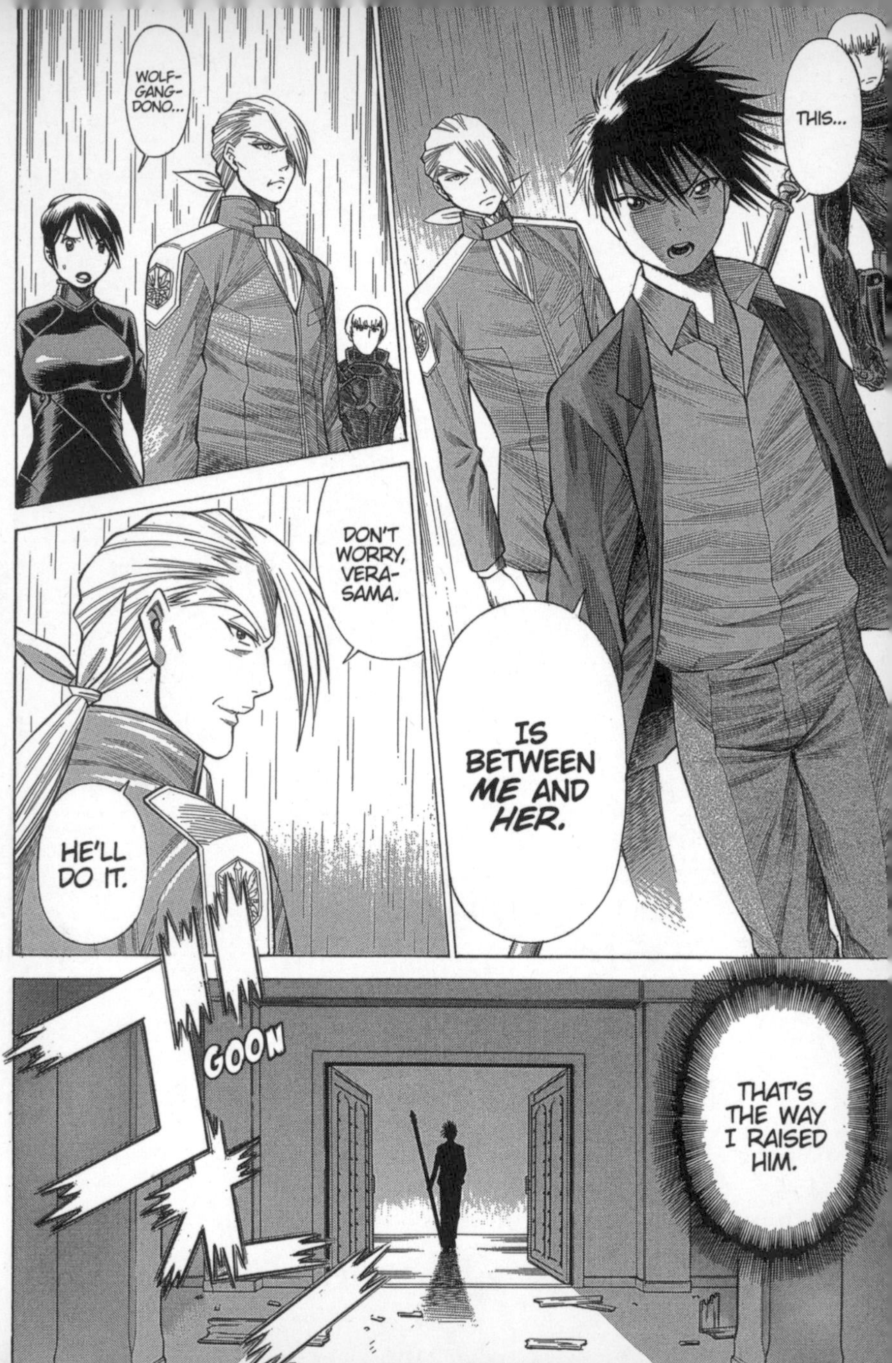
THIS...
IS BETWEEN *ME* AND *HER.*
WOLF-GANG-DONO...
DON'T WORRY, VERA-SAMA.
HE'LL DO IT.
THAT'S THE WAY I RAISED HIM.
GOON

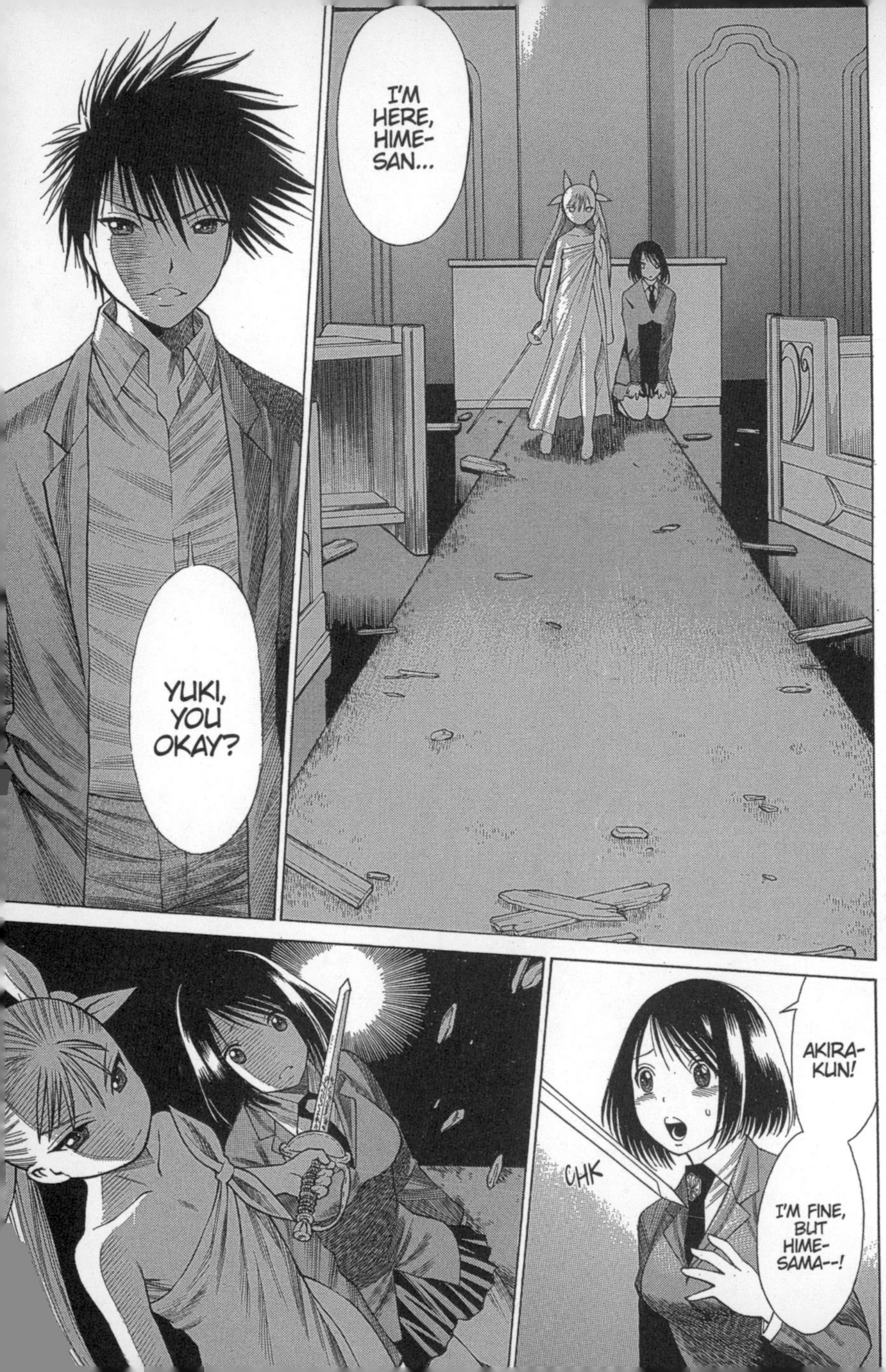
I'M HERE, HIME-SAN...
YUKI, YOU OKAY?
AKIRA-KUN!
CHK
I'M FINE, BUT HIME-SAMA--!

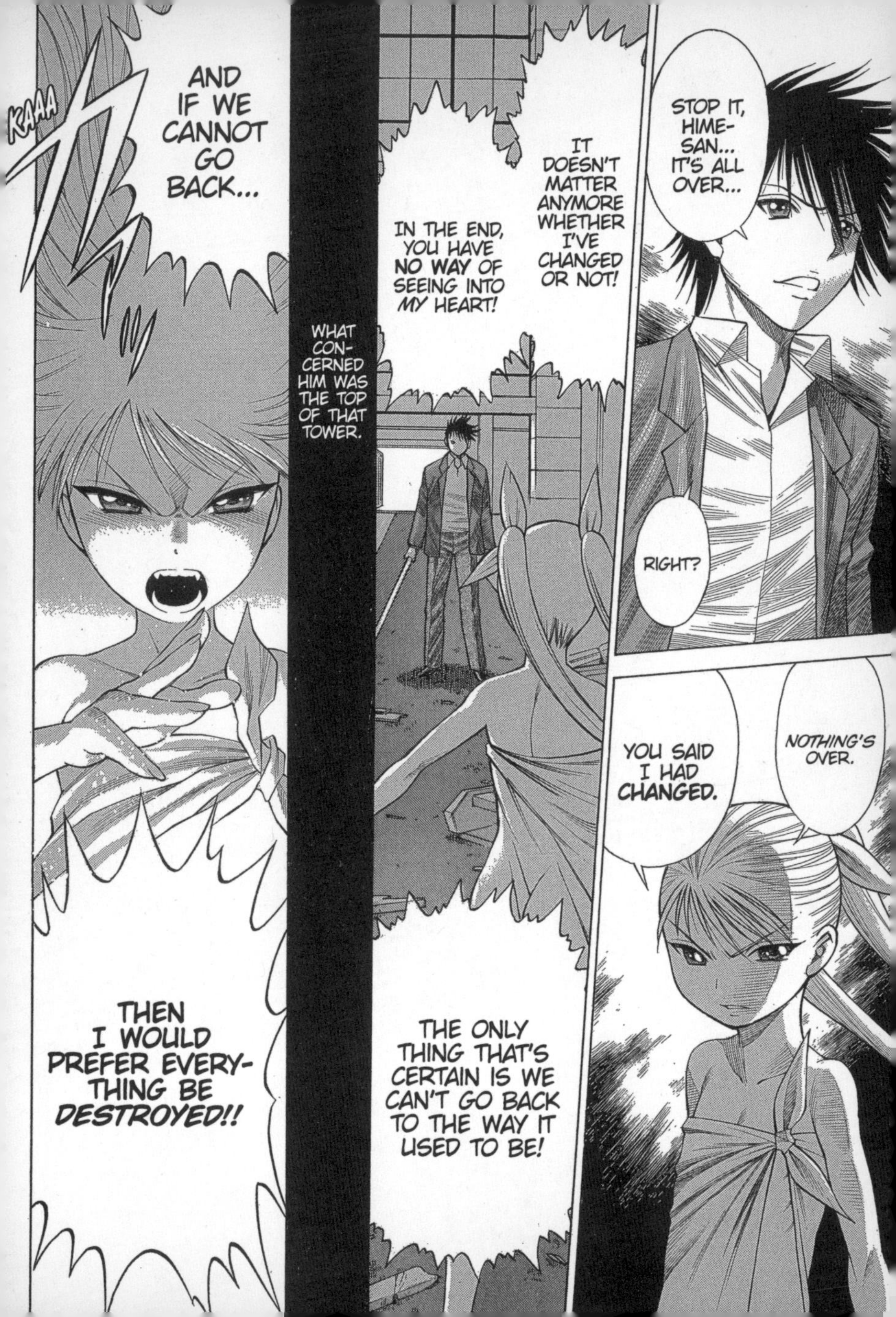
STOP IT, HIME-SAN... IT'S ALL OVER...
RIGHT?
NOTHING'S OVER.
YOU SAID I HAD CHANGED.
IT DOESN'T MATTER ANYMORE WHETHER I'VE CHANGED OR NOT!
IN THE END, YOU HAVE NO WAY OF SEEING INTO MY HEART!
THE ONLY THING THAT'S CERTAIN IS WE CAN'T GO BACK TO THE WAY IT USED TO BE!
WHAT CONCERNED HIM WAS THE TOP OF THAT TOWER.
KAAA
AND IF WE CANNOT GO BACK...
THEN I WOULD PREFER EVERYTHING BE DESTROYED!!

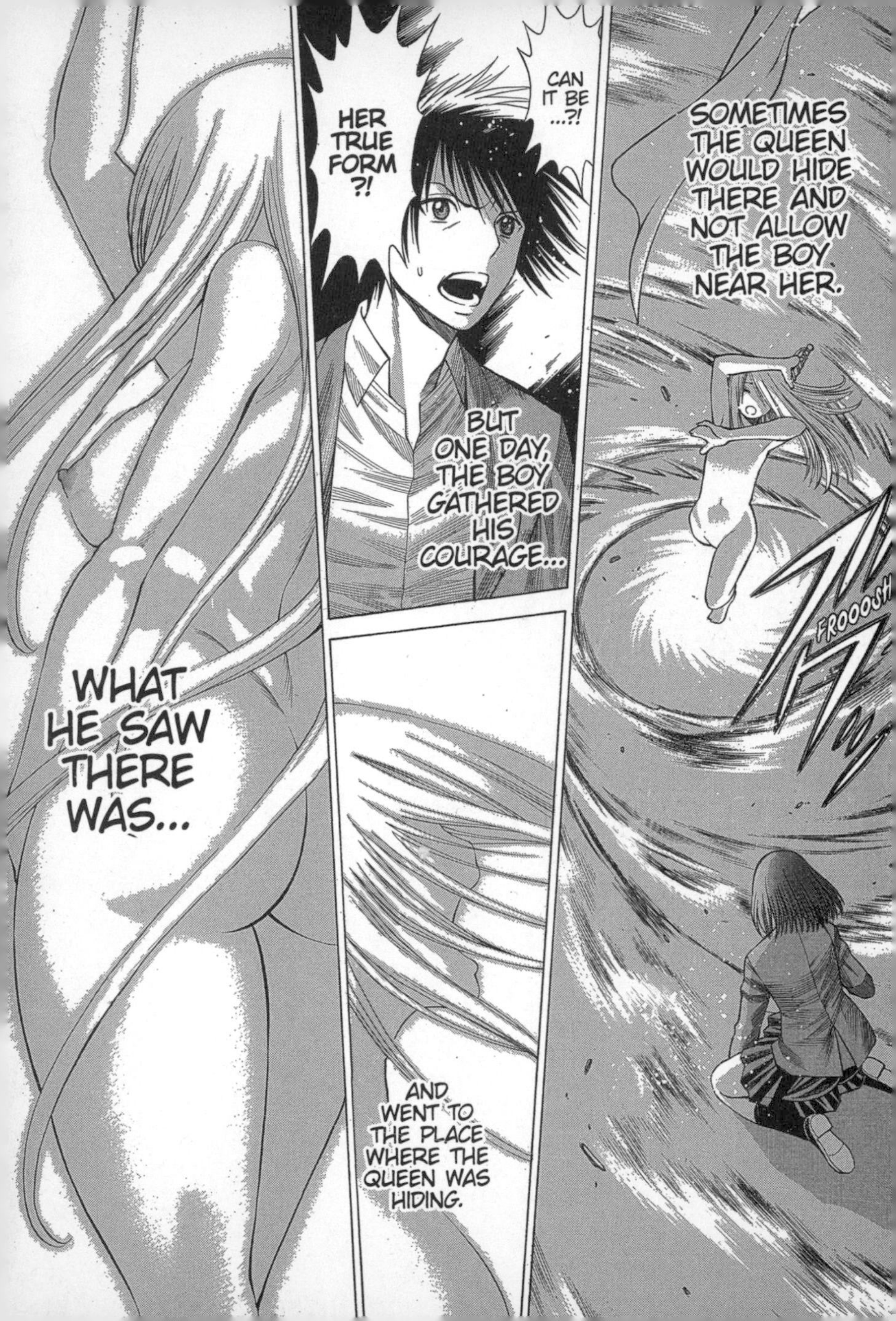
SOMETIMES THE QUEEN WOULD HIDE THERE AND NOT ALLOW THE BOY NEAR HER.
FROOOSH
CAN IT BE ...?!
HER TRUE FORM ?!
BUT ONE DAY, THE BOY GATHERED HIS COURAGE...
AND WENT TO THE PLACE WHERE THE QUEEN WAS HIDING.
WHAT HE SAW THERE WAS...

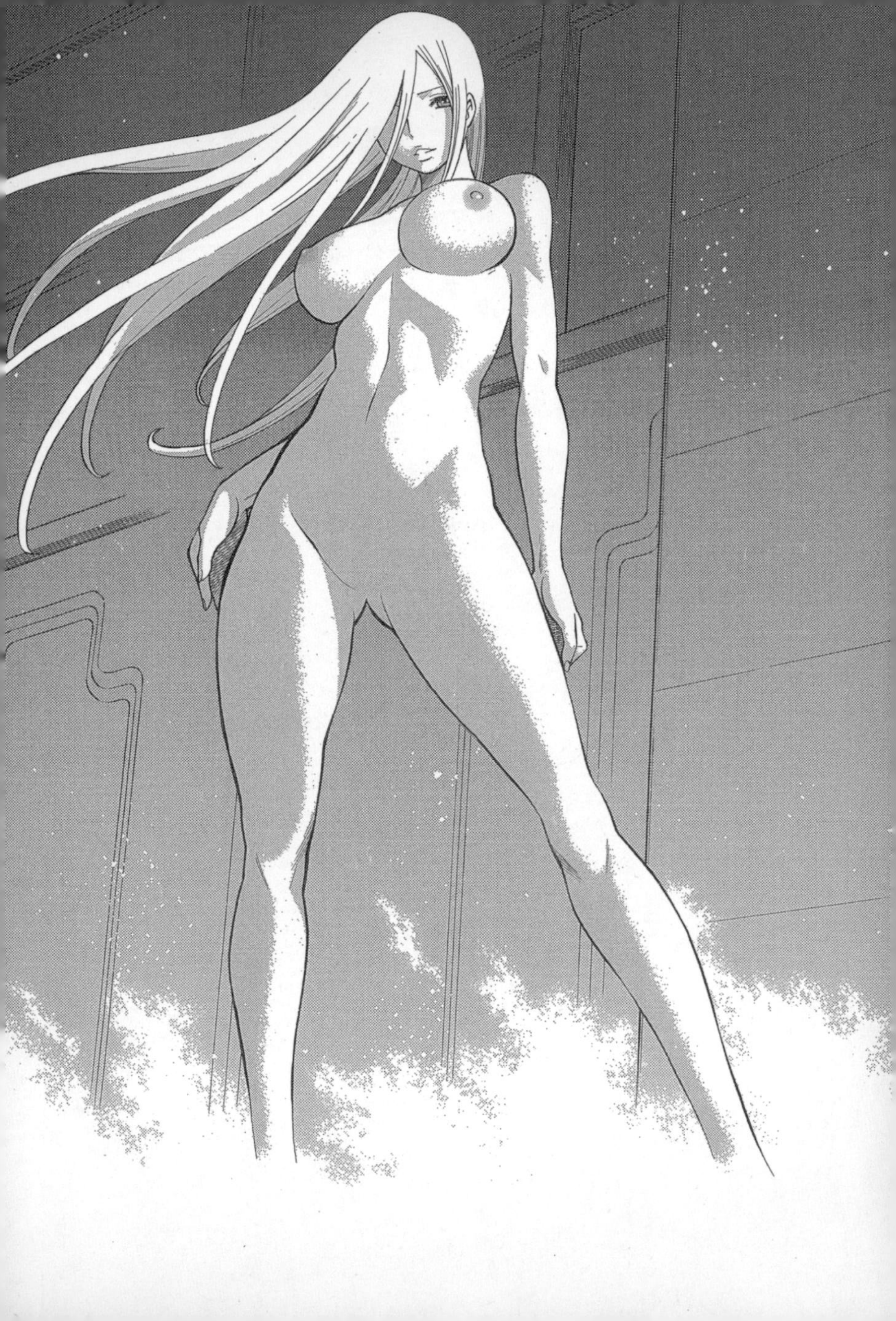

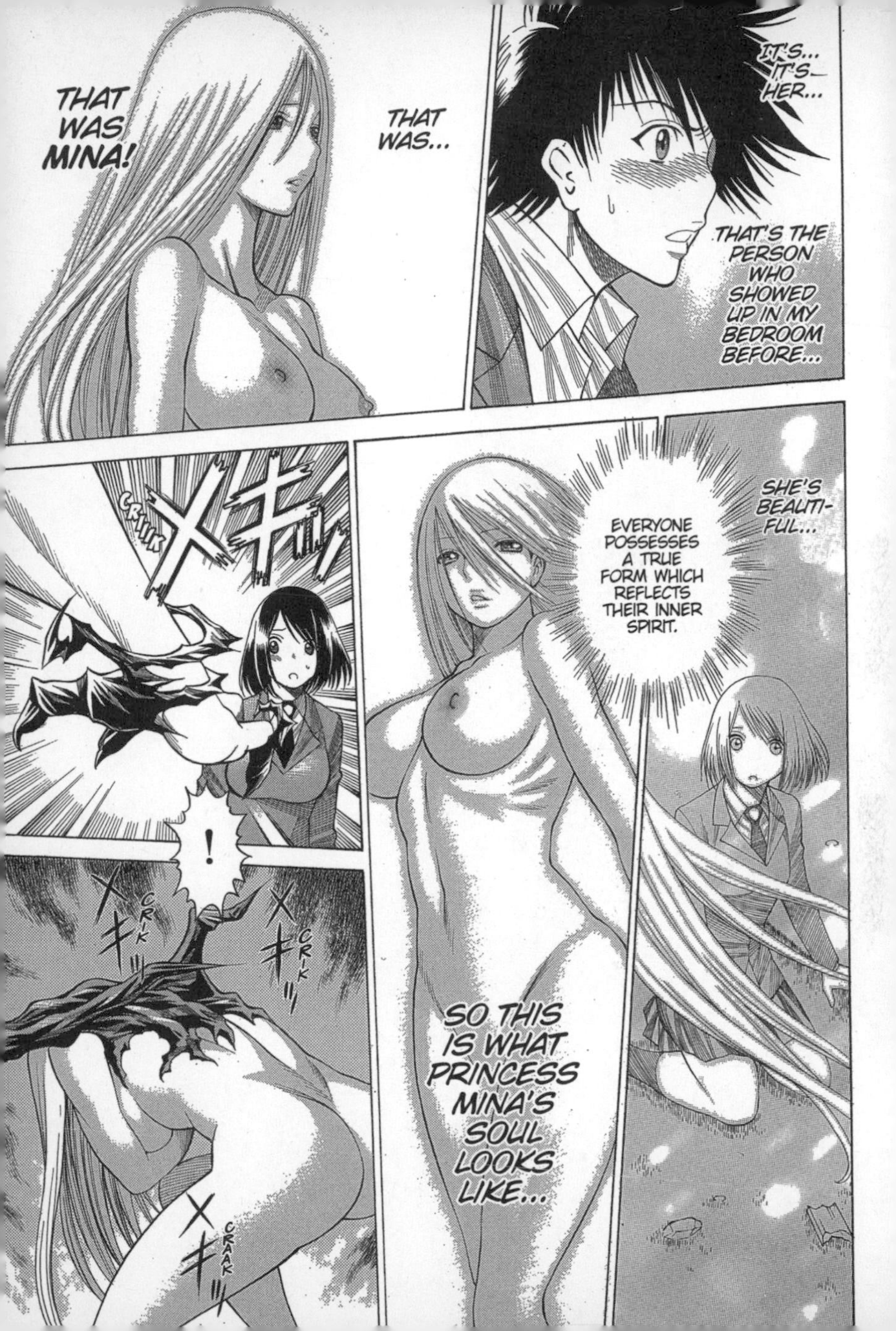

IT'S... IT'S—HER...
THAT'S THE PERSON WHO SHOWED UP IN MY BEDROOM BEFORE...
THAT WAS...
THAT WAS MINA!
SHE'S BEAUTI-FUL...
EVERYONE POSSESSES A TRUE FORM WHICH REFLECTS THEIR INNER SPIRIT.
SO THIS IS WHAT PRINCESS MINA'S SOUL LOOKS LIKE...
CRIIK
!
CRIK
CRIK
CRAAK

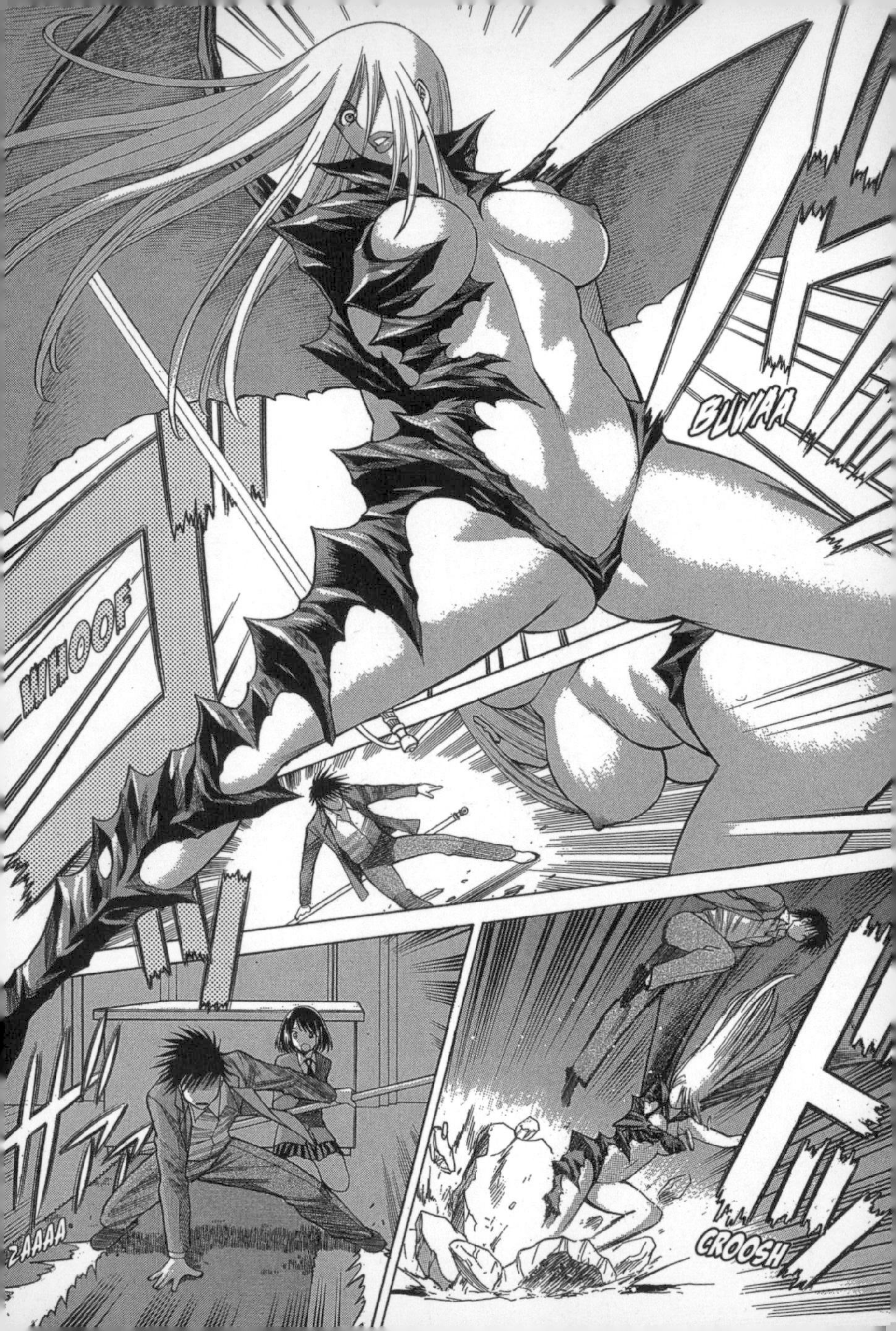
BUWAA
WHOOF
CROOSH
ZAAAA

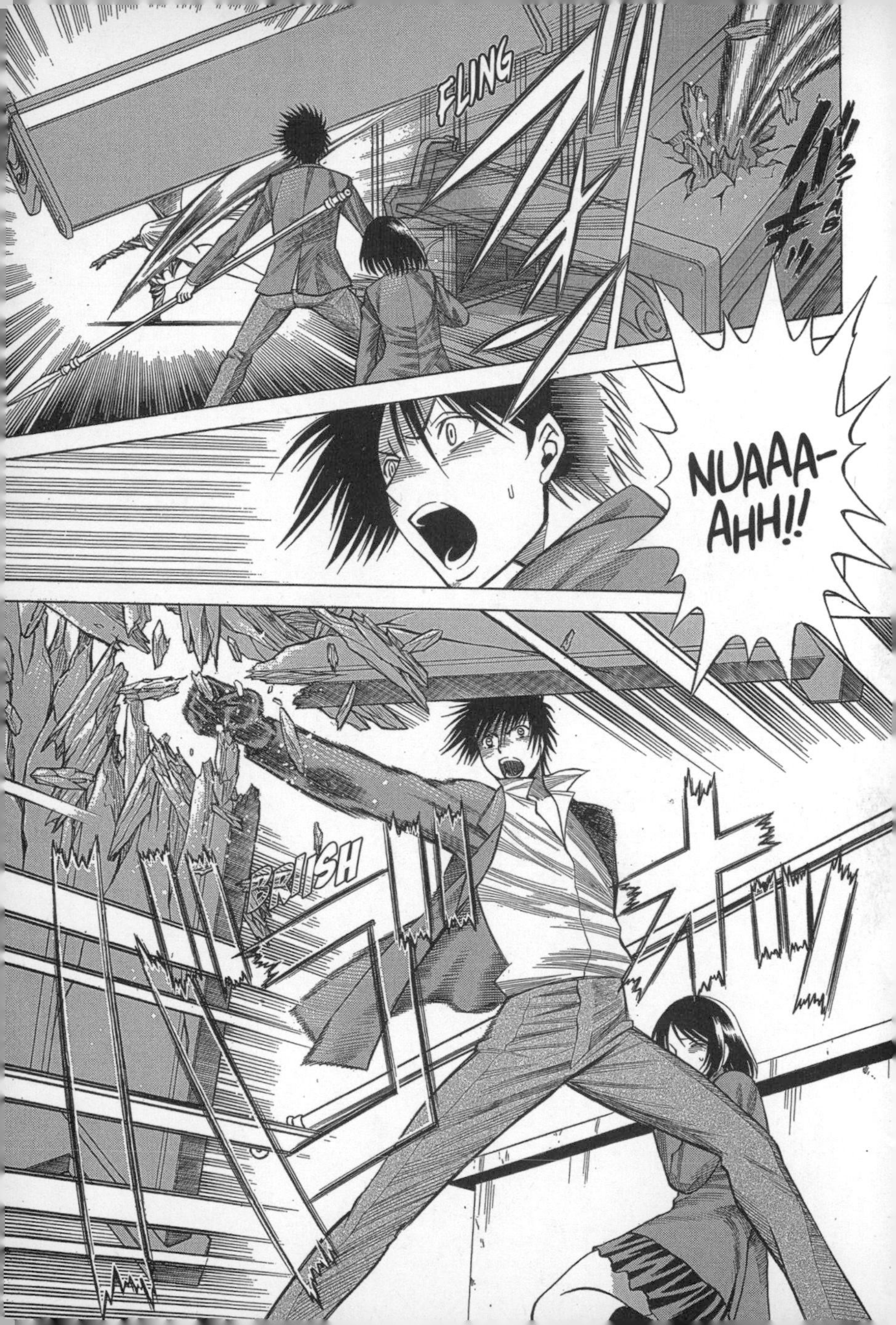
FLING
STAB
NUAAA-
AHH!!
BRIISH

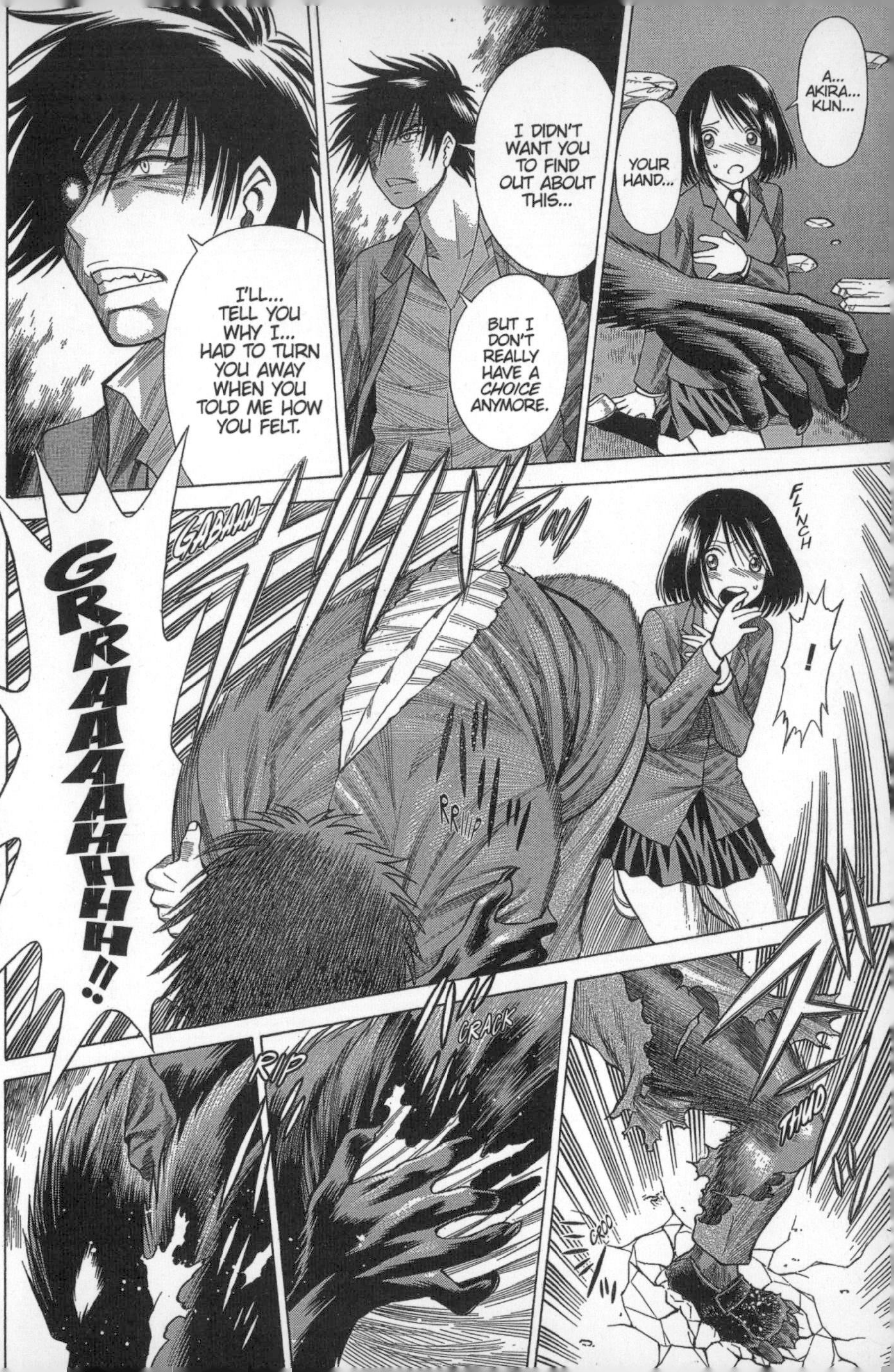
A... AKIRA... KUN...
YOUR HAND...
I DIDN'T WANT YOU TO FIND OUT ABOUT THIS...
BUT I DON'T REALLY HAVE A CHOICE ANYMORE.
I'LL... TELL YOU WHY I... HAD TO TURN YOU AWAY WHEN YOU TOLD ME HOW YOU FELT.
FLINCH
!
RRIIP
GRRAAAAHHHH!!
THUD
CRACK
RIP

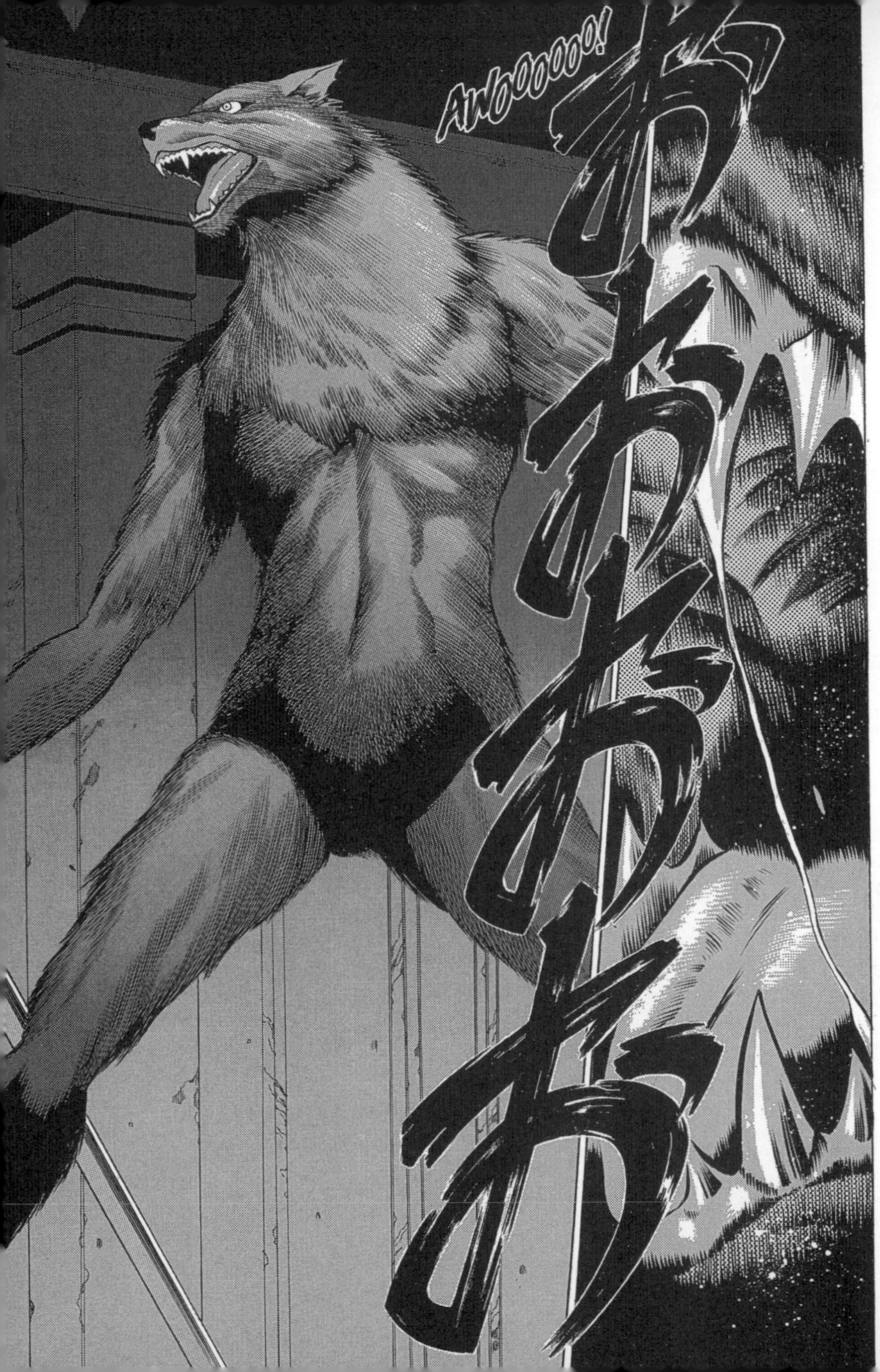
AWOOOOOOO!

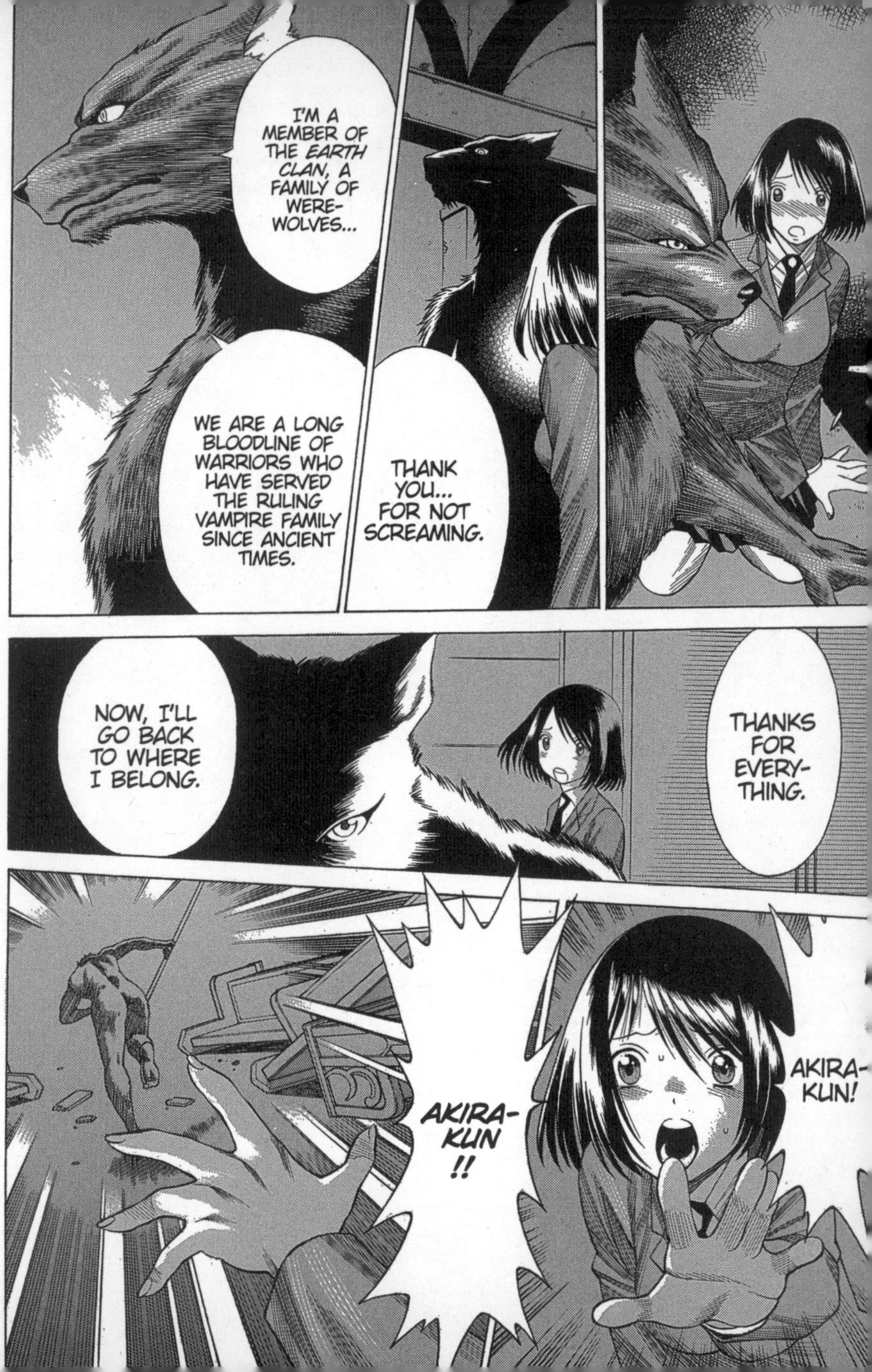
THANK YOU... FOR NOT SCREAMING.
I'M A MEMBER OF THE *EARTH CLAN*, A FAMILY OF WERE-WOLVES...
WE ARE A LONG BLOODLINE OF WARRIORS WHO HAVE SERVED THE RULING VAMPIRE FAMILY SINCE ANCIENT TIMES.
THANKS FOR EVERY-THING.
NOW, I'LL GO BACK TO WHERE I BELONG.
AKIRA-KUN!
AKIRA-KUN !!

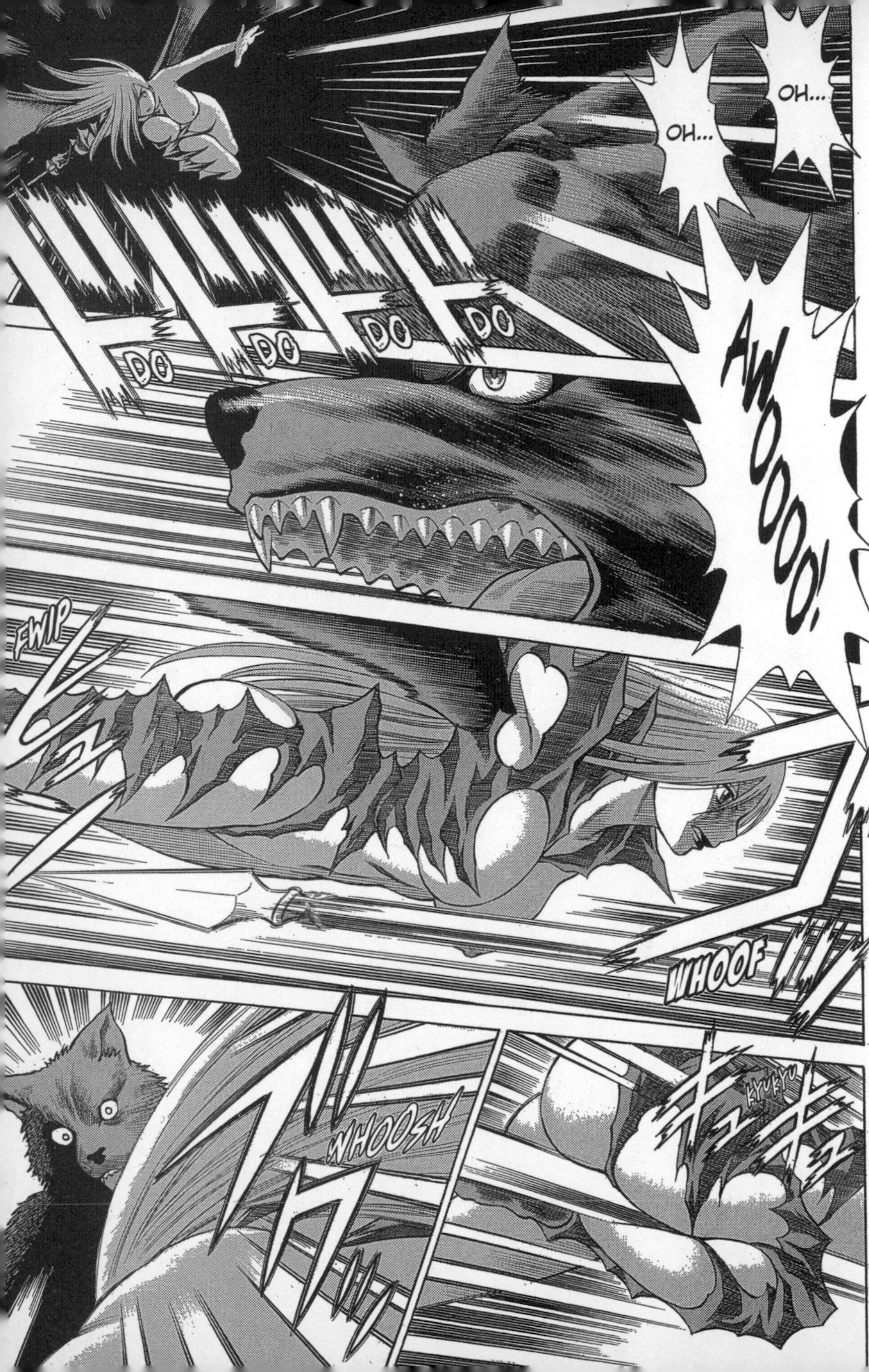
OH...
OH...
AWOOOOO!
DO
DO
DO
DO
FWIP
WHOOF
KYUKYU
WHOOSH

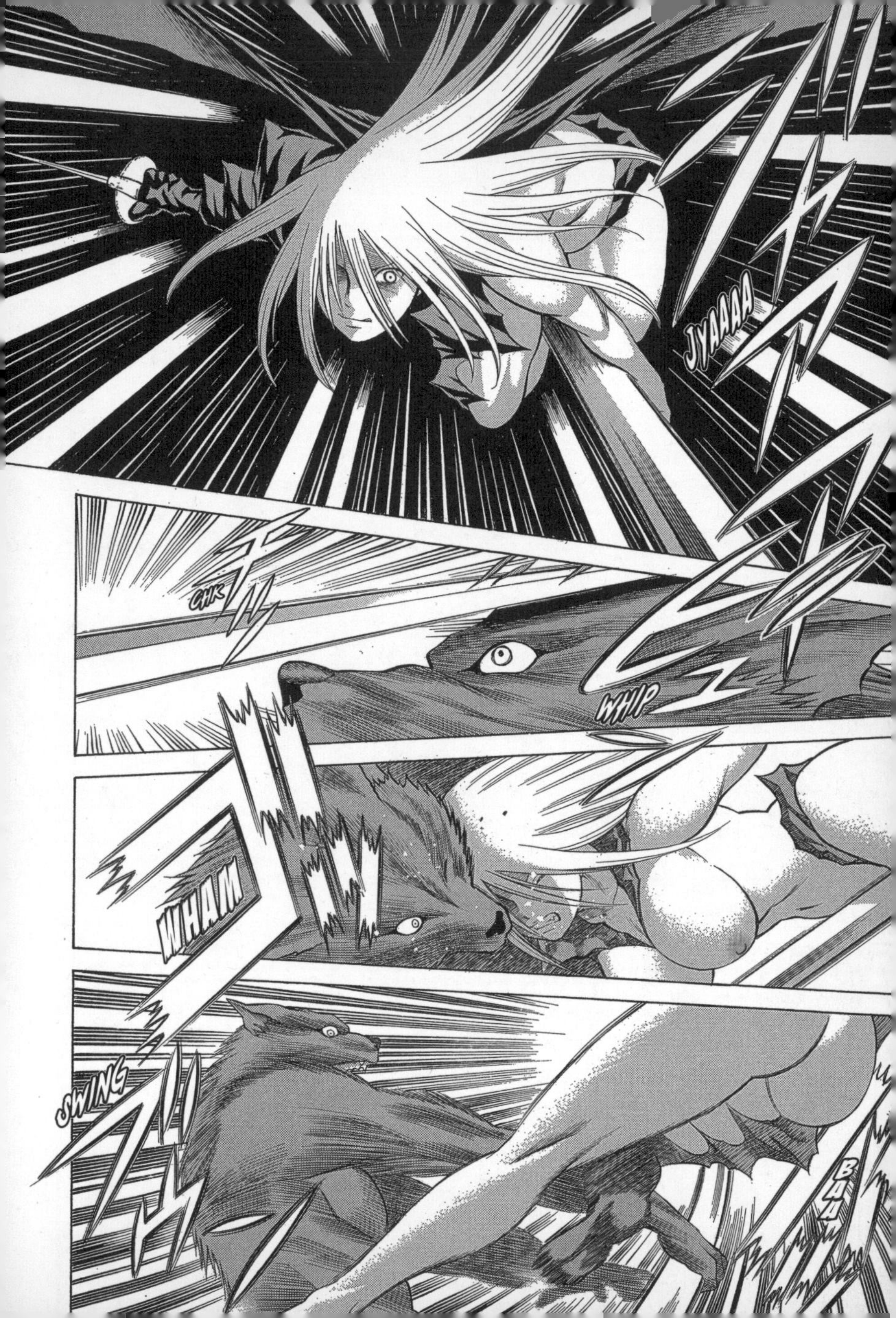
JYAAAA
WHIP
CHK
WHAM
BAA
SWING

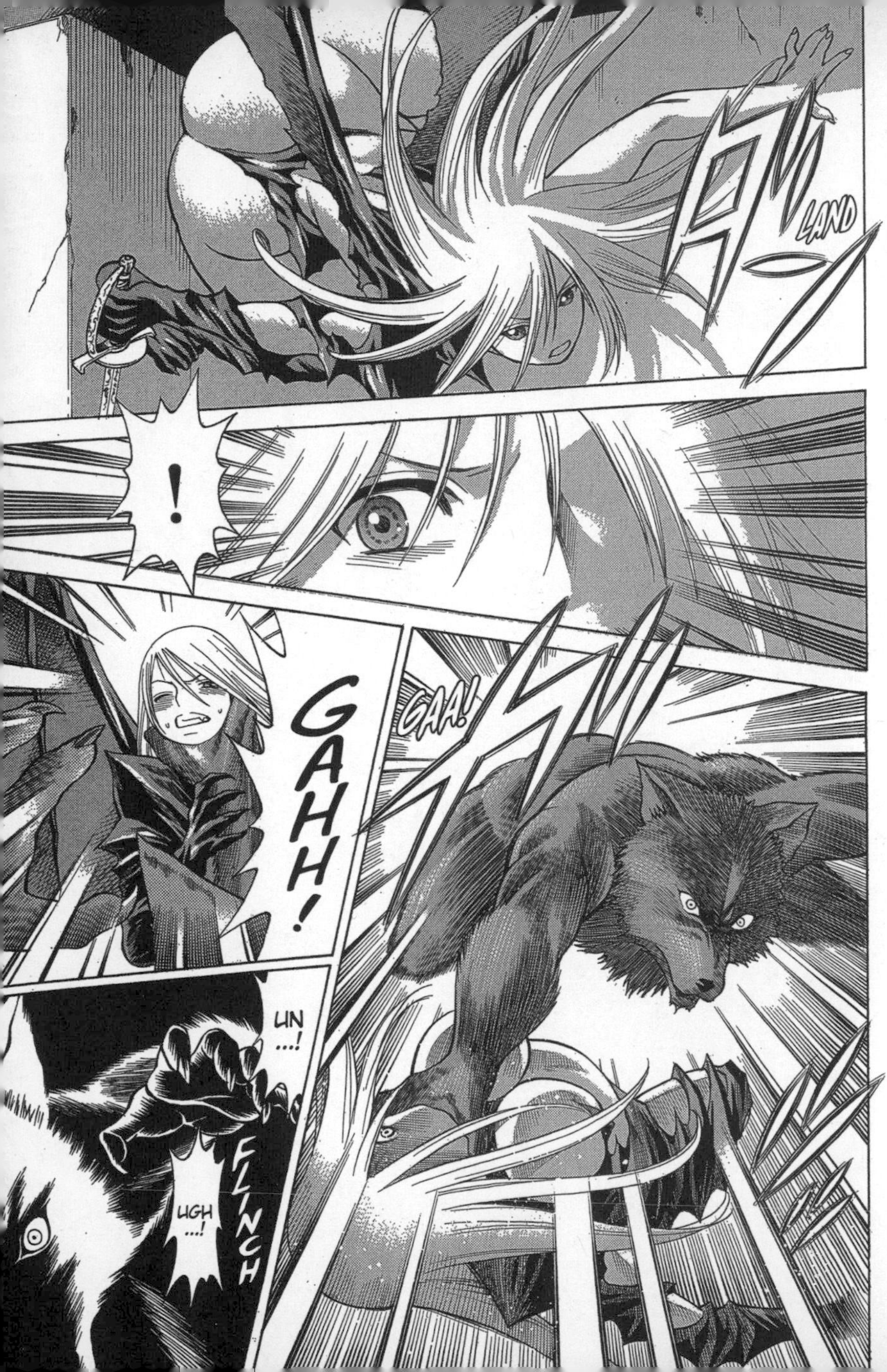
LAND
!
GAA!
GAHH!
UN...!
FLINCH
UGH...!

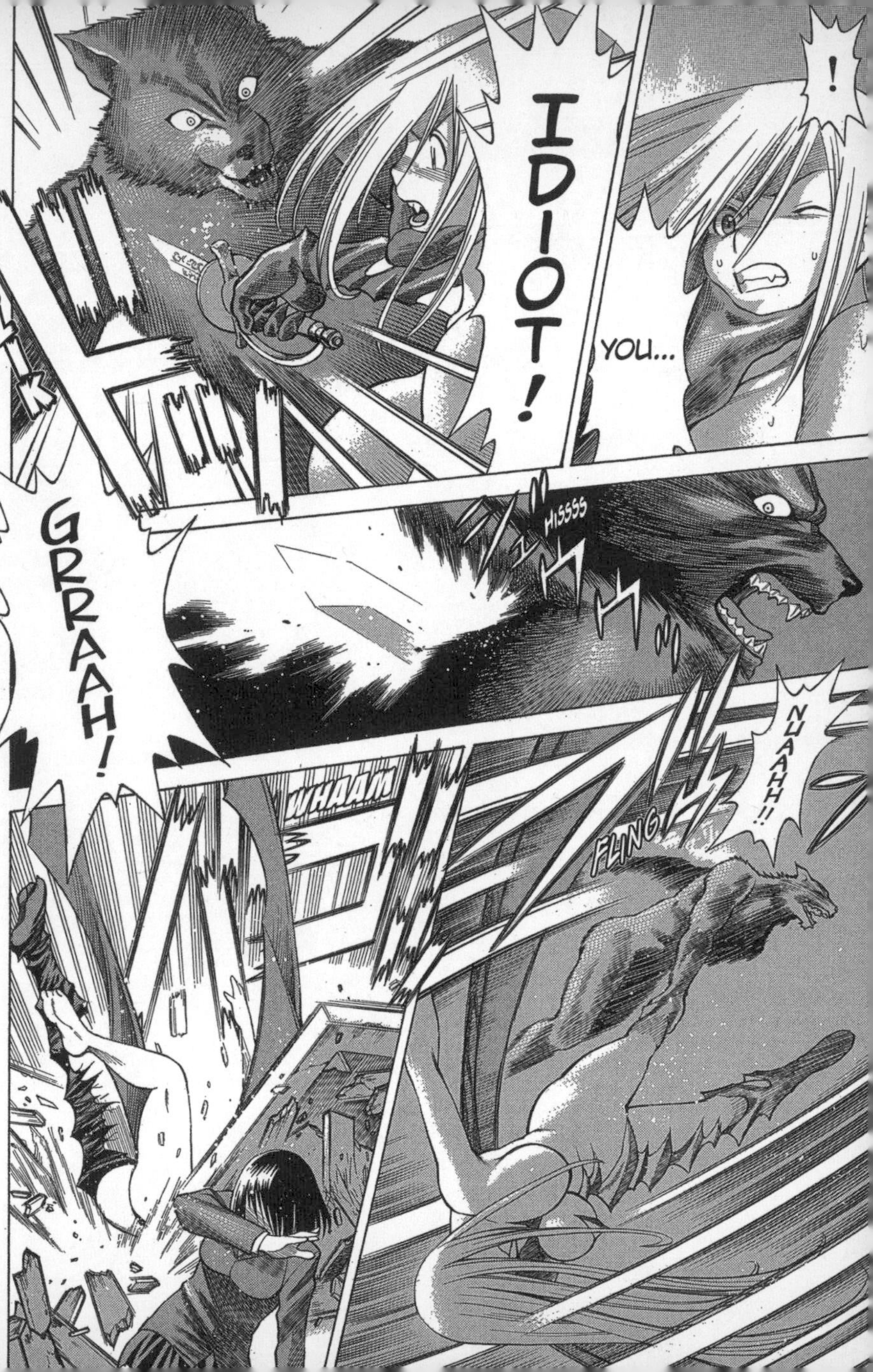
!
YOU...
IDIOT!
SLIK
HISSSS
GRRAAH!
NUAAAHH!!
FLING
WHAAM

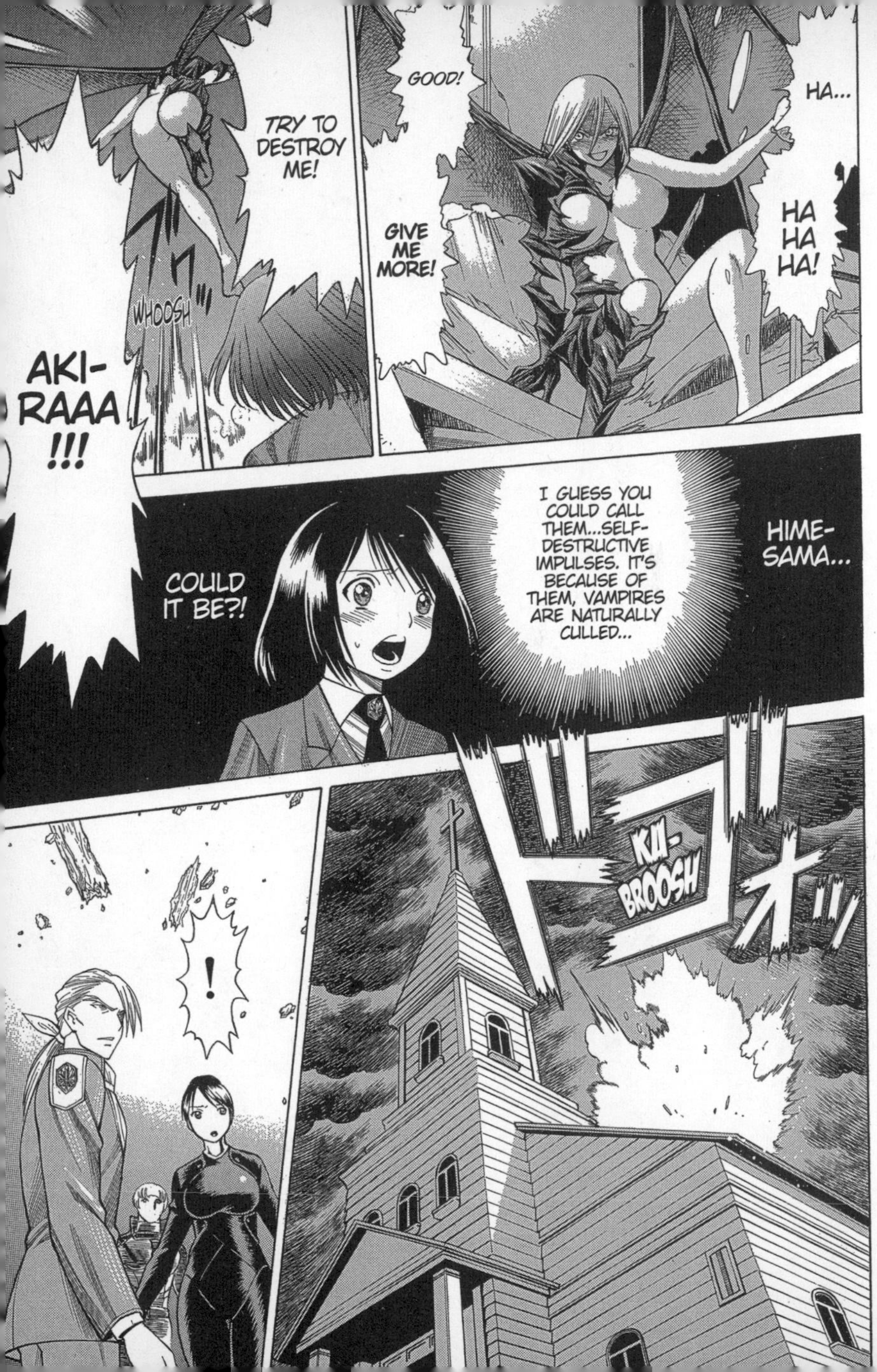

HA...
HA HA HA!
GOOD!
GIVE ME MORE!
TRY TO DESTROY ME!
WHOOSH
AKI-RAAAA!!!
HIME-SAMA...
I GUESS YOU COULD CALL THEM...SELF-DESTRUCTIVE IMPULSES. IT'S BECAUSE OF THEM, VAMPIRES ARE NATURALLY CULLED...
COULD IT BE?!
KA-BROOSH
!

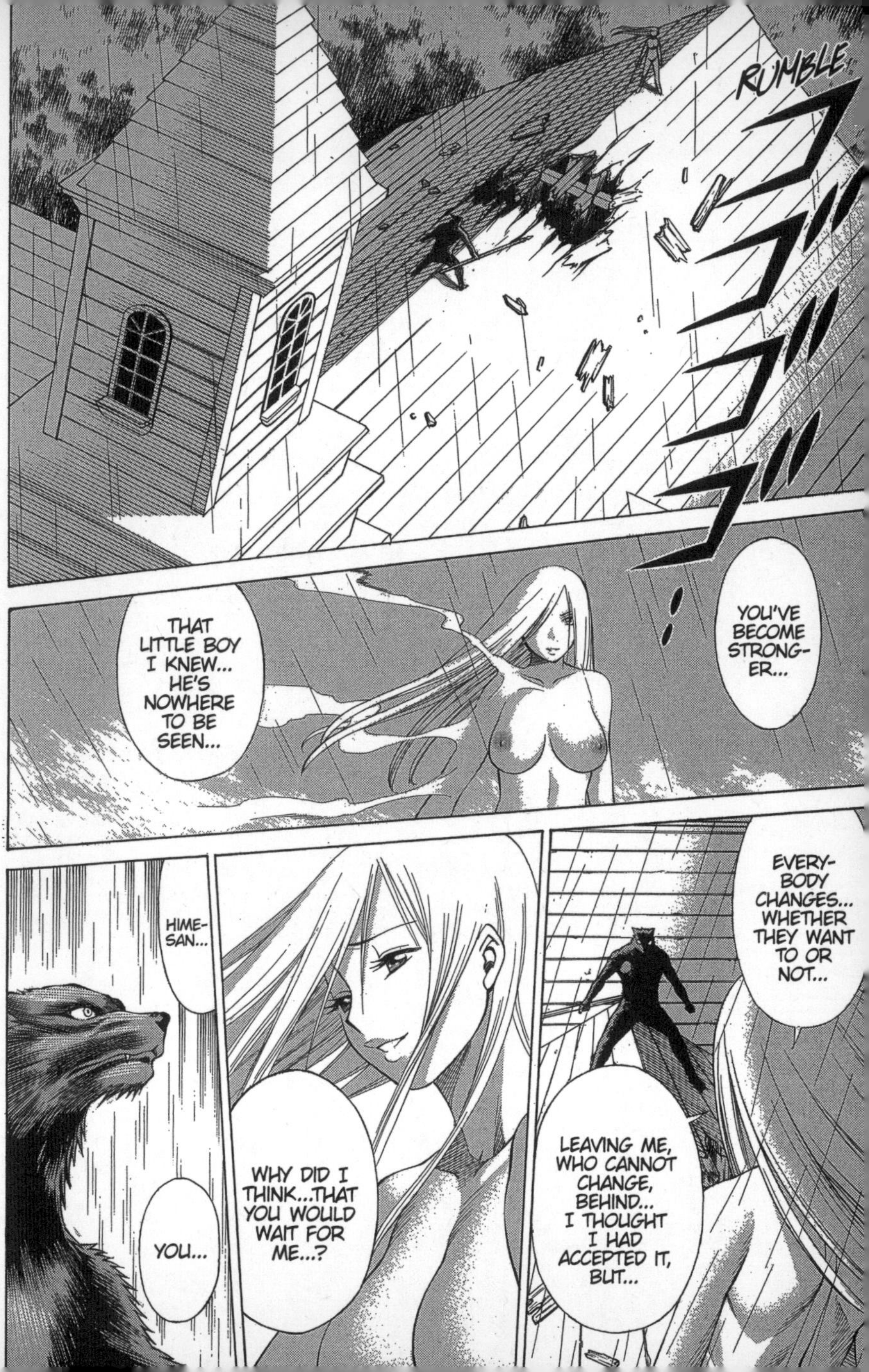
RUMBLE
YOU'VE BECOME STRONGER...
THAT LITTLE BOY I KNEW... HE'S NOWHERE TO BE SEEN...
EVERYBODY CHANGES... WHETHER THEY WANT TO OR NOT...
LEAVING ME, WHO CANNOT CHANGE, BEHIND... I THOUGHT I HAD ACCEPTED IT, BUT...
WHY DID I THINK...THAT YOU WOULD WAIT FOR ME...?
HIME-SAN...
YOU...

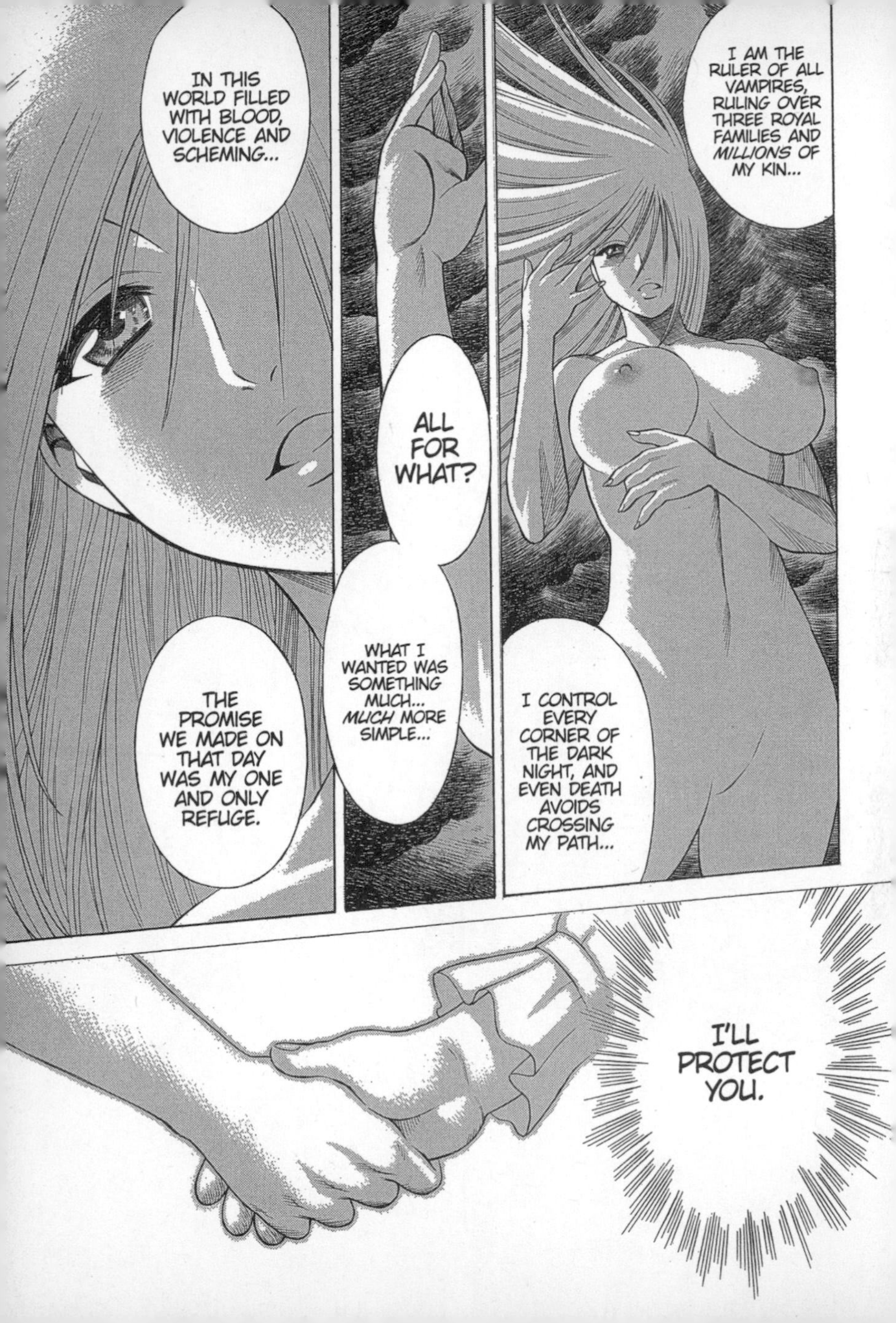
I AM THE RULER OF ALL VAMPIRES, RULING OVER THREE ROYAL FAMILIES AND *MILLIONS* OF MY KIN...
I CONTROL EVERY CORNER OF THE DARK NIGHT, AND EVEN DEATH AVOIDS CROSSING MY PATH...
ALL FOR WHAT?
WHAT I WANTED WAS SOMETHING MUCH... *MUCH* MORE SIMPLE...
IN THIS WORLD FILLED WITH BLOOD, VIOLENCE AND SCHEMING...
THE PROMISE WE MADE ON THAT DAY WAS MY ONE AND ONLY REFUGE.
I'LL PROTECT YOU.

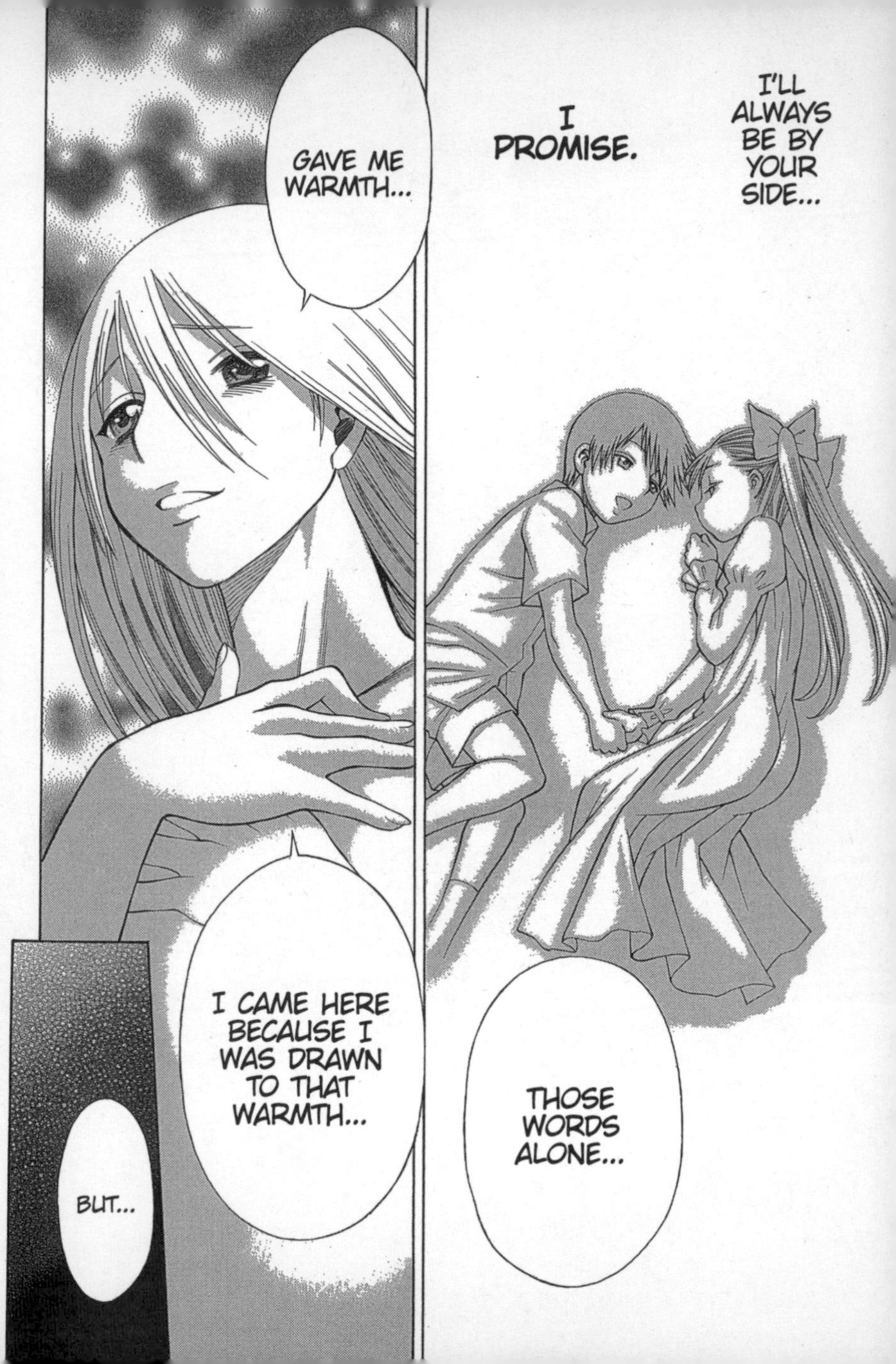
I'LL ALWAYS BE BY YOUR SIDE...
I PROMISE.
THOSE WORDS ALONE...
GAVE ME WARMTH...
I CAME HERE BECAUSE I WAS DRAWN TO THAT WARMTH...
BUT...

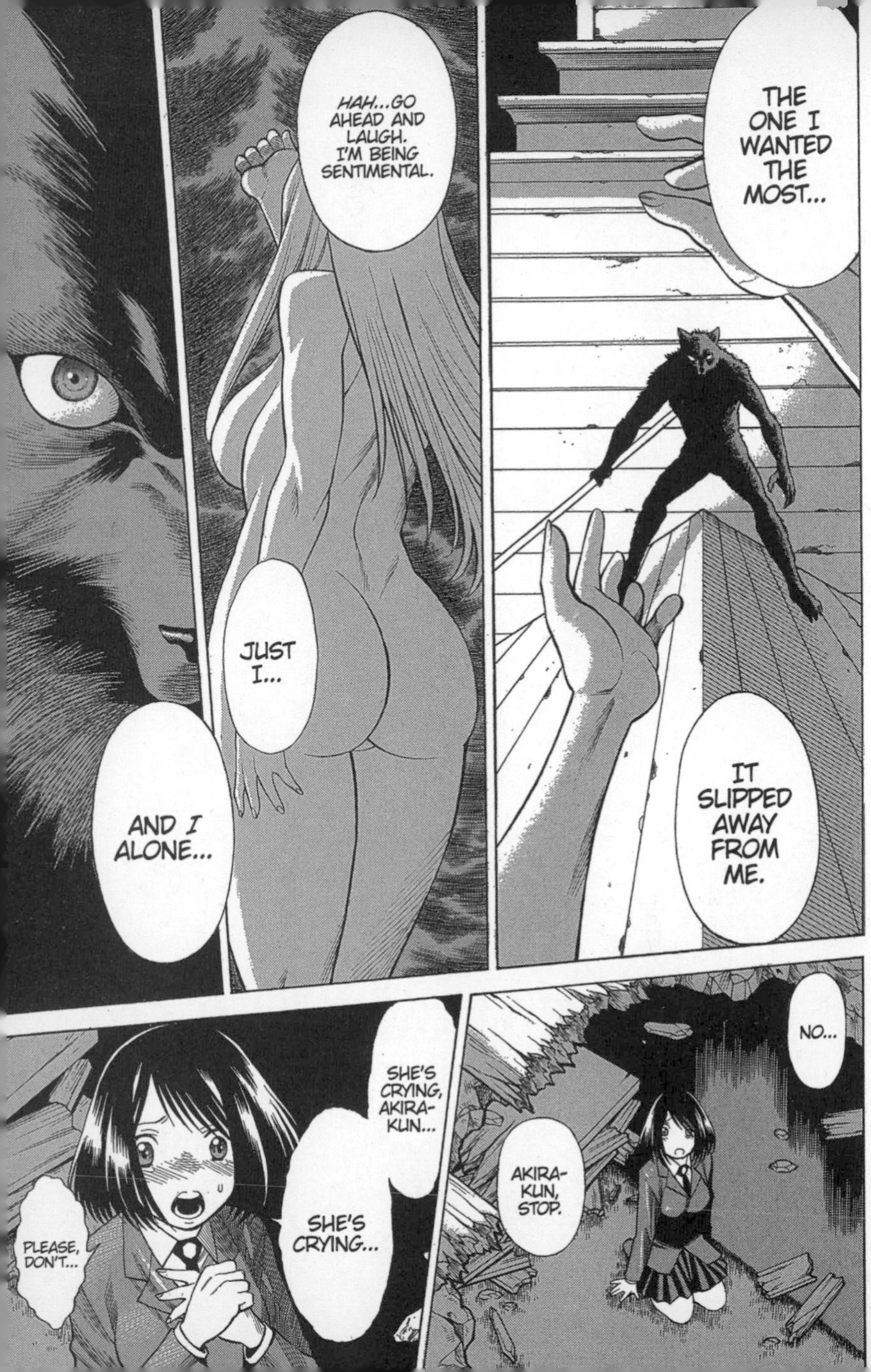
THE ONE I WANTED THE MOST...
IT SLIPPED AWAY FROM ME.
HAH...GO AHEAD AND LAUGH. I'M BEING SENTIMENTAL.
JUST I...
AND I ALONE...
NO...
AKIRA-KUN, STOP.
SHE'S CRYING, AKIRA-KUN...
SHE'S CRYING...
PLEASE, DON'T...

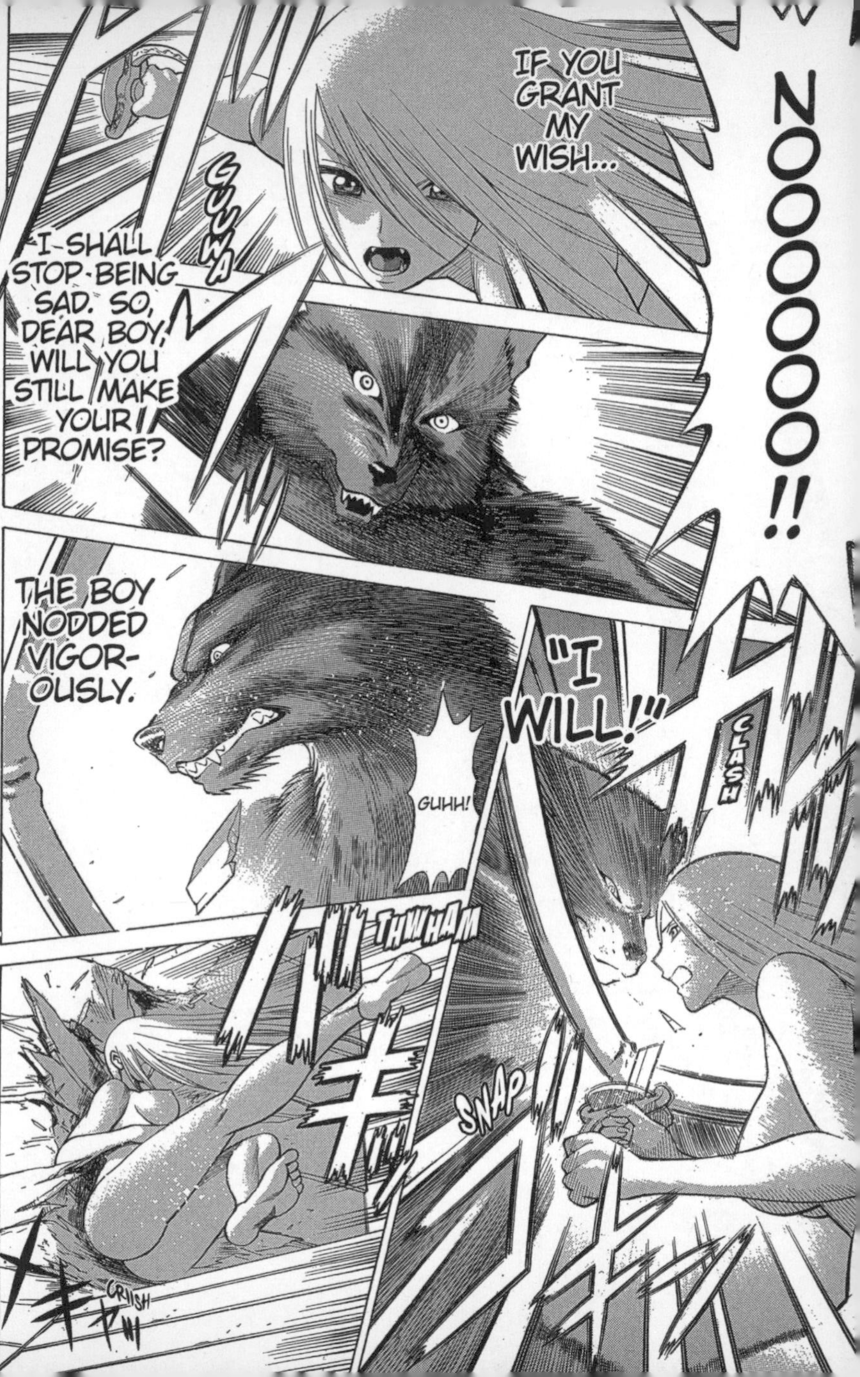
NOOOOOO!!
IF YOU GRANT MY WISH...
GUWA
I-SHALL STOP BEING SAD. SO, DEAR BOY, WILL YOU STILL MAKE YOUR PROMISE?
"I WILL!"
CLASH
THE BOY NODDED VIGOROUSLY.
GUHH!
THWHAM
SNAP
CRUSH

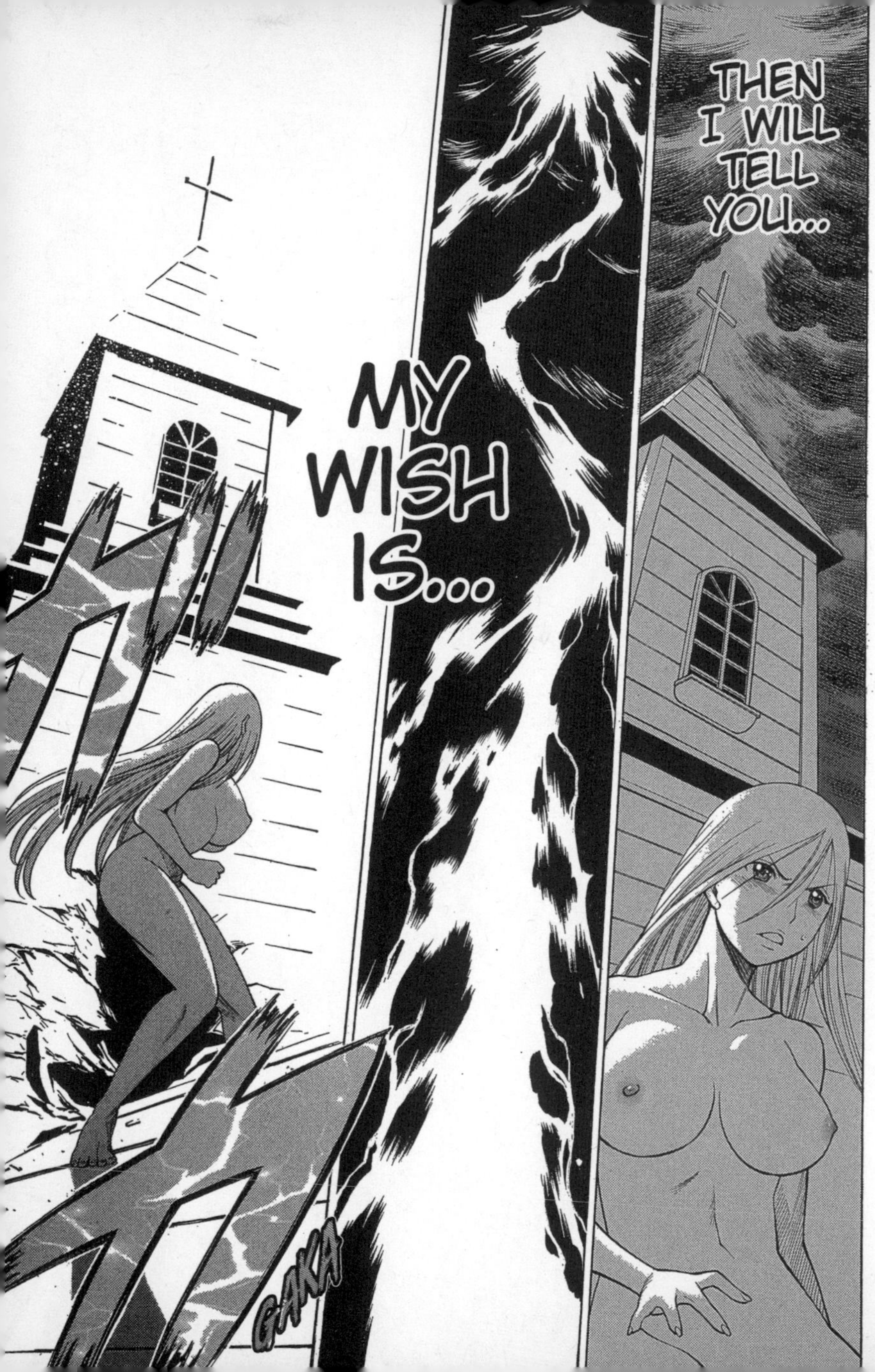
THEN I WILL TELL YOU...
MY WISH IS...
GAKA

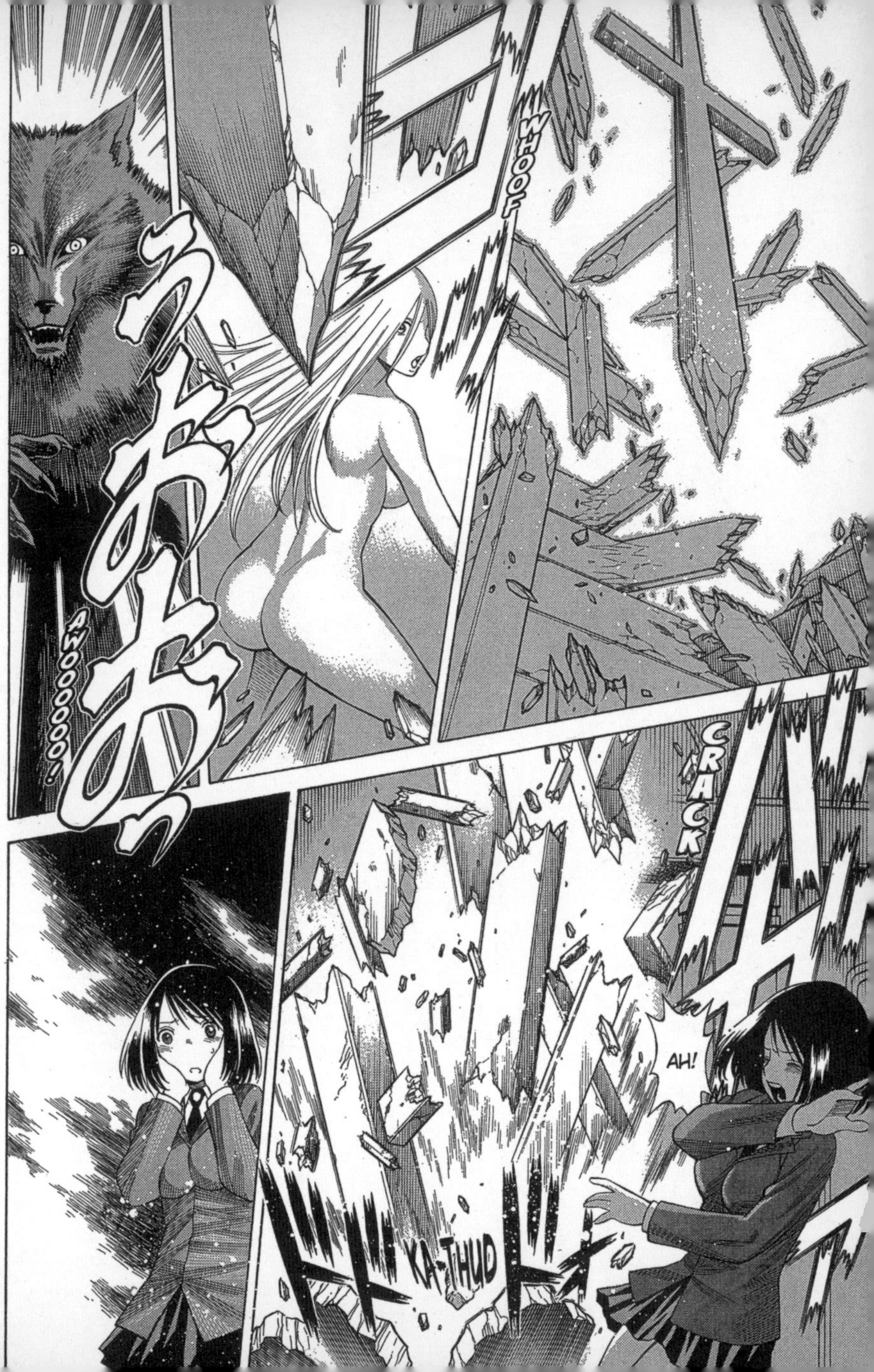
WHOOF
AWOOOOOOOO!
CRACK
AH!
KA-THUD

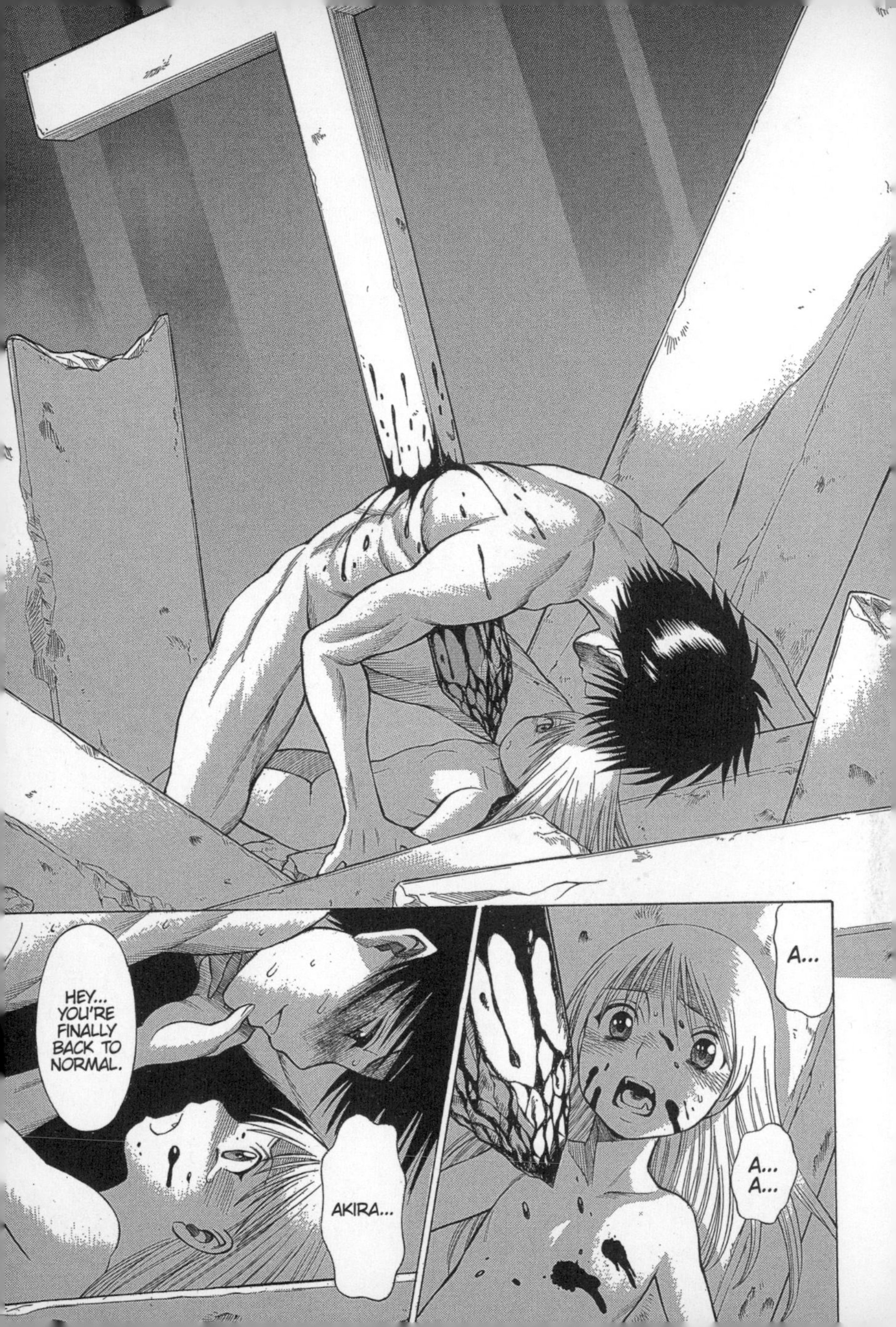
A...
A...
A...
HEY... YOU'RE FINALLY BACK TO NORMAL.
AKIRA...

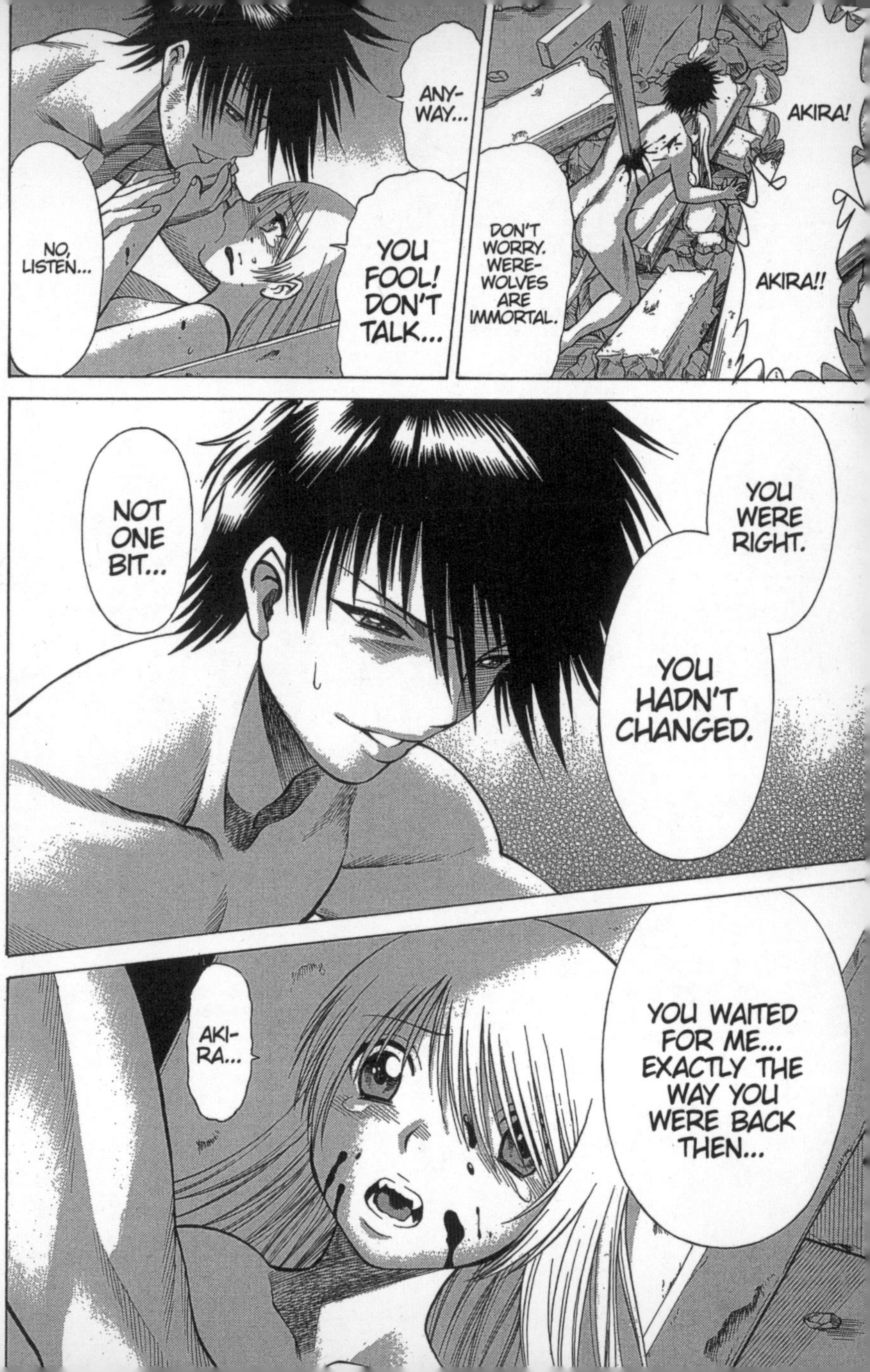
AKIRA!
AKIRA!!
DON'T WORRY. WERE-WOLVES ARE IMMORTAL.
YOU FOOL! DON'T TALK...
ANY-WAY...
NO, LISTEN...
YOU WERE RIGHT.
YOU HADN'T CHANGED.
NOT ONE BIT...
YOU WAITED FOR ME... EXACTLY THE WAY YOU WERE BACK THEN...
AKI-RA...

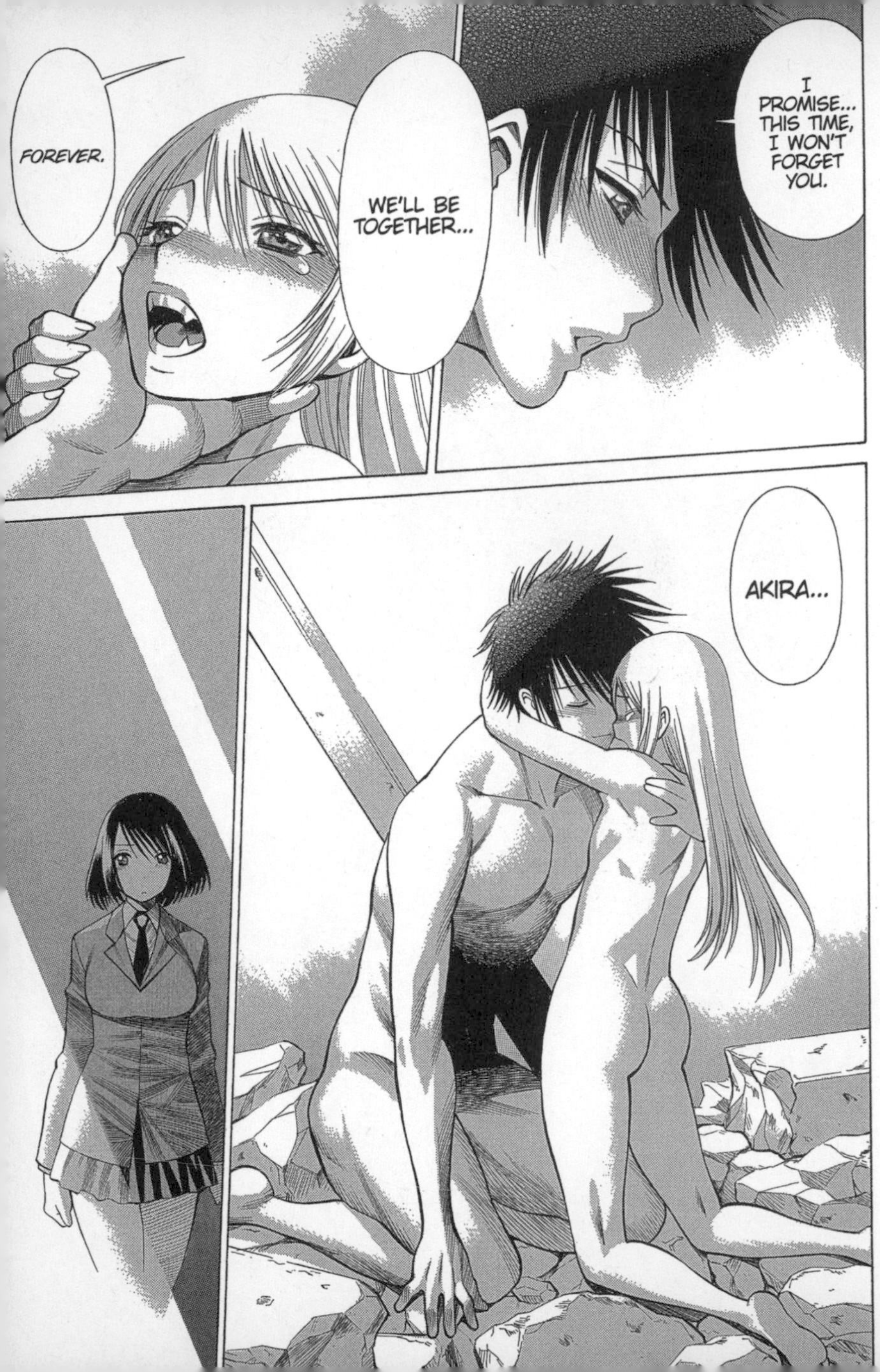

I PROMISE... THIS TIME, I WON'T FORGET YOU.
WE'LL BE TOGETHER...
FOREVER.
AKIRA...

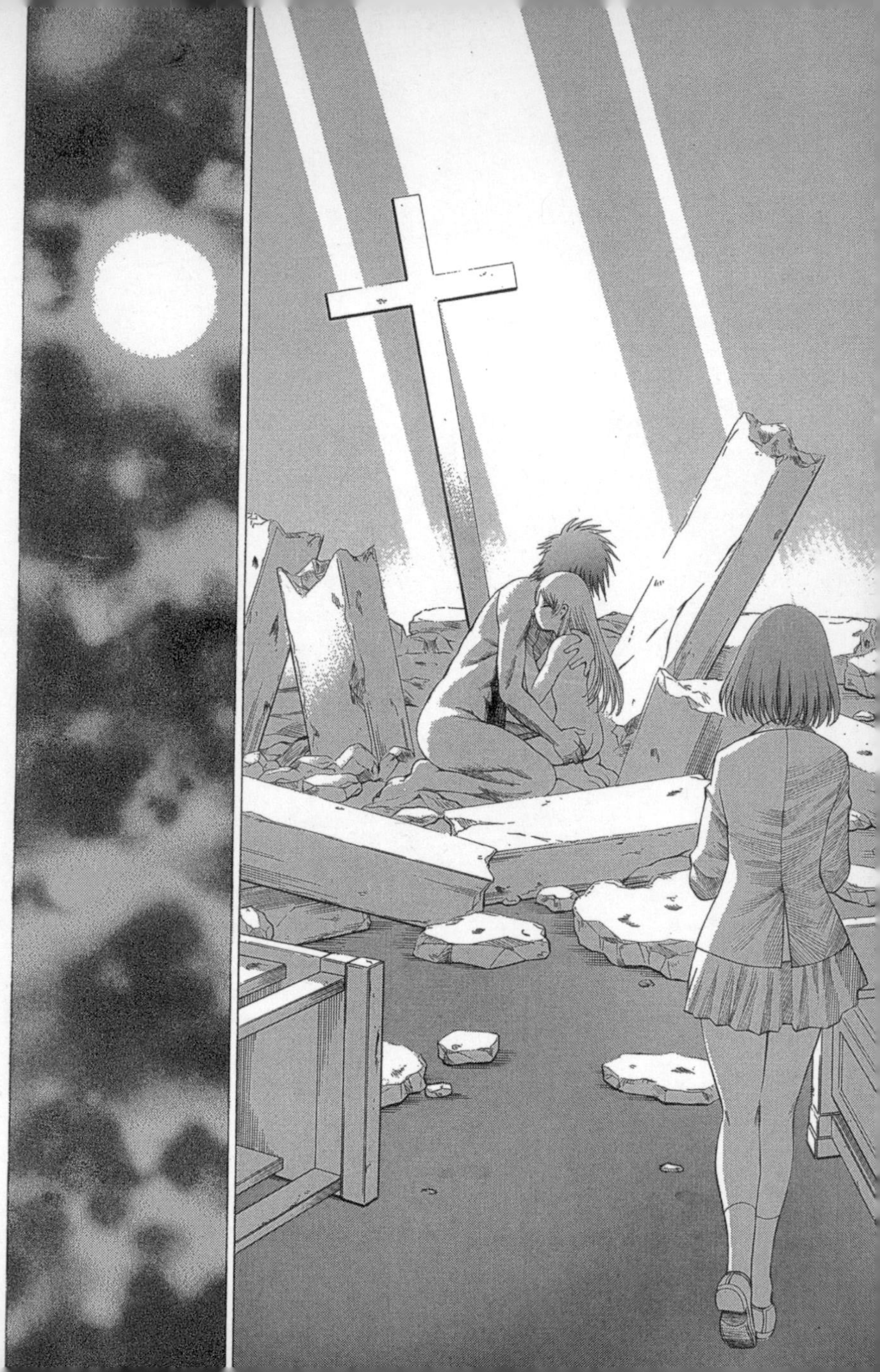

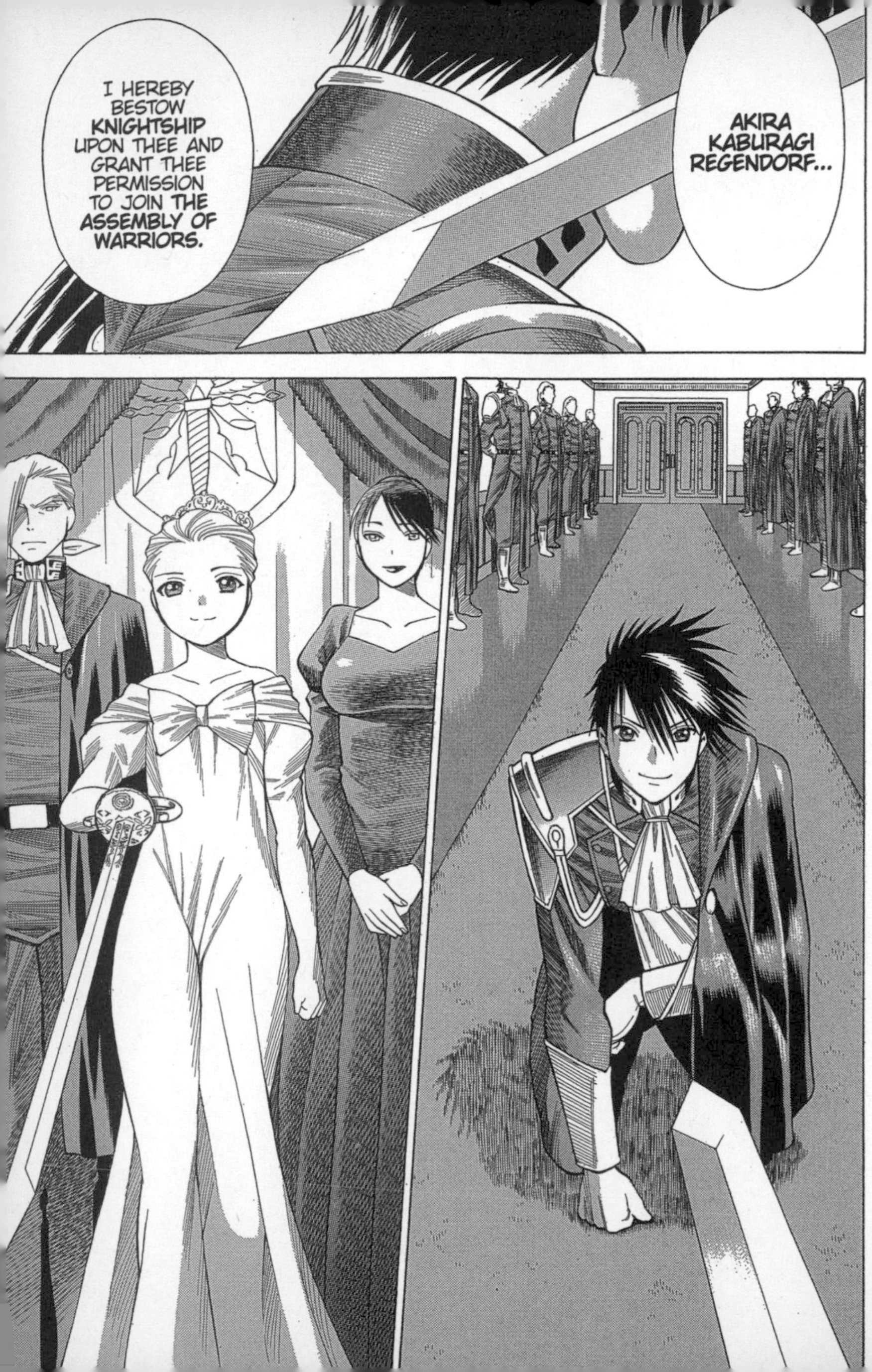
AKIRA KABURAGI REGENDORF...
I HEREBY BESTOW KNIGHTSHIP UPON THEE AND GRANT THEE PERMISSION TO JOIN THE ASSEMBLY OF WARRIORS.

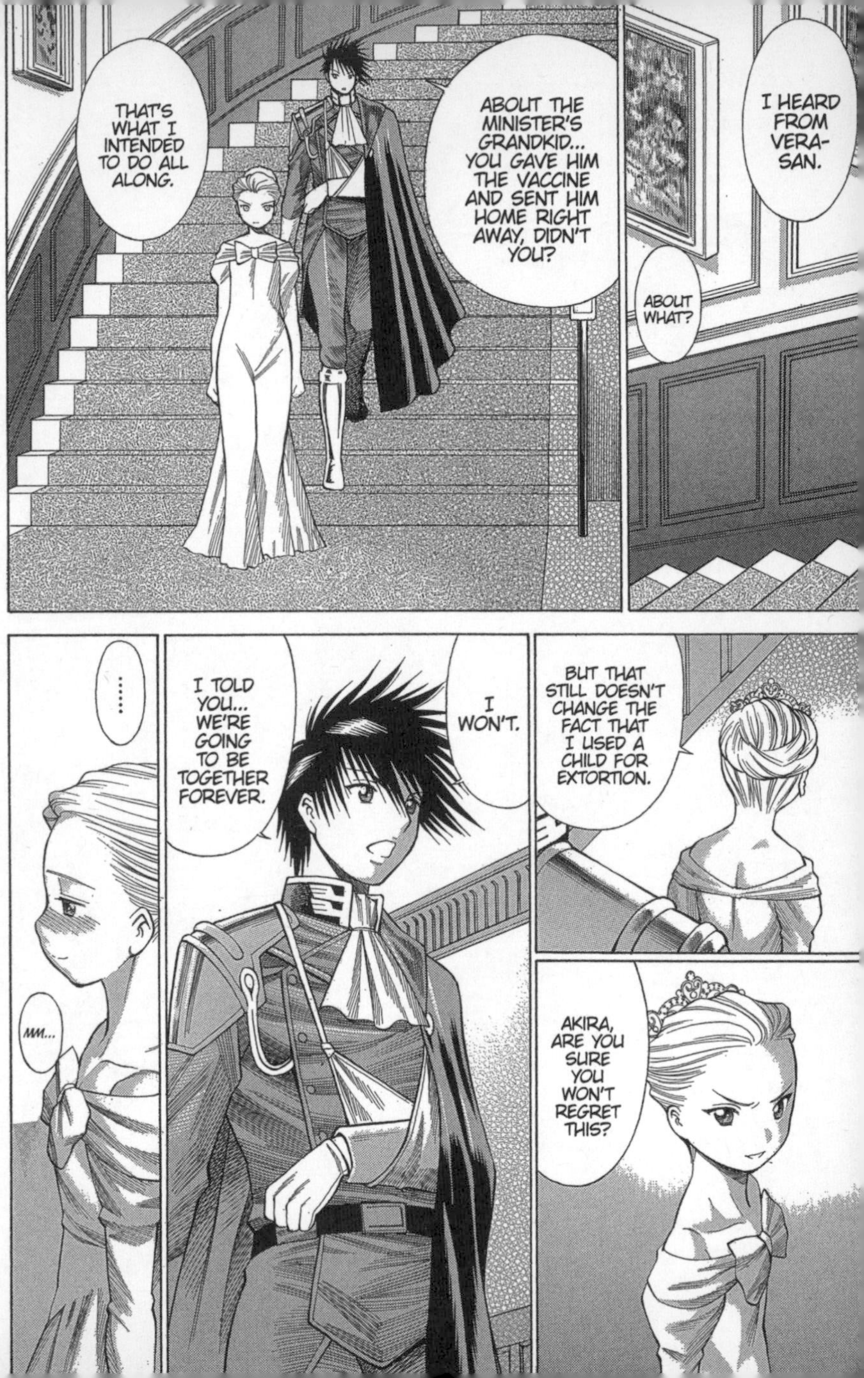
I HEARD FROM VERA-SAN.
ABOUT WHAT?
ABOUT THE MINISTER'S GRANDKID... YOU GAVE HIM THE VACCINE AND SENT HIM HOME RIGHT AWAY, DIDN'T YOU?
THAT'S WHAT I INTENDED TO DO ALL ALONG.
BUT THAT STILL DOESN'T CHANGE THE FACT THAT I USED A CHILD FOR EXTORTION.
AKIRA, ARE YOU SURE YOU WON'T REGRET THIS?
I WON'T.
I TOLD YOU... WE'RE GOING TO BE TOGETHER FOREVER.
......
MM...

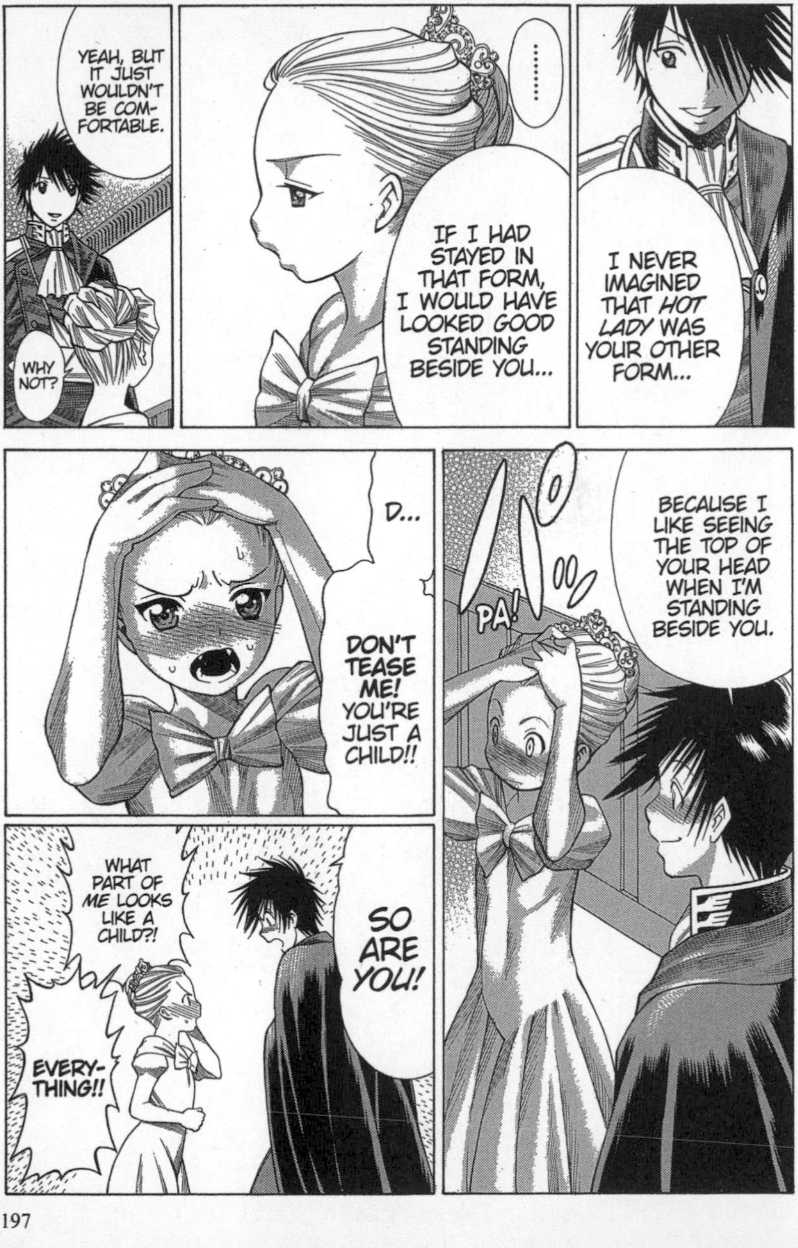

I NEVER IMAGINED THAT *HOT LADY* WAS YOUR OTHER FORM...
......
IF I HAD STAYED IN THAT FORM, I WOULD HAVE LOOKED GOOD STANDING BESIDE YOU...
YEAH, BUT IT JUST WOULDN'T BE COM-FORTABLE.
WHY NOT?
BECAUSE I LIKE SEEING THE TOP OF YOUR HEAD WHEN I'M STANDING BESIDE YOU.
PA!
D...
DON'T TEASE ME! YOU'RE JUST A CHILD!!
SO ARE YOU!
WHAT PART OF *ME* LOOKS LIKE A CHILD?!
EVERY-THING!!

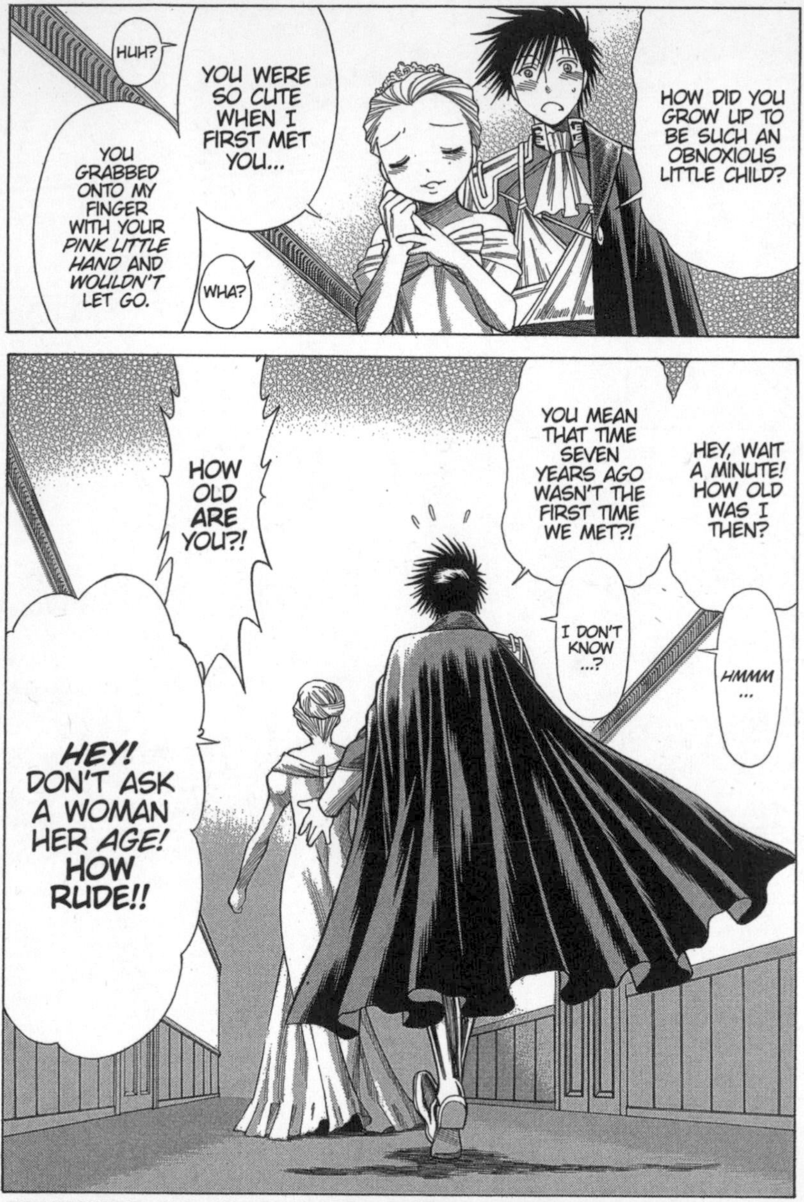
HOW DID YOU GROW UP TO BE SUCH AN OBNOXIOUS LITTLE CHILD?
YOU WERE SO CUTE WHEN I FIRST MET YOU...
HUH?
YOU GRABBED ONTO MY FINGER WITH YOUR *PINK LITTLE HAND* AND *WOULDN'T* LET GO.
WHA?
HEY, WAIT A MINUTE! HOW OLD WAS I THEN?
YOU MEAN THAT TIME SEVEN YEARS AGO WASN'T THE FIRST TIME WE MET?!
HMMM ...
I DON'T KNOW ...?
HOW OLD ARE YOU?!
HEY! DON'T ASK A WOMAN HER *AGE!* HOW RUDE!!

CONTINUED IN DANCE IN THE VAMPIRE BUND VOLUME 3

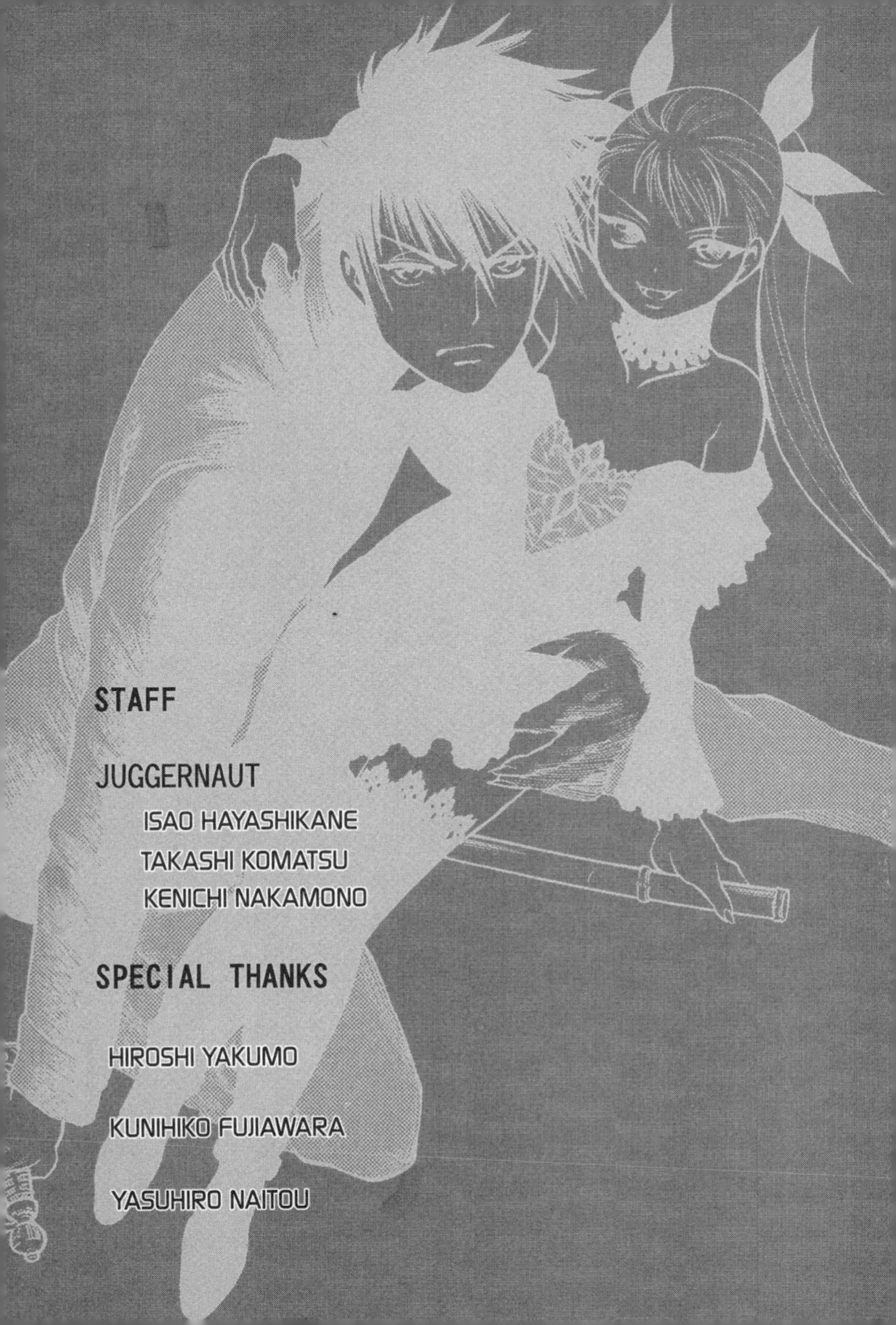

STAFF

JUGGERNAUT

ISAO HAYASHIKANE

TAKASHI KOMATSU

KENICHI NAKAMONO

SPECIAL THANKS

HIROSHI YAKUMO

KUNIHIKO FUJIAWARA

YASUHIRO NAITOU

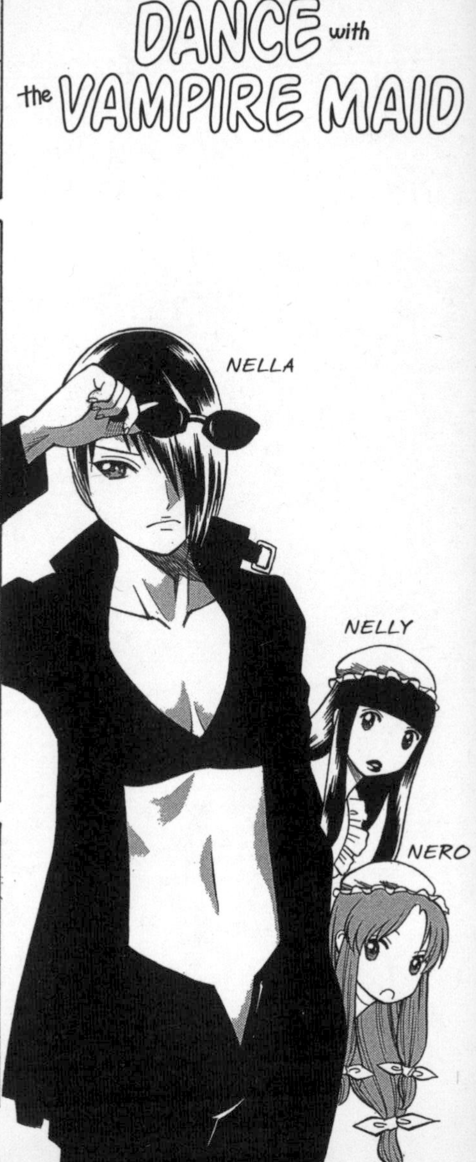
DANCE with the VAMPIRE MAID
NELLA
NELLY
NERO

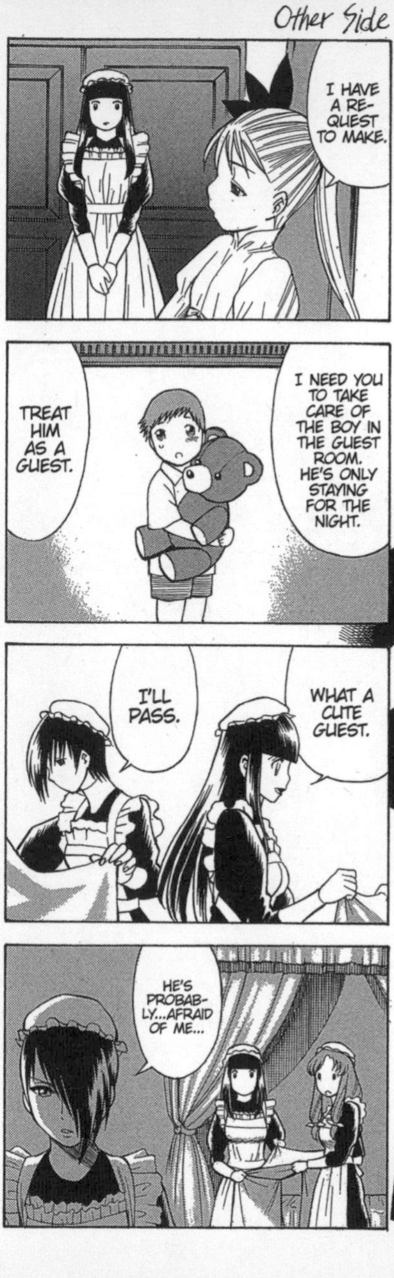
Other Side
I HAVE A REQUEST TO MAKE.
I NEED YOU TO TAKE CARE OF THE BOY IN THE GUEST ROOM. HE'S ONLY STAYING FOR THE NIGHT.
TREAT HIM AS A GUEST.
WHAT A CUTE GUEST.
I'LL PASS.
HE'S PROBABLY...AFRAID OF ME...

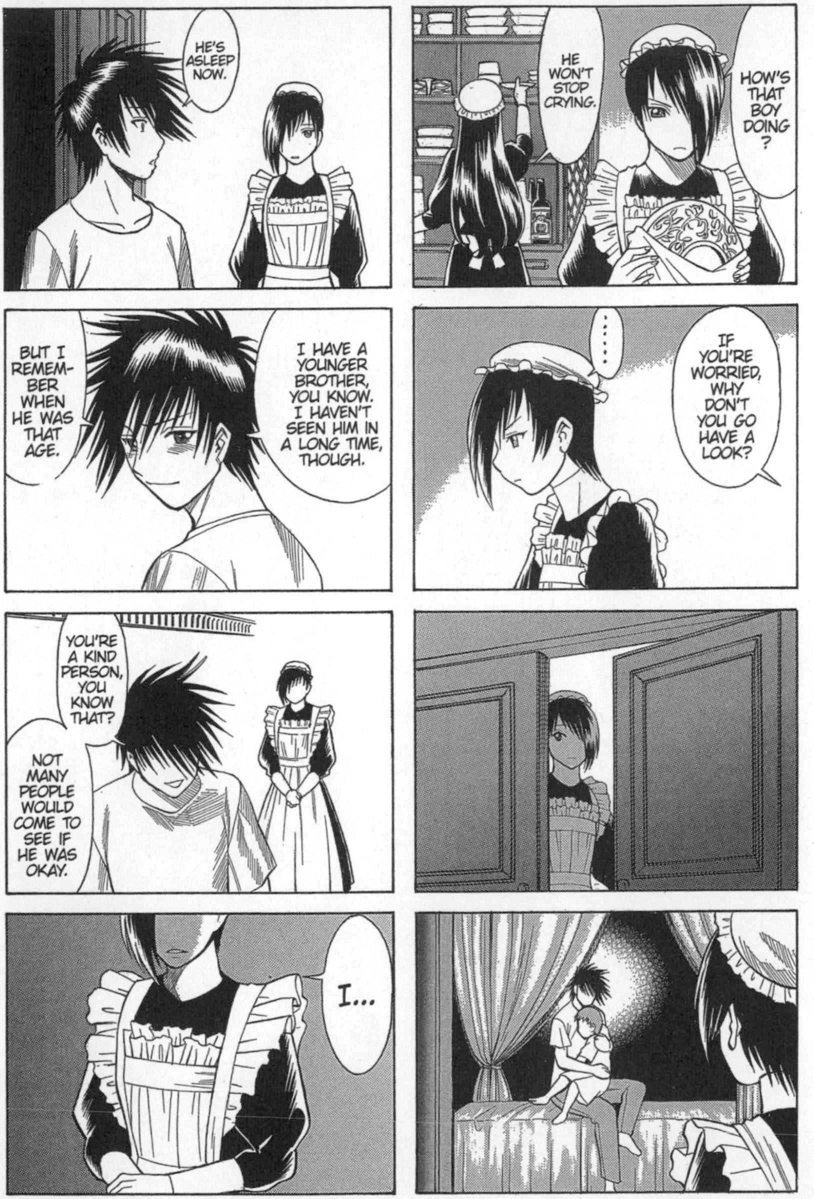
HOW'S THAT BOY DOING?
HE WON'T STOP CRYING.
HE'S ASLEEP NOW.
IF YOU'RE WORRIED, WHY DON'T YOU GO HAVE A LOOK?
......
I HAVE A YOUNGER BROTHER, YOU KNOW. I HAVEN'T SEEN HIM IN A LONG TIME, THOUGH.
BUT I REMEM-BER WHEN HE WAS THAT AGE.
YOU'RE A KIND PERSON, YOU KNOW THAT?
NOT MANY PEOPLE WOULD COME TO SEE IF HE WAS OKAY.
I...

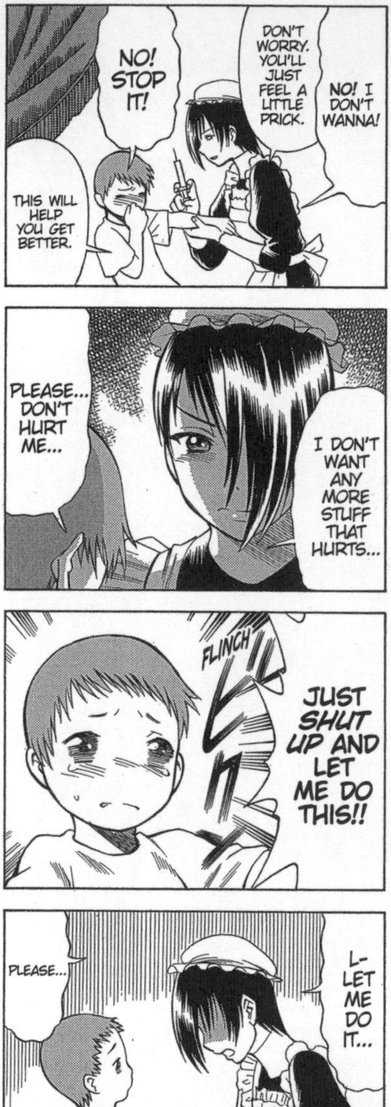
NO! I DON'T WANNA!
DON'T WORRY. YOU'LL JUST FEEL A LITTLE PRICK.
NO! STOP IT!
THIS WILL HELP YOU GET BETTER.
PLEASE... DON'T HURT ME...
I DON'T WANT ANY MORE STUFF THAT HURTS...
FLINCH
JUST SHUT UP AND LET ME DO THIS!!
L-LET ME DO IT...
PLEASE...
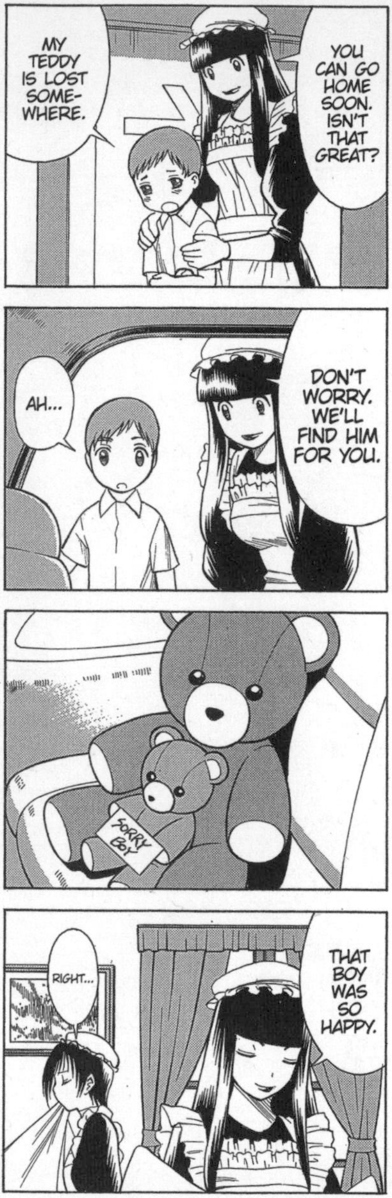
YOU CAN GO HOME SOON. ISN'T THAT GREAT?
MY TEDDY IS LOST SOME-WHERE.
DON'T WORRY. WE'LL FIND HIM FOR YOU.
AH...
SORRY BOY
THAT BOY WAS SO HAPPY.
RIGHT...

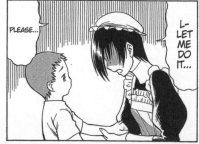

After Side

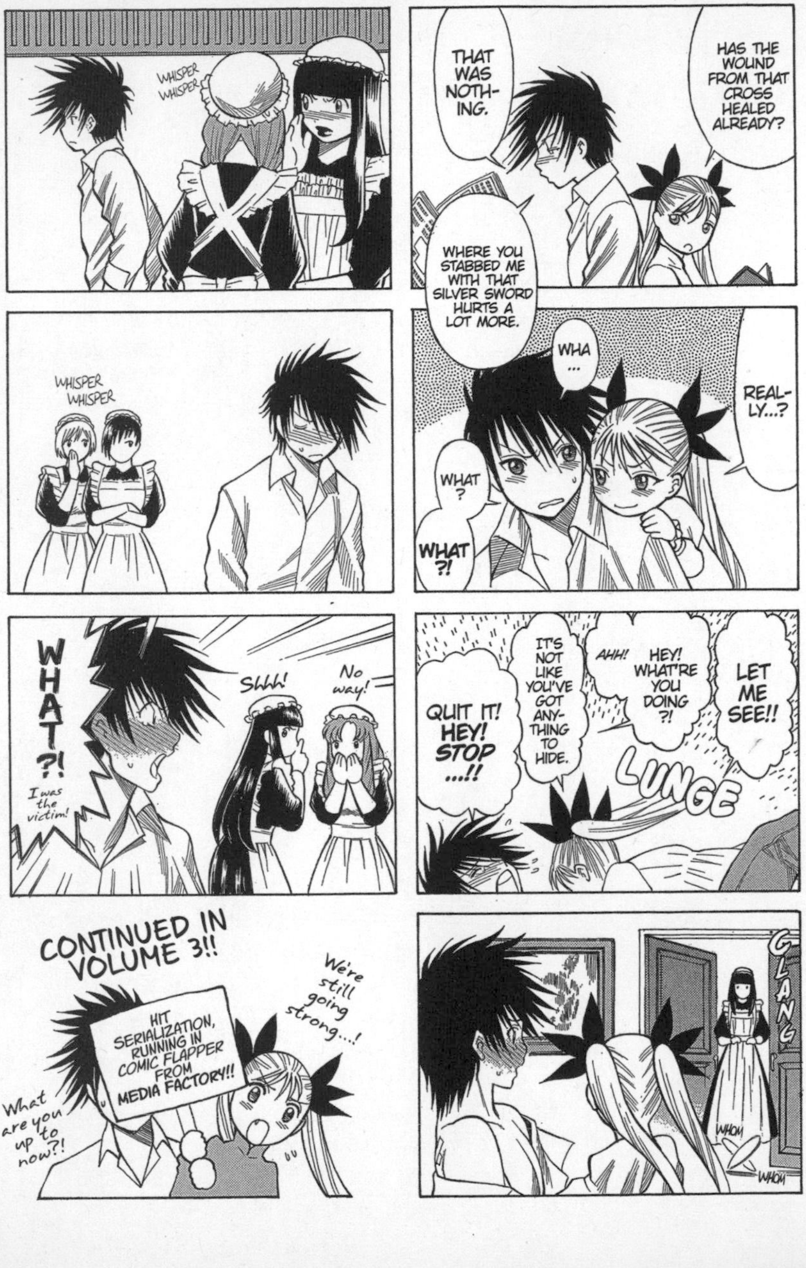
HAS THE WOUND FROM THAT CROSS HEALED ALREADY?
THAT WAS NOTHING.
WHERE YOU STABBED ME WITH THAT SILVER SWORD HURTS A LOT MORE.
WHISPER WHISPER
WHA...
REALLY...?
WHAT?
WHAT?!
WHISPER WHISPER
LET ME SEE!!
HEY! WHAT'RE YOU DOING?!
AHH!
IT'S NOT LIKE YOU'VE GOT ANYTHING TO HIDE.
QUIT IT! HEY! STOP...!!
LUNGE
No way!
Shhh!
WHAT?!
I was the victim!
GLANG
WHOM
WHOM
CONTINUED IN VOLUME 3!!
We're still going strong...!
HIT SERIALIZATION, RUNNING IN COMIC FLAPPER FROM MEDIA FACTORY!!
What are you up to now?!

TRANSLATION NOTES

VAMPIRE BUND

Bund refers to an embankment or embanked quay, and comes from the Urdu word *band*, which in turn is related to the German word bund ("federation" or "union") and the English words *bind* and *band.* A famous waterfront area in Shanghai, China is also named "The Bund."
In all cases, *bund* is a term used to describe some sort of colony or collective, and as such a Vampire Bund would be an area (in this case a man-made island) set aside for vampires to live on.

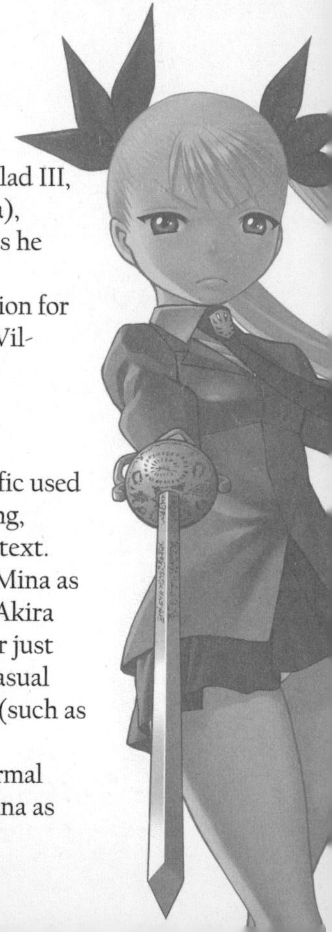

MINA TEPEŞ

The name Ţepeş comes from the common Russian nickname, *Vlad Ţepeş* (Vlad The Impaler) given to Vlad III, Prince of Wallachia (a state in what is now Romania), which he earned for the extremely cruel punishments he inflicted on his people. In the Western world he is probably better known as Vlad Dracula, the inspiration for Bram Stoker's famous novel. Mina is a reference to Wilhelmina Murray, also of Bram Stoker's novel.

HIME-SAMA

"Hime" is literally "princess" and "sama" is an honorific used to indicate respect towards a person of higher ranking, although it can also be used in a joking/sarcastic context. Several characters (such as Akira and Vera) refer to Mina as "Hime-sama" as a sign of respect and/or friendship (Akira also calls her by the less-respectful "san" honorific, or just plain "Hime" on occasion, to indicate his relatively casual relationship and attitude towards her) while others (such as Wolfgang and Juneau) refer to her more formally as "Princess" or "Her Highness." Similarly, in certain formal contexts even the characters who usually refer to Mina as "Hime-sama" will refer to her as "Princess" instead.

PAGE 7

Kasumigaseki is a district in Tokyo where most of the government ministry buildings are located.

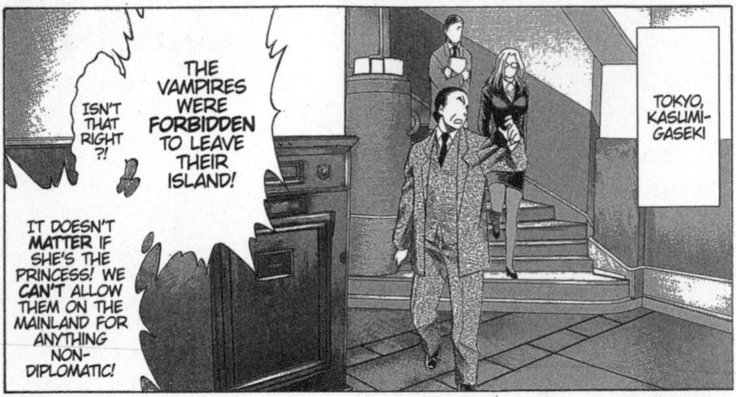
TOKYO, KASUMI-GASEKI
THE VAMPIRES WERE FORBIDDEN TO LEAVE THEIR ISLAND!
ISN'T THAT RIGHT ?!
IT DOESN'T MATTER IF SHE'S THE PRINCESS! WE CAN'T ALLOW THEM ON THE MAINLAND FOR ANYTHING NON-DIPLOMATIC!

PAGE 11

Kaichou is an honorific that literally means "president" and is used to refer to the head of a company or organization.

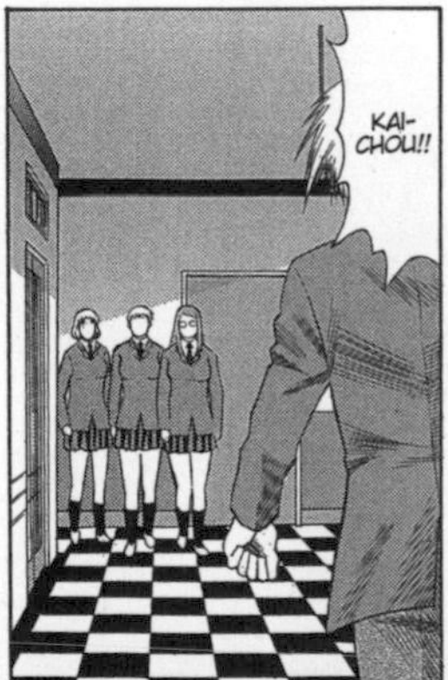
KAI-CHOU!!

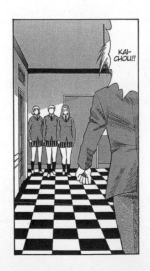

Dance in the Vampire Bund

Volume 2

story & art by Nozomu Tamaki

STAFF CREDITS

translation	Kenji Komiya
adaptation	Katherine Bell
retouch & lettering	Aristotle Licuanan
layout	Bambi Eloriaga-Amago
copy editor	Lori Smith
editor	Adam Arnold

publisher **Seven Seas Entertainment**

DANCE IN THE VAMPIRE BUND VOL. 2
© 2006 by Nozomu Tamaki
First published in Japan in 2006 by MEDIA FACTORY, Inc.
English translation rights reserved by Seven Seas Entertainment, LLC.
Under the license from MEDIA FACTORY, Inc., Tokyo.

Visit us online at www.gomanga.com

ISBN: 978-1-933164-81-6

Printed in Canada

First printing: August 2008

10 9 8 7 6 5 4 3 2 1

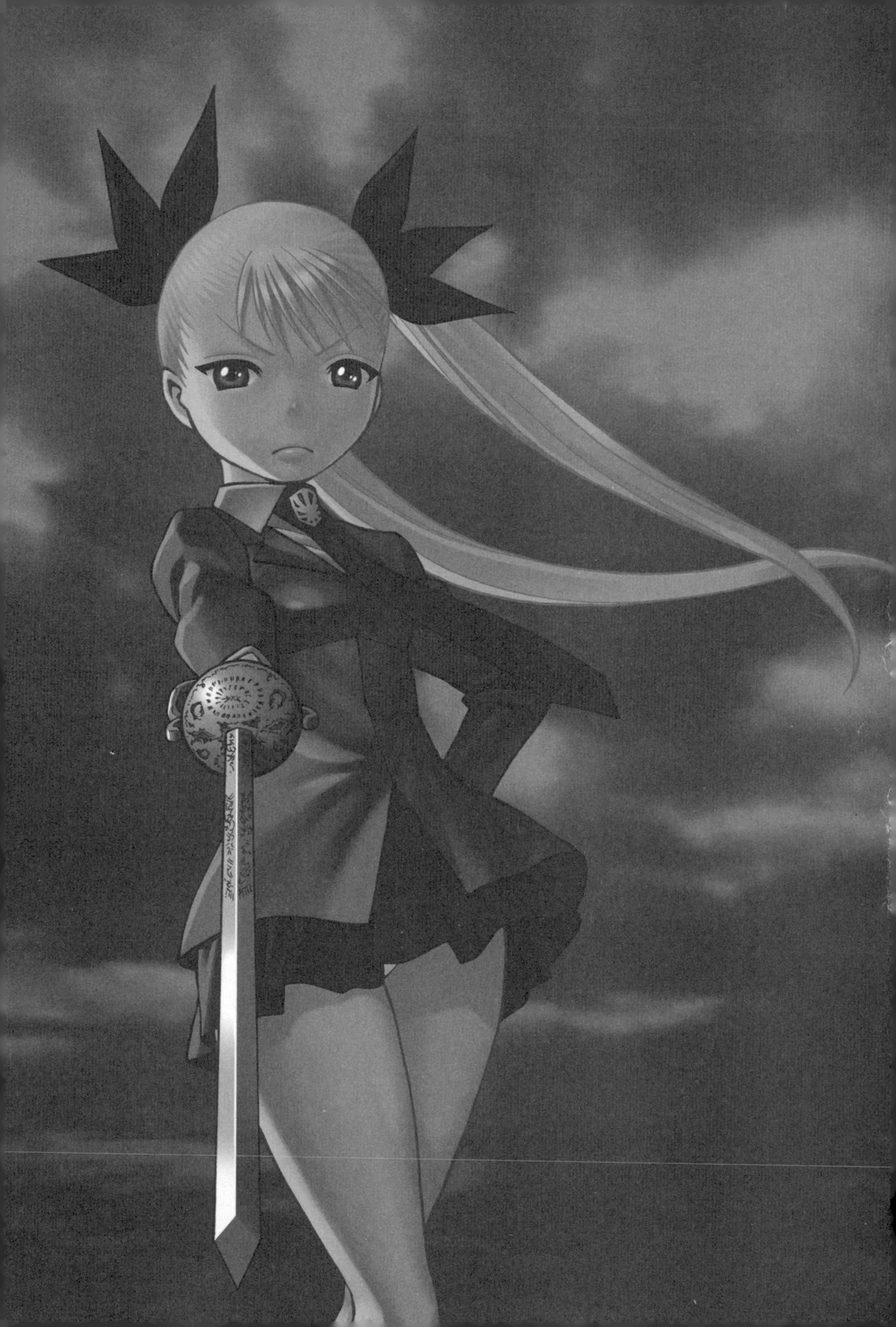

YOU'RE READING THE WRONG WAY

This is the last page of
Dance in the Vampire Bund
Volume 2

This book reads from right to left, Japanese style. To read from the beginning, flip the book over to the other side, start with the top right panel, and take it from there.

If this is your first time reading manga, just follow the diagram. It may seem backwards at first, but you'll get used to it! Have fun!